# Between Power and Plenty

Foreign Economic Policies of
Advanced Industrial States

# BETWEEN POWER AND PLENTY

Foreign Economic Policies of
Advanced Industrial States

Edited by
**Peter J. Katzenstein**

The University of Wisconsin Press

Published 1978
The University of Wisconsin Press
114 North Murray Street
Madison, Wisconsin 53715

The University of Wisconsin Press, Ltd.
1 Gower Street
London WC1E 6HA, England

Printings 1978, 1980, 1984, 1986

Printed in the United States of America

ISBN 0-299-07564-8; LC 77-91053

# Contents

# Preface

This volume analyzes how the domestic structures of advanced industrial states shape political strategies in the international political economy. Early outlines and preliminary drafts of papers were prepared for a panel of the Annual Meeting of the International Studies Association in Toronto in February 1976 and for a workshop held at Cornell University in June 1976. Full drafts were discussed at a conference held at Harvard University in October 1976. (Conference on Domestic Structures and the Foreign Economic Policy of Advanced Industrial States.) In light of these discussions the papers were extensively revised once more prior to publication.

This has been a collaborative effort from the very beginning. The contribution which the authors have made extends far beyond their individual essays. The arguments in the introductory and in the concluding essays incorporate many of the central themes in our discussions.

Maureen Appel Molot of Carleton University and Gabriel Sheffer of Hebrew University have also been members of the core group. For the Harvard conference they prepared excellent papers on Canadian and Israeli foreign economic policy. Unfortunately these essays could not be included in this volume simply for reasons of length.

All the essays have benefitted greatly from the criticisms and suggestions of the participants in the workshop and the conference: Douglas Ashford, Stephen Cohen, Mack Destler, Peter Gourevitch, Ted Greenwood, Barbara Haskel, Robert Isaak, Miles Kahler, Janet Kelly, James Kurth, Peter Lange, Carl Lankowski, Milton Leitenberg, Charles Lipson, Frank Long, Ian Lustick, John Odell, Robert Paarlberg, Robert Pastor, George Quester, Judith Reppy, Richard Rosecrance, Joan Spero, Sidney Tarrow, Ezra Vogel, Steven Warnecke, and Peter Weitz.

In the Summer of 1976 the editor of this journal, Robert Keohane, suggested to me that *International Organization* might be interested in publishing the revised conference papers as a special issue. His interest in the project was an important stimulant. Under his stewardship, a review committee consisting of Benjamin Cohen, Leon Lindberg, and Joseph Nye read each essay with great care and suggested numerous improvements.

Nicole Ball, Linda Rabben, and Jo Denham were perceptive editors of substance and style.

Financial support was an important concomitant to the intellectual assistance which this volume received from friends and colleagues. Funding was obtained from the Transnationalism Project at the Center for International Affairs and from the Center for European Studies—both at Harvard University, from the Rockefeller Foundation, and from the Peace Studies Program, the Carpenter Chair, and the Comparative Public Policy Project at Cornell University.

vii

# Between Power and Plenty

Foreign Economic Policies of
Advanced Industrial States

# 1
# Introduction: Domestic and International Forces and Strategies of Foreign Economic Policy

*Peter J. Katzenstein*

Why does a common challenge, such as the oil crisis, elicit different national responses in the international political economy? The domestic structure of the nation-state is a critical intervening variable without which the interrelation between international interdependence and political strategies cannot be understood. The essay justifies this volume's concentration on a few advanced industrial states of the North; from a broader historical perspective it looks briefly at the interaction of international and domestic forces in the shaping of the international political economy; it examines two theories of foreign policy (international approaches and bureaucratic politics) in order to highlight the gap which this volume intends to fill; and it details the theoretical orientation informing the essays which follow.

The management of interdependence is a key problem which all advanced industrial states have confronted in the postwar international political economy. Differences in their domestic structures and the international context in which they are situated have dictated the adoption of different strategies 'of foreign economic policy. The

Peter J. Katzenstein is Associate Professor of Government at Cornell University and a member of the Board of Editors, *International Organization*. Earlier drafts of this paper have benefitted from the comments, criticisms, and suggestions which I have received from the authors in this volume; from the participants in the Workshop and in the Conference on Domestic Structures and the Foreign Economic Policy of Advanced Industrial States; from my Cornell colleagues Theodore J. Lowi, T.J. Pempel, Richard N. Rosecrance, Sidney G. Tarrow and Edward Wonder; and from B.J. Cohen, Robert Gilpin, Robert O. Keohane, David D. Laitin, Leon N. Lindberg, Joseph S. Nye, and Hans-Jürgen Puhle.

rationale of all strategies is to establish a basic compatibility between domestic and international policy objectives. But since the domestic structures in the advanced industrial states differ in important ways, so do the strategies of foreign economic policy which these states pursue. This volume examines in depth the political strategies and domestic structures of six advanced industrial states—the United States, Britain, West Germany, Italy, France, and Japan.

In the contemporary international political economy increasing interdependence goes hand in hand with assertions of national independence. As was true of military policy in the previous era of "national security," in the present era of "international interdependence," strategies of foreign economic policy depend on the interplay of domestic and international forces.[1] The starting premise of this volume thus puts little value on a clear-cut distinction between domestic and international politics. A selective focus on either the primacy of foreign policy and the "internalization" of international effects or on the primacy of domestic politics and the "externalization" of domestic conditions is mistaken. Such a selective emphasis overlooks the fact that the main purpose of all strategies of foreign economic policy is to make domestic politics compatible with the international political economy.

But the literature on foreign economic policy has, in recent years, unduly discounted the influence of domestic forces. Explanations which focus on the persistence of international interdependence and the pervasiveness of transnational relations have failed to account for a paradox in our understanding of the international political economy. These international explanations do not adequately explain why an international challenge, such as the oil crisis, elicits different national responses. Despite the enormous growth of different forms of international interdependencies and transnational relations, the nation-state has reaffirmed its power to shape strategies of foreign economic policy. The central purpose of this volume is to fill this gap in our understanding of politics by offering a particular interpretation of the domestic structures of six advanced industrial states.

Why such a book at this time? True to Hegel's maxim, events rather than intellectuals have forced this reorientation in theoretical perspectives. All of the contributors to this volume received their professional training in the mid- or late 1960s when both the hegemonic position of the United States in world politics and the assumption of the primacy of international forces in political analysis simultaneously came into serious question. A process of accelerating change in the international security and economic systems illuminated the weakness of the established paradigm. The Vietnam War, it turned out, was not the product of strategic interaction between the superpowers but of Washington's institutionalization of a world order infused by an encompassing structure of "interest and

---

[1] Robert O. Keohane and Joseph S. Nye, *Power and Interdependence: World Politics in Transition* (Boston: Little, Brown and Company, 1977), pp. 6–8.

ideology."[2] In the 1960s, the foreign policies of the European states also illuminated the importance of domestic structures. General de Gaulle shifted the course of European politics by obstinately refusing to succumb to the force of European integration. And Japan's stunning rise to the position of one of the world's foremost commercial powers was evidently made possible by particular features in its domestic politics. In the 1970s, it is not possible to understand the international energy system without appreciating the domestic barriers which impede an American energy policy. Similarly, the persistent and enormous surplus in the West German trade balance (and the burden which it puts on other deficit countries) can be understood only when one knows of the strong forces in West German politics which are opposed to inflationary policies. The decline in America's influence in world politics is countered by the growing political importance of other nation-states. Today's international political economy remains unintelligible without a systematic analysis of domestic structures.

## *I  Why study the "North"?*

When we think about problems of the international political economy our imagination is captured by the current dialogue between North and South. Negotiations in Paris, Nairobi, and New York have wavered between confrontation and compromise and appear to be making only very slow progress. While the North will consider only marginal adjustments, the South insists on far-reaching modifications of present international economic arrangements. This difference is encapsulated in the political rhetoric of the two parties to the negotiations. The South speaks of *The* New International Economic Order; the North refers to it, typically, as *A* New International Economic Order. In asking for a redistribution of resources the South raises matters of substance. In talking about instrumentalities and procedures, the North has responded, until recently, by raising matters of style. The idea of a new "international class conflict" between North and South is intuitively plausible to many and may, over the long run, have important political consequences. But for the short- and medium-term it is important to separate fact from fiction. The notion that a new international class conflict could determine developments in the

---

[2] Franz Schurmann, *The Logic of World Power: An Inquiry into the Origins, Currents and Contradictions of World Politics* (New York: Random House, 1974), pp. 8–13. On the domestic sources of foreign policy more generally see, among others, Henry A. Kissinger, *American Foreign Policy* (New York: W.W. Norton, 1974), pp. 11–50. James N. Rosenau, ed., *Domestic Sources of Foreign Policy* (New York: The Free Press, 1967). James N. Rosenau, "Pre-Theories and Theories of Foreign Policy," in *Approaches to Comparative and International Politics*, R. Barry Farrell, ed. (Evanston, Illinois: Northwestern University Press, 1966), pp. 27–92. *Domestic Determinants of Foreign Policy (Third German-American Forum)* (Washington, D.C.: Georgetown University, 1974). Nicholas Wahl, "The Autonomy of Domestic Structures in European-American Relations," in *Atlantis Lost: US-European Relations after the Cold War*, James Chace and Earl C. Ravenal, eds. (New York: New York University Press, 1976), pp. 225–48.

international political economy during the years ahead is based on two questionable political assumptions.

First, the image of bloc conflict between North and South presumes a degree of international order which is lacking today. Both politically and economically the two camps are internally divided. There are vast differences, for example, in the economic circumstances of oil-producing states such as Saudi Arabia, Iran, Indonesia, Venezuela or, soon, Britain and Norway. They have different balance-of-payment objectives, growth potentials, and export dependencies. Differences of similar magnitude can be observed in the domestic social and political structures which condition the foreign economic policies of these states. Among the producer countries cartelization, it appears, is difficult; oil will be, for some time to come, "the exception."[3] The political and economic heterogeneity of raw-material exporters is a formidable barrier inhibiting the organization of cartels.

Among the advanced industrial states these differences in economic and political circumstances are equally striking. The economic crisis faced by Britain and Italy, for example, is much more serious than those of other states in the North. On the surface, differences in domestic social and political structures may be less glaring than among the countries of the South. But the essays in this volume illustrate that important differences affect foreign economic policy. These show little sign of disappearing. In sum, the image of bloc politics in the international political economy, of the confrontation between producer and consumer cartels, is deceptively simple and misleading.[4]

There is a second reason why the image of bloc politics between North and South is misplaced. In the past, major shifts in the distribution of power have occurred in domestic politics when the interlocking tripod of power, wealth, and status began to split not from the bottom but from the top.[5] The disorder in the current international political economy did not originate with the oil embargo in 1973 but dates back to the mid-1960s and the growing strains in the international

[3] Stephen D. Krasner, "Oil is the Exception," *Foreign Policy* No. 14 (Spring 1974): 68–84. Thierry de Montbriand, "For a New World Economic Order," *Foreign Affairs* Vol. 54, No. 1 (October 1975): 71.
[4] C. Fred Bergsten, "The Threat from the Third World," *Foreign Policy* No. 11 (Summer 1973): 102–24. C. Fred Bergsten, "The Threat is Real," *Foreign Policy* No. 14 (Spring 1974): 84–91. C. Fred Bergsten, "Response to the Third World," *Foreign Policy* No. 17 (Winter 1974–75): 3–34.
[5] Andrew Shonfield, ed., *International Economic Relations of the Western World, 1959–1971*, 2 vols. (London: Oxford University Press, 1976). David H. Blake and Robert S. Walters, *The Politics of Global Economic Relations* (Englewood Cliffs: Prentice-Hall, 1976). Joan Edelman Spero, *The Politics of International Economic Relations* (New York: St. Martin's Press, 1977). Klaus Knorr, *The Power of Nations: The Political Economy of International Relations* (New York: Basic Books, 1975). On the New International Economic Order see Karl P. Sauvant and Hajo Hasenpflug, eds., *The New International Economic Order: Confrontation or Cooperation between North and South?* (Boulder, Colorado: Westview Press, 1977). Roger D. Hansen, "The Political Economy of North-South Relations: How Much Change?" *International Organization* Vol. 29, No. 4 (Autumn 1975): 921–48. Tony Smith, "Changing Configurations of Power in North-South Relations Since 1945" *International Organization* Vol. 31, No. 1 (Winter 1977): 1–29.

monetary system. These strains resulted from the redistribution of economic power between the reconstructed economies of the European continent and Japan, on the one hand, and of the United States on the other. Increasing trade conflicts, especially in the area of agriculture, and growing antagonisms toward overseas investment of American multinational corporations were noticeable in the late 1960s. More recently, the imposition of the oil embargo and the diverging reactions of the rich countries illustrated the deep fissures which prevented the advanced industrial states from meeting the crisis in a coordinated fashion.

Despite the lack of coordination, the advanced industrial states still dominate the international political economy. Roughly two-thirds of global trade and direct investment is exchanged among a handful of advanced industrial states. In an era of rising concern over adequate international grain reserves, an overwhelming proportion of agricultural exports comes from the North American breadbasket. Only a small number of advanced industrial states has the technological capability for exporting nuclear reactors—a possible partial remedy for the global energy shortage and a likely stimulant to the proliferation of nuclear weapons. Figure 1 illustrates graphically the economic dominance of the advanced industrial states in the international political economy.

This volume analyzes in some depth the foreign economic policies of the United States, Britain, West Germany, Italy, France, and Japan. Although these six advanced industrial states have the biggest economies in the Organization for Economic Co-operation and Development (OECD), they do not comprise all of the North. Among others, the Scandinavian states and Canada, for example, are politically important in their own right and follow different political strategies in the international economy. But these six states illustrate the political heterogeneity and increasing potential for conflict which characterize the political relations within the North. Because of the overwhelming economic resources which they control, they constitute the core of the international economy.

## II International and domestic forces and foreign economic policy

Strategies of foreign economic policy of the advanced industrial states grow out of the interaction of international and domestic forces. That interaction is evident in the cycle of hegemonic ascendance and decline which we can trace in the international political economy over the last 150 years.[6] An open international

[6] Robert Gilpin, "Economic Interdependence in Historical Perspective," (Princeton, New Jersey: 1976). David P. Calleo and Benjamin M. Rowland, *America and the World Political Economy: Atlantic Dreams and National Realities* (Bloomington, Indiana: Indiana University Press, 1973). Stephen D. Krasner, "State Power and the Structure of International Trade," *World Politics* Vol. 28, No. 3 (April 1976): 317–47. For a broader historical treatment see Carlo M. Cipolla, ed., *The Economic Decline of Empires* (London: Methuen, 1970).

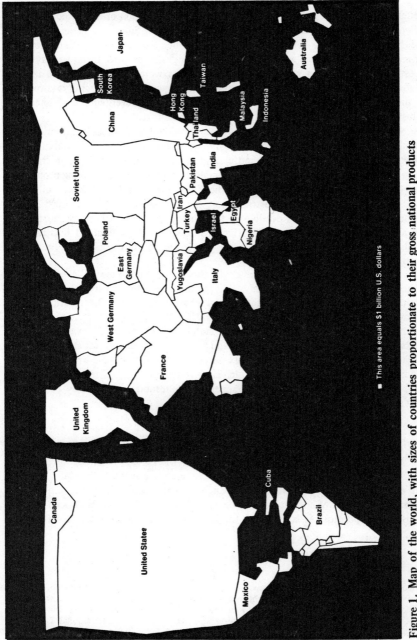

**Figure 1.** Map of the world, with sizes of countries proportionate to their gross national products © 1976 by The New York Times Company. Reprinted by permission.

political economy favoring the process of international exchange existed during Britain's hegemonic ascendance (1840–1880) and during the prominence of the United States after World War II. These periods were followed by movements toward international closure in periods of hegemonic decline marked by numerous challenges to the established institutions governing foreign economic policy. This was true of the late nineteenth century and the interwar years; some elements of this development can also be detected since the late 1960s. Periods of imperial ascendance are distinguished by the politics of plenty. A coalition within a rising hegemonic state is able to maintain an open international political economy. State power is largely invisible, for the nature of the problem in international economic affairs centers on distribution and regulation which occur within established structures.[7] The international political economy thus is orderly; this in turn facilitates the task of political management. Periods of hegemonic decline, on the other hand, are marked by the "politics of scarcity."[8] A coalition within a declining hegemonic power is, eventually, neither willing nor able to resist the forces pushing toward closure. State power becomes visible, for the nature of the political problem in the international economy centers on redistribution and constitutional debates which question established institutions. The lack of order in the international political economy in turn impedes the exercise of effective political leadership by the declining hegemonic state.

From the 1820s on, Britain's industrial prowess and its decision to shift gradually toward a low-tariff policy made it the leading state in the international political economy of the nineteenth century. That role reflected a realignment in Britain's domestic balance of power which gradually tilted in favor of its commercial, industrial, and financial elites. The defeat which Britain's aristocratic landowners suffered in the repeal of the Corn Laws in 1846 was a critical divide in British history. Until Britain's entry into the Common Market in the early 1970s the principle of no tariffs on food imports would not be questioned again. But the repeal of the Corn Laws also had important consequences for the international political economy, for it opened Britain's market to the Continent's grain exports, thus facilitating international trade. The interests of Britain's rapidly expanding industrial, commercial, and financial sectors, cast in the ideology of Manchester Liberalism, received their international sign of legitimation with the signing of the Cobden-Chevalier Tariff Treaty of 1860, which set the stage for numerous other bilateral tariff reductions throughout Europe. A realignment of political forces within Britain was, then, projected onto the international political economy, where Britain's preeminence assured order.

In comparison both to the United States (which decided not to assume its

---

[7] Robert O. Keohane and Joseph S. Nye, "World Politics and the International Economic System," in *The Future of the International Economic Order: An Agenda for Research,* C. Fred Bergsten, ed. (Lexington, Mass.: D.C. Heath, 1973), pp. 121–26.

[8] Myron Weiner, *The Politics of Scarcity: Public Pressure and Political Response in India* (Chicago: University of Chicago Press, 1962).

role as political leader until 1945) and to Germany (which became Britain's main political rival in the late nineteenth century) Britain's hegemonic power weakened from the 1880s onward. This was illustrated by its unwillingness and inability to counteract successfully the growing wave of protectionism which spread from the late 1870s in response to the Depression of 1873–1896.[9] Like economic liberalism, economic nationalism was the result of shifting coalitions in domestic politics. In Germany, for example, the (in)famous coalition between iron and rye was based on a high tariff policy and amounted to what has been called the Second Founding of the Empire.[10] This realignment of political forces was as important for Germany as the Corn Laws had been for Britain, and it was critical in pushing the international political economy off its liberal course. Germany's challenge to Britain eventually led to an intensive politicization of the international economy, as economic and military interests became insolubly linked both at home (as in the naval arms race) and abroad (as on the Baghdad Railway).

The absence of a hegemonic power and a protectionist international political economy was still more prominent during the Great Depression of the 1930s.[11] The flow of goods, capital, and labor was regulated not by market forces but by states engaging in competitive protectionism and devaluation policies, making the interwar international economy largely political. The breakdown of a liberal international economic order reflected the profound social upheaval which World War I had wrought on all of Europe. The weakening of the old middle class and the intensification of the conflict between organized capital and organized labor pushed more European states toward the Right. Fascist and authoritarian ideologies legitimized the pervasive role of the state in economic affairs, both domestic and international.

With the United States acting the part of international leader, the cycle of hegemonic ascendance and decline has repeated itself since 1945.[12] The Bretton Woods system, reinforced by free-convertibility achieved in 1959 and successive tariff reductions culminating in the Kennedy Round (completed in 1967), facili-

---

[9] Hans-Jürgen Puhle, *Politische Agrarbewegungen in kapitalistischen Industriegesellschaften* (Göttingen: Vandenhoeck and Ruprecht, 1975). Alexander Gerschenkron, *Bread and Democracy in Germany* (Berkeley: University of California Press, 1943). Charles P. Kindleberger, "Group Behavior and International Trade," *The Journal of Political Economy* Vol. 59, No. 1 (February 1951): 30–46. Peter A Gourevitch, "International Trade, Domestic Coalitions, and Liberty: Comparative Responses to the Great Depression of 1873–1896," *Journal of Interdisciplinary History* Vol. 8, No. 1 (August 1977, in press).

[10] Helmut Böhme, *Deutschlands Weg zur Grossmacht: Studien zum Verhältnis von Wirtschaft und Staat während der Reichsgründungszeit 1848–1881* (Cologne: Kiepenheuer and Witsch, 1966).

[11] Charles P. Kindleberger, *The World in Depression 1929–1939* (London: Allen Lane, The Penguin Press, 1973). Benjamin M. Rowland, ed., *Balance of Power or Hegemony: The Interwar Monetary System* (New York: New York University Press, 1976).

[12] Richard N. Rosecrance, "Introduction," in *America as an Ordinary Country: US Foreign Policy and the Future*, Richard N. Rosecrance, ed. (Ithaca: Cornell University Press, 1976), pp. 11–19.

tated a degree of openness in the international political economy and a growth in international transactions unprecedented in the twentieth century.[13] The multinational corporation, as the institutionalization of this liberal marketplace ideology, became the most dramatic symbol of an international political economy functioning smoothly under US auspices. This international economic order was based on a convergence of domestic and foreign policy interests on both sides of the Atlantic An open, depoliticized international market was perceived to be an essential precondition for the successful reestablishment of a "bourgeois Europe."[14] Supported by the flow of US government aid and private capital, the rapid economic recovery of the war-devastated states of Western Europe and Japan has led to a gradual diminution of the United States' hegemonic position since the mid-1960s. The oil crisis, however, halted the process of hegemonic decline vis-à-vis Western Europe. Through the adroit political maneuvering of Secretary of State Kissinger, the lesser dependence of the United States on raw material imports has temporarily arrested a further decline of the United States in international economic affairs. It remains to be seen whether the domestic stalemate on American energy policy will accelerate that decline in the near future.

International and domestic factors have been closely intertwined in the historical evolution of the international political economy since the middle of the nineteenth century. Shifts in domestic structures have led to basic changes in British, German, and American strategies of foreign economic policy. The international context in which these countries found themselves in turn influenced their domestic structures and thus, indirectly, the strategies they adopted in the international political economy. But the relative weight of domestic structures in the shaping of foreign economic policy increased in periods of hegemonic decline. As long as the distribution of power in the international political economy was not in question, strategies of foreign economic policy were conditioned primarily by the structure of the international political economy. But when that structure could no longer be taken for granted, as is true today, the relative importance of domestic forces in shaping foreign economic policy increased. Over the last decade the gradual shift from security issues to economic concerns has further increased the relative weight of domestic structures on foreign economic policy. Everywhere the number of domestic interests tangibly affected by the international political economy is far greater than it had been during the previous era of national security policy.

[13] Alex Inkeles, "The Emerging Social Structure of the World," *World Politics* Vol. 27, No. 4 (July 1975): 467–95. Peter J. Katzenstein, "International Interdependence: Some Long-Term Trends and Recent Changes," *International Organization* Vol. 29, No. 4 (Autumn 1975): 1021–34. Richard N. Rosecrance et al., "Whither Interdependence?" *International Organization* Vol. 31, No. 3 (Summer 1977), in press. Richard N. Rosecrance and Arthur Stein, "Interdependence: Myth or Reality?" *World Politics* Vol. 26, No. 1 (October 1973): 1–27.

[14] Charles S. Maier, *Recasting Bourgeois Europe: Stabilization in France, Germany, and Italy in the Decade after World War I* (Princeton: Princeton University Press, 1975). Maier is now working on a companion volume for the years after World War II.

## *III  International and bureaucratic politics approaches to the international political economy*

Our focus on the effect of domestic structures on foreign economic policy complements two other approaches enjoying wide currency in contemporary writings on international political economy. One approach focuses on different political, economic, and technological features of the international system which affect strategies of foreign economic policy. The second approach examines in detail domestic, bureaucratic factors and the policy-making process. These two approaches have different strengths. A focus on international developments is particularly useful for analyzing the range of choice of foreign economic policy strategies. An analysis of bureaucratic factors highlights the contingency of strategies. These essays focus on different policy choices rather than on the range or the contingency of strategies. This is why the primary focus of this volume is on domestic rather than on international or bureaucratic structures.

*International Approaches:* Recent analyses have begun to distinguish systematically between the different international forces conditioning foreign economic policy.[15] Derived from Realist, Marxist, and Liberal traditions, these analyses offer different explanations of the limits which the growing international division of labor has imposed on strategies of foreign economic policy. Some of the more recent analyses of transnational relations have attempted to construct eclectic explanations drawing on several of these intellectual traditions.[16]

Despite the increase in the international division of labor and the growth in international commerce and finance, political realists argue that America's hegemonic presence in the international political economy has affected the strategies of foreign economic policy of all advanced industrial states since 1945.[17] That hegemony rested on America's relative military and economic invulnerability, which has been evident even in recent years, for example, in the ending of the

---

[15] Robert Gilpin, "Three Models of the Future," *International Organization* Vol. 29, No. 1 (Winter 1975): 37–60. Stephen D. Krasner, *Raw Materials Investments and American Foreign Policy* (Princeton: Princeton University Press, forthcoming). Peter J. Katzenstein, "International Relations and Domestic Structures: Foreign Economic Policies of Advanced Industrial States," *International Organization* Vol. 30, No. 1 (Winter 1976): 4–13. Robert W. Cox, "On Thinking about Future World Order," *World Politics* Vol. 28, No. 2 (January 1976): 175–96.
[16] Keohane and Nye, *Power and Interdependence.*
[17] Robert Gilpin, *US Power and the Multinational Corporation: The Political Economy of Foreign Direct Investment* (New York: Basic Books, 1975). Raymond Aron, *The Imperial Republic: The United States and the World 1945–1973* (Englewood Cliffs: Prentice-Hall, 1973). Kenneth N. Waltz, "The Myth of National Interdependence," in *The International Corporation,* Charles P. Kindleberger, ed. (Cambridge: MIT Press, 1970), pp. 205–23. Albert O. Hirschman, *National Power and the Structure of Foreign Trade* (Berkeley: University of California Press, 1945). Stephen D. Cohen, *International Monetary Reform, 1964–1969: The Political Dimension* (New York: Praeger Publishers, 1970). Calleo and Rowland. Krasner, "State Power." Krasner, *Raw Materials Investments.* Jacob Viner, "Power versus Plenty as Objectives of Foreign Policy in the 17th and 18th Centuries," *World Politics* Vol. 1, No. 1 (October 1948): 1–29.

Bretton Woods system in 1971 and in the oil crisis of 1973. Marxist interpretations of the international political economy have viewed the internationalization of industrial and financial capital as both a reflection of and a constraint on political strategies.[18] Both the internationalization of industrial capital through multinational corporations with "global reach" and the internationalization of financial capital through a variety of banking institutions are rooted in the structure of capitalist economies, limiting the range of political choices.[19] Liberal interpretations, finally, have focused on the effects of technological change on increases in capital flows which reveal the sensitivity of national economies to international developments and also limit strategies.[20] In one of the first serious crises of the Bretton Woods system, for example, 300 million dollars were converted into Swiss francs in a four-day period in March 1961. In one of the most recent currency crises in February–March 1973, three billion dollars were converted into European currencies in a single day.[21] These enormous shifts of funds constrain governments in their choice in the international political economy.

Although these three interpretations highlight different features of the international political economy, their particular strength lies in focusing attention primarily on the different kinds of limitations which the world economy imposes. These interpretations are, however, not so helpful in explaining the different strategies which advanced industrial states actually pursue. This is the central objective of this volume. Its primary focus on domestic structures facilitates an

---

[18] Harry Magdoff, *The Age of Imperialism: The Economics of US Foreign Policy* (New York: Monthly Review Press, 1969). Paul A. Baran and Paul M. Sweezy, *Monopoly Capital: An Essay on the American Economic and Social Order* (New York: Monthly Review Press, 1966). Ernest Mandel, *America vs. Europe: Contradictions of Imperialism* (New York: New Left Books, 1970). Theodore Moran, "Foreign Expansion as an Institutional Necessity," *World Politics* Vol. 25, No. 3 (April 1973): 369–86. Steven J. Rosen and James R. Kurth, eds., *Testing Theories of Economic Imperialism* (Lexington, Mass.: D.C. Heath, 1974). Nicos Poulantzas, "Internationalization of Capitalist Relations and the Nation State," *Economy and Society* Vol. 3, No. 2 (1974): 145–79. Stephen D. Hymer, *The International Operations of National Firms* (Cambridge: MIT Press, 1976).

[19] Richard J. Barnet and Ronald E. Müller, *Global Reach: The Power of the Multinational Corporations* (New York: Simon and Schuster, 1974). Gerd Junne and Salua Nour, *Internationale Abhängigkeiten: Fremdbestimmung und Ausbeutung als Regelfall internationaler Beziehungen* (Frankfurt a.M.: Fischer Athenäum, 1974). Gerd Junne, *Der Eurogeldmarkt: Seine Bedeutung für Inflation und Inflationsbekämpfung* (Frankfurt: Campus Verlag, 1976).

[20] Richard N. Cooper, *The Economics of Interdependence: Economic Policy in the American Community* (New York: McGraw Hill, 1968). Richard N. Cooper, "Economic Interdependence and Foreign Policy in the Seventies," *World Politics* Vol. 24, No. 2 (January 1972): 159–81. Raymond Vernon, *Sovereignty at Bay: The Multinational Spread of US Enterprises* (New York: Basic Books, 1971). Raymond Vernon, "Storm over the Multinationals: Problems and Prospects," *Foreign Affairs* Vol. 55, No. 2 (January 1977): 243–62. Edward L. Morse, "The Transformation of Foreign Policies," *World Politics* Vol. 22, No. 3 (April 1970): 371–92. Werner J. Feld, *Nongovernmental Forces and World Politics: A Study of Business, Labor and Political Groups* (New York: Praeger Publishers, 1972). Lester R. Brown, *World without Borders* (New York: Random House, 1972).

[21] Robert W. Russell, "Crisis Management in the International Monetary System, 1960–1973," paper prepared for delivery at the International Studies Association Convention, New York City, March 16, 1973, pp. 3b, 35.

explanation of the different strategies; emphasis on international developments, on the other hand, often leaves unspecified the policy consequences of particular international developments for different advanced industrial states.[22] In the future, though, it will be necessary to develop the connections between limitations on strategies and actual policy choices more systematically than has been possible in this volume.

*Bureaucratic Politics:* A growing number of books and articles have also focused on the machinery of government which conditions strategies of foreign economic policy.[23] This literature is derived from Max Weber's ideal-typical concept of "rational" modern bureaucracy on the one hand, and the description of "irrational" bureaucracy in American organization theory on the other.[24] The "rational" and the "irrational" types define the end points of a continuum along which different models of foreign policy and foreign economic policy have been constructed.

The American state has been the prime testing ground for the development of this approach to the study of foreign policy making. The complexity of the foreign policy machinery of the modern American state, Graham Allison argued, can be illustrated even in times of extreme political crisis.[25] The rationality of bureaucracy imputed by the Weberian ideal type explains certain actions of the United States government, but it leaves many others unaccounted for. The size of this bureaucracy and the scale of its operations have become so large that they lead to a lack of control by central foreign policy decision makers. Informal networks and alliances, reinforced by idiosyncratic factors tied to the character and position of particular individuals, work in the same direction.[26] With the shift of power from Congress to the Executive, interest-group politics has simply moved too. The rule of law in democratic systems gives the bureaucracy a larger autonomy from the executive than it might enjoy in other forms of government, thus further encouraging a political process within the bureaucracy.

Models of bureaucratic politics are useful in detailing the intra-bureaucratic limitations which the contingency of numerous complex factors imposes on

---

[22] Katzenstein, "International Relations and Domestic Structures."
[23] Graham T. Allison, *Essence of Decision: Explaining the Cuban Missile Crisis* (Boston: Little, Brown and Company, 1971). Morton H. Halperin, *Bureaucratic Politics and Foreign Policy* (Washington D.C.: The Brookings Institution, 1974). Graham T. Allison and Morton H. Halperin, "Bureaucratic Politics: A Paradigm and Some Policy Implications," in *Theory and Policy in International Relations,* Raymond Tanter and Richard H. Ullman, eds., *World Politics* Vol. 24 (Supplement, Spring 1972): 40–79. John D. Steinbruner, *The Cybernetic Theory of Decisions: New Dimensions of Political Analysis* (Princeton: Princeton University Press, 1974). Wilfrid L. Kohl, "The Nixon-Kissinger Foreign Policy System and US-European Relations: Patterns of Policy Making," *World Politics* Vol. 28, No. 1 (October 1975): 1–43.
[24] Max Weber, *The Theory of Social and Economic Organization* (New York: The Free Press, 1964), pp. 324–41. Samuel B. Bachrach, "From Morphology to Cognitions: Toward a Political Framework of Intra-Organizational Analysis " (Ithaca, New York: New York School of Industrial Labor Relations, November 1975).
[25] Allison, *Essence of Decision.*
[26] The role of cultural values is explored in Michel Crozier, *The Bureaucratic Phenomenon* (Chicago: University of Chicago Press, 1964), especially Part IV.

strategies of foreign economic policy. These models are, however, less helpful in accounting for the different strategies pursued by the advanced industrial states. It is simply not clear to what extent the bureaucratic politics approach universalizes a particular American syndrome (the internal fragmentation of the American state) and how much it particularizes a universal phenomenon (the push and pull which accompany policy making in all advanced industrial states).[27] Models of bureaucratic politics abstract so little from the different strategies of foreign economic policy which need to be explained that they cannot clearly specify either the content of political strategies or the influence of particular intra-bureaucratic factors in the advanced industrial states. In the future, though, it will perhaps be possible to develop a way of thinking about bureaucratic limitations which can be linked systematically to the analysis of domestic structures lying at the heart of this volume.[28]

## IV State, society, and foreign economic policy

The essays in this volume share a theoretical orientation which we should make explicit at the outset. This common view includes both the problems in foreign economic policy worth explaining (the dependent variables) and the political and economic forces operating at home and abroad which make these problems intelligible (the independent variables).

In characterizing the problem one could focus on the specific decisions and events which constitute particular episodes in policy making. Or one could look at general features which characterize types of policies. In taking the first route, the case-study approach generates useful and important descriptive detail on specific phases of the policy process; but it often leaves the broader meaning of policy untouched. Discussion of the latter is the particular strength of the second approach, which derives from Theodore Lowi's work distinguishing between different types of policy. But comparative political research faces the problem of linking particular policies or phases of policy making to abstract definitions of different types of policies.[29]

---

[27] In this respect there exists a striking resemblance between the bureaucratic politics approach and the pluralist paradigm of the mid-1960s.

[28] As far as I know the work of William Wallace (Chatham House) on British, French, and German foreign economic policy making is currently the only sustained, comparative investigation outside Washington. See also *Commission on the Organization of the Government for the Conduct of Foreign Policy* (Murphy Commission), especially Appendix, Vols. 1 and 3 (Washington D.C.: US Government Printing Office, 1975).

[29] Theodore J. Lowi, "American Business, Public Policy, Case Studies and Political Theory," *World Politics* Vol. 16, No. 4 (July 1964): 677–715. Theodore J. Lowi, "Making Democracy Safe for the World," in Rosenau, *Domestic Sources*, pp. 295–331. Theodore J. Lowi, "Decision Making vs. Policy Making: Toward an Antidote for Technocracy," *Public Administration Review*, Vol. 30, No. 3 (May/June 1970): 314–25. William Zimmerman, "Issue Area and Foreign Policy Process," *American Political Science Review* Vol. 67, No. 4 (December 1973):

Between these two approaches the essays in this volume steer a middle course. Two components of strategies of foreign economic policy are singled out for analysis. The first is the definition of policy objectives or the ends of policy; the second is the instrument or means of policy. This distinction between objectives and instruments is an arbitrary analytical device; in many instances the defense of a means can become an end in itself, and ends can become means in the attainment of other objectives. In the case of British monetary policy, for example, it is virtually impossible to decide whether the defense of sterling was a means to defend the reserve status of the British currency, and with it Britain's international position, or whether it had become an end in itself. To different degrees each paper analyzes both components in national policy making. In search of broader patterns, the concluding essay classifies these strategies under broader descriptive categories.

The key problem for a comparative analysis is to understand the differences between the advanced industrial states. In *Social Origins of Dictatorship and Democracy*,[30] Barrington Moore postulated a democratic Liberal, a Fascist, and a Communist road to the present. However, today we find it hard to understand fully the varieties of domestic structures which Moore, emphasizing their similarities instead of their differences, referred to as "democratic." These varieties are analyzed here using the traditional distinction between "state" and "society."[31]

In the history of political thought there is a strand of theory associated with the rise of the absolutist state. The writings of Machiavelli or Bodin focus mainly on statecraft and discount civil society as a passive object for the instruments of rulers. During the Enlightenment, writers began to focus attention on the social conditions which facilitated or impeded the exercise of statecraft under different constitutional regimes. This in fact was one of Montesquieu's purposes in the *Spirit of the Laws*. In the nineteenth century this evolved into a sociological perspective on the state which became a core element of both Liberal and Marxist interpretations of politics. In addition to these two contrasting perspectives a third emerged which

---

1204–12. James Q. Wilson, *Political Organizations* (New York: Basic Books, 1973), pp. 327–346. Francesco Kjellberg, "Do Policies (really) Determine Politics? And Eventually How?" paper prepared for delivery at the ECPR London Joint Sessions, April 7–13, 1975. Geoffrey K. Roberts, "On the Definition and Classification of Policy Inputs " (Manchester, England, 1975). Thomas L. Brewer, "Issue and Context Variations in Foreign Policy: Effects on American Elite Behavior," *Journal of Conflict Resolution* Vol. 17, No. 1 (March 1973): 89–114. Dall W. Forsyth, "Taxation and Regime Change in America, 1781–1833: A Taxonomy of Political Events," Ph.D. Dissertation, Columbia University, 1974.

[30] Barrington Moore, *Social Origins of Dictatorship and Democracy: Lord and Peasant in the Making of the Modern World* (Boston: Beacon Press, 1966).

[31] Reinhard Bendix, "Social Stratification and the Political Community," *Class, Status, and Power: Social Stratification in Comparative Perspective*, 2nd ed., Reinhard Bendix and Seymour Martin Lipset, eds. (New York: The Free Press, 1966), pp. 73–86. Reinhard Bendix et al., eds., *State and Society* (Berkeley: University of California Press, 1973). J.P. Nettl, "The State as a Conceptual Variable," *World Politics*, Vol. 20, No. 4 (July 1968): 559–92. The difference between state and society is developed from other theoretical premises in Bruce Andrews, "Social Rules and the State as a Social Actor," *World Politics* Vol. 27, No. 4 (July 1975): 521–40.

focused on the state and on society as partly interdependent and partly autono-mous spheres of action. The intellectual giants of the nineteenth century—Tocqueville, Marx, Durkheim, and Weber—grappled with the problem of how state and society counterbalanced each other in different historical periods and in different places.

Although this dualism between "state" and "society" was postulated before and after him—for example in the writings of Rousseau and Weber—Hegel's distinc-tion between the public realm of freedom and the private realm of necessity was the cornerstone of his theory of the state and his philosophy of history.[32] Hegel's civil society strongly resembled the economic marketplace of Manchester Liberal-ism, for it was constituted of the complex interactions of individuals and groups for whom the pursuit of selfishness reigned supreme. On the other hand, according to Hegel, the state has revealed itself progressively in world history as the one organization predestined to identify the public good and private interests and to mediate between them.

If it is to generate fruitful insights, the analytical distinction between state and society needs to be amended in two ways. First, Hegel's analysis reifies the state. The "commanding heights" of state power are occupied by concrete actors, individuals belonging to real groups with particular interests and ideologies. The Prussian bureaucracy which Hegel admired so much was manned by members of the East Elbian gentry. The state thus offers to a particular class of people a mechanism of political organization and control which it denies to others. This does not mean that state interests will necessarily express only the particularistic interests of specific classes or status groups. But it makes it probable that in the pursuit of a strategy of foreign economic policy the national interest and the public good will not coincide.

The distinction between state and society connotes a gap between the public and the private sector which exists today in no advanced industrial state. The way in which state and society are actually linked is historically conditioned and that link determines to a large extent whether modern capitalism is atomistic, competi-tive, organized, or statist.[33] In pointing to the effect which private actors have on state policy, "societal" interpretations of foreign economic policy take two dif-ferent forms. The democratic explanation traces a direct causal chain from mass preferences (the private and public interests of all members of society) translated

[32] Shlomo Avineri, *Hegel's Theory of the Modern State* (London: Cambridge University Press, 1972).

[33] Andrew Shonfield, *Modern Capitalism: The Changing Balance of Public and Private Power* (London: Oxford University Press, 1970). Malcolm MacLennan, Murray Forsyth, and Geoffrey Denton, *Economic Planning and Policies in Britain, France, and Germany* (New York: Praeger, 1968). Raymond Vernon, ed., *Big Business and the State: Changing Relations in Western Europe* (Cambridge: Harvard University Press, 1974). Jack Hayward and Michael Watson, eds., *Planning, Politics and Public Policy* (London: Cambridge University Press, 1975). Hugh Patrick and Henry Rosovsky, eds., *Asia's New Giant* (Washington D.C.: The Brookings Institution, 1976). Heinrich A. Winkler, ed., *Organisierter Kapitalismus: Voraussetzungen und Anfänge* (Göttingen: Vandenhoeck and Ruprecht, 1974).

via elections into government policy (representing public and private interests of state actors).[34] But in the area of foreign economic policy parties and elections are often less important than interest groups in the formulation and implementation of policy. The interest group model of foreign economic policy traces the infusion of private interests into the definition of public preference and the exercise of public choice. It does so through an analysis which focuses on the interrelationships of social sectors and political organizations.[35] In sum, in both the interest group model and the democratic model, foreign economic policy is seen primarily to reflect societal pressures.

But the connection between state and society also runs the opposite way. Public policy can shape private preference. The locus of decisions in a state-centered model of policy lies in the public realm; in many ways states organize the societies they control. This "statist" interpretation of foreign economic policy discounts mass preferences, political parties, and elections, which are viewed as the effects rather than the causes of government policy. Interest groups are not autonomous agents exerting the pressure which shapes policy but subsidiary agents of the state. These two kinds of interrelationships between state and society are, in reality, always mixed. In the contemporary analysis of foreign economic policy, variants of the former (which reflect the Anglo-Saxon experience) usually are discussed in much greater detail than the latter (which reflect the experience of some countries on the European continent and Japan).

Although most prominent interpretations of state and society agree on the symbiotic relation between the two, they differ on questions of evaluation. Conservatives like Friedman or Hayek argue that the expanding role of government has caused the private sector of advanced industrial states to lose vitality in the twentieth century. Liberals like Galbraith dissent, viewing the new osmosis of state and society as a result of the power of the modern corporation. According to Galbraith's analysis, the economy of advanced industrial states is split between technologically advanced, capital-intensive, and oligopolistic segments and technologically backward, labor-intensive, and competitive sectors. Modern business is big, and big business requires big government. Yet modern governments are too weak to deal effectively with the modern corporation.[36] Neo-Marxists view the osmosis of state and society as the outcome of these two developments. Increasing government intervention in the economy not only reflects the inherent instability of modern capitalism, but also constitutes an attempt to compensate for it.

Since the papers in this volume illustrate the experiences of a number of advanced industrial states, they help to put the problems of any one country into a broader perspective. In recent writings on the international political economy, this

---

[34] For example see Assar Lindbeck, "Stabilization Policy in Open Economies with Endogenous Politicians," *American Economic Review* Vol. 66, No. 2 (May 1976): 1–19.

[35] Kindleberger, "Group Behavior," and Raymond A. Bauer, Ithiel de Sola Pool and Lewis Anthony Dexter, *American Business and Public Policy: The Politics of Foreign Trade* (New York: Atherton Press, 1963).

[36] John K. Galbraith, *The New Industrial State* (Harmondsworth: Penguin, 1969).

has not always been the case; categories of analysis were sometimes derived from the particular experience of one country. The French tradition, for example, would lead one to the conclusion that the politicization of the international economy is due to the important role which the state plays in regulating domestic society.[37] Although state and society also mesh closely in Japan, the depoliticization strategy adopted by the Japanese government appears to counteract that conclusion. Similarly, the focus on transgovernmental relations and bureaucratic politics in recent writings on transnational relations partly reflects the fragmentation of the American federal bureaucracy.[38] Yet Richard Neustadt has argued convincingly that White House politics and Whitehall politics are qualitatively different.[39] The papers in this volume offer a broader data base from which to compare systematically the effect of domestic structures on strategies of foreign economic policy.

The actors in society and state influencing the definition of foreign economic policy objectives consist of the major interest groups and political action groups. The former represent the relations of production (including industry, finance, commerce, labor, and agriculture); the latter derive from the structure of political authority (primarily the state bureaucracy and political parties). The governing coalitions of social forces in each of the advanced industrial states find their institutional expression in distinct policy networks which link the public and the private sector in the implementation of foreign economic policy. The notion that coalitions and policy networks are central to the domestic structures defining and implementing policy rests on the assumption that "social life is structured—not exclusively of course, but structured nonetheless—by just those formal institutional mechanisms. To disregard such structures at least implies the belief that social reality is essentially amorphous. This does not mean that institutions work as they are intended to work; it does mean that they have an effect."[40]

Central to the concerns of this volume is the analysis of actors in state and society. In focusing on the governing coalitions which define policy objectives and the institutional organization which conditions policy instruments, we are obviously indebted to both Marxist and Liberal interpretations of politics. However,

[37] For different interpretations of one country see Edward L. Morse, *Foreign Policy and Interdependence in Gaullist France* (Princeton: Princeton University Press, 1973) and John Zysman, *Political Strategies for Industrial Order: State, Market, and Industry in France* (Berkeley: University of California Press, 1977).
[38] Raymond F. Hopkins, "The International Role of 'Domestic' Bureaucracy," *International Organization* Vol. 30, No. 3 (Summer 1976): 405–32. Thomas G. Weiss and Robert S. Jordan, "Bureaucratic Politics and the World Food Conference: The International Policy Process," *World Politics* Vol. 28, No. 3 (April 1976): 422–39. Hadley Arkes, *Bureaucracy, the Marshall Plan, and the National Interest* (Princeton: Princeton University Press, 1972). Jessica P. Einhorn, *Expropriation Politics* (Lexington, Mass.: D.C. Heath, 1974). Ronald I. Meltzer, "The American Response to Granting Trade Preferences to Developing Countries: Bureaucratic Politics, Transgovernmental Relations, and the Politics of Policy Reversal," paper prepared for delivery at the XVII Annual Convention of the International Studies Association, Toronto, February 1976.
[39] Richard E. Neustadt, *Alliance Politics* (New York: Columbia University Press, 1970).
[40] Bendix, "Introduction" in Bendix, *State and Society*, p. 11.

neither the Marxist emphasis on private ownership of the means of production in capitalist states nor the Liberal focus on the market as a mechanism of distribution in advanced industrial societies is very helpful in explaining the different strategies which advanced industrial states pursue in the international political economy. The national studies in this volume point to an explanation, spelled out in the concluding essay, which steers between sociological types and a general theory of capitalism on the one hand and ideal types and a particularistic description of a number of advanced industrial states on the other. Between generality and specificity, comparative analysis offers comprehension of the unique, historically conditioned components common to the ruling coalitions and policy networks of all advanced industrial states.

This volume's comparative approach is also indebted to the tradition of political research which postulates the state as a central actor in all governing coalitions and a critical institution in all policy networks. The debate between mercantilists on one side and Marxists and Liberals on the other centers on the degree of autonomy of state power from class structure and group conflict.[41] Are the purposes and instruments of state power fundamentally autonomous although modified by the character of a society's class structure and group conflict before they find expression in strategies of foreign economic policy? Or are the purposes and instruments of state power not an independent but merely an intervening variable which aggregates and legitimizes the interests of particular classes or groups? Although I suspect that an answer to these questions does not depend on empirical evidence alone, it is certain that no answers can be tendered in the abstract. Many have understood Marx's *18th Brumaire* as an argument for the relative autonomy of state power. Yet, as a social scientist concerned with questions of empirical evidence, Marx argued for the relative autonomy of the French state in a particular phase of its historical evolution. Speaking generally, this is the kind of answer this volume gives. State power is stronger in some countries, such as Japan or France, than in others; it varies according to whether one analyzes the definition of objectives or the implementation of foreign economic policy.

In their political strategies and domestic structures, the United States, Britain, West Germany, Italy, France, and Japan fall into three distinct groups.[42] In pursuing a liberal international economy as a key objective, policy makers in the two Anglo-Saxon states rely, by and large, on a limited number of policy instruments which affect the entire economy rather than particular sectors or firms. Policy makers in Japan, on the other hand, can pursue their objective of economic growth with a formidable set of policy instruments which impinge on particular sectors of the economy and individual firms. The three continental states occupy an intermediary position with West Germany and Italy showing some affinity for the

[41] This was a central point of contention in the discussions among authors and participants in the workshop and the conference on Domestic Structures and Foreign Economic Policies of Advanced Industrial States.

[42] This organizing framework is elaborated further in the concluding essay of this volume.

Anglo-Saxon pattern and France sharing some resemblance to Japan. Corresponding differences also exist in the domestic structures of these six states. In the two Anglo-Saxon countries the coalition between business and the state is relatively unfavorable to state officials and the policy network linking the public with the private sector is relatively fragmented. In Japan, on the other hand, state officials hold a very prominent position in their relations with the business community and the policy network is tightly integrated. The three continental countries hold an intermediary position, with West Germany resembling the Anglo-Saxon pattern, France approximating more the Japanese model, and Italy falling somewhere in between.

These differences in political strategies and domestic structures have narrowed in comparison to the interwar years. In his analysis of the origins of the postwar international political economy, Charler Maier shows how the interrelations between domestic and international forces on both sides of the Atlantic and in Japan favored the American desire to redefine questions of political economy as questions of productivity. In his paper on the United States Stephen Krasner traces a forty-year cycle of American trade policy during which protectionist interest groups represented in Congress increasingly had to defer to policy makers in the White House and the State Department. The latter favored a liberal international trade regime for broad political reasons rather than narrow economic concerns. The greater centralization of power inherent in questions of monetary policy has also facilitated the pursuit of a liberal American policy until the early 1970s. The very success of America's liberal design for the postwar international political economy has strengthened the big corporations and banks as the major beneficiaries and proponents of a liberal policy. This explains why, in recent years, deviations from America's liberal orientation have occurred only very gradually. This indirect effect of state policy also lies, according to Stephen Blank, at the root of Britain's foreign economic policy and the "British disease." The prolonged defense of an overvalued sterling was made possible by a policy of domestic deflation—but it was based on a political decision made by the Prime Minister. He and his cabinet subscribed to a banker's view of the world, according to which London's City could profit only by defending international financial obligations rather than national industrial interests. The devaluation of the pound in 1967 and the recognition of the deleterious effects of the disguised reserve status of sterling in 1976 came so late that the productive capacity of the British economy and the legitimacy of the British system of party government are now in deep crisis.

T.J. Pempel's essay illustrates the way the liberal tenets to which the two Anglo-Saxon countries subscribed have been antithetical to the neo-mercantilism of Japan's foreign economic policy. After 1945, Japanese policy makers did not concern themselves with international hegemony, but focused instead on extracting maximum benefits from the international political economy. The exclusion of what Pempel calls "the other Japan" (the clientele served elsewhere by the welfare state) from equitable distribution of growth dividends at home and increasing resistance to Japan's single-minded commercial expansion abroad are beginning to pose serious questions about the future of Japan's foreign economic policy.

In attenuated form, the three states of the European continent reflect the differences between Anglo-Saxon liberalism and Japanese neo-mercantilism. Michael Kreile's analysis of West Germany's policy of export-led growth reveals the pervasive market orientation to which export industries and government officials subscribe. The Eastern trade policy and imported inflation created conflict in the 1950s and 1960s. But only recently have the acceleration of West Germany's capital exports, large wage increases, and the revaluation of the Deutschmark created the dilemma of implementing a sectoral industrial and manpower policy which provides a stiffer challenge to West Germany's liberal orientation. On the other hand, John Zysman argues that France has succeeded in extracting resources from her European partners (e.g., West Germany) for the modernization of French agriculture and in shaping critical sectors of French industry to the requirements of international competition. Although the strident tones of Gaullism and Jobertism no longer mark French foreign economic policy and although international inflation has left France in a more precarious economic position in recent years, its basic position has remained largely unchanged since the late 1950s. Just as Europe as a whole holds an intermediate position between the Anglo-Saxon countries and Japan, Italy occupies an intermediary position between West Germany and France. Alan Posner shows that the flabbiness of the Italian state is a result of the Christian Democratic (DC) electoral coalition and Italy's clientelistic politics. Italy's liberal foreign economic policy is thus fashioned by private or para-statal corporations which, together with Italy's banking sector, circumvent an ineffective and inefficient state bureaucracy. It remains to be seen whether the official or unofficial participation of the Communist party (PCI) in government will alter the passivity which Italy has adopted.

These essays converge on one central point.[43] The loss of control deplored in the foreign ministries of all advanced industrial states is rooted not only abroad but at home. Lack of action, or inappropriate action, taken in domestic politics often leads to serious consequences in the international political economy. In itself a global approach to meeting global needs appears to be an inefficient and ineffective way of trying to cope with the problems of the international political economy. The management and the analysis of interdependence must start at home.

[43] Robert L. Paarlberg, "Domesticating Global Management," *Foreign Affairs* Vol. 54, No. 3 (April 1976): 563–76.

# 2
# The Politics of Productivity: Foundations of American International Economic Policy after World War II

*Charles S. Maier*

The years immediately after World War II provided American policy makers with a unique opportunity to help shape the international economic order for a generation to come. United States objectives are usually described in terms of enlightened idealism or capitalist expansionism. But much of the way policy makers envisaged international economic reconstruction derived from the ambivalent way in which domestic economic conflict had been resolved before and during the New Deal. In the inconclusive struggle between business champions and the spokesmen for reform, Americans achieved consensus by celebrating a supposedly impartial efficiency and productivity and by condemning allegedly wasteful monopoly. Looking outward during and after World War II, United States representatives condemned Fascism as a form of monopoly power, then later sought to isolate Communist parties and labor unions as adversaries of their priorities of production. American blueprints for international monetary order, policy toward trade unions, and the intervention of occupation authorities in West Germany and Japan sought to transform political issues into problems of output, to adjourn class conflict for a consensus on growth. The American approach was successful because for almost two decades high rates of growth made the politics of productivity apparently pay off. Whether an alternative approach could have achieved more equality remains an important but separate inquiry.

Charles S. Maier is a member of the Department of History at Duke University. This essay draws upon papers the author presented in 1975–76 while a Fellow of the Lehrman Institute in New York City. The title of that series, which is intended to serve as the base for a future book, was *The United States and the Reorganization of European Institutions after World War II.*

The ground rules of a liberal international economic system may establish formal equality among participants but they also reflect the disparity of power and resources. Just as significant, they reveal the inequalities and conflicts within the dominant national societies of the system. The primary objective of this article is to suggest how the construction of the post-World War II Western economy under United States auspices can be related to the political and economic forces generated within American society. A second focus must be to demonstrate how those American impulses interacted with the social and political components of the other nations, European and Japanese, covered in this volume.

The close of World War II brought American policy makers a rare and heady opportunity to reshape the guidelines of the international economic order. The pretensions of the Axis powers to organize continental Europe and East Asia had collapsed. Soviet Russia seemed preoccupied with its own huge tasks of reconstruction and the establishment of a glacis in Eastern Europe. Great Britain depended upon Washington's assistance to maintain its own international role and could not durably oppose American policies. Spared the losses incurred by the other belligerents, the United States inherited a chance to secure Western economic ground rules according to its own needs and visions.

What determined those needs and visions? Historians and political scientists have often argued that they represented either an enlightened idealism or a nationalistic and capitalist expansionism. Thus polarized, the debate remains inconclusive because the same policies could serve both aspirations. Washington's neo-Cobdenite mission did aim at higher world levels of exchange and welfare. Simultaneously, it was intended to benefit American producers who could compete vigorously in any market where the "open door" and the free convertibility of currencies into dollars facilitated equal access.[1] Both the defenders and the critics of American objectives, moreover, have recognized the traumatic legacy of a Depression that only wartime orders finally overcame. Indeed, Donald Nelson of the War Production Board and Eric Johnston of the Chamber of Commerce encouraged the Soviets to believe that American businessmen wanted their orders lest mass unemployment recur after the wartime stimulus ended. Nor was international commerce solely an economic objective: trade restrictions, argued New Deal spokesmen, brought political hostility. "Nations which act as enemies in the market place cannot long be friends at the council table," said Assistant Secretary of State William Clayton, a wealthy cotton dealer sympathetic at first hand to the needs of exporters.[2] He echoed Cordell Hull's assessment that the establishment of a closed

[1] For critical analyses, Lloyd C. Gardner, *Economic Aspects of New Deal Diplomacy* (Madison: University of Wisconsin Press, 1964); Gabriel Kolko, *The Politics of War: The World and United States Foreign Policy, 1943–1945* (New York: Random House, 1968); William Appleman Williams, *The Tragedy of American Diplomacy* (New York: Dell Publishing Co., 1962).

[2] For Johnston and Nelson, see John Lewis Gaddis, *The United States and the Origins of the Cold War, 1941–1947* (New York: Columbia University Press, 1972), pp. 176–77, 185–89. Clayton cited in Thomas Paterson, *Soviet-American Confrontation: Postwar Reconstruction and the Origins of the Cold War* (Baltimore: The Johns Hopkins University Press, 1973), p. 4.

trading bloc comprised an essential aspect of Fascism: "The political line up followed the economic line up."[3] Thus, a compelling objective in 1945 was to do away with protected trading areas outside the United States, thereby to banish domestic depression and international conflict. The United States would lead the United Nations to a lofty plateau of peaceful intercourse and economic expansion.

This eschatology of peaceful prosperity—with its amalgam of nationalist and universal aspirations usefully termed "Wilsonian"[4]—is not sufficient, however, to account fully for the ideological sources of American foreign economic policy. (Nor, I hope to show, is growing anti-Communism a sufficient ideological explanation.) American concepts of a desirable international economic order need to be understood further in terms of domestic social divisions and political stalemates. United States spokesmen came to emphasize economic productivity as a principle of political settlement in its own right. They did this not merely because of the memory of harsh unemployment, nor simply to veil the thrust of a latter-day "imperialism of free trade,"[5] nor even because wartime destruction abroad made recovery of production an urgent objective need. Just as important, the stress on productivity and economic growth arose out of the very terms in which Americans resolved their own organization of economic power. Americans asked foreigners to subordinate their domestic and international conflicts for the sake of higher steel tonnage or kilowatt hours precisely because agreement on production and efficiency had helped bridge deep divisions at home. The emphasis on output and growth emerged as a logical result of New Deal and wartime controversies, just as earlier it had arisen out of inconclusive reform movements.

## I The domestic sources of American economic concepts

In retrospect, it is easy to point out that the international economic arrangements the United States sought in the years after the Second World War would benefit a capital-intensive and resource-rich economy. Wartime leadership and British dependence brought the opportunity to press for the Treasury and State Department's preferred multilateralism. These policies had not originally been ascendant. At its inception, the New Deal had adopted a course of monetary unilateralism as Roosevelt refused cooperation with the London Economic Conference in 1933 and embarked upon the almost capricious gold purchases of 1934.

---

[3] *The Memoirs of Cordell Hull*, 2 vols. (New York: Macmillan Co., 1948), Vol. I, p. 364.
[4] To see the implications of Wilsonianism, see N. Gordon Levin, Jr., *Woodrow Wilson and World Politics. America's Response to War and Revolution* (New York: Oxford University Press, 1970).
[5] For the earlier analogue: John Gallagher and Ronald Robinson, "The Imperialism of Free Trade," *Economic History Review*, 2nd series, 6 (1953): 1–15; objections in D.C.M. Platt, "The Imperialism of Free Trade: Some Reservations," *Economic History Review*, 2nd series, 11 (1968): 296–306, and "Further Objections to an 'Imperialism of Free Trade,' 1830–1860," *Economic History Review*, 2nd series, 26 (1973): 77–91.

Such initiatives represented, in part, a reaction to Britain's floating of the pound and regrouping of a Commonwealth trading bloc in 1931–1932. They also reflected the Democrats' distrust of the New York banking elites (the Federal Reserve leadership and J.P. Morgan, Co., etc.) that had sought to work with the British toward monetary stabilization in the 1920s and seemed to emphasize international cooperation rather than domestic growth. Nonetheless, a common British and American need to limit competitive devaluation after France departed from the gold standard led to a Tripartite currency agreement in 1936. The danger of Nazi expansionism further impelled Neville Chamberlain to solicit Washington's cooperation and conclude the Anglo-American trade agreement of November 1938.[6] With the advent of World War II, Britain had to become even more insistent a suitor. For its Lend-Lease assistance, Washington pressed for further dismantling of the Commonwealth trading bloc. London finally had to rely upon shared political values and plucky sacrifices to temper American demands for the liquidation of its international financial position.[7]

Noisy disputes sometimes obscured the underlying thrust of United States policy, but foreign economic objectives generally reflected Cordell Hull's unceasing emphasis upon the virtue of lowering tariff barriers. This program was consistent with the lessons of comparative advantage and a universalist vision of economic advance, even as it served to encroach upon the British Commonwealth. Roosevelt needed Hull because of his excellent relations with Congress; and the official who offered an alternative program of international commodity bartering, George Peek, the Administrator of the Agricultural Adjustment Act, resigned in late November 1935. The disputes between Hull and Henry Morgenthau, Jr. at the Treasury appear more those of bureaucratic rivalry than fundamental policy disagreements. Hull was originally willing to allow the British monetary flexibility in return for free-trade commitments; in 1935 he dissented from the dollar's competitive devaluation against the pound. But while Hull afterward urged the postwar elimination of the Westminster system as a condition for Lend-Lease, Morgenthau was less insistent. The Treasury emphasized economic leadership through a pivotal role for the dollar. Rather than impose Section VII of the Lend-Lease agreement which committed Britain to move toward free trade, the Secretary of the Treasury sought to extract London's agreement not to rebuild its foreign currency reserves during the period of American aid.[8] Nonetheless, the Treasury's quest for monetary leadership was

---

[6] Benjamin M. Rowland, "Preparing the American Ascendency: The Transfer of Economic Power from Britain to the United States," in *Balance of Power or Hegemony: The Interwar Monetary System,* Benjamin M. Rowland, ed. A Lehrman Institute Book (New York: New York University Press, 1976), pp. 195–224, and, in the same volume, Harold van B. Cleveland, "The International Monetary System in the Interwar Period," esp. pp. 54–56; Lowell M. Pumphrey, "The Exchange Equalization Account of Great Britain," *American Economic Review,* 32 (December 1942): 803–16.

[7] Richard N. Gardner, *Sterling-Dollar Diplomacy: Anglo-American Cooperation in the Reconstruction of Multilateral Trade* (Oxford: Clarendon Press, 1956), offers the best account of this relationship.

[8] Rowland in Rowland, pp. 202–04, 213–15.

not fundamentally inconsistent with the State Department's stress on the "open door" and the importance of free trade. Both policies envisaged using the American abundance of food and cotton and the productivity of labor to establish a benign economic dominance that would raise the welfare of all nations. Neither agency had reason to sanction an exhausted Britain's maintaining imperial pretensions at US expense. Both policies derived from a Wilsonian globalism. In Morgenthau's concepts, for example, a Britain prosperous but on reduced monetary tether accompanied a Germany shorn of its heavy industry and a Russia reconstructed with American credits.[9] The premise for all policy makers was American economic preeminence. This preeminence was felt to arise naturally from the nation's energy and resources, not from the exercise of coercion.

Yet this very emphasis on economic potential itself emerged from deeper divisions. The productivist view of America's postwar mission arose naturally out of the domestic modes of resolving social conflict, or, rather, the difficulty of resolving conflicts cleanly. Neither an insistence upon conflict nor upon consensus adequately conveys the dialectical interplay of both social conditions, such that unresolved disputes brought contestants to apolitical areas of common endeavor. Most immediately, the emphasis on the benevolent mission of America's productive leadership reflected the stalemate of New Deal reform and even wartime politics. By the late 1930s, the New Deal thrust to displace economic power from private capital to either corporatist National Recovery Administration (NRA) institutions or to countervailing private forces (i.e., labor unions) was rapidly dissipating. The severe recession of 1937–38 intensified political infighting between "spenders" such as Harry Hopkins, Harold Ickes, Marriner Eccles, and Leon Henderson and those such as Morgenthau who urged tax cuts for business. Outside the White House, the Democratic coalition began to fray and the President failed to persuade Congress to enact several key proposals during 1938–39. In November 1938 Republicans won 81 new seats in the House and eight in the Senate. As the political situation in Europe became more preoccupying, it provided a further incentive for the President to turn back to a business community that a few years earlier he had labelled "economic royalists." Harry Hopkins, newly installed as Secretary of Commerce in early 1939, chose Averell Harriman as a close advisor, in part to reconstruct bridges to business leadership. Edward Stettinius, Jr. of US Steel, James Forrestal of Dillon Reed, Donald Nelson of Sears Roebuck, and William Knudsen of General Motors were only a few of the "tame millionaires" the Administration summoned to run the ever-shifting agencies designed to coordinate defense production. With Pearl Harbor, Roosevelt could announce that "Dr. Win the War" was replacing "Dr. New Deal."[10]

---

[9] For Morgenthau's ideas, see John Morton Blum, ed., *From the Morgenthau Diaries*, Vol. 3: *Years of War 1941–1945* (Boston: Houghton Mifflin Company, 1967), pp. 228–30, 324–26, 333 ff; cf. Kolko, pp. 323–40.

[10] William E. Leuchtenburg, *Franklin D. Roosevelt and the New Deal, 1932–1940* (New York: Harper and Row, 1963), pp. 243 ff.; J. Joseph Huthmacher, *Senator Robert F. Wagner and the Rise of Urban Liberalism* (New York: Atheneum, 1971); Robert Sherwood, *Roosevelt and Hopkins* (New York: Harper & Brothers, 1948), pp. 110–11.

The infusion of industrialists, however, could not automatically adjourn old conflicts over social and economic policy. Critics of business found the new organizers unimpressive and laggard in the task of converting industry to wartime production. The new participants from banking and industry regarded the inveterate New Dealers as partisan and woolly-headed. As Forrestal reported about the provocative Henderson in July 1941: "He is trying to use the Office of Civilian Requirements to get a foothold and control of the defense effort and incidentally to fight a social as well as a military war."[11] The role of labor was particularly controversial. The Office of Production Management (OPM) and its successor, the War Production Board, resisted the policies of the trade union Left. The CIO and AFL sought representation in the key industry divisions of the OPM but had to be content with participation in the less central labor advisory committees. Labor delegates did become important on the War Manpower Committee, but after a production crisis in 1943, Roosevelt's solution of placing James Byrnes in charge of an overarching Office of War Mobilization again kept labor spokesmen from the center of decisions.[12]

From one perspective these struggles were bureaucratic rivalries with multi-million-dollar appropriations and unprecedented regulatory control as the important stakes. Yet it would be misleading to forget the ideological implications. The war imposed a common task upon all contenders but could not nullify the profound struggles over business and labor power that had continued for over a decade. Nor could it cleanly resolve them. Symptomatic of the continuing ideological and social disputes was the stormy career of Henry Wallace. By 1942 Wallace had established himself as the spokesman for a messianic liberalism of abundance; America's war was an act of millennial liberation that would usher in "the century of the common man." Not merely a visionary, the Vice-President and his aides had accumulated key economic supervisory positions. But the State Department resented the inroads of Wallace's Bureau of Economic Warfare. And the long, public quarrel with Jesse Jones, the conservative Texas millionaire who served as Secretary of Commerce and directed the Reconstruction Finance Committee (RFC), finally led Roosevelt to abolish the Bureau of Economic Warfare, limit the RFC's role, and establish a new Foreign Economic Agency under Jones's protege, Leo Crowley. The struggle was a bureaucratic and personal one but its upshot disheartened the New Deal Left and set back potential precedents for future economic regulation and planning. At Thanksgiving 1942 Wallace had approached FDR "in the spirit of Queen Esther approaching King Ahasuerus, only I was going to speak on behalf of

---

[11] Letter to Averell Harriman, July 7, 1941, in James Forrestal papers, Princeton University Library, Box 56. For a liberal, journalistic account of Washington wartime economic conflicts, see Bruce Catton, *The Warlords of Washington* (New York: Harcourt, Brace, 1948).

[12] Paul A. C. Koistinen, "Mobilizing the World War II Economy: Labor and the Industrial-Military Alliance," *Pacific Historical Review*, 42 (November 1973): 443–78, esp. 446–60. Cf. Barton J. Bernstein, "America in War and Peace: The Test of Liberalism," in *Toward a New Past: Dissenting Essays in American History*, Barton J. Bernstein, ed. (New York: Random House-Vintage, 1968).

the liberals rather than the Jews."[13] He did not recall that since the laws of the Medes and the Persians were immutable, the Jews won only the right to defend themselves, not the cancellation of the attacks already ordered.

In Congress the fate of New Deal reform under wartime conditions was also problematic. Price controls and rationing under the Office of Price Administration (OPA) remained a sore point for conservatives, especially since OPA became a refuge for New Deal exponents such as Henderson and Chester Bowles. Senator Robert Wagner, chairman of the Banking and Currency Committee, managed to renew the OPA and price-control legislation. He failed, however, to secure passage of the Wagner-Murray-Dingell bill, which would have enacted an equivalent of Britain's Beveridge Plan if it had not remained a dead letter in 1943, 1944, and 1945. When the National Resources Planning Board, deeply influenced during the war years by Harvard Keynesian Alvin Hansen, brought forward its 1943 proposals for continued welfare reforms and countercyclical spending, it won applause from *The New Republic*. Congressional conservatives, on the other hand, responded by gutting the agency. By 1944, with further Republican gains at the polls, Congress reflected a taut division between Liberals and Conservatives. The result was typified by the fate of the Liberals' proposed full-employment bill. Originally designed to mandate government spending to prevent joblessness, it emerged, after much horse-trading, as the Employment Act, which merely targetted maximum feasible job levels. With the creation of the Council of Economic Advisors it remained more a technical than a political measure.[14]

This stalemate of forces precluded any consistent social-democratic trend for the American political economy. Coupled with the impressive record of the domestic industrial plant as the "arsenal for democracy," it made it easier for American leaders to fall back upon the supposedly apolitical politics of productivity. The theme of productivity as a substitute for harsh questions of allocation was a venerable one. It had emerged in the Progressive Era and pervaded the War Production Board of 1918. It was championed by Herbert Hoover under the form of a business "associationism" that would transcend wasteful competition, and be given institutional expression once again in the NRA concept of industrial self-government. The recurrent ideas all stressed that by enhancing productive efficiency, whether through scientific management, business planning, industrial cooperation, or corporatist groupings, American society could transcend the class conflicts that arose from scarcity. The coinage of politics—power and coercion—was

[13]John Morton Blum, ed., *The Price of Vision: The Diary of Henry A. Wallace, 1942–1946* (Boston: Atlantic-Little Brown, 1973), p. 137. See also Norman D. Markowitz, *The Rise and Fall of the People's Century: Henry A. Wallace and American Liberalism, 1941–1948* (New York: Free Press, 1973), pp. 47ff.; Frederick H. Schapsmeier and Edward L. Schapsmeier, *Prophet in Politics: Henry A. Wallace and the War Years, 1940–1945* (Ames, Iowa: The University of Iowa Press, 1970), pp. 55–71.

[14]Bernstein in Bernstein for Congressional conservatism; Markowitz, pp. 57–65 on NRPB; Huthmacher, pp. 285–302; Stephen Kemp Bailey, *Congress Makes a Law: The Story behind the Employment Act of 1946* (New York: Columbia University Press, 1950).

minted only in the kingdom of material necessity and would have no function in the realm of abundance.[15]

Although the Depression discredited the claims to foresight and acumen on the part of America's business elites, the wartime experience suggested again that the United States could enjoy productive abundance without a radical redistribution of economic power. The neo-Progressives in the business community organized a Committee on Economic Development (CED) to urge continuing governmental responsibility (including advantageous tax benefits) for maintaining high investment and employment. Charles E. Wilson of General Electric and the War Production Board and Paul Hoffman of Studebaker, later head of the Economic Cooperation Administration, became major CED spokesmen for the new government-business partnership.[16] Not surprisingly, it was the emergency priorities of wartime that rendered this celebration of a business-oriented commonwealth initially acceptable to American Liberals. The wartime celebration of production and output, its rehabilitation of the large corporation, and its evocation of an overarching national commitment, all facilitated a new consensus on interventionist planning. As Harriman noted in his first unofficial press conference after becoming Secretary of Commerce in October 1946, "People in this country are no longer scared of such words as 'planning.' ... people have accepted the fact the government has got to plan as well as the individuals in the country."[17]

It is important to emphasize, however, that planning was accepted only in a restricted sense. During the 1930s, the Department of Agriculture under the guidance of Rexford Tugwell and Mordecai Ezekiel, the National Resources Planning Board as influenced by Gardiner Means, and the Tennessee Valley Authority (TVA) had emerged as foyers for the planning enthusiasts. But the impact of the would-be planners was concentrated in natural resource issues; for in questions of environmental resources, providing ever-normal granaries, or halting erosion, planning could claim a conservation-related justification it could not in industry. Likewise, planning seemed more acceptable on the regional level: TVA became a New Deal showcase not merely because of its cheap power but its incubation of

---

[15] See Ellis Hawley, "Herbert Hoover, the Commerce Secretariat and the Vision of an 'Associative State,' 1921–1928," *The Journal of American History*, 61 (June 1974): 116–40; also Hawley's own essay in *Herbert Hoover and the Crisis of American Capitalism*, Ellis Hawley et al. (Cambridge, Massachusetts: Schenkman, 1973); Barry D. Karl, "Presidential Planning and Social Science Research: Mr. Hoover's Experts," *Perspectives in American History*, 3 (1969): 347–409; Charles S. Maier, "Between Taylorism and Technocracy: European Ideologies and the Vision of Industrial Productivity in the 1920's," *Journal of Contemporary History*, 5 (April 1970): 27–61.

[16] Karl Schriftgeisser, *Business Comes of Age: The Story of the Committee for Economic Development and its Impact upon the Economic Policies of the United States* (New York: Harper and Row, 1960); also Herbert Stein, *The Fiscal Revolution in America* (Chicago: University of Chicago Press, 1969), Chapters 8–9; Robert Lekachman, *The Age of Keynes* (New York: Random House, 1966).

[17] Secretary of Commerce files in W. Averell Harriman papers, Washington, National Press Club Luncheon, October 15, 1946.

local democracy. Its exuberant director, David Lilienthal, foresaw TVA-like developments helping to leapfrog the more exploitative and wasteful stages of growth outside the United States as well:

> There seems to be a definite sequence in history in the change from primitive or non-industrial conditions to more highly developed modern industrial conditions. Whether all of those steps have to be taken and all the intervening mistakes made is open to question. . . . Don't we have enough control over our destinies to short-cut those wasted steps?[18]

The same buoyant belief in the power of economic rationality would mark Marshall Plan administrators. But precisely because they and other American Liberals usually envisaged planning as a step toward productive efficiency, it became apolitical. Planning would overcome the waste that CED industrialists saw in restrictive labor practices or needless competition, that Lilienthal measured in overpriced kilowatt-hours, or that Keynesians perceived in idle savings and unemployed workers. In each case, the mission of planning became one of expanding aggregate economic performance and eliminating poverty by enriching everyone, not one of redressing the balance among economic classes or political parties. When they turned to European difficulties after 1945, American advisors enjoyed greater opportunity to reshape the ailing economies abroad than to influence the domestic one. But even in confronting European needs, they reaffirmed the general premises of American economic thinking. United States aid was designed to remove "bottlenecks," and to clear away the obstacles left by war and political demoralization by temporary coal shortages and transitory dollar gaps. Prosperity was available for Europeans too, once the impediments to production were limited. The true dialectic was not one of class against class, but waste versus abundance. The goal of economic policy, abroad as at home, was to work toward the latter.

American opinion generally viewed the transition to a society of abundance as a problem of engineering, not of politics. Nonetheless, as Americans ended the Second World War, they recognized one major institutional impediment to peacetime prosperity—monopoly. Denunciation of monopoly was a recurring ideological theme. John Taylor of Caroline, Andrew Jackson, the Progressives, and the New Deal successively assailed monopoly as an affliction of democracy. The criticism of monopoly presented the same rhetorical advantages as the stress on productivity and efficiency. Instead of depicting political society as subject to complex interest

[18]*The Journals of David E. Lilienthal*, Vol. I: *The TVA Years, 1939–1945* (New York: Harper & Row, 1964), p. 471, entry of April 14, 1942. On the conservation justification, see Robert F. Himmelberg essay in Hawley et al., pp. 63–82; for planning in the '30s: Ellis W. Hawley, *The New Deal and the Problem of Monopoly* (Princeton: Princeton University Press, 1966), pp. 122–27, 130–46; Lewis L. Lorwin and A. Ford Hinrichs, *National Economic and Social Planning* (Washington: GPO, 1935); Charles F. Roos, *NRA Economic Planning* (Bloomington, Indiana: Principia, 1937); Charles Merriam, "The National Resources Planning Board: A Chapter in American Planning Experience," *American Political Science Review*, 38 (December 1944): 1075–88.

cleavages, it posited a rallying of all productive elements against one isolated enemy. Spokesmen for reform found it easier to lead a crusade against monopoly than persevere in, or even fully confront the implications of, a contest against the more pervasive inequalities of power and wealth.

By the mid-1930s, the theme of monopoly became preoccupying anew on several grounds: the new literature on imperfect competition and oligopoly,[19] the relapse into severe recession in 1938, and, finally, the American diagnosis of the nature of Fascism. In his study for the Secretary of Agriculture, *Industrial Prices and their Relative Inflexibility*, Gardiner Means contrasted the competitive market in agriculture with the administered markets where prices were not allowed to fall with slackening demand.[20] The result was reduced purchasing power that might explain persistent depression. When manufacturing prices rose faster than wages, Henderson and Ezekiel both correctly predicted renewed recession.[21] The setback to New Deal hopes prompted Roosevelt to propose a major investigation of the economic obstacles to recovery. An attack on monopoly was not only relatively cost-free in political terms; it seemed appropriate in the light of the latest economic analysis. In April 1938 the President asked Congress to open a major inquiry into American economic structures with a message that stressed the inequality among corporations (less than 0.1 percent of corporations owned 52 percent of the assets) and attributed unemployment to rigid administered prices.

Monopoly, Roosevelt suggested further, was politically dangerous: "The liberty of a democracy is not safe if the people tolerate the growth of private power to a point where it becomes stronger than their democratic state itself. That, in its essence, is Fascism—ownership of government by an individual, by a group, or by any other controlling private power."[22] This warning naturally reflected the anxieties of 1938. The *Anschluss* had taken place a month earlier. The idea also fit in with Cordell Hull's view of the German threat, which the Secretary interpreted as a political outgrowth of strivings for autarky. In syllogistic terms, Hull argued that economic nationalism reduced living standards, led to unemployment and despair, and, finally, provoked the use of political violence as an alternative to disorder.[23]

By the late 1930s Liberals thus connected Fascism with monopolistic economic tendencies. The Depression had obviously been instrumental in bringing Hitler to power. In addition, remarked Thruman Arnold, the new head of the

---

[19] Joan Robinson, *The Economics of Imperfect Competition* (London: Macmillan, 1933); Edward H. Chamberlain, *The Theory of Monopolistic Competition* (Cambridge, Massachusetts: Harvard University Press, 1938).

[20] US Congress, Senate, *Industrial Prices and their Relative Inflexibility*, by Gardiner Means, Sen. Doc. 13, 74th Congress, 1st. Sess. 1935; cf. Adolph Berle and Gardiner Means, *The Modern Corporation and Private Property* (New York: The Macmillan Co., 1937); also Maurice Leven, Harold G. Moulton, Clark Warburton, *America's Capacity to Consume* (Washington: The Brookings Institution, 1934), pp. 126–28.

[21] David Lynch, *The Concentration of Economic Power* (New York: Columbia University Press, 1946), pp. 1–34; Hawley, *The New Deal and the Problem of Monopoly*, pp. 404–19.

[22] Temporary National Economic Committee, *Hearings*, Vol. I, appendix, p. 105.

[23] *The Memoirs of Cordell Hull*, I, p. 364.

Anti-Trust division of the Justice Department, the effort to protect special-interest groups, which the New Deal had pursued misguidedly under the NRA, had also been an objective of the ill-fated Weimar Republic.[24] When Roosevelt listened to Morgenthau plead for a cut in business taxes to restore industry's confidence, the President backed away. Appeasing business "would put a man in as President who," as he called it, "would be controlled by a man on horseback, the way Mussolini and Hitler are.... This simply would mean that we would have a Fascist President."[25]

It was foreordained that the anti-monopoly theme would weaken at home with economic mobilization. On the one hand, Keynesians themselves came to stress that persistent unemployment lay in the failure to invest and not with rigid prices or inadequate consumer power. The Temporary National Economic Committee (TNEC) hearings laboriously continued, producing dozens of monographs on industries, patents, and taxation, but without much legislative result. The Committee had begun with the assumption that a conflict-free solution to unemployment, price rigidity, and unhealthy concentration of power might be found in attacking monopoly. Instead, they encountered complexity and uncertainty about the relation of size to efficiency or monopoly to depression. Thurman Arnold's vigorous antitrust prosecutions languished as the War Production Board insisted that price competition had to be relaxed for the duration.[26]

Nonetheless, the theme of monopoly continued to play a strong role in the analysis of European developments. Robert Brady, who had earlier analyzed the Nazi regime and the German rationalization movement, which also involved growing mergers and concentration, spotlighted the political role of the leading industrial interest groups in his *Business as a System of Power*. Franz Neumann's *Behemoth* helped to make a quasi-Marxist analysis of National Socialist power the intellectual basis for much of American planning for the postwar occupation of Germany. These and similar discussions in the press continued to elaborate Roosevelt's 1938 conclusions that Fascism was essentially an outgrowth of modern private economic power.[27]

Thus by 1945 the two themes of productivity and monopoly formed the conceptual axes along which Americans located economic institutions. At home there was the inconclusive confrontation between the popularly mandated New Deal and the long-sanctioned tradition of free enterprise, between the wartime

---

[24] Lilienthal, p. 324, entry of May 22, 1941.

[25] John Morton Blum, ed., *From the Morgenthau Diaries, Vol. 1: Years of Urgency, 1938–1941* (Boston: Houghton Mifflin Company, 1965), p. 20.

[26] Lynch describes the TNEC results; for antitrust see Hawley, *The New Deal and the Problem of Monopoly*, pp. 420–25.

[27] See three books by Robert Brady, *The Rationalization Movement in German Industry* (Berkeley and Los Angeles: University of California Press, 1933); *The Spirit and Structure of German Fascism* (New York: The Viking Press, 1937); *Business as a System of Power* (New York: Columbia University Press, 1943); Franz Neumann, *Behemoth: The Structure and Practice of National Socialism* (Toronto and New York: Columbia University Press, 1942). Cf. Lutz Niethammer, *Entnazifierung in Bayern: Säuberung und Rehabilitierung unter amerikanischer Besatzung* (Frankfurt am Main: S. Fischer Verlag, 1972), pp. 37 ff.

rehabilitation of industrialists and the distrust of monopoly. This domestic stalemate made recourse to metapolitical notions of economic organization natural and
appealing. Monopoly explained political and economic setbacks; productivity promised advance.

Nevertheless, the conjugate themes would be applied to different areas. The
politics of productivity beckoned originally in the non-Axis countries. The ineffi-
ciencies of production that would be vexing in Europe after 1945 did not appear as
a result of concentrated power but as the consequences of a hidebound traditional-
ism attributed to small and backward businessmen. Moreover, the indices of
production and growth allowed supposedly apolitical criteria for dealing with the
rivalries among the postwar contenders in France, Italy, and elsewhere. They
provided a justification for separating constructive growth-minded labor movements
(Social-Democratic or Christian) from divisive and allegedly self-seeking Communist
ones.

Americans would draw upon the anti-monopoly orientation, on the other
hand, in establishing plans for transforming the political economies of defeated
Germany and Japan. Until 1948–49, the Occupation authorities imposed decartelization in their German zone and moved to break up the Zaibatsu across the Pacific.
As Edwin Pauley's reparation mission concluded in the months after V-J Day:

> Japan's Zaibatsu (literally, 'financial clique') are . . . the greatest war potential
> of Japan. It was they who made possible all Japan's conquests and aggres-
> sions. . . . Not only were the Zaibatsu as responsible for Japan's militarism as
> the militarists themselves, but they profited immensely by it. Even now, in
> defeat, they have actually strengthened their monopoly position. . . . Unless
> the Zaibatsu are broken up, the Japanese have little prospect of ever being
> able to govern themselves as free men. As long as the Zaibatsu survive, Japan
> will be their Japan.[28]

Not only did the anti-monopoly concepts find service in the Occupation, but some
of the trust-busters themselves left the unpromising Justice Department to pursue
their work in defeated Germany and Japan.[29] The Axis powers offered a laboratory
in which to pursue the reforms that had been shelved at home. Within a few years,
of course, they would be shelved abroad. Faced with the Cold War, Americans
ultimately would actually carry out one further dialectical transformation. They
would subordinate their crusade against monopoly in the ex-Fascist powers precisely to advance the cause of productivity. Just as during the war the Administration had dropped antitrust prosecutions for the sake of industrial mobilization,
after 1948, policy makers would tacitly abandon the anti-monopoly drive in
Germany and Japan in order to spur the non-Communist economies as a whole. By

---

[28] Jerome B. Cohen, *Japan's Economy in War and Reconstruction* (Minneapolis: University of
Minnesota Press, 1949), p. 427.
[29] For the embittered reaction of one see James Stewart Martin, *All Honorable Men* (Boston:
Little, Brown, 1952).

that time, however, Americans had already constructed the scaffolding of the Western economic order they were seeking.

## II  The arena for American policy

"Americans are inclined to believe that the period at the end of the war will provide a tabula rasa on which can be written the terms of a democratic new order. The economic and political institutions of 1939 and before are clearly in suspension and need not be restored intact after the war."[30] This assessment, which was offered during an October 1942 study group session of the Council on Foreign Relations, was typical of much American thinking. And by 1945, looking at Berlin and Warsaw, or Caen, who could doubt that Europe was a tabula rasa?

In fact, however, Europe was not a blank slate, and the economic policies that the United States thrust upon it could not avoid partisan implications even when they were deemed apolitical. The major issues Washington sought to influence in economic reconstruction concerned new monetary arrangements and trade agreements (the whole complex structure of multilateralism) and the role of foreign assistance. Also at issue were the nature of labor representation (specifically, how to organize trade union support for plans consonant with American leadership) and the total reconstruction possible in West Germany and Japan. Each of these massive and perplexing set of issues tested the American postulates of productivity.

*Multilateralism and monetary reorganization:* The return to a system of stable exchange rates was high on the agenda for both American and British leaders from the beginning of US involvement in the war. Yet, within the Anglo-American alliance, there were sharp differences of interest. If Congress or the United States Treasury were going to endorse unprecedented foreign aid first in the Lend-Lease agreements, then in the $3.75 billion loan of 1945–46, they saw no reason not to compel London to give up commercial advantages that excluded American producers. Section VII of the Lend-Lease agreement had insisted upon postwar trade liberalization (although specifics remained omitted). The Treasury did not want British reserves to rise, and American negotiators were to attack such British assets as the dominion reserves held in sterling in London. The British, on the other hand, invoked the notion of "equality of sacrifice" in the common war effort. What Washington was being asked to bear appeared small in comparison to their losses, financial and otherwise.

It would be wrong to bifurcate the positions too absolutely. After their own devaluation decisions during 1933–34, Roosevelt and his advisors agreed that high employment should take precedence over the stability of international exchange. Veterans of the 1930s understood that they could not allow the cost of stable currency parities to be a wrenching deflation of the home economies. This meant

---

[30]Council on Foreign Relations: Studies of American Interests in the War and the Peace, Memoranda of Discussion; Economic and Financial Series, E-A 36, October 27, 1942.

that as natural postwar leader and source of the potential key currency, the United States would bear a special responsibility. It must be prepared to rediscount the deficits in international account of the weaker economies and to provide the international liquidity that would get its own goods abroad. Was Washington ready for that responsibility? And if Roosevelt himself, bound by ties of sentiment and flattery to Churchill, was, would Republican Conservatives and Western Democrats endorse the policies?

The record was mixed. From the outset the differences between Keynes's plan for a postwar clearing union and Harry Dexter White's proposed stabilization fund reflected the divergent national interests. In Keynes's concept, the burden of currency stabilization was to be shared with the creditor nation (much as later the United States would pressure West Germany and Japan for upward revaluation of their respective exchange rates). Keynes envisaged a large pool of international reserves, which, like later Special Drawing Rights (SDRs), could be created as needed. To discourage countries from maintaining an undervalued currency he proposed that the large creditors of the clearing union pay interest along with the debtors. This was a suggestion that most of his colleagues saw as more playful than serious. Finally, Keynes envisaged automatic overdraft rights on the clearing union by national banks, much as British businessmen might overdraw their own accounts. The United States plan included only a modest fund without overdraft rights; but by mid-December 1942 White proposed a "scarce currency" clause that would have allowed debtor nations to discriminate in trade against a creditor nation that persisted in piling up balances with the stabilization fund. "The Americans," noted Roy Harrod, who felt the concession truly epochal, "have, happily, played a card which according to the rules of the game we could not play."[31] The scarce currency provision was actually accepted by the Congress in the Bretton Woods Act of July 1945. This action suggested that the majority understood it could not demand that an exhausted Europe simultaneously "buy American" and maintain currency stability. In contrast with the 1920s, this represented a significant insight, or concession, on the part of the United States, albeit a limited one. The International Monetary Fund (IMF) remained inadequately funded and entrusted with procedures that enforced a deflationary unorthodoxy upon debtors; and Washington was to keep up pressure on Britain to restore the pound to a disastrous convertibility.

The ambivalent pattern of pressure and support on the West Europeans remained characteristic of United States policy from the war until the 1950s. Increasingly, the more restrictive policies became identified with the Treasury while those more sympathetic with European reflationary needs influenced the Marshall Plan administration. The policy makers in these agencies had to confront a variety of European monetary initiatives after 1945. For all the countries the root problem

---

[31] Cf. Gardner, *Sterling-Dollar Diplomacy;* Rowland in Rowland, pp. 213–22; Paterson, pp. 159–73; Roy Harrod, *The Life of John Maynard Keynes* (New York: Harcourt, Brace, 1951), p. 547 (letter to Keynes, March 2, 1943).

was the same: apportioning the costs of the war by cancelling various claims to wealth and income. In Belgium and Holland a resolute amputation of bank accounts and monetary claims facilitated quick reconstruction of stable currencies. This was a solution that America and Britain would impose upon West Germany three years later.[32] In France, equivalent measures were proposed by Pierre Mendès-France but met opposition from a Communist Party in search of middle-class votes and found no support from De Gaulle. Instead, France muddled through with a chronic inflation that amounted to a disguised capital levy. Italy's postwar financial policy initially followed the pattern of French irresolution, for the liberation of Italy restored a group of traditionalist *liberisti* economists as policy makers. They were untainted by Fascism but retained the laissez-faire convictions of the pre-1925 era. Once the Left had been forced out of the governing coalition in 1947, they embarked upon a severe scheme of monetary stabilization. Their restrictions of private credit indeed halted the inflation that had shrunk the lira to one-seventieth of its 1938 value, but also provoked a recession that bottled up potential labor in the South and left existing industrial capacity badly under-utilized. Recent monetarists have judged the results as a necessary cleansing for the heady growth of the 1950s. However, Economic Cooperation Administration (ECA) critics of the time (and subsequent Keynesian-type analysts) sharply condemned a policy that seemed to waste Marshall Plan resources on building up currency reserves.[33] The heirs of Franklin Roosevelt did not really wish simply to restore the counterparts of Herbert Hoover.

On the other hand, there was American consensus on the general value of multilateral exchange and as much currency convertibility as possible. The creation of intra-European payment mechanisms that were to culminate in the European Payments Union of 1952 appeared just the logical steps toward an expansion of trade that all desired. These clearing mechanisms, however, raised new conflicts with London. Authorities there feared that the intra-European accounts would expose Britain's hazardous reserve position to further depletion, as had occurred when, under Washington's pressure, the pound had been made convertible for

---

[32] Leon H. Dupriez, *Monetary Reconstruction in Belgium* (New York: The Carnegie Endowment for International Peace and the King's Crown Press, 1947), esp. Chapters 3–4; Fritz Grotius, "Die europäischen Geldreformen nach dem 2. Weltkrieg," *Weltwirtschaftliches Archiv,* Vol. 63 (1949 II): 106–52, 276–325; J.C. Gurley, "Excess Liquidity and European Monetary Reforms," *The American Economic Review,* 43 (March 1953): 76–100; Hans Möller, "Die westdeutsche Währungsreform von 1948," in *Währung und Wirtschaft in Deutschland 1876–1975,* Deutsche Bundesbank, ed. (Frankfurt am Main: Fritz Knapp GmbH, 1976), pp. 433–83.
[33] For criticism, Marcello De Cecco, "Sulla politica di stabilizzazione del 1948," *Saggi di politica monetaria* (Milan: Dott. A. Giuffrè Editore, 1968), pp. 109–41; Economic Cooperation Administration, *Country Study (Italy)* (Washington, 1950); Bruno Foa, *Monetary Reconstruction in Italy* (New York: The Carnegie Endowment for International Peace and King's Crown Press, 1949); favorable judgments in George H. Hildebrand, *Growth and Structure in the Economy of Modern Italy* (Cambridge, Massachusetts: Harvard University Press, 1965), Chapters 2 and 8. On France, see Maurice Parodi, *L'économie et la société française de 1945 à 1970* (Paris: Armand Colin, 1971), pp. 66ff. For general coverage of postwar policies, A.J. Brown, *The Great Inflation, 1939–1951* (London: Oxford University Press, 1955), pp. 227–48.

several weeks in the Summer of 1947. Belgium especially, by dint of its early currency reform and the continuing influential role of its orthodox central bank, had achieved the strongest balance-of-payments position within Europe; London feared that Brussels might present its accumulation of sterling for conversion. British Labour spokesmen Stafford Cripps and Hugh Gaitskill also feared a renewal of Washington's earlier efforts to break into the sterling area. They felt that the United States sought to undermine the currency restrictions that allowed Britain to pursue socialist experiments without worrying about a flight from the pound. After a mini-crisis in June 1950, a compromise agreement between American negotiators and London limited the convertibility of intra-European claims, and Brussels and Washington spared London the burden of converting Belgium's accumulated sterling.[34]

The record of American policy thus remains ambivalent. On the one hand, United States negotiators pressed Britain to renounce its special protection for the pound and for its trade. This occurred between 1941 and 1945, again in 1946–47, and during 1950. On the other hand, credits did come through and the American demands were repeatedly modified in practice. US Treasury authorities pursued a rigid Bretton Woods multilateralism most vigorously, perhaps because key Treasury officials of the Truman years came not from academic economics (as had Harry Dexter White) or gentleman farming (as had Morgenthau) but from the world of banking. John Snyder (succeeding the cautious Southerner Fred Vinson) emerged from a mid-West banking milieu. His special assistant for international finance and later US executive director of the International Monetary Fund, Andrew Overby, had also begun as a banker and then served as a Vice-President of the New York Federal Reserve. In contrast, the Marshall Plan authorities who dealt with the individual European countries after 1948 derived from a more expansionist industry background and had endorsed Keynesian-type reflation. They also included labor union representatives to work with European trade union leaders. The debate between Treasury and Marshall Plan officials thus tended to reflect the unresolved differences between Keynesians and conservatives at home, between the New Deal and its critics.

Another indication of the same disputes and policy ambiguity was provided by American resistance to ratification of the International Trade Organization (ITO) draft charter. It was signed at Havana in March 1948, but it finally had to be removed from Congressional consideration by Truman in December 1950. The scuttling of the ITO, however, did not mean that the United States was turning its back on the laborious efforts to lower trade barriers; indeed the country remained committed to the interim General Agreement on Tariffs and Trade (GATT) concluded in 1947. But the more ambitious architecture of the ITO sought also to

[34] William Diebold, Jr., *Trade and Payment in Western Europe* (New York: Harper and Row, 1952), esp. pp. 64–69. I have also drawn upon an oral-history interview with Averell Harriman, Milton Katz et al.

regulate commodity agreements and to make allowances for the weaker partners in the international economic system. American business critics felt it had the disadvantage of committing the United States to free trade while allowing escape clauses for less robust countries. Especially disturbing was the fact that the ITO would have allowed nations to keep exchange controls and continue inflationary policies to avoid the recessions that might attend a return to full convertibility. If American businessmen were to prolong the US commitment to low tariffs, they wanted Hull's implicit compact: the open door at home would be compensated for by the open door abroad.[35]

*Foreign aid:* Crudely summarized, American policy sought to maximize currency stability and international trade. This would enhance the welfare of all and the predominance of the United States. The price of Bretton Woods, however, had to be foreign assistance. Initially, Americans did not realize or confess the full extent of support they would have to provide. Only after two years of false starts did they face up to the problem of Europe's dollar gap in its full magnitude. But the issue of expanding foreign aid beset their postulates with new difficulties. Originally an apolitical aid was thought to secure the broad range of American objectives. Once, however, the Soviet Union was acknowledged as a threat, the liberals' image of a healthy political economy became strained. It was no longer clear that simple maximization of output adequately answered American interests. Increasingly, policy makers rejected those forms of international assistance which provided no direct political dividend, such as the UN Relief and Rehabilitation Administration (UNRRA). Harriman and others criticized this form of aid early on.[36] On the other hand, foreign aid could not become purely subordinate to politics, for it followed from all the earlier axioms that problems of political stability and capitalist recovery were resolved by efficient and neutral applications of planning or social engineering.

The difficulties became significant when Léon Blum came to plead for coal and funds in Washington during March 1946. As the American Ambassador in Paris warned, a rebuff to Blum would benefit the Communists significantly. Assistant Secretary of State Clayton endorsed generous assistance on behalf of the State Department. In the meetings of the National Advisory Council on International Monetary and Financial Problems, however, Marriner Eccles objected that "he would dislike to have the Government accused of undertaking to buy a foreign election." (This was a scruple soon to vanish.) Clayton answered that "he had great difficulty in separating political from economic conditions in thinking about Europe. If he thought that country X was in danger of economic and social chaos he would favor a loan if it were reasonable in amount and there were a reasonable chance of repayment." Secretary of Commerce Henry Wallace was also willing to go

---

[35] On this issue, see William Diebold, Jr., *The End of the ITO*, Princeton University, Department of Economics and Social Institutions, Studies in International Finance (Princeton: Princeton University Press, 1952).

[36] Paterson, pp. 94–98.

along, provided that a "bad" loan would not be extended merely to stabilize political conditions.[37] Hesitation about using loans for partisan or anti-Communist goals was expressed in Council on Foreign Relations discussions as late as December 1946. Some speakers felt that Washington should decide on the groups it favored and extend aid selectively. Others found Dean Acheson's food policy "exerting too much direct pressure on European politics."[38]

It is notable that a selective policy still raised controversy at the end of a year of growing tension over Germany and Eastern Europe, atomic weapons, Iran, and the role of Communism in general. Nonetheless, the rationale for foreign aid now involved both Cold War objectives and the commitment to productivity. When George Kennan's Policy Planning Staff worked up a paper on aid to Western Europe in May 1947, it argued that "it does not see Communist activities as the root of the difficulties of Western Europe." Blame was instead placed on the effects of the war and the "profound exhaustion of physical plant and of spiritual vigor." Thus, it advocated "that American effort in aid to Europe should be directed not to the combatting of Communism as such but to the restoration of the economic health and vigor of European society."[39] When the European Recovery Program was launched, it was theoretically offered to the Communist states as well, although most in Washington probably did not expect Soviet adhesion and were probably relieved when Molotov quit the preliminary talks. But at least the Marshall Plan allowed American liberals to endorse an implicitly anti-Communist aid program on the older grounds of economic assistance. Aid could remain simultaneously apolitical in motive and political in result. The point is not to deny that the antagonism with Soviet Russia deeply influenced American objectives. It is easy to catalogue the Cold War initiatives of the period (whether ultimately they were taken in response to Soviet threats is not the issue here): they included firmness over Iran, formation of the Bizone, and exclusion of the Communists from the coalitions in France, Belgium, and Italy. Wrangling at the Foreign Ministers' Conferences, the Truman Doctrine, moving toward establishment of a West German state, and limiting Socialist outcomes in the Western zones were other important milestones. This escalation confirmed the division of Europe and Asia and the formation of a United States hegemony in "the West." Nonetheless, if the politics of the Cold War in a sense took over the economic rationale of American policy, it also logically continued the politics of productivity. Both were efforts to align universalist aspirations with United States preponderance.

*The issue of European labor:* The politics of productivity, as it set the guidelines for American policy during the formative postwar years, had necessarily to include a trade union dimension. Ultimately, the American prescriptions for

---

[37] US Department of State, *Foreign Relations of the United States,* 1946, V, 440–43. (Minutes of the Twenty-Fourth Meeting of the National Advisory Council on International and Monetary Problems, Washington, May 6, 1946.)
[38] Council on Foreign Relations archives, Records of Groups, XII G.
[39] US Department of State, *Foreign Relations of the United States,* 1947, III, 224–25.

Europe postulated that economic relations could be free of conflict, hence, could transcend earlier class divisions. This was never really true in the US, although observers during the war might be excused for thinking class antagonisms had been superseded. More accurately, the challenge of American labor had not shaken the society's consensus on the value of private enterprise as in Europe. After 1945, the view of Europe as a tabula rasa suggested an equivalent opportunity to build consensus there as well.

What such a perspective suggested was that those labor groups willing to endorse growth and productivity should continue as a component of the European coalitions. Those who dissented were held to be regrettably partisan, obstructionist, and by 1947, subversive. During the period of liberation, it was precisely the French and Italian Communists who insisted upon the imperatives of production and summoned striking coal miners and workers back to their jobs. At the same time, Catholic, Social-Democratic, and Communist labor representatives strenuously worked to unify their trade unions as they emerged from an era of Fascist suppression. But this unity proved ephemeral and broke down on both the political and the trade union levels.[40] In France Communist Party acquiescence in policies of wage restraint provoked criticism from left-wing militants as the harsh Winter of 1946–47 set back economic recovery. Following hesitating support for a strike of Renault workers, the Party was excluded from the French government, and, in constant touch with the State Department, De Gasperi performed analogous surgery in May of 1947.[41]

In the flurry of messages over American aid in the Spring of 1947, the issue of Communist participation in government had emerged as implicitly critical. It was not surprising that by the Fall of 1947, the Communist labor confederations should make rejection of the Marshall Plan a major issue in the demonstrations and strikes that shook France and Italy. The strike movement, however, further crystallized the internal divisions within the trade union movements. Non-Communist members had already organized their own journal in France, *Résistance Ouvière*, now redubbed *Force Ouvrière*. By late 1947 acceptance of the Marshall Plan became the major touchstone of division between the non-Communists and Communists, and Force Ouvrière leaders felt that the Communists had engaged labor's sacrifices to support a policy dictated by Moscow. At the end of 1947 they left the Confédération Générale du Travail (CGT) to organize their own federation the following April.

[40] Trends can be followed in Georges Lefranc, *Le mouvement syndical de la libération aux événements de mai–juin 1968* (Paris: Presses Universitaires de France, 1969), pp. 41–76; Fabio Levi, Paride Rugafiori, Salvatore Vento, *Il triangolo industriale tra ricostruzione e lotta di classe 1945/48* (Milan: Feltrinelli, 1974); Adolfo Pepe, "La CGIL della ricostruzione alla scissione (1944–1948)," *Storia Contemporanea*, 5 (1974): 591–636; Alfred J. Rieber, *Stalin and the French Communist Party, 1941–1947* (New York: Columbia University Press, 1962), Chapter 14.

[41] Besides the above, see Ambassador Caffrey's report to the State Department in *Foreign Relations of the United States*, 1947, III, p. 703, and Ambassador Dunn (Rome) on May 28, 1947, in ibid., pp. 911 ff.

In Italy, Catholic and socialist trade unionists left their federation, the General Confederation of Italian Labor (CGIL), a few months thereafter.[42]

Throughout this interval United States officials and AFL leaders encouraged the non-Communist unions to secede and establish their own federations. CIA agent Thomas Braden later estimated that $2 million was channeled to the pro-Western elements.[43] Ambassador Caffrey in Paris condemned the CGT as "the fortress" of the French Communist Party. Ambassador James Clement Dunn in Rome saw the local working class demand for factory councils as a "Communist framework for fomenting disorder and attacking the authority of the state."[44] American CIO leaders were initially reluctant to join in the concerted pressure against the unified labor federations and for a while resisted official pleas that they enlist against the Communists. But by late 1948 the CIO was wracked by the struggle against Communist-led unions within its own ranks, and its leaders felt a greater Communist danger. Secretary James Carey also served on the Harriman Committee that helped outline the European Recovery Program after Marshall's famous address of June 1947, and he became angry over the obstruction to the plan that the fellow-traveling Secretary-General of the World Federation of Free Trade Unions seemed to be raising. By the Spring of 1949, the CIO and the AFL met with the Force Ouvrière and the British Trade Union Congress to charter a new non-Communist international labor federation.[45]

The Marshall Plan thus irrevocably split the European labor movement between 1947–49. More precisely, it sealed a division that was probable in any case; but it did so on the questions of economic recovery that Americans found easiest to defend. Given the United States axioms, what men of good will could legitimately reject the concept of assistance to stimulate investment and production? The Communists, in a sense, placed themselves outside the continuum of normal politics. On the other hand, the premises of the Marshall Plan, as well as the make-up of the Truman Administration, imposed limits on the political reaction of 1947–49. No Democratic Administration in the United States, especially one facing a challenge from its Left, could have alienated labor. Nor would it thereafter have been able to work with any anti-Communist government abroad that needed to preserve some working-class support. From this derived the imperative of constructing a Social-Democratic center, even if this strategy meant, as Dunn argued from Italy, that socialization would be accelerated.[46] The British Labour Party, finally, remained a key factor in organizing a "third force," and its members believed, in

---

[42] Lefranc, pp. 51–76; Sergio Turone, *Storia del sindacato in Italia(1943–1969)* (Bari: Laterza, 1973), pp. 177–89; Daniel L. Horowitz, *The Italian Labor Movement* (Cambridge, Massachusetts: Harvard University Press, 1963), pp. 214 ff.

[43] *The New York Times*, May 8, 1967, p. 1, for Braden revelations.

[44] *Foreign Relations of the United States*, 1947, III, 690–91 (Caffrey cable, February 19), and 747–48 (Dunn report, December 11, 1948), III.

[45] Evolution of the CIO leadership can be followed in *Foreign Relations of the United States*, 1948, III, 847–48, 867 (reports of March 10 and 24).

[46] *Foreign Relations of the United States*, 1948, III, p. 863 (March 28, 1948).

the words of Dennis Healey, that Europe could be reconstructed only as Democratic Socialist or Communist.[47] Far from turning out to be an infinitely malleable society, Europe and its divisions forced the American politics of productivity in a clear centrist direction.

*Germany and Japan:* The influence that Washington exerted through foreign aid in most of Europe could be imposed directly in the two societies that would later form the strongest building blocks of the Western economy along with America, specifically West Germany and Japan. During the very months that the division of Germany was becoming irremediable (Spring 1947 to Spring 1948), the future political economy of the West German state was also being decided. The outcome depended upon a complex interplay between a number of groups and individuals. General Lucius Clay was proconsul of the American zone. The Department of the Army in Washington supported Clay. The Department of State heeded the Paris Embassy's warnings about the dangers of compelling the shaky French government to accept too quick a German recovery. Finally, the British government controlled the industrial heartland of North-Rhine-Westphalia. It was clear that Clay would seek to limit Socialist initiatives inside the *Länder* of the American zone. The formation of the Bizone, moreover, allowed him to determine effectively the outcome within North-Rhine-Westphalia as well, even though it lay inside the British administrative sphere. During 1947 Clay forestalled British Labour Party intentions to establish the Ruhr mines under public German control. Once Clay's views prevailed in Washington, French and British dependence upon American aid precluded their resisting his framework for a capitalist and federalist West German state. The implications for future West German politics were crucial; for coupled with the diminishing chances for reunification, the new constraints on West German collectivism effectively condemned the left wings of the SPD and of the CDU to a political desert. Who remembers today the vibrant Christian Socialism of the North-Rhine-Westphalian CDU before 1949?[48]

Comparable developments took place in Japan. The revival of trade unionism that Occupation authorities originally encouraged became unwelcome when labor protested against the deterioration of living conditions that had occurred after the end of the war and that had reached a crisis (in all countries) during the Winter of 1946–47. When the militant, Communist-oriented Sambetsu union federation announced a general strike for February 1, 1947, MacArthur prohibited the demonstration. The Socialist Party won a plurality in the April elections (the Liberals and

---

[47] Ibid., p. 855 (March 17, 1948).
[48] For Clay's opposition to British plans, and Washington discussions, see *Foreign Relations of the United States,* 1947, II, pp. 910–11, 924ff; also Jean Edward Smith, ed., *The Papers of Lucius D. Clay: Germany 1945–1949,* 2 vols. (Bloomington, Ind.: The Indiana University Press, 1975), Vol. I, pp. 341–43, 352–63, 411–13. For German political ramifications see, among others, Hans-Peter Schwarz, *Vom Reich zur Bundesrepublik. Deutschland im Widerstreit der aussenpolitischen Konzeptionen in den Jahren der Besatzungsherrschaft 1945–1949* (Neuwied and Berlin: Luchterhand, 1966), pp. 297–344, 551–64; also Eberhard Schmidt, *Die verhinderte Neuordnung 1945–1952* (Frankfurt am Main: Europäische Verlagsanstalt, 1970).

Democrats had not yet consolidated) and participated in the government during 1947–48. It was the last time for a generation that they were to do so. Both Japanese business and the Supreme Allied Command-Pacific endeavored successfully to encourage a schism in the Sambetsu. They achieved a secession by the moderates and the formation, by 1950, of the Sōhyō federation. This was analogous to the contemporary formation of Force Ouvrière in France or the Social Democratic Party in Italy.[49]

In both Germany and Japan the policy of industrial deconcentration was slowly jettisoned. By the Fall of 1947, the Harriman-Draper mission to Germany recommended a new emphasis on rebuilding German industry and protests rose against dismantling and reparations (even to the Western allies). Draper visited Japan in early 1948 and made similar recommendations. He was followed by Secretary of the Army Kenneth Royall and by fiscally orthodox Detroit banker Joseph Dodge in early 1949. The campaign against the Zaibatsu faltered as did the effort to reorganize durably the German iron and steel industry.[50] The logic of the new policy was persuasive. If the United States were to commit itself to a great effort to restore economic production in Europe and Asia, how could it plausibly persevere in crippling the most productive centers of those continents?

Indeed, West Germany and Japan remained the states where the United States' politics of productivity could be transplanted most triumphantly. Perhaps because of the visible destruction all around or the labor pool formed by the immigrants from the East, German labor demonstrated consistent restraint. The Social Democrat Party (SPD) did not press its program in Bizonia. Indeed, it reverted to the opposition. The trade union federation (DGB) accepted a far more circumscribed co-determination law than it originally wanted. As German industrial and banking leaders would themselves testify, trade union wage restraint became a major component of the economic miracle.[51] The post-Korea take-off in Japan condemned the Left in that country to a noisy but marginal status.

American policy in Germany and Japan was thus a resounding success. The whole thrust of Washington's effort in the emerging Federal Republic, the new Japan, and the members of the Organization for European Economic Cooperation (OEEC)–later the Organization for Economic Cooperation and Development

[49] Jon Halliday, *A Political History of Japanese Capitalism* (New York: Pantheon Books, 1975), pp. 206–19, is useful from a Marxist perspective. See also Eitaro Kishimoto, "Labour-Management Relations and the Trade Unions in Post-War Japan (1)," *The Kyoto University Economic Review* Vol. 38, No. 1 (April 1968): 1–35, which emphasizes the role played by "seniority wages" in encouraging enterprise unions at the expense of more class-oriented labor coalitions; also Iwayo F. Ayusawa, *A History of Labor in Modern Japan* (Honolulu: East-West Center Press, 1966), pp. 257–75, 281–301, 315–23; Koji Taira, *Economic Development and the Labor Market in Japan* (New York: Columbia University Press, 1970), pp. 183–87.

[50] Halliday, *A Political History of Japanese Capitalism*, pp. 182–90; John Gimbel, *The American Occupation of Germany, 1945–1949* (Stanford, Calif.: Stanford University Press, 1968), pp. 147 ff., 163 ff., 174–85.

[51] See, for example, Herman Abs's presentation to the Council on Foreign Relations, December 5, 1949, Council on Foreign Relations Archives, Records of Meetings, Vol. 10.

(OECD)—was to ensure the primacy of economics over politics, to de-ideologize issues of political economy into questions of output and efficiency. The two occupied states offered the most promising ground for accomplishing the conversion of politics into economics. Especially in West Germany, the political structure developed as a scaffolding for economic reconstruction; the Federal Republic emerged as a proto-state built upon organs for economic administration. Even today both the Federal Republic and Japan are nations which represent massive economic forces that lack concomitant political weight. From states in which military-bureaucratic establishments, pursuing objectives of prestige and expansion, called upon the resources of production for statist ends, they have become political economies in which the concept of state has become virtually otiose.

In the last analysis, the politics of productivity that emerged as the American organizing idea for the postwar economic world depended upon superseding class conflict with economic growth. By bringing West Germany and Japan into a community of nations as dynamos of wider regional recovery, the United States aided other societies to adjourn their own distributive conflicts and to move from scarcity to relative abundance. By helping to establish West Germany and Japan as nexuses of economic transactions and the most efficient accumulators of capital, rather than as centers of political power, America most completely carried out its postwar economic postulates.

The success of this politics of productivity can be judged by the fact that the 1950s and the 1960s turned out to be periods of unparalleled growth and capital formation. Investment was a major objective of the European Recovery Program.

### Table I  Gross national capital formation

|  | *1950–58* | *Previous maxima* |
|---|---|---|
| UK | 16.2% | 14.0% (1900–14) |
| German Federal Republic | 26.8 | 24.1 (1891–1913) |
| Italy | 19.8 | 17.3 (1901–10) |
| United States | 18.4 | 21.9 (1889–1908) |
| Sweden | 21.4 | c. 20.4 (1941–49, inferred) |
| Japan | 30.2 | 15.3 (1927–36) |

Source: Simon Kuznets, *Modern Economic Growth: Rate, Structure, and Spread* (New Haven: Yale University Press, 1966), pp. 236–39.

Without capital formation, American aid might ease immediate balance-of-payment crises but would have to continue indefinitely, whereas the premise of the Marshall Plan as presented to Congress was that after four years Europe's self-sufficiency would be restored. By 1948–49, it was clear that Europe was investing 20 percent of its GNP, whereas from an equal social product in 1938, its societies had ploughed back only 12 percent. (And military expenditures in 1948–49 were only 1 percent less than 1938's 6 percent.) Indeed, the ambitious British investment levels of 1948–49, when gross domestic capital formation (less overseas deficit) reached 22.8 percent (1948) and 21.4 percent (1949), or roughly twice that of 1938, seemed excessive to American Keynesians. The memory of the Depression, when aggregate demand did not keep pace with productive capacity, sobered the observers of British efforts under the Marshall Plan.[52]

Insofar as much of post-World War II politics can be viewed as a debate between growth and equality, between collective investment or public consumption, at least until the late 1960s, the argument was largely resolved so as not to endanger investment. This can be inferred not only from electoral returns that excluded the Left, but from the slow percentage growth of wage shares as a component of national income. In the stately half-century decline of the return on capital, the 1950s represented a decade of redress. Reviewing the reverses of Socialism in 1959, Richard Titmuss found increasing privilege, inequality, and concentrations of power.[53] The other side of the story was unparalleled economic growth (albeit outside Great Britain) and the rise of real incomes. Germany and Japan, above all, achieved record growth and accumulation. These were, of course, precisely the arenas in which the American politics of productivity could be most thoroughly instituted.

In retrospect the 1950s, and even the 1960s, must be judged a great era for the stabilized growth capitalism of the West. Conservative governments ruled in London, Bonn, Rome, for a time in Paris, and certainly in Washington. This was not right-wing leadership, but solid men of the center committed to growth after wartime destruction and exhaustion with ideological conflict. The United States encouraged this trend but did not have to impose it. Had these impulses not been present it seems unlikely that Americans could have built a breakwater in Europe any more than they were able to dam up different aspirations in Asia. On the other hand, the social basis for the politics of productivity was present in Europe, as it was not in mainland Asia. The war and Nazi occupation had shaken, but not uprooted, a prevailingly bourgeois society with broad middle-class patterns of ownership and culture.

## III The limits of American hegemony

Perhaps the best term for the postwar Western economy would be that of consensual American hegemony. "Consensual" can be used because European leaders accepted Washington's leadership in view of their needs for economic and security assistance. Hegemony derives from Washington's ability to establish policy guidelines binding on the West. In what respects, however, did hegemony really mean influence exerted to alter European policies that might otherwise have turned

---

[52] Howard Ellis, *The Economics of Freedom* (New York: Harper, 1952), pp. 129, 135.
[53] Richard Titmuss, "The Irresponsible Society," *Essays on the Welfare State* (Boston: Beacon Press, 1969).

out differently? Certainly in the years 1944 to 1947 the emphasis on free convertibility of currencies and stable exchange rates, as stipulated in the Bretton Woods arrangements and aid to Britain, were designed, in part, to limit London's capacity to organize a separate trading bloc. Pained British protests made American *force majeure* abundantly clear, although they did not necessarily justify British preferences in terms of broader criteria of economic welfare. In the years after 1947, when the objectives of some American policy makers became more politically conservative, Washington's continuing pressure on behalf of the dollar as an international currency, the political signals which accompanied its foreign aid, and its direct intervention in West Germany and Japan could inhibit leftist experiments in societies that might have tried alternative principles of economic organization. These would in turn have ultimately been less susceptible to United States influence. Usually Washington did not have brutally to abort a series of promising Socialist initiatives. Instead, it more subtly rewarded a generation of centrist "Atlantic" oriented European leaders (and Japanese Liberal Democrats) who found the American preferences rational and humane. Moreover, the United States could benefit from some of the economic arrangements generated in wartime Europe and Japan. For if the wartime experiences provoked a left-wing resistance mystique, paradoxically they reinforced corporatist patterns of social bargaining that persisted afterward. Labor relations in Germany, Japan, the Netherlands, and other countries were to bear the wartime impression, and the United States would ultimately benefit from the collaborative tendencies thus bequeathed.[54] In the last analysis, the means of exercising hegemony may be as critical as the fact of dominance itself: the architects of the American-sponsored international economic order exerted a gentlemanly persuasion. Moreover, it was one enjoying most of the mystical aura of an "invisible hand," which usually attends smoothly running cybernetic systems, much as had been the case with the Gold Standard before World War I.[55]

Hegemony remains successful, however, only when it achieves advances for the whole international structure within which it is exercised. Hegemony imposed in a zero-sum cockpit, that is, at the expense of the secondary members of the system, must finally prove less durable. (Alternatively, it requires overt force; viz., Hungary, 1956, and Czechoslovakia, 1968.) The quarter-century of relatively frictionless American domination depended partially upon the fact that the technologies of the era (including the capitalization of agriculture) permitted the growth

---

[54] These continuities in Europe comprise a major theme of my own current research; for the Japanese case, see Taira, p. 188, drawing upon the Japanese work of Ryohei Magota.

[55] For the issue of whether international monetary systems do or do not require "hegemonic" leadership see the essays in Rowland, ed., *Balance of Power or Hegemony;* also Stephen D. Krasner, "State Power and the Structure of International Trade," *World Politics* Vol. 28, No. 3 (July 1976): 317–43. Insights into the regulatory capacity of the earlier system are derived from Arthur Bloomfield, *Short-Term Capital Movements under the Gold Standard,* Princeton University, Department of Economics and Social Institutions, International Studies No. 16 (Princeton, N.J., 1952), esp. pp. 72ff.; Peter Lindert, "Key Currencies and Gold, 1900–1913," *Princeton Studies in International Finance,* No. 24 (Princeton, N.J.: Princeton University Press, 1969).

that was its underlying premise. Ironically, too, the destruction left by World War II allowed rapid catch-up recovery that could be attributed to the American role. The result was that the politics of productivity rested upon the reality of productivity. The system paid off.

Indeed, once the system ceased to pay off, it began to founder. Between 1944 and 1971 the structures of American leadership could serve the United States in one of two ways: one accepted as legitimate and one as less legitimate by the secondary participants. Insofar as the United States was prepared to furnish European societies goods and services without real economic counterpart, it could ask policy compliance in return. This was the situation of the "dollar gap" in the late 1940s and early 1950s, when Washington provided more than $20 billion of assistance and secured more open trading areas. The other way that Americans could utilize the Bretton Woods framework was precisely the reverse: by exacting tribute through seigneurage, i.e., accumulating dollar liabilities abroad and purchasing European assets with an overvalued currency. This was the situation of the late 1960s when, in effect, the United States taxed its allies for part of the costs of the Indochina War (combined with other public commitments) by trying to insist upon the unaltered reserve status of an eroding dollar. Since, however, the system remained one of consensual hegemony (contrasted, for example, with the German organization of continental Europe between 1940 and 1944), the United States could not easily enforce the power of unlimited overdrafts. The French refused to pay the levy from 1965 on, and it was primarily the special West German dependence upon US security presence that enabled the Bretton Woods framework to last as long as it did. (That West German need, both objective and subjective, in turn reflected the special circumstances in which the Federal Republic of Germany had emerged under US auspices.)

With the partial relinquishing of American claims to leadership, the divergent patterns of foreign economic policy that are the subject of the other essays in this volume became more visible. While Washington's politics of productivity helped to reorient the Western economies in the postwar era, characteristic national preferences and approaches persisted. Of course, as American predominance relaxed, it would have been logical for the secondary countries to revert to a more mercantilist conduct in the absence of forceful leadership. Such trends, though, were to be further reinforced by traditional historical patterns of economic policy making. For all its economic vigor, for example, the business leadership of West Germany continued to reemphasize the primacy of exports and only secondarily the importance of domestic purchasing power and expansion. Italian and Japanese policy makers likewise tended to pursue policies in which relatively cheap labor played a major role. The American politics of productivity applied abroad had originally encouraged labor restraint to secure ultimate economic growth. As American leadership became more diffuse, entrepreneurs and political leaders in Europe tended to emphasize the restraint more than the growth.

Perhaps it is ungracious to ask whether what was originally a successful and, I believe, broad and generally beneficial policy had serious costs. But all grand policy structures must at least exclude alternatives, and this particular international economic system probably served to stabilize the inequalities of income and power within each society of the West and Japan. A contrast with the British imperial structure before 1914 may help to reveal the mechanism and also establish its proportions. Britain's financial preponderance rested upon real growth but also upon the society's willingness to live with sharply skewed distributions of income and wealth. Had there been sharper challenges to domestic inequality over the half-century before World War I, it might have proved far more difficult to generate the social savings that established the reserve position of sterling. By the 1920s, the costs of continuing were excessive, even for a society as cohesive as the British. American hegemony, on the other hand, was a child of Wilsonianism and the New Deal. Politically, it could not demand renunciation on the part of the American working classes for the sake of providing the liquidity of the West. Nor, initially, did it have to; the discrepancy in productivity and output between Europe and the US left by the Second World War made American leadership relatively painless in domestic terms. Conservatives complained about taxes, but the sacrifice even to support the Marshall Plan was comparatively slight. It was not the fiscal burden, but the departure from political traditions that represented the major domestic hurdle. When, by the end of the 1960s, real sacrifices at home in terms of taxation or restrictions on use of the dollar abroad might have been necessary to restore credibility in the dollar's reserve status, the Nixon Administration chose to renounce a degree of economic primacy.

Yet the contrary-to-fact query remains. Might the progress of reducing inequality within the United States as well as Europe not have been faster or surer without the quarter-century of economic domination? It is impossible to be confident. While periods of quick growth do not usually reduce income disparities, neither does stagnation, which might have been the result of a less forward American policy. Nonetheless, the question must be posed. "Welfare" criteria apply, most easily, to whole societies. Alone they cannot measure the costs of hegemony on particular components but can only confirm the triumph of productivity for the aggregate. But this, indeed, was all Americans sought to know. The cohesiveness of our politics lay in the reluctance to suggest alternative questions. In the terms that all significant sectors of opinion would have posed the issue, US foreign economic policy was beneficial as well as potent. This judgment should not be surprising; it followed from the ideological beliefs that rescued national cohesion in a society of great material differences.

# 3
# United States Commercial and Monetary Policy: Unravelling the Paradox of External Strength and Internal Weakness

*Stephen D. Krasner*

The fundamental objective of American foreign economic policy after the Second World War was to establish a regime in which impediments to the movement of capital and goods were minimized. In this quest American central decision makers were largely successful because of America's external power. However, because of the weakness of the US political system, that is, the ability of private groups to check state initiatives, public officials were constantly faced with domestic political constraints. These constraints were more apparent in the area of commercial policy, where decisions involved Congress and executive agencies susceptible to societal influences, than in monetary policy, where decisions were made in a more insulated environment. The decline of America's external power, which became evident in the mid-1960s, was accompanied by growing demands for protection as more sectors of the American economy were adversely affected by foreign trade. This has led to increasing incoherence in US policy and greater instability in the international economic regime.

Stephen D. Krasner is a member of the Department of Political Science at the University of California, Los Angeles. He would like to thank Benjamin Cohen, John Conybeare, I.M. Destler, Peter Katzenstein, Robert Keohane, Kenneth Oye, and Robert Pastor for their comments on an earlier version of this article. Completion of this study was facilitated by a grant from the Rockefeller Foundation Program in Conflict in International Relations. The author is solely responsible for the contents.

There are makers, breakers, and takers of international economic regimes. Economic transactions do not take place in a political vacuum. Political power is needed to establish a system or regime—a pattern of rules, norms, and practices. In international affairs that power can only come from a state or group of states. Historically, a stable international economic regime has been associated with a hegemonic maker of the system. Medium-size states can be breakers of the system. They do not have the power to establish a regime, but by changing their policies they may be able to undermine an ongoing pattern of rules and behavior: they can move international economic relations from the pole of order toward the pole of chaos. Small states are takers of the system. They can adjust their own policies to try to maximize their particular objectives, but, for them, the general nature of the regime is a given.

In the period after the Second World War, the United States was the maker of the system. Its power and policies shaped the international economic regime. While the other country studies in this volume deal with potential breakers, an exposition of American foreign economic policy must examine its external consequences in terms of establishing, maintaining, and undermining the international economic regime, as well as the domestic determinants of US policy.

The fundamental objective of American central decision makers was to create a liberal international economic regime. This meant that barriers to the movement of goods, services, capital, and technology would be minimized. It also meant that these transactions would be carried out by private, as opposed to state-owned, firms. American leaders sought this objective not only because it was initially in the economic interest of the US, but also because America's liberal ideology led them to believe that such a regime would promote prosperity and peace around the world.

In pursuing this goal American central decision makers confronted external and internal constraints—resistance from other international actors and from particular domestic interest groups. This dual challenge of external and internal resistance must be faced by any state leader.[1]

The US was more constrained by internal than by external factors, at least from 1948 until the last ten years. The US emerged from the Second World War in a position of unprecedented international power. The economies of all of the other major industrial states had been severely strained or destroyed by the global conflagration. It was not until the late 1960s or the 1970s that the decline in America's relative international position began to impose limits on the ability of the US to maintain a liberal global order.

---

[1] The approach to foreign policy analysis that has been used in this essay, which begins with the needs of the state and then looks to external and internal dangers and opportunities, is suggested by mercantilist writings of the 16th, 17th, and 18th centuries. Mercantilist policies were designed to strengthen and unify the state against both the universalism of the Church and the particularism of medieval society. See Eli F. Heckscher, *Mercantilism*, Vol. I (London: G. Allen and Unwin, 1935), p. 21.

However, US central decision makers were persistently confronted by challenges from domestic groups. This endemic problem was a product of the structure of the American political system. The key characteristic of that structure is that power is fragmented and decentralized. The American state—those institutions and roles that are relatively insulated from particularistic pressures and concerned with general goals (primarily the White House and the State Department and to a lesser extent the Treasury and Defense Departments)—is weak in relation to its own society. In comparison with their counterparts in other industrial countries, US central decision makers have difficulty extracting the domestic resources that they need to implement state policies. The potential international power of the state—the ability of central decision makers to change the behavior of other international actors and to provide collective goods for the international system if *all* of the society's resources could be used for state purposes (that is, if there are no domestic constraints)—is great. But the actual power of the state—the power resulting from the resources that central decision makers can actually extract from their own society—is much less. The difference between the two is probably larger for the United States than for any other advanced industrial society.

The problems presented by domestic political weakness were more manifest for commercial policy than for monetary policy. American monetary policy and the orderliness of the international monetary regime very closely paralleled the rise of American external power through the early 1960s and the decline that followed. But commercial policy, where Congress was a relatively more important decision arena, always presented American central decision makers with domestic constraints: it was necessary to buy off some import-competing industries that were being hurt by the pursuit of a liberal global order. However, even here, the pervasiveness of ideology, the vision of peace and prosperity flowing from a free and open international economic system, offered US leaders a lever of power that dampened, even if it did not entirely suppress, demands for protectionism.

America's foreign economic policy has moved through four stages during the postwar years, distinguished by changes in specific international economic policies. Each of these shifts reflected changes in the international position of the United States and in the constraints imposed by domestic pressure groups.

1. *1945–1947, A False Start.* Initial efforts to create a liberal order failed because US leaders were unable to extract from their domestic society the resources necessary for postwar reconstruction. By 1948, the international institutions which they had envisioned as the centerpieces of the new order were either inactive, such as the International Monetary Fund (IMF) or the World Bank (IBRD), or nonexistent, like the International Trade Organization (ITO).

2. *1947–1962, An Opening Wedge.* In 1947 American central decision makers broke with the amorphous Wilsonianism that had animated their previous activities and redefined international economic issues in terms of a global struggle with Communism. They moved from the World Bank and the IMF to the Marshall Plan. By changing the nature of the debate, US political leaders were able to extract much higher levels of resources from their own society. These resources facilitated

the creation of a liberal economic order by promoting European and Japanese economic growth. International liquidity for higher levels of world trade was provided by the American balance of payments deficit. However, commercial policy was still trammelled by domestic resistance.

3. *1962–1971, Apogee and Decline.* In the early 1960s, the United States still enjoyed an extraordinary international position. During the 1950s, growing international trade and investment made the benefits of a liberal order a reality or an immediate promise for American business rather than a long-term and uncertain vision. Both international and domestic constraints were low. This made possible the passage of the Trade Expansion Act in 1962 and the Kennedy Round. However, during the 1960s the relative economic position of the US declined. Balance of payments difficulties became more apparent. More domestic industries faced stiff foreign competition. Protectionist demands increased and policy became less coherent.

4. *1971–, Growing Strains, International and Domestic.* The problems for domestic groups, which first developed in the 1960s, became more severe during the 1970s, and the decline in America's potential international power continued. In August 1971, the US broke the Bretton Woods system. The 1974 Trade Act was more protectionist than the 1962 Act. During the early 1970s, the world monetary system became more disorderly and little progress was made in multilateral trade negotiations.

## *I  The goals of American central decision makers*

The most important and consistently pursued policy of American central decision makers since the Second World War has been the creation and maintenance of a liberal international economic regime. Such a system has two basic characteristics. The first is the minimization or elimination of barriers to the movements of goods, services, technology, and capital across international boundaries. The second is the control of such movements by private, as opposed to state-owned, corporations.

The desire to construct a liberal regime stemmed from three different sources. The first was the historical experience of American decision makers. The Depression had been accompanied by a sharp increase in economic nationalism as countries moved to protect themselves from the ravages of a malevolent global economy. The economic crisis was also associated with Hitler's rise to power. Nazi Germany had not only caused the Second World War, it had also followed international policies that were highly discriminatory and nationalistic and that were heavily influenced by the state. One lesson that American leaders drew from this experience was that economic nationalism was a threat to both peace and prosperity.[2]

---

[2] Joseph Marion Jones, *The Fifteen Weeks* (New York: Harcourt, Brace, and World, 1955), p. 92; Richard N. Gardner, *Sterling-Dollar Diplomacy* (New York: McGraw-Hill, 1969), pp. 19–20; Mira Wilkins, *The Maturing of Multinational Enterprise: American Business Abroad from 1914 to 1970* (Cambridge, Massachusetts: Harvard University Press, 1974), p. 289.

The second source of America's commitment to a liberal international order was more closely related to definable American interests stemming from America's international structural position. America emerged from the war as a hegemonic power; it was much larger and more technologically advanced than any of its rivals. Such a state is likely to prefer an open international economic regime. Such a regime will increase its static economic well-being and help to promote its economic growth. It will also further its political power by locking other countries into economic relationships that they cannot break without greater cost to themselves than to the hegemonic state.[3]

The third reason for the commitment to a liberal international economic regime was ideological. A new world economic order was one aspect of the general vision animating US leaders after World War II. It was a vision that had its roots in America's own historical experience. As Louis Hartz has argued, that experience has been heavily colored by Lockian liberalism, by a world view that has emphasized individual liberty and the minimization of state interference in the society. This ideology has had a "fixed, dogmatic" hold on Americans' view of the social and political order.[4]

Liberalism has not always been manifest in American foreign policy in general or foreign economic policy in particular. During the nineteenth century, the costs of openness, in terms of stifling America's own industrialization, were too great. It was not until Woodrow Wilson's presidency that Lockian ideas strongly affected international economic policy. Although Wilson did not succeed, those leaders who came after him held the same beliefs. Ideology became so important after World War II because American power was so great. Unlike the nineteenth century, the US was not concerned about foreign competition. It could seek not just to protect its own narrow objectives but also to create an international system in its own image: a system that reflected the virtues of liberalism.[5]

Of the three factors affecting the objectives of American central decision makers since the Second World War, ideology has turned out to be the most important. Historical memories have faded. The structural position of the United States has changed; it is no longer clear that American interests are furthered by a laissez-faire system.[6] Nevertheless, American leaders have continued to pursue this policy, although the explicit rationale has changed from Wilsonianism to anti-Communism to building democracy to interdependence, all of which are facets of America's liberalism. While American leaders have been concerned with specific objectives ranging from balance-of-payments equilibrium to the import of instant

---

[3] See Stephen D. Krasner, "State Power and the Structure of International Trade," *World Politics* Vol. 28, No. 3 (April 1976): 318–21, for an elaboration of this argument.

[4] Louis Hartz, *The Liberal Tradition in America* (New York: Harcourt, Brace, and World, 1955).

[5] Gardner, pp. 8–12; Franz Schurmann, *The Logic of World Power* (New York: Pantheon, 1974), Part I.

[6] For an argument along these lines see Robert Gilpin, *U.S. Power and the Multinational Corporation: The Political Economy of Foreign Direct Investment* (New York: Basic Books, 1975), Chapter 8.

coffee, they have not seriously entertained any alternative to a liberal order. Furthermore, central decision makers have not adopted policies that they perceived as being antithetical to such an international regime. While more and more groups within the United States have advocated protectionism, none has been able to offer a world view that can replace liberalism, not only in terms of specific American economic interests, but also in terms of preserving world peace and prosperity.[7]

## II  The international structure

With the exception of the United States, the Second World War devastated the economies of all major industrial states. While the US had become the world's largest producer of manufactures in the 1880s and the most important source of international credit after World War I, the impact of the Second World War elevated America to a position of potential power unprecedented in the modern era.[8] Once the Soviet Union and its allies had withdrawn into their own international order, the relationship of the US to other states with which it carried on active economic interchange was even more asymmetrical.

The extraordinarily powerful position of the United States with respect to the rest of the non-Communist world is brought out by the following table.

These aggregate indicators alone do not show America's *potential* international power—its ability to influence the behavior of other states and provide collective goods for the international system, if *all* of these resources could be utilized by central decision makers.[9] Such an evaluation would require a detailed study of the vulnerabilities of other countries relative to those of the US[10] but Table I does give a picture that is indicative of general trends. The US emerged from the Second World War in an unchallenged position. Its economy was much larger and more prosperous than that of any other country. Furthermore, it enjoyed a dominant position in virtually every economic issue-area ranging from capital to manufacturing to raw materials.

During the 1960s America's potential international economic power began to decline. In some areas, such as wheat and energy consumption, there is not much change from the 1950s to the 1970s. But in others, such as iron ore, steel, and petroleum, the relative position of the US in the world was much different in 1973 than it was in the late 1940s. This is not to say that America has become a

---

[7] Such alternatives have been offered by academics. For example, see Gilpin, Chapter 8, and Robert W. Tucker, *The New Isolationism: Threat or Promise?* (Washington: Potomac Associates, 1972).

[8] Krasner, "State Power and the Structure of International Trade," pp. 333–34.

[9] It is obviously necessary to distinguish between power resources and power itself, the ability to influence the behavior of others. For an elaboration of this point see Klaus Knorr, *The Power of Nations: The Political Economy of International Relations* (New York: Basic Books, 1975), pp. 9–14.

[10] For sophisticated analyses of this kind see ibid., and Albert Hirschman, *National Power and the Structure of Foreign Trade* (Berkeley: University of California Press, 1946).

second-rate power, but it is to say that America has become more like a normal nation-state. No longer does American power dominate in virtually every issue-area. No longer can the US simply impose its will on others.

## III Domestic constraints

The potential or maximum international power of the state, the power that could be derived from all the resources controlled by its citizens relative to those of other societies, establishes only the outer boundaries of state power. Central decision makers cannot utilize resources that are beyond their sovereign control, but they may not even be able to mobilize all of the capabilities nominally within their jurisdiction. While political leaders must look outward toward external dangers and opportunities, they must also look inward toward their own domestic societies. In the extreme, a regime may be threatened by civil disorder and dissolution. Short of that, however, political leaders may find that they are unable to mobilize the resources that are needed to achieve the state's international goals because of resistance from domestic groups.

The ability of political leaders to mobilize domestic resources is a function of a) the structure of the domestic political system, and b) the convergence between private and public interests. In the following section we will consider the former; in the succeeding section, we will turn to the question of private and public interests.

### The domestic weakness of the American state

The defining characteristic of a political system is the power of the state in relation to its own society.[11] This power can be envisioned along a continuum ranging from weak to strong. The weakest kind of state is one which is completely permeated by pressure groups. Central government institutions serve specific interests within the country, rather than the collective aims of the citizenry as a whole. Lebanon even before the civil war of 1975–76 can be thought of as such a state. Public functions and positions were divided between Moslems and Christians. There was little or no general agreement on what constituted the general good or the collective interest of the country. The situation was exacerbated during the early 1970s, when the Palestinians were able to establish de facto control over some areas.

[11] I realize that this hardly conforms with conventional notions. Liberal analysts treat the state, at worst, as an epiphenomenon whose behavior is explained by societal pressures and, at best, as another interest group or as an arbitrator among competing interests. See Theodore Lowi, "The Public Philosophy: Interest-Group Liberalism," *American Political Science Review* Vol. 61, No. 1 (March 1967): 5–24. Marxists regard the state as a servant of particular economic interests or as an agency preserving the general structure of capitalist society. Both liberals and Marxists deny the assumption of this paper that the state is an independent, autonomous entity with powers and objectives that are distinct from any particular societal groups.

# Table I  Some indicators of United States potential external power

| | A National Income | | B Per capita income | C Crude petroleum production | | D Crude steel | |
|---|---|---|---|---|---|---|---|
| | RATIO OF US TO TOTAL MARKET ECONOMIES | RATIO OF US TO NEXT LARGEST | RATIO OF US TO NEXT HIGHEST | RATIO OF US TO TOTAL WORLD PRODUCTION | RATIO OF US TO NEXT LARGEST PRODUCER (EXCL. E. BLOC) | RATIO OF US TO TOTAL WORLD PRODUCTION | RATIO OF US TO NEXT LARGEST PRODUCER (EXCL. E. BLOC) |
| 1937 | | | | | | | |
| 1945 | | | | | 3.81 (Ven.) | .64 | 6.02 (UK) |
| 1948 | | | | | | | |
| 1949 | | | | | | | |
| 1950 | | | | | | | |
| 1953 | | 6.43 (UK)⁴ | 1.58 (Switz.)⁵ | .51 | 3.33 (Ven.) | .45 | 5.31 (UK) |
| 1955 | | | | | | | |
| 1958 | .45 | 6.33 (UK)⁴ | 1.52 (Switz.)⁵ | .43 | 2.91 (Ven.) | .39 | 4.98 (W. Ger.) |
| 1960 | | 6.96 (UK) | 1.78 (Swed.) | .33 | 2.33 (Ven.) | .26 | 2.64 (W. Ger.) |
| 1965 | | 6.59 (W. Ger.) | 1.51 (Switz.) | | | .26 | 3.23 (W. Ger.) |
| 1966 | | | | .25 | 3.42 (Saudi Arabia) | | |
| 1970 | .39 | 5.23 (W. Ger.) | 1.14 (Swed.) | .21 | 2.48 (Iran) | .20 | 1.27 (Japan) |
| 1973 | | 3.27 (Japan) | .98 (Swed.) | .16 | 1.25 (Saudi Arabia) | .20 | 1.15 (Japan) |

| | E Iron ore production | | F Energy consumption | | G Wheat | |
|---|---|---|---|---|---|---|
| | RATIO OF US TO TOTAL WORLD PRODUCTION | RATIO OF US TO NEXT LARGEST PRODUCER (EXCL. E. BLOC) | RATIO OF US TO TOTAL WORLD CONSUMPTION | RATIO OF US TO NEXT HIGHEST CONSUMER (EXCL. E. BLOC) | RATIO OF US TO TOTAL WORLD PRODUCTION | RATIO OF US TO NEXT LARGEST PRODUCER (EXCL. E. BLOC) |
| 1937 | .49 | 6.14 (Swed.) | .44[1] | 3.72 (W. Ger.) | | |
| 1948 | | | | | .24[3] | |
| 1949 | | | .49[1] | 4.77 (UK) | | |
| 1950 | .42 | 5.06 (Fr.) | .51[1] | 5.22 (UK) | | 2.20 (Can.) |
| 1955 | .31[2] | 3.28 (Fr.) | .40 | 5.05 (UK) | .17 | 1.80 (Can.) |
| 1960 | .19 | 2.20 (Fr.) | .34 | 5.63 (UK) | .12 | 2.61 (Can.) |
| 1965 | .15 | 2.29 (Can.) | .34 | 6.42 (UK) | .15 | 2.43 (Fr.) |
| 1970 | .13 | 1.82 (Can.) | .33 | 6.83 (Japan) | .13 | 1.83 (India) |
| 1973 | .11 | 1.13 (Aust.) | .32 | 6.45 (Japan) | .12 | 1.88 (India) |

[1] World Excl. USSR, China, and Korea
[2] World Total Excl. China
[3] Excl. USSR
[4] GDP
[5] GDP/capita

Sources: Columns a and b, United Nations, *Statistical Yearbook* and United Nations, *Yearbook of National Account Statistics*, various years. Columns c,d,e,f, and g, United Nations, *Statistical Yearbook*, various years. Countries in parentheses indicate the next highest non-Communist producer.

At the other extreme from a state which is completely permeated by political pressure groups is one which is able to remake the society and culture in which it exists; that is, to change economic institutions, values, and patterns of interaction among private groups. Such extraordinarily powerful states only exist immediately after major revolutions. It is not that the state is so strong during such periods, but that the society is weak because existing patterns of behavior have been shattered. The clearest examples are the Soviet Union after 1921 and China after 1948. Both countries had suffered many years of war. In China, the old regime had been disintegrating for a century, unable to cope with pressure from the West. In Russia, the First World War had devastated the country and demonstrated the incompetence of the Czarist government. The Communist regimes which were able to seize power made fundamental changes in economic, cultural, and even familial relationships.

Obviously, most states are neither as weak as Lebanon, nor as strong as post-revolutionary Communist regimes. All advanced market economy countries fall someplace in between. The domestic strength of the state can be indicated by the answer to three questions:

1. Can the state formulate policy goals independent of particular groups within its own society?
2. Can the state change the behavior of specific groups?
3. Can the state directly change the structure of the society in which it operates?[12]

Obviously, the answer to any of these questions may vary with the issue-area that is being considered. But if the answers to all three are generally positive, then one is dealing with a relatively strong state. Of the countries examined in this volume, Japan comes closest to the pole of strength, at least for the period before 1976. Japanese leaders have been able to pursue a coherent set of objectives. They have not been confronted with serious domestic resistance. They have been able not only to influence the behavior of specific groups but also to change the structure of the Japanese economy. This power has reflected several characteristics of Japanese polity and society. Until the 1976 elections, Japan essentially had a one party state minimizing the problems presented by executive-legislative clashes. Japanese interest groups accepted the legitimacy of state intervention in the economy. The state controlled a wide range of policy instruments, most importantly the dispensation of credit, which allowed it to influence private behavior and to change economic structures.

With the exception of the control of the Liberal Democratic Party, all of these factors are integral products of Japan's historical experience. As a late industrializer, the Japanese state played a decisive role in bringing modernity to

---

[12] With regard to the economy, structure can be defined in terms of the nature of ownership (public versus private), the degree of concentration within an industrial sector, and the importance of particular sectors in the economy as a whole.

Japan. The pattern of intervention established during the Meiji restoration has persisted to the present day, although the external forms have changed dramatically.[13] Furthermore, Japan has always been confronted with scarce resources. It could not avoid involvement in the world economy without seriously sacrificing economic prosperity and growth, and this involvement has been accompanied by a high degree of state intervention.

Of the countries examined in this volume, the United States is probably closest to the pole of weakness. American policy makers have had a clear objective, the creation and maintenance of a liberal international economic order. Indeed, if the state cannot formulate a set of coherent goals, it is difficult to defend the concept of the state at all. But implementation in the face of domestic political opposition has been another matter. It has been very difficult for American central decision makers to change the behavior of non-state domestic actors. Political leaders have relatively little command of material resources, such as the control of credit, that can be used to offer incentives or to make threats. The most important mechanism through which American leaders have affected private actors and the Congress has been ideology: they have been able to appeal to a liberal vision of the world order to change the perceptions of interest held by non-state actors. Furthermore, the US political system offers its leaders few opportunities directly to change the structure of the economy. Some macro-economic policies, such as the determination of the money supply, do have an *indirect* impact over time, but central decision makers have rarely been able to act *directly* at the level of the industrial sector or the firm. When such intervention has occurred, as in the case of regulatory agencies or particular tax laws, the initiative has come from the private sector more often than from the state.

The central feature of American politics is the fragmentation and dispersion of power and authority. This has been recognized by pluralists such as Polsby and Truman, who tend to emphasize the system's virtues, as well as by writers such as Huntington and Burnham, who see the American polity as basically flawed. Polsby argues that the different branches of the American government were designed so that they "would be captured by different interests."[14] Truman notes that the "[d]iffusion of leadership and disintegration of policy are not hallucinations."[15] Huntington summarizes the situation as one in which there is a "fusion of functions and division of power."[16] Burnham argues that the political system has been "in domestic matters at any rate—dispersive and fragmented . . . dedicated to the defeat,

[13] On the relationship between late industrialization and state intervention see Alexander Gerschenkron, *Economic Backwardness in Historical Perspective* (Cambridge, Massachusetts: Harvard University Press, 1962), Chapter 1.

[14] Nelson Polsby, *Congress and the Presidency,* 2nd ed. (Englewood Cliffs, New Jersey: Prentice-Hall, 1971), pp. 140–41.

[15] David B. Truman, *The Governmental Process: Political Interests and Public Opinion,* 2nd ed. (New York: Knopf, 1971), p. 529.

[16] Samuel P. Huntington, *Political Order in Changing Societies* (New Haven: Yale University Press, 1968), p. 110.

except temporarily and under the direct pressure of overwhelming crisis, of any attempt to generate domestic sovereignty. . . ."[17]

The Constitution is a document more concerned with limiting than enhancing the power of the state. The founding fathers were wary of power. They sought to deal with its temptations by limiting legal authority, dividing power within the government, and dividing power among groups in the society. This is reflected by their preserving the states, giving Congress and the President specific, not unlimited, legal powers, denying some power to Congress, establishing a bicameral legislature, and creating an independent judiciary. While the concept of dividing power among societal groups is not explicitly reflected in the Constitution, it was voiced by Madison at the Convention and clearly explicated in Federalist Paper Number 10.[18]

Within the executive branch it is unclear whether the President or the Congress controls particular bureaus. Permanent bureaucracies have their own interests. Some have their own independent ties with particular societal groups and Congressional committees.[19]

The dispersion of power is even more striking in the American legislature. Bills can be blocked at any one of a number of decision-making nodes. In the House, these include subcommittees, full committees, the Rules Committee, the full House, the Rules Committee again for a bill going to a conference committee, and the conference committee. The situation is similar in the Senate, except that there is no direct parallel with the Rules Committee. The jurisdictional authority of individual committees is often not clearly differentiated. The Appropriations and Government Operations Committees, the House Rules Committee, and the Joint Economic Committee all have virtually universal scope in the matters they can consider. There is usually little cooperation between committees with the same jurisdiction in the two Houses.[20]

There are several reasons for the fragmentation of power and authority, and thus the weakness, of the American political system. First, this situation is as integral a part of America's historical experience as Japan's strength is of its. American society was born modern; it was not necessary to have a strong state to destroy a traditional society. Early Americans were favorably disposed to change and to

[17] Walter Dean Burnham, *Critical Elections and the Mainsprings of American Politics* (New York: W.W. Norton, 1970), p. 176.

[18] Robert Dahl, *Pluralist Democracy in the United States* (Chicago: Rand-McNally, 1967), p. 39.

[19] On the bureaucratic problem see Richard Neustadt, *Presidential Power: The Politics of Leadership* (New York: Wiley, 1960); Graham Allison, *Essence of Decision: Explaining the Cuban Missile Crisis* (Boston: Little Brown, 1971); and Morton Halperin, *Bureaucratic Politics and Foreign Policy* (Washington: Brookings Institution, 1974). For discussions of the tendency to overemphasize autonomous bureaucratic goals as opposed to general beliefs and societal pressures see Stephen D. Krasner, "Are Bureaucracies Important?," *Foreign Policy* 7 (Summer 1972): 159–79, and Robert J. Art, "Bureaucratic Politics and American Foreign Policy: A Critique," *Policy Sciences* Vol. 4 (1973): 467–90.

[20] Richard F. Fenno, Jr., "The Internal Distribution of Influence: The House," in *The Congress and America's Future*, 2nd ed., edited by David B. Truman (Englewood Cliffs, New Jersey: Prentice-Hall, 1973), pp. 63–90; Ralph K. Huitt, "The Internal Distribution of Power: The Senate," in Truman, ed., *The Congress and America's Future*, pp. 91–117.

social status based on achievement rather than birth. Commitment to social classes was weak. There were neither feudal institutions nor an aristocracy that blocked social and economic development. America was an early industrializer. Economic change took place slowly and with relatively little state direction. In comparing Europe with America, Huntington argues that "[i]n Europe the opposition to modernization within society forced the modernization of the political system. In America, the ease of modernization within society precluded the modernization of political institutions."[21]

A second reason for the persistence of a weak political structure is that America has not, until recently, confronted a serious external threat to its territorial and political integrity. On the European continent, the great impetus to the centralization of political authority during the sixteenth and seventeenth centuries was the constant threat of war. Fledgling states could not defend themselves without a standing army. To raise and maintain such forces, it was necessary to strengthen the political system.[22] The United States, on the other hand, enjoyed the protection of Britain's maritime dominance during the nineteenth century. By the time America was thrown upon the world scene in the twentieth century, its size and mastery of technology made it possible to create the world's most formidable military force. Curiously, the very weapons that have, for the first time, made the territorial integrity of the United States vulnerable may also, because of their capital intensity, allow the state to maintain its defenses with a weak political structure. The burdens imposed upon the domestic population by hardened missile sites and nuclear submarines are less than those resulting from large armies and extensive reserve corps.

A third reason for the persistence of a political system with diffused power has been material abundance and high levels of social equality. Tocqueville was struck by America's egalitarianism. He found a high level of literacy and relatively little social deference outside the cities of the eastern seaboard.[23] This social equality is intimately related to the abundance of American society. America has been rich from its beginnings. In terms of per capita income, it surpassed Britain in the middle of the nineteenth century. It then fell back as a result of immigration and other factors but regained its lead by the outbreak of the First World War. Abundance and rapid growth facilitated more equal opportunity and the belief that things would always improve. Social problems were often solved by technological and economic changes rather than political initiatives. The country was well-endowed with natural resources. All of this reinforced the myth of social equality and mobility. It was possible to believe that things would always get better because they usually did for most people. The pressures brought upon the political system were usually modest because the level of social dissatisfaction was mitigated by economic growth. A weak political system could exist because politics was less necessary for a citizenry that perceived itself dividing an expanding rather than stagnant national product. In the words of David Potter, "Economic abundance is

[21] Huntington, p. 129.
[22] Ibid., pp. 122 ff.
[23] Dahl, pp. 58–61.

conducive to political democracy"[24] and, one might add, a democratic system that diffused rather than concentrated power and authority.

The laws and practices affecting America's foreign commercial policy illustrate the fragmentation and diffusion of power that can exist for particular issue-areas in the American political system. The problem has been much less acute for monetary policy.

The number of institutions involved in US trade policy is very large. The power to impose countervailing duties against foreign goods that are receiving a "bounty or grant" from their own government is vested in the Treasury Department by the Tariff Act of 1897. The 1921 Anti-Dumping Law also gives the Treasury the responsibility for protecting the American market from goods that are unfairly exported.[25] Under the 1974 Trade Act, the Commerce Department is charged with judging applications for adjustment assistance from businesses and communities, and the Labor Department with applications from labor. The Office of the Special Trade Representative (STR) was established by the 1962 Trade Expansion Act because Congress felt that the State Department, which had carried the main responsibility for multilateral negotiations to that date, was not sufficiently responsive to domestic needs. The 1974 Act makes the STR a cabinet level post ·subject to Senatorial approval.[26] The agricultural advisory committees established by the 1974 Act are chaired by the Agriculture Department; the industry committees by Commerce. A former Administration official, writing for the Peterson Commission in 1971, outlined the involvement of administrative agencies in the area of international trade and investment as depicted in Table II.

## Table II  Executive departments involved
in international economic policy

| *Issue-area* | *Agencies* |
| --- | --- |
| Revenue and expenditure | Treasury and Office of Management and Budget |
| Injury | Commerce, Labor, Council of Economic Advisors, STR |
| Negotiability | State, STR, Treasury, Commerce |
| International trade effect | Commerce, State, STR, Agriculture |
| Foreign policy effect | State, National Security Council |

Source: US Commission on International Trade and Investment Policy, *United States International Economic Policy in an Interdependent World*, Compendium of Papers: Vol. II (Washington: Government Printing Office, 1971), p. 424.

[24] David M. Potter, *People of Plenty: Economic Abundance and the American Character* (Chicago: University of Chicago Press, 1954), p. 112.

[25] Robert A. Pastor, "Legislative-Executive Relations and US Foreign Trade Policy: The Case of the Trade Act of 1974," Paper prepared for delivery at the 1976 Annual Meeting of the American Political Science Association, Chicago, Ill., September 2–5, 1976, p. 17; and Mathew J. Marks and Harald B. Malmgren, "Negotiating Nontariff Distortions to Trade," *Law and Policy in International Business* Vol. 7, No. 2 (1975): 348.

[26] Gordon L. Weil, *American Trade Policy: A New Round* (New York: Twentieth Century Fund, 1975), p. 56; and Pastor, p. 16.

The decision-making structure for foreign economic, and particularly commercial, policy also gives representatives of the private sector more than ample access. The most significant point of entrance is the Congress. Congressmen may try to put off constituency entreaties, but they cannot ignore them. Various laws have given domestic groups formal standing with regard to some trade issues. The 1951 Trade Act provided that the Tariff Commission could investigate a motion under the escape clause (the provision that the US could withdraw a trade concession if a domestic industry were seriously injured) instigated by the President, a resolution of either House, a resolution of the Senate Finance or House Ways and Means Committees, or by the application of *any interested party*.[27] Although the Executive had always consulted with private groups before entering trade negotiations, the 1974 Act mandated the establishment of a system of advisory committees. The Executive has established a 45-member advisory Committee for Trade Negotiations with representatives drawn from industry, agriculture, and labor. It has also established separate committees for industry, labor, and agriculture. As of January 1976, 27 industry sectoral committees, eight agricultural sector committees, and six labor sectoral committees had been created.[28]

Private groups can also affect foreign economic policy through the judicial system. Rulings of the International Trade Commission can be appealed to the US Customs Court, then to the Court of Customs and Patent Appeals, and ultimately to the Supreme Court. Recently, consumer groups have brought legal suits against trade controls. They have challenged the President's authority to conclude voluntary export agreements on the grounds that they violate US antitrust and due process laws.[29] In sum, the laws give Congress, the President, Treasury, Commerce, Labor, Agriculture, State, the Special Trade Representative, the courts, and private groups access to US commercial policy making.

In contrast, there is less diffusion of power with respect to international monetary policy making. Only during the period from 1945 through 1947 was domestic restraint a significant factor for central decision makers. At other times, it was America's position in the structure of international power that primarily determined US policy and its impact on the global monetary regime. Decisions about monetary policy have been taken in the White House, the Treasury Department, and the Federal Reserve Board, arenas that are well insulated from particular societal pressures. Once the system of stable exchange rates, based more on the US dollar than on Bretton Woods, was established, there were not many issues that came before the Congress. Private actors rarely saw how monetary decisions related to their specific interests and therefore did not press for greater access to the decision-making machinery. In fact, until the late 1960s, virtually all sectors of the

[27] John W. Evans, *The Kennedy Round in American Trade Policy: The Twilight of the GATT?* (Cambridge, Massachusetts: Harvard University Press, 1971), pp. 17–18; and Weil, pp. 37–38.
[28] *National Journal Reports,* January 18, 1975, pp. 77–78; and US Congress, Senate, Committee on Finance, *United States International Trade Policy and the Trade Act of 1974,* Committee Print, 94th Cong., 2nd sess., p. 19.
[29] *National Journal Reports,* May 10, 1975, p. 696.

American elite regarded both the value of the dollar and fixed exchange rates as graven in stone and beyond the tampering of mere mortals.

In summary, the American political system is relatively weaker than that of most other industrial countries. Central decision makers in Japan and France can more easily manipulate their own domestic societies. Even the British regime, at least before the deterioration of the 1960s described by Stephen Blank, was probably stronger than the American. In the US, private groups can penetrate the decision-making process more easily. There are many decision-making nodes where state initiatives can be vetoed. US leaders have relatively few policy instruments for intervening in the economy. This is not to say that American central decision makers are hapless victims of societal pressure groups. They are not. US leaders have been able to formulate clear policy objectives. They have been able to sway private groups through appeals to a widely shared ideological vision. In international monetary issues, they have had a relatively free hand because of the arenas in which decisions have been made.[30] However, the structural characteristics of the American polity allow domestic groups to impose more constraints on the state than in most other advanced countries.

## The changing nature of domestic interests

The structure of the political system is only one variable determining the ability of central decision makers to carry out their preferences without regard to domestic societal pressures. The other is the extent of convergence between the policy goals of public and private actors. More specifically, the issue for this paper is the extent to which private preferences have converged with the desire of American leaders to create a liberal international economic system. If there is complete agreement between private and public actors, then the weakness of the political structure will not create many difficulties for central decision makers.

In the United States, private support for a liberal international economic order reached its peak around 1960. At that time, few import-competing industries were seriously threatened by foreign competition, and export industries and multinational firms saw many opportunities for foreign activities. Before 1960, support for a liberal order was lower because the involvement of the American economy in world trade and investment was still modest. After the early 1960s, the consensus for an open global economic regime began to decline because more sectors of the American economy were negatively affected by imports.

---

[30] On the importance of decision-making arenas see E.E. Schattschneider, *The Semi-Sovereign People: A Realist's View of Democracy in America* (New York: Holt, Rinehart and Winston, 1960), Chapter 1. For the US, monetary policy is unusual in that it is decided in a small number of arenas that are insulated from societal pressures. Other aspects of foreign economic policy, including investment and aid as well as commercial policies, are fought over in a larger number of arenas.

The following tables give some indication of the changing pattern of domestic interests with respect to foreign economic activities. Obviously, they do not show the policies followed by particular domestic groups. But they do give some indication of the impact of international economic activities on different groups within the US. This impact is suggested by patterns of trade, direct investment, and banking.

Table III shows American imports, exports, and trade balances for single digit Standard International Trade Classification (SITC) numbers as well as five specific industries that have been the subject of controversy and demands for protection. These five are crude and partly refined petroleum, textiles and clothing, iron and steel, road motor vehicles, and footwear.

1949 is the first postwar year for which statistics are available from the United Nations. It is more indicative of the situation immediately following the Second World War than is 1950, by which time American trade was already affected by the Korean War. The most striking aspect of the 1949 data is not just that the US was running a heavy overall surplus, but that it had a positive trade balance for every major (single digit) category of commodities. For the other items shown on the table, only crude and partly refined petroleum shows a negative balance, but this was a trivial percentage of total American oil consumption. Europe and Japan had hardly begun their postwar recoveries. The only economy capable of generating a wide variety of goods for export was that of the United States.

By 1960, the situation had changed. The US had a negative trade balance for food, crude materials, fuels, and basic manufactures (SITC numbers 0, 2, 3, and 6). However, except for fuels, none of these deficits was very large relative to exports. There were positive trade balances for beverages and tobacco, animal and vegetable oils, chemicals, miscellaneous manufactured goods, and machines and transport equipment (SITC numbers, 1, 4, 5, 7 and 8). SITC number 7, machines and transport equipment, includes the most technologically sophisticated group of products. However, some of the technologically older sectors of the American economy were suffering from foreign competition even in 1960. American shoe manufacturers had ceased exporting altogether, and imports were nine times greater in 1960 than 1955. Textiles and clothing went from a positive balance in 1955 to a negative one in 1960. While iron and steel still showed a positive balance, the ratio of exports to imports had fallen from 3.27 to 1.17. Road motor vehicles, a more technologically sophisticated product, continued to show a strong surplus. American dependence on foreign petroleum continued to grow and had reached about 20 percent of consumption. In sum, by 1960, technologically older industries, such as textiles and footwear, were already showing trade deficits. Goods utilizing advanced and intermediate technologies had positive balances.

By 1970, the US economy was still more exposed to foreign competition. There were strong negative balances not only for unprocessed goods but also for basic manufactures. Textiles and iron and steel showed negative balances even though both were protected by "voluntary" export agreements negotiated during the 1960s. The value of imported road motor vehicles now significantly exceeded

# Table III  US sectoral trade balances

| SITC number | Class of goods | 1949 Imports | 1949 Exports | 1949 Balance | 1960 Imports | 1960 Exports | 1960 Balance |
|---|---|---|---|---|---|---|---|
| 0 | Food | 1986 | 2105 | 119 | 3004 | 2668 | −336 |
| 1 | Beverages & tobacco | 166 | 320 | 154 | 397 | 482 | 85 |
| 2 | Crude materials inedible, except fuels | 1859.5 | 1346 | −513 | 3155 | 2774 | −381 |
| 3 | Minerals fuel, lubricants, related material | 484.9 | 872 | 388 | 1570 | 830 | −740 |
| 312 or 331 | Petroleum crude & partly refined | 348.1 | 116 | −232 | 951 | 8 | −943 |
| 4 | Animal & vegetable oil & fats | 84.8 | 147 | 62 | 95 | 306 | 211 |
| 5 | Chemicals | 113.2 | 742 | 629 | 451 | 1749 | 1298 |
| 6 | Basic manufactured goods | 1491 | 2030 | 539 | 3432 | 2756 | −676 |
|  | Textiles & clothing | 686 | 1547 | 861 | 866 | 618 | −248 |
| 681 or 67 | Iron & steel | 47.9 | 611 | 563 | 566 | 662 | 96 |
| 7 | Machines, transport equipment | 136 | 3522 | 3386 | 1460 | 6987 | 5527 |
| 732 | Road motor vehicles | 14 | 719 | 715 | 645 | 1243 | 598 |
| 8 | Misc. manufac. goods | 179.7 | 618 | 438 | 1057 | 1303 | 246 |
| 851 | Footwear | 6.2 | 20.9 | 15 | 141 | – | −141 |
| 9 | Goods not classified by kind | 95.2 | 232 | 137 | 393 | 450 | 57 |
| TOTAL | | 6598 | 11885 | 5287 | 15016 | 20308 | 5292 |

| SITC number | Class of goods | 1970 | | | 1973 | | |
|---|---|---|---|---|---|---|---|
| | | Imports | Exports | Balance | Imports | Exports | Balance |
| 0 | Food | 5374 | 4451 | −923 | 7986 | 12101 | 4115 |
| 1 | Beverages & tobacco | 855 | 716 | −139 | 1213 | 1026 | −187 |
| 2 | Crude materials inedible, except fuels | 3306 | 4663 | 1357 | 4986 | 8444 | 3458 |
| 3 | Minerals fuels, lubricants, related materials | 3074 | 1695 | −1379 | 8101 | 1672 | −6429 |
| 312 or 331 | Petroleum crude & partly refined | 1448 | – | −1448 | 4581 | – | −4581 |
| 4 | Animal & vegetable oil & fats | 159 | 495 | 336 | 493 | 692 | 199 |
| 5 | Chemicals | 1450 | 3840 | 2390 | 2437 | 5779 | 3342 |
| 6 | Basic manufactured goods | 8539 | 5179 | −3360 | 13199 | 7444 | −5755 |
| | Textiles & clothing | 2404 | 801 | −1603 | 3748 | 1503 | −2245 |
| 681 or 69 | Iron & steel | 2030 | 322 | −1708 | 3008 | 74 | −2934 |
| 7 | Machines, transport equipment | 11 171 | 18 018 | 6847 | 20969 | 28078 | 7109 |
| 732 | Road motor vehicles | 5480 | 3573 | −1907 | 10009 | 6045 | −3964 |
| 8 | Misc. manufac. goods | 4846 | 2692 | −2154 | 8184 | 4229 | −3955 |
| 851 | Footwear | 629 | – | −629 | 1079 | – | −1079 |
| 9 | Goods not classified by kind | 1273 | 1472 | 199 | 1790 | 1839 | 49 |
| TOTAL | | 39 951 | 43 224 | 3273 | 69127 | 71314 | 2193 |

Source: United Nations, *U.N. Yearbook of International Trade Statistics*, various years, except for Textiles and Clothing, which is from US Census Bureau, *Statistical Abstract of the United States*, various years.

exports. Industries with intermediate levels of technology were confronting significant foreign competition. SITC number 7, machines and transportation equipment,
continued to show the largest positive balance. Hence, by 1970, many sectors of
the American economy faced significant foreign competition, while others had
become very heavily involved in export markets. The convergence of interests in an
open system among advanced, intermediate, and even some technologically older
industries, which had existed as late as 1960, had disappeared. At least through
1973, the devaluations of the early 1970s had not changed this pattern.

Trade figures alone are a misleading indicator of the way in which America's
changing place in the world economy has affected different societal actors. Trade
balances do suggest the interests of labor, but not necessarily those of industry.
Accompanying the growth of world trade since the Second World War has been a
massive increase in foreign investment. While some sectors of the American economy, such as shoes, were unable or unwilling to try to end-run foreign competition
by buying foreign plants, others were far from reluctant. In some areas, such as raw
material exploitation, US firms were already well established. While SITC number
2, crude materials excluding fuels, has consistently shown a negative trade balance,
until 1970 almost all imports involved the flow of goods within vertically integrated
companies, mostly American. With the exception of Shell, and later British Petroleum, virtually all American imports of fuels (SITC number 3) were controlled by
US companies. In other areas, particularly manufacturing, many firms have significantly increased their overseas activities during the last three decades. Table IV
shows the net capital outflows, value, and earnings of US direct investment.

### Table IV  US foreign direct investment (millions of dollars)

| Period | Average annual net capital outflow | Year | Value of US direct investment | Earnings of US direct investment |
|--------|-----------------------------------|------|------------------------------|----------------------------------|
| 1950–54 | 676 | 1950 | 11788 | 1766 |
| 1955–59 | 1553 | 1955 | 19395 | 2878 |
| 1960–64 | 1823 | 1960 | 32765 | 3546 |
| 1965–69 | 3227 | 1965 | 49217 | 5431 |
| 1970–74 | 5034 | 1970 | 75456 | 8023 |
| | | 1975 | 133168 | 17433 |

Sources: US Department of Commerce, *Survey of Current Business*, various issues. Average
annual net capital outflow derived from annual figures.

American banks rapidly began to expand their foreign activity after major
European currencies became convertible in 1958. This is shown in Table V.

## Table V Foreign activities of US banks

| Year | Number of banks with overseas branches | Number of overseas branches | Assets of overseas branches ($ billions) | Total assets commercial banks in US ($ billions) | Assets of foreign branches as a percent of total assets of all commercial banks in the US |
|------|------|------|------|------|------|
| 1960 | 8 | 131 | 3.5 | 255.7 | 1.3 |
| 1965 | 13 | 211 | 9.1 | 374.1 | 2.4 |
| 1970 | 79 | 536 | 52.6 | 576.2 | 9.1 |
| 1973 | 125 | 699 | 118.0 | 827.1 | 14.2 |
| 1974 (Sept.) | 129 | 737 | 155.0 | 872.0 (June) | |

Source: Andrew F. Brimmer and Frederick R. Dahl, "Growth of American International Banking: Implications for Public Policy," *Journal of Finance* Vol. 30, No. 2 (May 1975): 345.

These tables suggest why the private consensus for a liberal international economic order was greatest around 1960. In the early 1950s, the international involvement of American corporations, and particularly American banks, was still relatively small. But by 1960, it was substantial for corporations, and banks were on the verge of a great foreign expansion. Once these institutions became involved in foreign direct investment, their stake in a liberal international regime became increasingly apparent. During the 1950s, virtually all US industries enjoyed a positive trade balance. However, during the 1960s, the number and variety of industries that had to deal with foreign competition increased sharply. In cases where US manufacturers had established foreign subsidiaries, this created an ambiguous set of interests. An open international order was beneficial for their international activities, but more protectionism would help their domestic ones. For American labor, the situation was clearer. Whether imports came from foreign-owned firms or American multinational corporations (MNCs) was immaterial. Jobs were being lost. As more and more sectors of the American economy confronted a negative trade balance during the 1960s, the attractions of protectionism became greater for the American labor movement. Hence, in 1960, US economic groups, with the exception of a few technologically older industries, found a liberal order attractive. During earlier periods many firms, including banks, were not heavily involved in foreign activities. Later, more sectors of the US economy faced foreign competition.

In sum, three basic factors bear on the analysis of American foreign economic policy after the Second World War:

1. The state (group of central decision makers) wants to create and maintain a liberal international economic regime.
2. These central decision makers have at their command potential international power that is overwhelming immediately after the war, but erodes thereafter. This erosion becomes apparent during the 1960s.
3. US central decision makers must act in a weak domestic political system that limits their ability to extract resources from their own society when their goals conflict with private ones. Such conflicts are least apparent around 1960.

*IV  The historical evolution of American policy*

The interplay of state objectives, international economic power, and domestic political constraints is revealed by an examination of four periods of American foreign economic policy. Each of these periods is defined by some decisive policy choice: Bretton Woods in 1944, the Marshall Plan in 1947, the Trade Expansion Act of 1962, and the new economic policy of August 1971. The first, from the war years to the Marshall Plan, was an unsuccessful attempt to construct a new international economic order. The second period, from the Marshall Plan through the 1950s, saw the reestablishment of economic stability in Europe and Japan, at least in part because of American assistance. During these same years, the external power of the United States almost automatically led to a well-functioning international monetary system. However, domestic support for a decisively open commercial policy did not yet exist. The third period, the 1960s, saw the apogee and decline of support for a liberal order. At the beginning of the decade, there was a very strong domestic consensus for freer trade, which led to the passage of the Trade Expansion Act. By the end of the decade, increasing protectionist pressures were coming from American labor and from US industries that were suffering from foreign competition. While a number of ad hoc measures were used to deal with international monetary problems, they were not fully successful. The last period, ushered in by the proclamations of August 1971, has been one of growing tensions. The relative decline of America's power has been translated into international monetary disorder almost as automatically as its preponderant power had been translated into stability during the 1950s and early 1960s. In commercial policy, internal cleavages were reflected in the Trade Reform Act of 1974, which moved to protect specific economic sectors without abandoning a general commitment to freer trade.

## A false start: the war years to the Marshall Plan

During the Second World War, American central decision makers developed an unambiguous commitment to a more liberal international economic order. They wanted to lower trade barriers, eliminate discrimination, and establish currency convertibility. Their strong belief in this set of goals stemmed from US interests, the immediate experience of the Depression and World War II, and, most important, a Lockian view of political and social life.

Planning for postwar economic arrangements reflected the desire to create a liberal order. The Atlantic Charter, signed in 1941 by Roosevelt and Churchill, called for equal access for trade and raw materials and full cooperation in "the economic field." Article 7 of the 1942 Mutual Aid Pact between Britain and the United States, which governed the dispensation of Lend-Lease, committed Britain to working toward an end to discriminatory trade practices, a phrase directed at the Imperial Preference system.[31]  By the middle of 1942, Treasury Department offi-

[31] Gardner, pp. 65–67.

cials had drawn up plans for an international bank and an international monetary fund designed to prevent the disruption of exchange systems and the collapse of credit, and to provide capital for reconstruction.[32] The charters of the World Bank and the IMF were approved at an international meeting held at Bretton Woods, New Hampshire, in 1944. Work on an organization to deal with trade began in 1943. The differences between the US and Great Britain were more manifest here than elsewhere, and a charter for an International Trade Organization was not concluded until 1948. The General Agreement on Tariffs and Trade (GATT), which was expected to be an interim arrangement, had been signed in early 1948.

These efforts to construct a new international economic order were a nearly complete failure. The International Bank for Reconstruction and Development, as the World Bank was officially known, was funded only at the very modest level of $10 billion. Its resources were completely unequal to the task of postwar reconstruction. By the middle of 1947, its funds were nearly exhausted. After an initial burst of activity in 1947 and 1948, IMF activities sank to very low levels until the Suez crisis nearly a decade later. Britain did establish convertibility on July 15, 1947, in accordance with the terms of a $3.75 billion loan received from the United States. But convertibility was suspended on August 20 because of a tremendous outflow of dollars from London. The International Trade Organization was never brought to a vote in the American Congress, much less ratified. The GATT, an institution with few resources, in which American participation was based on an executive agreement rather than a treaty or a Congressional-Executive agreement, became the most important postwar institution dealing with commercial practices.[33]

Why were America's first steps to create a liberal global economic order so unsuccessful? Part of the answer involves a failure of perception. As late as 1946, US officials were far more optimistic about the resources that would be needed for their plans than was warranted. They felt that the Fund and the Bank, with an additional $3–4 billion from the Export-Import (EXIM) Bank, would take care of the world's dollar needs. They also believed that the extra $3.75 billion for Britain would be enough to establish convertibility and promote reconstruction.[34] They were wrong. The dislocations caused by the war were far more serious than American leaders had anticipated.

However, there is a second reason for American failure, one more relevant to the analysis in this paper: domestic opposition prevented US leaders from extracting the resources needed to create a liberal global regime. The period before 1948 is the only one examined in this paper in which monetary as well as commercial policy was constrained by domestic political considerations. These constraints reflected the active role played by Congress and Congress' sensitivity to the values

[32] Alfred E. Eckes, Jr., *A Search for Solvency: Bretton Woods and the International Monetary System, 1941–1971* (Austin: University of Texas Press, 1975), Chapter 2.

[33] Gardner, pp. xxx–xxxi, 118, and 312 ff; Eckes, pp. 220–22.

[34] Jones, p. 95; Gardner, pp. 288–93; and Dean Acheson, *Present at the Creation: My Years in the State Department* (New York: W.W. Norton, 1969), pp. 230–71.

of its members and to particularistic pressures. While central decision makers were committed to an open international system, many societal groups were not. A liberal order could not be established without the appropriation of funds. These funds were necessary to try to restore convertibility in international exchange markets and to coerce or entice European colonial powers to give up their systems of Imperial Preferences, as well as to enable reconstruction. The appropriation of funds required the approval of Congress. And many Congressmen did not share the goals and visions of central decision makers.

In 1945, as the previous section of this paper suggests, the actual stake of American business and labor in foreign economic activities was small. The war had not interrupted a healthy and growing world economy but rather one that had not moved out of the Depression. US businesses were leary of overseas investment.[35] Their primary concern was the domestic market and adjustment to a peacetime economy.

Furthermore, American leaders encountered difficulties because their international efforts became embroiled in domestic political struggles. The Fund and the Bank were philosophically related to the Roosevelt Administration's domestic programs. Both involved greater state management of the economic order. Groups opposing the New Deal were also suspicious of the new international arrangements. Large private bankers in New York feared that the Fund and the Bank would encroach on their activities. From the outset, American officials rejected British efforts to create an international monetary fund with very liberal credit provisions (the Keynes Plan) because they felt it would never pass the Congress. US economic interests opposed the ITO because of provisions calling for full employment, host-country control of foreign investments, international commodity agreements, and foreign aid.[36]

Midwest isolationists also opposed the Administration. This became an acute problem when the Republicans won control of the Congress in 1946, and a number of powerful committee chairmanships, including that of the Senate Finance Committee, passed into the hands of men unsympathetic to efforts to create a liberal global order.[37]

US leaders were not completely unsuccessful in extracting resources from their domestic society. Bretton Woods did pass the Congress. EXIM Bank authorizations were increased. A $3.75 billion loan was made to Great Britain in 1946. However, given the devastation of the war, this was not enough. What was involved in the late 1940s was the establishment of a new international economic regime, not simply the maintenance of an ongoing pattern of rules and behavior. Before other advanced states could lower trade barriers and make their currencies convertible, they needed to reconstruct their own societies. And for that, a very high level of resources was needed from the US. Hence, despite the enormous potential

---

[35] Wilkins, pp. 300–01.
[36] Gardner, pp. 77, 87 ff; Eckes, pp. 220–22; and Wilkins, p. 288.
[37] Gardner, pp. 194, 349.

external power of the US in the period immediately after World War II, the actual resources at the disposal of central decision makers were not adequate for the establishment of a liberal economic regime because of misperception of central decision makers and the resistance of domestic groups.

## An opening wedge: the Marshall Plan and the 1950s

The vague Wilsonianism that had informed the Bretton Woods agreements was not sufficiently compelling to enable American central decision makers to extract the resources necessary for European reconstruction. They had to transform the basic way in which international economic relations were perceived. It was necessary to move from the Wilsonianism of the Fund and the Bank to the hard-headed anti-Communism of the Truman Doctrine and (despite the disclaimers of its progenitors) the Marshall Plan. Only by picturing American aid as part of a global struggle against Communism were American central decision makers able to get the resources necessary to create a prosperous economic order in Western Europe.

The events that precipitated the Truman Doctrine and the Marshall Plan, in what J.M. Jones has immortalized as the *Fifteen Weeks,* February 21st to June 5th, 1947,[38] were closely associated with the danger of Communist takeovers in Europe. On February 21, 1947, Britain informed the US that it could no longer carry the burden of aid to Greece and Turkey. Intelligence data suggested that Greece could "go Communist" in a matter of weeks. There were already Communists in the Italian cabinet. The first government appointed by the French Fourth Republic included four Communists. American leaders became starkly aware of the inadequacy of existing levels of aid to Europe and of the weakness of Britain, a country which only two years before they had treated as a proto-rival.[39]

In 1947, the external world presented great dangers for US leaders, but they feared that domestic constraints would prevent them from responding. Roosevelt's death, not popular votes, had brought Truman to power. The Republicans had won control of the Congress in the 1946 elections. A majority of them had voted against the Reciprocal Trade Agreements Act and its renewals, Bretton Woods, the 1945 increase in Export-Import Bank credits, and the 1946 loan to Great Britain. American leaders were not naive anti-Communists. Many had a grasp of the realist view of international politics. But they felt that only by shocking the American people could they get the resources that they needed. The only sentiment strong enough to give such a jolt was anti-Communism. Truman harped on the theme in his presentation of the Truman Doctrine to Congress. The Marshall Plan was also explicated in terms of a global struggle with an implacable and malevolent enemy. In his memoirs, Dean Acheson writes:

[38] Jones, *The Fifteen Weeks.*
[39] Ibid., pp. 5–11 and 96; Acheson, p. 226.

I have probably made as many speeches and answered as many questions about the Marshall Plan as any man alive, except possibly Paul Hoffman, and what citizens and the representatives in Congress alike always wanted to learn in the last analysis was how Marshall aid operated to block the extension of Soviet power and the acceptance of Communist economic and political organization and alignment.[40]

The weakness of the American political system, the inability of the President to secure domestic resources for reconstruction without painting the world situation in lurid colors, inevitably led to what Theodore Lowi has termed the tendency to "oversell" policies to the American public.[41]

Nevertheless, the result was the transfer of enormous sums to Europe. By 1953, the World Bank had made $1.2 billion in disbursements, while the US had transferred $41.3 billion. Marshall Plan aid amounted to about 33 percent of Europe's imports.[42] Most of these funds were given as outright grants. At the same time, American leaders also toned down their expectations. Rather than constructing a global open order, they were now willing to settle for one that included only their European and Asian allies. In the Marshall Plan, the US explicitly pushed European integration rather than globalism. Thus, in the issue-area of reconstruction, US policy was a success.

In the monetary issue-area, American policy makers were also fairly successful during this period. By the end of 1958, convertibility had been restored for all major currencies. The US supported European arrangements for multilateral clearings that began in 1947, most importantly the European Payments Union. During the 1940s, Marshall Plan funds were used not only to cover payment deficits with the Western Hemisphere, but also to facilitate the extension of credit among European countries. In 1950, the US granted $350 million to the European Payments Union to facilitate its multilateral clearings. Furthermore, by 1949 the US had forced substantial devaluations of all major European currencies. This contributed to a persistent American balance-of-payment deficit that began in 1950 and continued for the next two decades. One product of this deficit was an increase in world liquidity because of the excess dollars being held by foreign central banks.[43] Hence, the critical developments for monetary affairs during the 1950s were the devaluations of foreign currencies, the dispensation of Marshall Plan aid, and the dollar's central role as an international reserve currency. The first two were policy decisions taken largely within the Executive branch and the third

---

[40] Acheson, p. 233.

[41] Theodore J. Lowi, *The End of Liberalism: Ideology, Policy and the Crisis of Public Authority* (New York: W.W. Norton, 1969), pp. 174–75.

[42] Eckes, pp. 224–25; Leland B. Yeager, *International Monetary Relations: Theory, History and Policy*, 2nd ed. (New York: Harper and Row, 1976), pp. 385–86.

[43] Ibid., pp. 410–13; Sidney E. Rolfe and James L. Burtle, *The Great Wheel: The World Monetary System, A Reinterpretation* (New York: McGraw Hill, 1975), pp. 67–68.

was an almost automatic consequence of the strength of the American economy. Domestic political groups did not constrain US central decision makers in this issue-area.

In the area of commercial policy, US leaders were less successful. The Trade Agreements Act was renewed in 1948, 1949, 1951, 1954, 1955, and 1958. Virtually every instance touched off a political struggle. While the President was given some additional tariff cutting authority during the 1950s, other protectionist elements were introduced into the legislation. In 1947, there was the escape clause which allowed the US to rescind a concession if it resulted in injury to a domestic industry. There was the peril point in 1948 which provided that the Tariff Commission establish a rate prior to trade negotiations below which a domestic industry would be injured. In 1951, Congressional action forced the President to impose quotas on some agricultural exports in violation of GATT rules.[44]

The continued conservatism of American trade legislation reflected isolationism in Congress, pressure from industries that were being threatened by imports, and the inaction of groups that would benefit from greater openness. In 1953, domestic coal and oil producers began asking for quotas on oil imports. This eventually led to the establishment of quotas in the late 1950s. In 1955, Southern textile manufacturers began to put heavy pressure on their Congressmen. With a technology that was widely dispersed, textile manufacturers were among the first to feel foreign competition. Both the coal and textile campaigns were industry-wide, supported by both corporations and labor unions.[45] In addition, there were still strong isolationist sentiments in the Republican Party. In 1953 and 1954, both the Finance and Ways and Means Committees were controlled by legislators who had no sympathy for a more expansionary trade policy.

The support for a more liberal order was weak. Large American companies and banks with growing exports or investments were reluctant to take a strong stand. In part, this was because such enterprises are prone to follow risk-avoiding policies and taking very explicit public stands can be a risky business. Perhaps more important, as Tables IV and, especially, V indicate, the benefits of an open order became apparent gradually. Only as the prospects for foreign trade and investment became clearer, by 1960, did large American businesses take a more decisive positive stand on commercial legislation. Politics has few laws, but one of them is that people are willing to fight harder to avoid giving up what they have than they are to get new benefits in the future. During the 1950s, this meant that those who wanted to avoid foreign competition were willing to fight more fiercely than those who had not yet tasted the full fruits of foreign activity.

In sum, American foreign economic policy during the 1950s did promote a liberal international economic system. The precondition for this success was America's unchallenged international position in the non-Communist world. Still, US

[44] Evans, p. 72.
[45] Raymond A. Bauer, Ithiel de Sola Pool, and Lewis Anthony Dexter, *American Business and Public Policy: The Politics of Foreign Trade* (New York: Atherton, 1967), pp. 60–61, 363–72.

leaders had to deal with their own society. Funds for reconstruction were secured by defining US aims in Manichean terms. Monetary policy was successful because decisions were taken by the Executive, and because the size of the US economy led to the dollar's role as a reserve currency without an explicit policy choice. In commercial policy, progress was slow because the influence of import-competing industries was felt through the Congress.

## Apogee and decline: 1960–1971

The most unambiguous support for a liberal world order came during the early 1960s. This was a reflection both of America's still prodigious potential international economic power and of wide domestic support for state goals. However, by the mid-1960s, America's potential international economic strength was clearly waning. In addition, as the decade progressed, more and more domestic groups were negatively affected by imports and by foreign direct investment. Protectionist sentiments grew.

The central development of the early 1960s was the enactment of the Trade Expansion Act of 1962. It set the stage for the Kennedy Round of multilateral trade negotiations, the most successful ever held. The Act empowered the President to make 50 percent tariff cuts and to eliminate duties entirely on goods where the US and the EEC provided 80 percent of world trade.[46] It introduced adjustment assistance for domestic groups that were adversely affected by tariff cuts. It eliminated the peril point. It tightened the conditions under which the escape clause could be invoked. And, finally, it allowed negotiations on the basis of broad categories rather than item by item.[47]

A number of factors prompted the Kennedy Administration to press for more liberal trade legislation. The first was the fear that the EEC and the European Free Trade Association (EFTA) would limit American sales in Europe. Second, there was a need both to find a solution to the persistent American balance-of-payments deficit and to spur the domestic economy. Finally, and more generally, the commitment to a liberal regime continued to exist.[48] However, the desires of central decision makers are not a sufficient explanation for the passage of the Trade Expansion Act and the success of the Kennedy Round. The aims of foreign economic policy were not much different in 1962 than what they had been in earlier years when commercial policy had faltered.

What was different in the early 1960s was the structure of interests in the American economy. The expansion of trade and foreign investments during the 1950s had extended the benefits of a liberal international economic order more

---

[46] Because Great Britain did not enter the Common Market in the mid-1960s, this provision had little practical effect.

[47] Evans, pp. 142–43.

[48] Ernest H. Preeg, *Traders and Diplomats: An Analysis of the Kennedy Round of Negotiations Under the General Agreement on Tariffs and Trade* (Washington D.C.: Brookings Institution, 1970), pp. 31–32; Evans, pp. 138–44.

widely and deeply. At the same time, as Table III shows, only a few industries were experiencing serious foreign competition. Manufacturing sectors with intermediate levels of technology, like steel and automobiles, still enjoyed a trade surplus. Many corporations and banks were increasing their foreign investments. The 1962 Act enjoyed very broad support, including the endorsement of organized labor.

Even with this backing, the Kennedy Administration was not able to formulate an unambiguously liberal trade policy. The fragmentation of the political structure, which gives powerful domestic groups the ability to block the initiatives of central decision makers, made it necessary to implement selective protectionist measures. The oil industry had already gotten a mandatory import quota program. The 1962 Act prohibited any concessions in this area. The fears of the textile industry were assuaged in a number of ways. The Long-Term Cotton Textiles Agreement of 1962 limited import increases to six percent per year. In March 1962, Kennedy used the escape clause to levy higher tariffs on carpets. There was also a ban on eight varieties of cotton imports from Hong Kong and an 8.5 cent a pound subsidy to cotton growers.[49] Still, these were rather modest concessions. The 1962 Act did open the way for the Kennedy Round, which resulted in tariff cuts averaging 35 percent.

However, even before the Kennedy Round was concluded, protectionist sentiment in the US was becoming more evident. The increasing openness of the international economy was subjecting more domestic sectors to international competition. By the mid-1960s, some industries with intermediate levels of technology began encountering serious competition from imports. For instance, the trade balance for iron and steel shifted from a small surplus in 1960 to a substantial deficit in 1965. The Congress failed to approve agreements involving American Selling Price (ASP) valuations and an anti-dumping code that had been concluded at the Kennedy Round. The Tariff Commission relaxed its definition of injury in anti-dumping cases in 1967. The number of judgments of injury increased from a total of three for the years 1965 through 1967 to a total of twelve for the years 1968 through 1970.[50] A number of new sectoral trade restrictions were put in effect after 1966. In 1967, quotas were imposed on some dairy products. In early 1969, a "voluntary" steel export agreement was concluded with major exporters from Japan and Europe. It provided that their sales to the US would be limited to increases of 5 percent a year from 1969 through 1971. On February 24, 1970, the President suspended tariff reductions on pianos under the escape clause. This was the first positive escape clause recommendation from the Tariff Commission since 1962.[51]

During the 1960s, America's international monetary policy also showed signs of strain. The establishment of convertibility for major currencies in 1958 quickly

---

[49] Evans, pp. 167, 201–02, 230–31; Pastor, p. 28.
[50] Marks and Malmgren, p. 375.
[51] Information from the International Monetary Fund, *Annual Report on Exchange Restrictions*, various years, US country pages.

revealed that the dollar shortage of the early 1950s had been replaced by a dollar glut; the US balance of payments deficit was excessive. To deal with the growing deficit, American policy makers implemented several programs during the 1960s. The most important were an Interest Equalization Tax which limited European access to the New York capital market; voluntary, and later mandatory, controls on direct foreign investments; and controls on banks. In addition, a number of new devices including the Gold Pool, swaps, and Roosa bonds were concocted to aid in supporting the existing regime.

Domestic political constraints were less important for monetary than for commercial policy. It was external, not internal, factors that caused monetary problems. The issues were decided in very different decision-making arenas. While the Congress played a major role in commercial policy, monetary policy was set by the White House, the Treasury, and the Federal Reserve Board. Controls on direct investment were imposed by Presidential proclamation. Controls on banking activity were set by the Federal Reserve Board. The Secretary of the Treasury announced that the US would suspend the purchase and sale of gold from private sources in 1968. The only two monetary decisions that involved Congressional action were the Interest Equalization Tax and the creation of Special Drawing Rights (SDRs). The most careful empirical study of US monetary policy during this period concludes that it was very much in the hands of the President and his close advisors.[52]

A second reason why domestic fragmentation did not constrain monetary policy was that the groups that could have been adversely affected by capital export controls, multinational corporations and banks, were able to adjust to most of the new regulations. Constraints on the export of dollars from the US quickly led to the development of the Eurodollar market. Banks in Europe, many of them branches of US financial institutions, rapidly increased their dollar deposits. US companies could obtain their capital from this market rather than from New York. MNCs did protest the mandatory Foreign Direct Investment Program in 1968; but, since the program was established by an Executive Order, they could not stop it. By 1973, when a Federal Court in Washington ruled the program illegal, controls were being dismantled.[53]

In sum, the 1960s saw a transition of American foreign economic policy. During the first part of the decade, American central decision makers were able to take advantage of a domestic consensus for a more liberal trading order to secure passage of the Trade Expansion Act and conclude the Kennedy Round negotiations. By the end of the decade, more and more sectors of the American economy were facing foreign competition. To prevent Congressional action, the Executive

---

[52] John Odell, "The United States in the International Monetary System: Sources of Foreign Policy Change" (Ph.D. Dissertation, University of Wisconsin, 1976).

[53] John A.C. Conybeare, "United States Foreign Economic Policy and the International Capital Markets: The Case of Capital Export Controls, 1963–1974" (Ph.D. Dissertation, Harvard University, 1976), Chapter 5 and pp. 231–37.

was compelled to implement a number of measures that protected certain domestic groups. In the monetary area, policy was free of domestic constraints, but ultimately unsuccessful in dealing with balance-of-payments problems. The American economy could not sustain both the Vietnam War and high domestic expenditures, and still maintain balance-of-payments equilibrium or an acceptable deficit, without, at the least, exchange rate adjustment.

## 1971–: growing strains, international and domestic

During the 1970s, the fundamental objective of foreign economic policy for American central decision makers has remained the maintenance of a liberal international economic regime. This goal is now most frequently explained in terms of interdependence, the notion that at least all non-Communist countries are locked into a complex network of relationships whose rupture would be extremely costly for everyone. While this rationale is different from the anti-Communism of the late 1940s and 1950s, the policy implications are identical. However, American leaders have found it increasingly difficult to implement their preferences because, as Table I indicates, America's potential economic power has declined. Simultaneously, as Table III indicates, the number of groups within American society that would benefit from protection has increased.

By the middle of 1971, a realignment of exchange rates was long overdue. In 1971, the US merchandise balance showed a deficit for the first time since 1894.[54] On August 15, President Nixon officially brought the Bretton Woods system to an end. He announced that the US would no longer buy and sell gold. He imposed a temporary 10 percent surcharge on American imports. American leaders were not interested in moving away from a liberal order, but they did want a change in exchange rates and an improvement in America's balance-of-payments situation. They did not foresee the violent foreign reaction that developed against the import surcharge. Most members of the Administration saw the surcharge as a device that would not only jolt America's trading partners, but that would also stave off protectionist legislation in Congress.[55]

The crisis precipitated by these announcements was temporarily resolved by a realignment of exchange rates in December 1971 known as the Smithsonian Agreement. But it was short-lived. By the end of 1973, international exchange rates were related by snakes, worms, and dirty floats. In addition, the quadrupling of oil prices in the Fall and Winter of 1973–74 led to very large deficits for almost all non-oil Third World countries, as well as some industrial ones. Some oil-exporting

[54] Charles P. Kindleberger, "U.S. Foreign Economic Policy, 1776–1976," *Foreign Affairs* Vol. 55, No. 2 (January 1977): 413. The overall balance had been in deficit almost continuously after 1949.

[55] Linda S. Graebner, "The New Economic Policy, 1971," in US Commission on the Organization of the Government for the Conduct of Foreign Policy, *Appendices,* Vol. 3 (Washington, D.C.: Government Printing Office, 1975), pp. 160–61.

states recorded enormous surplus revenues, which entered the international monetary system as a new and volatile source of liquidity, petrodollars. At Jamaica in early 1976, the IMF Articles of Agreement were amended to recognize actual practices, but no serious effort was made to construct a new order.[56]

The international monetary system no longer functions smoothly. There have been sharp swings in foreign exchange rates during the last few years despite very heavy official intervention in the dirty floating system. In March 1976, the French were compelled to withdraw their currency from the European snake to preserve their foreign exchange holdings. The Swiss have been unable to stifle an unwanted flood of foreign exchange into their country. In June of 1976, the Bank of England identified shifts in funds by oil-exporting states as the largest cause of the pound's decline from $2.40 to $1.70.[57] Even multinational corporations were having difficulties dealing with this uncertain environment.[58] This is not to say that the actual flow of goods, services, and capital has collapsed. World trade has recovered since the mid-1970s recession. Petrodollars are, on the whole, being successfully recycled by the private banking system. But it is to say that the international monetary order is much more troublesome and fragile today, much more subject to a serious breakdown, than at any time since the Second World War.

The fragility of the international monetary system is inherently related to the declining international power of the US. As in the case of most other monetary decisions, domestic constraints were less important than international ones because of the arena in which policy was set: the August 1971 package was imposed through Presidential authority, not Congressional legislation. But at the international level, the US no longer had the ability to control events. It could not get its trading partners, particularly the Japanese, to revalue their currencies enough to restore equilibrium to the US balance of payments. This contrasts sharply with 1949 when the US had been able to dictate exchange rates by threatening to withhold Marshall Plan aid. Once August 1971 had violated extant norms, they could not be restored. The international monetary system became increasingly disorderly. While the US has not suffered relative to other countries, and the dollar has remained the most important international currency, the effective power that the US can utilize is not sufficient to reestablish an international monetary system in which there is clear agreement on rules and norms.

Changes in US power and developments in the international monetary system are also reflected in the petrodollar problem. American dominance in the immediate postwar period existed in virtually every important issue-area. An attempted Arab oil production cutback in 1967 was prevented by increasing output in the US and other countries. By 1973, there was no surplus capacity. The October cutbacks and embargo revealed how high oil prices could actually go. The quadrupling of oil

---

[56] Tom de Vries, "Jamaica, Or the Non-Reform of the International Monetary System," *Foreign Affairs* Vol. 54, No. 3 (April 1976): 577–605.

[57] *Wall Street Journal,* March 16, 1976, p. 4:3; June 14, 1976, p. 7:2; and *New York Times,* June 17, 1976, p. 1:6.

[58] *Wall Street Journal,* June 7, 1976, p. 1:6; December 8, 1976, p. 1:6; and *New York Times,* December 13, 1975, p. 37:8.

prices greatly increased the number of petrodollars in the world monetary system. Given both the liquid form in which most oil-exporting states are holding their assets and their potential manipulation for political purposes, petrodollars have made the international monetary system much more subject to wide exchange rate swings. What the US almost single-handedly prevented in 1967 was out of its control by 1973.

American commercial policy during the 1970s has also been less successful in maintaining a liberal international order. As in earlier periods, the primary constraints on American central decision makers were domestic. However, these domestic constraints reflected a change in America's international economic position. As Table III indicates, the number of sectors of the American economy threatened by foreign competition has increased over time. Foreign countries, including some in the Third World, have been able to master more sophisticated levels of technology. Innovations developed in the US, such as color television tubes, have very quickly spread to other countries. The technological lead that the US enjoyed in the 1940s and 1950s, which gave America a strong balance of trade surplus, has eroded.

The result is that more groups within the US have been demanding protection. However, the pattern is confused, and the confusion has been reflected in policy. Most of the American labor movement has become protectionist, giving up a long history of support for free trade. Labor has also advocated measures to cut foreign direct investment. However, labor has not always had the support of management in sectors of the economy that are threatened by imports. In a number of industries, there has been heavy foreign investment by US corporations. These companies become torn between their domestic and foreign interests. Often there are differences within specific industries.[59] Furthermore, there are many sectors of the US economy, including agriculture, aircraft, and sophisticated machinery, which run a heavy trade surplus. They want an open system.

Given the weakness of the American domestic political system, it is not surprising that, during the 1970s, US commercial policy has become more confused and less coherent.[60] The divisions within the society have been mirrored in official policy. Explicit efforts at protectionism such as the Mills Bill and the Burke-Hartke Bill have been defeated. However, the 1974 Trade Act reflects societal cross pressures and is clearly less liberal than the Trade Expansion Act of 1962. First, the 1974 Act increases the decision-making role of the Congress for the first time since 1934, when the Reciprocal Trade Agreements Act gave the President real power to negotiate tariff levels. The Congress rejected a Presidential proposal that would have implied consent for changes in non-tariff barriers negotiated by the President if they were not explicitly rejected within 90 days. Instead, the 1974 Act requires Congress' acceptance or rejection within 60 days. For the first time, the law states that

---

[59] For example, Sylvania has supported quotas to protect the US color television industry, while RCA, which earns considerable sums from licensing fees in Japan, has opposed them. See *Wall Street Journal*, December 16, 1976, p. 21:3.

[60] For coherence as an important criterion for assessing policy see Peter J. Katzenstein, "International Relations and Domestic Structures: Foreign Economic Policies of Advanced Industrial States," *International Organization* Vol. 30, No. 1 (Winter 1976): 1–46.

members of Congress (ten) must be fully accredited members of the US trade delegation at Geneva. The Congress may override a Presidential rejection of a recommendation of the International Trade Commission (formerly the Tariff Commission). A majority of one House of the Congress can override a Treasury decision not to retaliate against foreign dumping.[61]

Congress is not the mere handmaiden of particular interest groups. In fact, one of the reasons that Congress gave more power to the President in 1934 was that it wanted to free itself from the naked exposure to interest group pressure and the petty and time-consuming wrangling that had been a part of tariff legislation.[62] Nevertheless, Congress is bound to be more sensitive to particularistic societal pressures than the President or the Secretary of State. The geographical system of representation guarantees that this will be the case. Hence, the increase in legislative power is both a reflection of growing protectionism and likely to lead to less liberal policies in the future.

Aside from procedural changes, the Trade Act of 1974 includes a number of measures that are less liberal than those of the 1962 legislation. The Act makes it easier for a domestic group to claim injury under the escape clause. The Trade Expansion Act of 1962 required that imports be the result of trade concessions and be "the major cause" of injury. The 1974 Act requires only that imports be a "substantial cause" of injury and does not require that imports be related to tariff concessions. The new legislation stiffens the procedures for imposing countervailing duties against exports that receive some form of subsidy by compelling the Treasury to make a judgment within twelve months. Previously, the Treasury had sat on some cases for years. The Trade Act also tightens US anti-dumping provisions.[63]

However, it would be an error to regard the 1974 Act as an unambiguously protectionist measure. It authorizes the President to reduce tariffs up to 60 percent for rates above five percent and to eliminate imposts altogether for rates below five percent. The Act also makes it easier for companies and workers to get adjustment assistance. During periods of economic prosperity, adjustment assistance can blunt protectionist sentiments by providing businesses and workers with funds to retrain or retool. During slack periods its effectiveness is likely to be less, because alternative opportunities are scarce.

The incoherence that is inherent in the 1974 Trade Act has also been reflected in a number of actual policy decisions. In June 1976, the specialty steel industry forced President Ford to accept an International Trade Commission recommendation for quotas because the Administration thought that the industry had enough votes in Congress to override a Presidential rejection of this recommendation. This was the culmination of an escape clause case brought by the United Steel Workers and

[61] Weil, pp. 53–56.

[62] William B. Kelly, Jr., "Antecedents of Present Commercial Policy, 1922–1934," in *Studies in United States Commercial Policy*, William B. Kelly, Jr., ed. (Chapel Hill: University of North Carolina Press, 1963), p. 15; Bauer, Dexter and Pool, pp. 27, 37.

[63] *National Journal Reports*, April 17, 1976, pp. 502–04.

nineteen companies. A small but united industry (speciality steel imports), with Congressional support, could prevail against the preferences of central decision makers.[64] However, an anti-dumping case brought by the United Auto Workers (UAW) against automobile companies in Belgium, Britain, Canada, France, Italy, Japan, Sweden, and West Germany resulted in an extremely ambiguous Treasury ruling against eight companies. They agreed to raise prices; countervailing duties were not imposed. The auto union was not supported by the four big US automobile companies, all of which have substantial foreign investments.[65]

The 1970s have seen the greatest strain on American efforts to create and maintain a liberal international economic regime. Constraints on US central decision makers have come from both the international system and from domestic groups. The declining international power of the US has been reflected in monetary relations which have become more fragile and disorderly. Domestic dissatisfaction with foreign competition has been reflected in the 1974 Trade Act and in the success some import-competing groups have had in forcing the Executive to accede to their demands. Progress at the current round of multilateral trade talks is now far behind schedule, and US officials are not in a position to offer strong leadership because they might not have the necessary domestic political support to sustain such initiatives.

## V Conclusions

A liberal international economic system could not have been established after the Second World War were it not for the power and policies of the US. The dollar has been the world's key currency. At the most important multilateral trade talks, which were held in 1947 and during the 1960s (the Kennedy Round), the US was able to take the lead in negotiations that led to very dramatic reductions in tariff levels. During the postwar period, world trade has grown very rapidly.

However, in more recent years, very serious strains have developed in the international economic system. The most obvious has been the quadrupling of oil prices. This action has contributed to inflation and to the creation of unmanageable debts for many Third World countries. It has led to lower rates of growth and to a more volatile international monetary system. Even more generally, the Third World has become an autonomous actor on the world scene; most of its members reject the vision and specific policies that have animated American leaders. At least 75 percent of the holdings of US raw materials corporations located in Third World countries have been nationalized. In violation of liberal tenets, institutions and firms that are directly controlled by governments are playing a more prominent role in the world economy.

---

[64] *Wall Street Journal,* January 1, 1976, p. 4:2; March 12, 1976, p. 24:2; March 17, 1976, p. 2:2; and *New York Times,* June 12, 1976, p. 29:5.

[65] *Wall Street Journal,* May 5, 1976, p. 3:1; May 6, 1976, p. 5:2; July 6, 1976, p. 9:1; August 11, 1976, p. 2:2.

It is possible that a new equilibrium will be established. It will not necessarily be one considered ideal by American policy makers, but, at least, it will be one in which liberal principles would hold for the industrial market economies. Perhaps, over the long term, some Third World countries could be enticed into this system. The relative volume and value of international exchange could continue to grow. The costs of undermining the system could increase for all actors. The world could grow ever more interdependent. Indeed, the rhetoric that the US has directed at OPEC countries reflects this scenario. US leaders have argued that oil-exporting and oil-importing states are locked into a mutual relationship in which "irresponsible" action by OPEC, that is, precipitous price increases, could have a disastrous impact on everyone.

The underlying logic of this argument is profoundly liberal. It assumes that a stable regime can grow out of economic interests. That is, it assumes that interests rather than power can be the basis for order. Just as for Locke individuals move from the state of nature to a political order by giving up some of their natural rights to achieve certain benefits, the logic of interdependence is that states will give up some of their right to self-help (and thereby establish a stable regime) to secure certain economic goods or to avoid the costs of isolationism. Individual actors will refrain from purely self-serving acts that can harm the system as a whole, because any weakness in the whole system would have a substantial impact on all of its members.

The arguments and assumptions of this paper are incompatible with such a liberal vision of the evolution of the global economy. Interests, alone, have not been enough to constitute an international order. It has always been necessary to have some political power that can provide collective goods and enforce rules and norms. The question, then, is whether the US can play the same role that it has in the past or whether some new political coalition can be constructed to sustain a new regime.

In terms of *potential* economic power resources, a serious case can be made that effective US leadership is still possible. At the end of 1975, the American economy was still more than twice as large as that of the Soviet Union and more than three times as large as that of the next largest non-Communist state, Japan.[66] The dollar continues to be the most important international reserve currency. At the end of 1974, dollars composed 74 percent of the Eurocurrency market, down only 6 percent from the proportion of a decade earlier.[67] The oil crisis has strengthened the position of the US relative to most other industrial countries because of its greater energy self-sufficiency. The US still holds a position that appears much more commanding than Britain's, even at the peak of British power in the 1860s and 1870s; and the London-oriented international economic system of

---

[66] *New York Times*, December 27, 1976, p. D4:4.
[67] Bank for International Settlements, *Fortieth Annual Report* (Basle: 1970), p. 151; *Forty-fifth Annual Report* (Basle: 1975), p. 131.

the nineteenth century persisted long after Britain's potential international economic power had begun to decline.

Unfortunately, an assessment based solely on aggregate resources ignores the domestic constraints that confront US central decision makers. While the potential power of the US remains formidable, the resources that its leaders can actually utilize to achieve state purposes are less, and the gap between potential and available resources is growing. This gap is a function of domestic political processes. The American political system is relatively weak: state leaders cannot easily overcome domestic opposition. The number of domestic groups that would be disenchanted with significant American sacrifices to maintain a liberal international economic regime is growing. Although the devaluations of the early 1970s provided some surcease, there has not been a basic change in the pattern of increased import competition for more sectors in the American economy.

To establish a new liberal order, US leaders would have to engage in complex bargaining across issue-areas. They would need discretionary control over a wide range of resources. Perhaps, if the American political system were stronger, they could extract a level of resources equal to the task. But policy is not made in counter-factual environments. US leaders will not be able to construct a stable order as open and liberal as the one that existed in the 1960s. If they persist in extolling the virtues of liberalism and interdependence, the result could be chaotic. The present situation is very fragile and any one of a number of events, such as another war in the Middle East, or Communist victories in Western Europe, could set off capital flights and other developments that would sharply curtail world commerce.

The international economic system is no longer congruent with the underlying political power that sustains it. There is too much openness, too much interdependence. The ideal policy for the US would be to press for a lessening of international involvements and greater regulation of the flows of goods, services, and capital. Such a system could be sustained by the existing distribution of power among states. This would require a new definition of goals by US leaders. It would require dealing with domestic groups such as banks and corporations that are heavily involved in foreign activity. Unfortunately, given the weakness of the American domestic political system and the pervasiveness of Lockian ideals, a policy of controlled closure is no more likely to be successfully pursued than one of renewed liberalism. In the future, US policy is likely to become less coherent and the world economy more unstable.

# 4
# Britain: The Politics of Foreign Economic Policy, the Domestic Economy, and the Problem of Pluralistic Stagnation

*Stephen Blank*

Economic policies in Britain after World War II, both domestic and international, were dominated by foreign policy goals. This provides the primary explanation for Britain's poor economic performance in the postwar years. Commitments made in the late 1940s and 1950s, particularly with regard to Britain's international position and responsibilities, and domestic economic policies devised to support these commitments, locked Britain into a low-growth situation. In the late 1950s and early 1960s, the widespread consensus supporting these commitments began to disintegrate and efforts were made to develop new policies directed toward stimulating domestic economic growth. These efforts were unsuccessful—largely because of the unwillingness of government leaders to shift national priorities away from traditional international commitments. This failure made it impossible for the British economy to meet the rising expectations of the British population and contributed, after 1967, to a widespread increase in social conflict. Compared to other advanced industrial nations, Britain's economic performance since 1945 has been poor. Britain's poor economic performance is due, however, not to the weakness of British governments or to their inability to resist demands made by interests groups, but rather to a series of policy choices, especially in the international area, that were inappropriate for Britain's resources but to which successive governments adhered with remarkable stubbornness and rigidity.[1]

Stephen Blank is a member of The Conference Board in New York City.
[1] This essay forms part of a wider study on the "political framework of economic policy making in advanced industrial nations." A much earlier draft of this paper was presented at the 1975 annual meeting of the British Politics Association. The support of the Council on Foreign Relations and the Center for West European Studies at Harvard University is gratefully acknowledged. In addition, I wish to thank the Rockefeller Foundation for permitting me to work on this project as a resident at the Villa Serbelloni.

There were two sets of constraints on Britain's economic performance after 1945, one internal and the other external. The internal constraints included inefficiently organized industries, dated capital structures in many industries, low levels of replacement of capital goods, widespread restrictive practices, an outmoded system of industrial relations, and trade union and management practices that inhibited industrial modernization and economic expansion. The external constraints related primarily to Britain's extraordinarily vulnerable international financial position (a function of limited reserves), consistently unfavorable balance of payments, and extensive international financial and economic commitments.

The history of the British economy in the 30 years after 1945 is, for the most part, the story of Britain's inability to overcome the internal constraints on its economic development. This failure has thus increased Britain's vulnerability to the external constraints. Most analyses of the British economic situation focus on the failures of the domestic economy. Included here would be the failure to increase production, to maintain stable prices, to invest more, to get more satisfactory returns in productivity from investment, to export more, and so on. But economic issues per se are not always seen to be the primary reasons for these failures. Increasingly, observers of Britain have come to believe that the fundamental reasons for the problems of the British economy are more political than economic. It is argued that the structure of British society and, more particularly, the way in which the political system operates have made it possible for groups representing limited interests to warp or undermine government policy. These groups are even seen to assume the powers of government and, thus, to inhibit or prevent governments from carrying out policies which are in the interests of the entire nation. Organized groups, workers or businessmen, ruthlessly exploit their power within the British political system to enhance their welfare at everyone else's cost. Political parties have made this situation still worse by promising far more than governments can deliver and, thus, by creating expectations doomed to be frustrated.

This essay argues that a major source of the constraints on British economic performance since 1945 has indeed been political. It disagrees, however, with those who say that the difficulties lie primarily in the abilities of groups in British society, particularly industrial or labor organizations, to thwart or undermine government policies. It suggests that frustrated expectations and the actions to which they give rise are the result more than the cause of Britain's economic and political difficulties. The argument of this essay is that Britain's economic problems in the postwar years have been caused in large measure by the policies of successive governments, especially those policies which dealt with Britain's role in the world.

It is not meant to suggest by this that organized industrial and labor groups in Britain have had no influence on government policies or that they have never undermined economically and socially productive policy objectives. In particular cases, under particular circumstances (not necessarily unique or even infrequent), trade unions and industrial associations have been able to influence policy outcomes substantially. When issues are finely focused rather than broad, administrative rather than political, when the expert knowledge of the group can be brought to bear, or when government's own policy is uncertain or the members of the government divided, there is considerable scope for influence. Regardless of policy outcomes, groups can also influence policy as it is implemented.

But these groups had little influence on the determination of domestic or international economic objectives or on the formulation of the broad outlines of national economic policy. In Britain, the permeability of the economic policy-making process has been considerably less of a problem than the insulation of the policy-making process from the impact of criticism and new ideas. What one finds in postwar Britain is not so much weak government, unable to resist the demands made by powerful interest groups, as government which made many wrong policy choices and persisted in following these policies with remarkable stubbornness. In the field of economic policy, British government has been neither weak nor vacillating. It rigidly adhered to the policies which it determined, even when the adverse impacts of those policies had become all too clear.

The external constraints on British economic performance differed from the internal constraints in that, to a large extent, they were the result of a series of political choices made by postwar governments to restore and preserve Britain's role as a world power. For much of the postwar period, domestic and international economic policy was dominated by and subordinated to the goals of foreign policy, goals which Britain was incapable of realizing. Yet, the attempt to achieve these goals led successive governments to sacrifice the domestic economy again and again. By the end of the 1950s, a vicious cycle had evolved in which efforts to maintain its international position became themselves the very causes of Britain's continuing international financial vulnerability. Efforts to create new policies and institutions whose purpose was to confront the problems of the domestic economy and to improve domestic economic performance foundered on the willingness of political leaders to abandon the most cherished symbol of Britain's international position by devaluing the pound.

Eventually, although not until the second half of the 1960s, British political leaders came to see that the international role Britain had sought to play since 1945 was beyond its capacity. By then, however, enormous damage had been inflicted on the domestic economy. Moreover, largely because of the retardation of economic growth that had been the result of these earlier policies, Britain was in a poor position to cope effectively with the new challenges of the 1970s, domestic and international.

This essay, to a certain extent, reverses the focus of the other papers in this volume. It looks much more at the impact of elite attitudes, particularly those dealing with Britain's international role, on domestic economic policy than at the major structural determinants of foreign economic policy. The essay seeks to examine the interrelationships of international and domestic economic and political objectives and policies. It looks, in particular, at the impact of foreign policy goals upon international and domestic economic policies. It contends that economic policies in Britain after World War II, both domestic and international, were dominated by foreign policy goals and that this domination provides the primary explanation for Britain's poor economic performance during the postwar years. Without the constraints which were the result of British foreign policy goals, Britain's economic performance would surely have been more satisfactory. But it still would have been limited by internal economic factors, not least of which are attitudes and values concerning the role of the state in the economy and the relationship of public and private power. Equally important are the rights and responsibilities of such bodies as the trade unions and the appropriate limitations, if any, on collective bargaining and price setting throughout the economy. To alter these attitudes as well as the practices and institutions in which they are embodied is perhaps the most vital task of national economic policy. The heightened level of social conflict in British society, the failure of governments to give adequate consideration to the needs of institutional development, and the politicization of economic policies and the instruments of economic management have made this task far more difficult at the present time than it might have been earlier.

In the end, in large part as a result of the continued failure of the economy to perform more successfully, Britain may be approaching a point at which its governments are exhausted, the legitimacy of its political leadership undermined, and its political parties deeply divided. Britain may thus be reaching a point at which there are no longer effective political barriers to protect society from groups which seek to defend themselves at all costs from a continuously declining economic situation. At such a point, the basic structure of Britain's economy and democracy will be undermined.

## I  The international setting of Britain's economic policy

There is an extensive and well-known literature which deals with Britain's long-term descent as a leading economic power. Much of this rests on the notion of Britain's precipitous industrial decline, relative to the expanding industrial economies of such nations as the United States and Germany, sometime during the last decades of the nineteenth century—the British "Climacteric."[2] E.J. Hobsbawm sums up the theme of this literature by suggesting that "this sudden transformation of the leading and most dynamic industrial economy into the most sluggish and conservative, in the short space of thirty or forty years (1860–90/1900), is the crucial question of British economic history."[3] Because of the loss of industrial preeminence, the nature of Britain's economy and its economic relations with other countries altered dramatically. Hobsbawm notes that "The British economy as a

[2] See E.H. Phelps Brown and S.J. Handfield-Jones, and D.J. Coppock, "The 'Climacteric' in the British Economy of the late Nineteenth Century: Two Interpretations," in *The Experience of Economic Growth,* Barry E. Supple ed. (New York: Random House, 1963), pp. 203–25.
[3] E.J. Hobsbawm, *Industry and Empire* (London: Penguin Books, 1968), p. 178.

whole tended to retreat from industry into trade and finance." Robert Gilpin has built from this and similar analyses a superb discussion of the role, and dangers, of the increasing outflow of foreign investment which resulted from the decline of the domestic economy.[4]

The analysis of Britain's "climacteric" of the late nineteenth century, because it is so well-documented and compelling, has had the unfortunate effect of encouraging scholars and, even more, a large number of non-scholars to see Britain's present economic situation solely in terms of this long drawn out economic collapse. Since 1945, Britain has been playing out the final act of this sad drama of decline and fall. Anglophiles brush away a tear, while an increasing number of would-be Gibbons in America are all too eager to dissect the corpse. They call up the image (clearly to make their own political hay) of some dying beast which, on its very death bed, feeds upon itself in a last orgy of lust and socialism.

The major problem with the analysis of long-term collapse, aside from a frequent vulgar economic determinism, is that it simply misses the subtle parts. The real story is better and, perhaps, sadder. Many indications exist to suggest that Britain's economy has not been in a state of continuous decline since the end of the nineteenth century. Rather, they suggest that it was substantially revitalized in the period which began in the late 1930s and continued through the Second World War into the late 1940s.

Britain's interwar economic record was not very good, but it was better, for example, than that of the French. Losses in the First World War were not as severe as those France had suffered and postwar economic dislocations had ended by the mid-1920s. The Depression hit Britain hard, but economic recovery was substantial between 1933 and 1935. Manufacturing output in 1938–39 was almost one-third higher than in 1929 and almost 40 percent more than in 1914.[5]

Through the interwar period, the problem of unemployment dominated British minds. "From 1921 on, unemployment was never less than 9 percent of the work-force; there seemed to be a hard core of one million jobless, good times or bad."[6] In fact, unemployment rates were not much greater in Britain than in France, at least among union members, but the political and social impact of unemployment was more severe in Britain. The unemployed urban worker in France drifted back to the countryside. In Britain, he was forced to stay in the city and on the dole. But total output and industrial output per head increased impressively in the interwar years, despite unemployment and depression. Moreover, there was a beginning of a shift in the British economy toward newer, more technologically intensive industries which were organized in a more modern fashion.

---

[4] Hobsbawm, p. 191. Robert Gilpin, *U.S. Power and the Multinational Corporation* (New York: Basic Books, 1975), pp. 85–97.
[5] David S. Landes, *The Unbound Prometheus* (Cambridge: Cambridge University Press, 1969), p. 394. See Hobsbawm, Chapter 11.
[6] Landes, pp. 368–69.

It is difficult to evaluate the economic impact of wars. British losses between 1939 and 1945 were serious indeed. Perhaps 10 percent of the nation's wealth at home was destroyed by enemy action or by overuse, and 400,000 British citizens were killed. But there were positive economic effects, too.[7] The war brought about a remarkable resurgence of confidence in Britain. Among the European participants in the war, only Britain had not suffered invasion or defeat. The British had stood alone against Hitler in the very darkest moment of the night. Together they had shared in Britain's "finest hour." The war had been a triumph for traditional British virtues: strength of character, tenacity, cooperation. Perhaps most important of all, the scourge of unemployment had ended. In 1945, three million more Britons were employed than in 1939. For the next 25 years, unemployment levels did not reach half the figure of the interwar years. Despite the bombing, the loss of resources, and the lack of replacement and new investment, Britain's economy had performed miracles of production. Even more, major technological advances had been made during the war. In many cases (for example, in electronics, radar, and jet propulsion) there was the promise of important peacetime applications. Thus A.J.P. Taylor concludes his study of Britain from 1914 to 1945 by stating: "During the Second World War, and not before, Great Britain took the decisive jump industrially from the nineteenth into the twentieth century. Before the war, Great Britain was still trying to revive the old staples. After it, she relied on new developing industries."[8]

Despite the enormous economic losses of the war, Britain's postwar economic recovery was remarkable by any standards. Indeed, one can, with some justice, speak of Britain's recovery in the first postwar years as Europe's first "economic miracle." The economic instability which had characterized Britain after 1918 was avoided, and impressive gains were made in total production, in productivity, and in exports. Between 1945 and 1950, industrial production increased by between 30 and 40 percent. (Indeed, between 1948 and 1960, the rate of real growth in total industrial output was 3.7 percent, compared to 3.1 percent between 1920 and 1937 and 1.6 percent between 1877 and 1913.) The rate of increase in industrial productivity was almost 3 percent between 1949 and 1960. Between 1924 and 1935 it had been 2.2 percent and was 1.6 percent between 1907 and 1924.[9]

Perhaps most significantly (and frequently overlooked), Britain's international trade performance improved dramatically. Visible exports increased by 75 percent over prewar levels in the first postwar years, with no increase in imports. Although British exports declined after the late 1940s as a percentage of all world exports, they continued to increase absolutely and imports into Britain rose no

[7] On this question in general, see Alan S. Milward, *The Economic Effects of the Two World Wars on Britain* (London: Macmillan, 1970).

[8] A.J.P. Taylor, *English History 1914–1945* (Oxford: The Clarendon Press, 1965), p. 600.

[9] K.S. Lomax, "Growth and Productivity in the United Kingdom," in *Economic Growth in Twentieth Century Britain,* Derek Aldcrott and Peter Fearnon, eds. (New York: Humanities Press, 1970), pp. 12 and 26. See also E.H. Phelps Brown, "Labour Policies: Productivity, Industrial Relations, Cost Inflation," in *Britain's Economic Prospects Reconsidered,* Sir Alec Cairncross, ed. (London: George Allen & Unwin, 1971).

more rapidly than in other developed nations. Britain's net trade gap had run around 30 percent in 1900–1910 (that is, there were 30 percent fewer visible exports than imports), 20–30 percent in 1920–1930, and 40–45 percent in 1930– 1939. Since 1945, it has run consistently below 10 percent, and often lower than 5 percent.[10] The remaining deficit has been more than made up each year by an invisible surplus. As a result, Britain consistently ran a *surplus* balance on the *private* account after the war (at least through the late 1960s) as favorable as that of France or Germany.[11]

All of this was accomplished against the background of the creation of the welfare state, a fairly large redistribution of personal income in favor of wage earners, and the maintenance of full employment. Although some observers of the British economy saw the economic crises of 1947 and 1949 as stages in a longer term process of decline, others believed these problems to be more temporary and caused by the inevitable difficulties of adjustment after the war. The going was tough enough in Britain after the war, particularly in the Winter of 1947. But the achievements of these years were clear, too, and there was a widespread sense of national purpose in the country. Besides, compared to the political and economic situation in Europe, Britain's difficulties hardly seemed insurmountable. In view of these achievements, the standard interpretations of these years is puzzling. As Sidney Pollard observes, it is "not a little surprising that the period appears in much contemporary literature as a period of chaos and failure."[12] It is even more surprising that this image has not been greatly revised.

British economic policies after World War II were dominated and shaped by two overriding policy objectives. British governments were committed to consolidate and maintain the welfare state, the system of economic and social security which ensured that the human suffering and deprivation of the interwar years would not be repeated. Its most vital element was the policy of full employment. The domestic roots of these commitments are obvious, but they have significant international foundations as well. By the end of the war, the British were convinced that the fundamental causes of the war were the economic and social conditions of the interwar years. British economic commitments and policies in the postwar years were greatly influenced by the belief that it was necessary to avoid the recurrence of such conditions at almost any cost. Thus, the consolidation of the welfare state and the guarantee of full employment at home went hand in hand with Britain's efforts to recreate a stable and liberal international commercial and financial order.

---

[10] W.A.P. Manser, *Britain in Balance: The Myth of Failure* (London: Penguin Books, 1973), p. 11. See also Lawrence Krause, "British Trade Performance," in *Britain's Economic Prospects,* Richard Caves and Associates (Washington: The Brookings Institution, 1968).

[11] Britain ran a surplus on its *private* account. The overall balance of payments, which includes government spending and lending abroad, was normally in deficit. See Manser, Chapters 1–5 for a detailed but comprehensible analysis of British trade accounts since 1945.

[12] Sidney Pollard, *The Development of the British Economy, 1914–1945,* 2nd ed. (New York: St. Martin's Press, 1969), p. 375.

British governments after World War II were committed, in the second place, to restore and protect Britain's international position. This was necessary not only in diplomatic and military terms (where it soon became clear that Britain would have to play second fiddle to the Americans) but in commerce and finance as well. Britain would maintain the "special relationship" with the US and would continue to play, alongside the United States but also independently, a major world political and economic role. The Commonwealth provided a power base which was independent of the US and Europe and, in particular, enabled Britain to maintain its position as the world's foremost commercial and financial center. Within this arena, the sterling system served as the prime mechanism which linked the Commonwealth into a coherent economic entity. Thus, the sterling system, resting on fixed exchange rates and London's role as banker, was seen as the key support for Britain's position as a world power.[13] The stability of the international financial and commercial system that was created under Anglo-American supervision at the end of the war was felt to be essential for the operation of the sterling system and, thus, for the maintenance of Britain's international role. This was so despite the fact that Keynes and others had been aware of the system's defects insofar as British interests were concerned. The continued successful operation of the international financial system both ensured a better world and guaranteed that Britain would be one of its leaders. These had been the two linked aims of British international economic policy since the early nineteenth century.

All of this—the consolidation of the welfare state at home, the recreation of a liberal world economic system with sterling at its center, and the restoration of Britain as a major world power—represented enormous commitments whose economic cost seems never to have been calculated. The 1950 budget, for example, which committed the nation to massive rearmament, led to the resignation of three members of the Cabinet. But the resignations focused on much more minor (although symbolically important) domestic issues, and the debate over these new defense and military commitments was minimal. Similarly, William Wallace observes that Eden's pledge in 1954 that Britain would maintain a sizable defense force on the continent for an unlimited period was given "almost without reference to the future cost to the balance of payments." The same was true, he states, in the negotiations which led to Germany's admission to NATO as well as to Britain's military commitments in the Far East.[14] Conservative governments in the 1950s continued to press for the restoration of full convertibility, but it does not seem that the burdens this would create for the domestic economy were carefully evaluated. It is impossible to disagree with Andrew Shonfield's remark in 1958 that:

---

[13] See J.B.D. Miller, *Survey of Commonwealth Affairs: Problems of Expansion and Attrition 1953–1965* (Oxford: Oxford University Press, 1974), Chapter 14.

[14] William Wallace, "Britain's Foreign Economic Policy," *International Affairs*, Vol. 50, No. 4 (April 1974): 260–61.

Looking back over the decade following the war, one of the strangest aspects of British politics now appears to be the mood of insouciance in which a whole series of political decisions was taken, regardless of their effect in adding to the existing overload of economic burdens on the country. The politicians and even more the officials responsible, just assumed grandly that "a way would be found" of paying for the decisions that were taken in the interest of the nation.[15]

It is not difficult, however, to comprehend British perceptions of their world role in the early postwar years. Britain had been one of the victors in the war and remained a member of the Big Three. Postwar recovery had been rapid. The errors of 1918 had been avoided. The welfare state had been put into place. Britain was a major military power and a world leader in technology. In 1945, the British were well aware of their weakness and the Labour government had struggled to reduce the nation's immediate foreign and military responsibilities. But, as Frankel states, it was assumed "that Britain's domestic arrangements, the international system, and Britain's role within it would all return to some approximation of prewar 'normalcy.' "[16]

The weight of tradition was extremely powerful. Britain had been a dominant international and imperial power since the early nineteenth century. Although its own resources were clearly insufficient to support this role after 1945, its position at the center of the "three circles" provided Britain with unique access to resources and a basis for international power and influence. The "three circles" were, of course, Churchill's description of the strategic bases of Britain's power in the postwar world, those overlapping circles of Britain's relations with the United States, with Western Europe, and with the Commonwealth.

It was by no means obvious during the first postwar years that Britain's international position had been fundamentally altered. Various factors served to disguise the situation. These included the image of British political and economic superiority over Japan and the nations of Western Europe, and the belief that the Commonwealth would provide Britain with a major source of strength. Finally, "The British political system militated against a public admission that Britain's status had been reduced, either by the government of the day or by the Opposition, although some of their members may have held and privately expressed much more skeptical views than those in public announcements."[17] No government would, or could, announce that it was presiding over the decline of Britain from a first- to a second-class power.

There were few differences, in any case, among party leaders, officials, or leaders of the major producer groups with regard to Britain's postwar international commitments. Frankel notes that:

---

[15] Andrew Shonfield, *British Economic Policy Since the War* (London: Penguin Books, 1958), p. 89.

[16] Joseph Frankel, *British Foreign Policy 1945–1973* (London: Oxford University Press, 1975), p. 91.

[17] Ibid., p. 155.

Both parties agreed that it was Britain's role to maintain peace, law and
stability in the world. . . . Not only did the leaderships and majorities of the
two main parties appraise Britain's major national interests in fundamentally similar terms, they also held similar views on maintaining her world role.
Whichever party had been in power, the general trends of her postwar policy
would probably not have been appreciably different. . . .[18]

Although some officials in the Foreign Office and Treasury were deeply concerned
at the end of the war about Britain's capacity to resume a leading world role, their
voices remained in a minority. There was little debate about Britain's international
role and the commitments this involved, either within government or Parliament or
outside of Westminster and Whitehall.

There is another dimension to these perceptions of Britain's role as a world
power. The British tended, in the early postwar years in particular, to envisage their
international role very much in terms of a range of responsibilities, the responsibilities of a world power. They were determined not to duck these responsibilities.
This was especially true in so vital an area both to the future of world peace and to
British interests as the reestablishment of a liberal world trading and financial
system. Younger observes that, while Britain's power to discharge its responsibilities
might have been limited, "She nonetheless rightly felt herself to be still the same
sort of power that she had been before, handicapped indeed by lack of resources,
but still cast for a world part, which no one else, for the time being, could play in
her stead."[19]

## II  Britain's domestic political structures and economic policy

There has been no shortage of explanations for Britain's economic problems
since the end of World War II. Businessmen complain about the poor quality of
British management. Historians link Britain's postwar economic performance to a
longer term pattern of relatively slow economic growth. Students of industrial
relations point to the organization of trade unions in Britain and to the archaic
character of industrial relations there. Sociologists discuss the continued saliency of
class divisions in British society and of the "us and them" outlook which pervades
class relations. Economists offer a wide range of causes including low levels of
investment, lack of adequate control over the monetary supply, and high propen-
sities to consume.

Political scientists on both sides of the Atlantic have recently advanced still
another explanation for Britain's economic difficulties, "pluralistic stagnation."

---

[18] Ibid., pp. 33–34.
[19] Kenneth Younger, *Changing Perspectives in British Foreign Policy* (London: Oxford University Press, 1964), p. 3.

The concept of pluralistic stagnation was used by Samuel Beer to suggest the dangers implicit in the "new group politics" in Britain. The "new group politics" describes the contemporary pattern of British politics in which interest groups have come to play a greater and greater role in the processes of government and policy making. Given the particular circumstances of British government and politics in this period, the role of interest groups has been seen to be largely functional for the political system. They have been particularly useful, as Beer observed, as a counterbalance to the growing and increasingly centralized nature of government.[20] But, in the Epilogue to the second edition of *British Politics in the Collectivist Age*, Beer writes that "It takes no very acute observer . . . to see that the danger may now not be oppressive efficiency, but *pluralistic stagnation.*" He observes that he is "thinking particularly of the reasons for Britain's economic problems" and concludes that "The responsibility of the new group politics for the failure of the economy is far from negligible."[21] The Epilogue was written in 1968, in the midst of severely worsening relations between the Wilson government and the trade unions, and the analysis was not developed in detail.

Others, however, have been more specific in their charges that interest groups, particularly trade unions and industrial associations, bear substantial responsibility for the state of the British economy. They suggest that, because of Britain's historical development and political culture, it is especially vulnerable to a form of *immobilisme* in which strong and broadly based interest groups are able to block government policies by exploiting its need for their "advice, acquiescence, and approval" and its limited ability to exercise effective control over them.[22] Gerald Dorfman's study of wage politics in Britain, for example, claims that British governments since World War II have been "dependent on their relationships with competing producer groups for the success of their economic policies." He illustrates how trade unions were able to undercut national economic policy by withholding their cooperation on wage restraint.[23] Jack Hayward's recent work on national aptitudes for planning in Britain, France, and Italy argues that the "initiative" in economic policy making in Britain "was surrendered to business organizations and trade unions who were elevated into corporatist veto groups,

[20] See Samuel Beer, *British Politics in the Collectivist Age*, revised edition (New York: Random House, 1969), Chapter 12. See Gabriel Almond, "A Comparative Study of Interest Groups and the Political Process," *American Political Science Review* Vol. 3, No. 1 (March 1958) for the basic functionalist view of interest groups in the "Anglo-American political systems."

[21] Beer, p. 408.

[22] See Samuel Finer, *Anonymous Empire*, revised edition (London: Pall Mall Press, 1966). This analysis, especially as it has been directed at the trade unions in recent years, is similar—although it emanates from a different point on the political spectrum—to that directed at "the political power of private capital" 30 years earlier. See, for example, Robert Brady, *Business as a System of Power* (New York: Columbia University Press, 1943). The best review of these arguments is Samuel Finer, "The Political Power of Private Capital," *Sociological Review* Vol. 3, No. 4 (December 1955) and Vol. 4, No. 2 (July 1956).

[23] Gerald Dorfman, *Wage Politics in Britain 1945–1967: Government vs. TUC* (Ames: Iowa State University Press, 1973), p. 75.

capable of frustrating public policy or at least modifying it so that it becomes acceptable."[24]

This analysis does not seem unreasonable. Private interests have long played an important part in British politics, and extensive interaction between interests and government has been encouraged by the structure of British political institutions and the values of British political culture. Students of British politics have frequently characterized the British political system as "quasi-corporatistic." [25] Thus, the new group politics is the development of traditional patterns of behavior in British politics in an era of new patterns of policy—the managed economy and the welfare state—and of vastly heightened social complexity and interdependence.

The extent of this network of interest group-government relations is remarkable. But the existence of the network in itself explains little about the *effectiveness* of groups in influencing the outcomes of public policy. Such networks may serve as readily as vehicles for government to exert influence on groups as for groups to influence governments. Alternatively, they may be irrelevant to outcomes altogether.[26] The *structure* of the new group politics in Britain provides little evidence in itself to support the view that some of the groups bear particular responsibility for certain policy outcomes.

In the early postwar period, however, there were few traces of the social strife or stagnation which seem to have become characteristic of British society. There existed, in fact, a remarkable consensus among the main producer groups and the political leadership of Britain on the major economic issues of the day.

Relations between British governments and organized business and industrial groups after World War II were characterized, to the end of the 1960s at any rate, by a high degree of effective collaboration. These relationships were by no means incongruent with wider patterns of social organization and behavior but were representative of a general pacification of social and class conflict in British society after 1945. The relationships rested on substantial areas of agreement on national goals and policies that linked the postwar British political elites, which now included, of course, trade union leaders.[27]

---

[24] Jack Hayward, "National Aptitudes for Planning in Britain, France and Italy," *Government and Opposition* Vol. 9, No. 4 (Autumn 1974): 401. See also Jack Hayward and Michael Watson, eds., *Planning, Politics and Public Policy: The British, French and Italian Experience* (Cambridge: Cambridge University Press, 1975).

[25] See, for example, Harry Eckstein's discussion of British political culture in Samuel Beer and Adam Ulam, eds., *Patterns of Government* (New York: Random House, 1962).

[26] See, for example, Enoch Powell's ironic and bitter article, "Capitalist Spokesmen and Socialist Government," *The Director*, February 1965. Theodore Marmor and David Thomas suggest that, at least in certain policy areas, the structure of negotiations between interest groups and governments has little to do with outcomes. See their "Doctors, Politics and Pay Disputes: 'Pressure Group Politics' Revisited," *British Journal of Political Science* Vol. 2, No. 4 (1972).

[27] On trade union-government relations from 1945 to the mid-1960s, see Irving Richter, *Political Purpose in Trade Unions* (London: George Allen & Unwin, 1973) and Dorfman. See also Colin Crouch, "Trade Unions and Politics in Britain," Discussion Paper for Working Group

A broad consensus on the structure of the postwar economic system, the objectives of economic policy, and the instruments of economic control had developed among leaders in the public and private sectors during the last years of the war. The policies of the 1945 Labour government scarcely constituted a revolution and were easily assimilated into this broad consensus. Debates over nationalization, for example, were largely symbolic. It was widely recognized that the means of production would remain almost entirely in private hands but that government would assume responsibility for a broad spectrum of economic and social goals, including social security, full employment, and rising standards of living. It would exercise this responsibility by "managing" the economy, but it would do this "indirectly," mainly by regulating the overall level of demand in the economy. Governments would not intervene directly in the affairs of individual firms or in collective bargaining.

This consensus predicated a very delicate balance between public and private power in the British economy. The Labour government's social reforms did not essentially alter this balance and, as the wartime economy was dismantled, the clear demarcation between the public and private sectors was reestablished. From 1947 until the very end of the 1950s, government policy makers as well as business and labor leaders sought to restore the traditional distance between government and the economy. They also tried to minimize government's role in the entire range of decisions affecting investment, the determination of wages and the conditions of work, and industrial relations. They attempted to limit the government's economic policy instruments to global mechanisms which would minimize administrative discretion. Government's economic policies, it was widely believed, should function globally, as simply and as automatically as possible. It was this dramatic reassertion of the liberal state after World War II that prompted Andrew Shonfield to remark in 1965 that "The striking thing about the British case is the extraordinary tenacity of older attitudes towards the role of the state."[28]

These liberal views were emphasized much more by the Conservatives, who would recall how they returned to power in 1951 under the banner of Free Enterprise, but they were widely shared among British leaders. Attlee's government never seriously attempted to institute a more interventionist style of economic management. The British Labour movement had not developed an economic strategy which focused on planning or on more selective forms of state interven-

---

12 (session III) of the VIII World Congress of Sociology, Toronto, August 1974, and Lewis Minkin, "The British Labour Party and the Trade Unions: Crisis and Compact," *Industrial and Labor Relations Review*, Vol. 28, No. 1 (October 1974). On industry-government relations, see Stephen Blank, *Government and Industry in Britain: The Federation of British Industries in Politics 1945–1965* (Farnborough: Saxon House, 1973), and Leonard Tirey and Ernest Wohlgemuth, "Trade Associations as Interest Groups," *Political Quarterly*, Vol. 29, No. 1 (January 1958). On "voluntarism" in government-industry relations after 1945, see Allan Flanders, "The Tradition of Voluntarism," *British Journal of Industrial Relations*, Vol. 8, No. 4 (November 1974): 358–61, and Sir Norman Kipping, *Summing Up* (London: Hutchison, 1972), Chapter 4.

[28] Andrew Shonfield, *Modern Capitalism* (Oxford, Oxford University Press, 1965), p. 88.

tion. The Left opposition within the Labour Party continued to call for further nationalization and the imposition of physical controls rather than economic planning. The trade unions sought, above all, to preserve maximum autonomy in the determination of wages and in all aspects of industrial relations.[29]

The movement away from sectoral wartime economic regulation was well underway by the time the Conservatives returned to power in 1951. It had been Harold Wilson who, as President of the Board of Trade, had lit the "bonfire of controls" in November 1948. The Conservatives, after 1951, tried to rely almost exclusively on global forms of economic regulation and emphasized, in particular, monetary policy as the master control of the level of economic activity. They were uninterested in developing sectoral policies in areas such as industrial structure and organization, investment, or industrial relations. Increasingly, they sought to make domestic economic management automatic as well, by utilizing the external strength of the pound as the principal regulator of the level of activity in the domestic economy.[30]

The consensus in Britain in the late 1940s and 1950s on the objectives and mechanisms of international economic policy was perhaps even more broadly based than that on domestic economic policy. The function of international economic policy was to restore and enhance Britain's role as a world power and, in particular, to contribute to the maintenance of the Commonwealth and sterling systems (as well as the "special relationship" with the United States), upon which Britain's international power rested so heavily. To be sure, there were differences in emphasis between the international economic policies of the first postwar Labour governments and the Conservative governments of the 1950s. In the years just after the war, the outstanding problems were still reconversion and shortages and the government was prepared to rely on physical controls to guide the economy. The emphasis at that time had been on the Commonwealth and overseas sterling area as a "defensive currency area," where, in particular, scarce dollars would be pooled and conserved. After 1951, the emphasis shifted to the achievement of convertibility and multilateral trade, to "the re-establishment of sterling as a general international currency and of London as an open financial market-place."[31]

But while emphases differed and evolved through time and changing conditions, basic commitments did not. What these came to involve was the creation of an interlocking network of policies which related to the preservation of Britain's role as a world power. Included were the restoration of sterling's international

[29] On the Labour government's economic management, see D.N. Chester, "Machinery of Government and Planning" and G.D.N. Worswick, "Direct Controls," in *The British Economy 1945–50*, G.D.N. Worswick and P.H. Ady, eds. (Oxford: Oxford University Press, 1952); Beer, pp. 189–200; on the role of the trade unions under the Labour government, see Beer, pp. 200–12. See also Shonfield, *Modern Capitalism*, Chapter 6.

[30] See Shonfield, *British Economic Policy Since the War*, Chapter 8; also C. Kennedy, "Monetary Policy," in *British Economic Policy in the Nineteen Fifties*, G.D.N. Worswick and P.H. Ady, eds. (Oxford: Oxford University Press, 1962).

[31] Susan Strange, *Sterling and British Policy* (London: Oxford University Press, 1971), p. 64. See also Miller, pp. 271–72.

transaction and reserve functions, fixed exchange rates, overseas investment directed particularly toward the sterling area, government spending and lending in the Commonwealth and sterling area, and the maintenance of a British military and defense presence in these areas.

There was little debate, and little discussion, in Britain about these international economic policies. International (and domestic) economic policies emerged in large measure as a response to perceptions about Britain's position, interests, and responsibilities as a great power in the international arena. But postwar economic policies were also shaped by the nature of the policy-making process, by commitments to particular techniques of economic management and by the nature, as well as the objectives, of national economic policy.

There are few case studies of policy making within the British government, and little material is available to illuminate the decision-making process. At best, a few general notions can be provided. Within the British government, the Treasury has had primary responsibility for the implementation of both domestic and international economic policy. The Foreign Office has not had the economic expertise, even if it had the will (which is doubtful), to contest this role. The Board of Trade played a far less central role in international economic policy, limited largely to the area of overseas commercial and trade policy. Twice in the postwar years, efforts were made to create a rival center within the government which would have primary responsibility for domestic economic, as opposed to financial, policy. The first was the formation of the Ministry of Economic Affairs under Cripps in 1947; the second, the Department of Economic Affairs, with George Brown as Minister, in 1964. In both cases, the Treasury soon reasserted its traditional control over the entire scope of domestic economic and financial policy.[32] In neither case, however, was the Treasury's preponderant responsibility for international economic policy and, in particular, for the defense of sterling questioned.

The Treasury has had primary responsibility for the implementation of economic policy rather than for the determination of policy objectives. The very efficiency of the government machinery in Britain, and especially of the Treasury, frequently leads observers to misunderstand the role of the civil service in policy making in Britain. The Treasury, in particular, is superbly efficient at carrying out policy. Indeed, sometimes it is so efficient at running the machine and implementing policy that insufficient attention is paid to the basic policy decisions themselves. Hugh Heclo and Aaron Wildavsky have recently observed that the great weakness of the American political system lies in implementation, in executing policy which is so laboriously pieced together. The danger in the British system, they note, is just the opposite: "The government may agree all too quickly, before

---

[32] See William Wallace, *The Foreign Policy Process in Britain* (London: The Royal Institute of International Affairs, 1975), Chapter 6. See also Roger Opie, "The Making of Economic Policy," in *Crisis in the Civil Service*, Hugh Thomas, ed. (London: Anthony Blond, 1968), passim.

the major implications of the policy are understood or the affected interests realize what is about to happen to them, leaving all concerned agape and aghast as the machine implements the policy with its usual splendid impartiality, that is, with equal harm all round."[33]

Perhaps this takes the point a little too far. Obviously, in a government in which the number of political leaders and senior officials is so small, there is no absolutely clear distinction between the policy makers and the policy implementors. Yet, despite the small number of people involved at the peak of the policy process and the absence of absolute clarity between functions, the different roles are deeply internalized. Civil servants carry out policies made by their masters, although, like a fine horse or automobile, the master who is not strong or able enough will soon find that the machinery has run away with him.

There are, of course, important feedback links. Officials in government, especially in the Treasury, have been less concerned with ultimate objectives than with means and instrumentalities. But this very concern for means or instruments of implementation can influence the shape of policy objectives. Indeed, given a lack of strong policy guidance from the political leadership, it can determine policy objectives by default. Certainly, the strong commitments of Treasury officials with regard to the means and techniques for the management of the economy influenced the shape of Britain's domestic and international economic policies after World War II. There are a number of reasons why this was undoubtedly so. "High foreign policy" was relatively insulated from international economic policy and political leaders (particularly Prime Ministers) lacked interest in international economic issues. There was also very little discussion and argument in the government about the whole structure of British economic policies and about the implications of political decisions (especially foreign policy) on economic policy.[34]

For the Treasury, domestic and international economic priorities and policies are closely linked, and its highest priorities were clearly focused on protecting sterling's international position. Britain's international role and its international commitments and responsibilities were all symbolized in the pound sterling and the sterling system. The domestic economy was viewed largely in response to international developments, particularly international confidence in the pound. What this seems to indicate is an extraordinary primacy of political over economic considerations within the Treasury itself. Treasury thought was dominated by a variety of "political myths" about Britain's role in the world, sterling, and so on, which, in fact, operated against Britain's economic interests. The Treasury's approach, far from being ruled by narrow economic considerations, too often evaded such economic realities as Britain's capacity to pay the costs of its international role.

The Treasury had readily assimilated a Keynesian approach to economic management during the war. Keynesian techniques, *as interpreted by officials,*

[33] Hugh Heclo and Aaron Wildavsky, *The Private Government of Public Money* (Berkeley and Los Angeles: University of California Press, 1974), p. 12.
[34] Wallace, "Britain's Foreign Economic Policy," p. 251.

provided government with the capacity to overcome the economic problems of the 1930s—unemployment, overproduction, the downside of the economic cycle—and yet to preserve the basic structure of the liberal economy. By regulating a single macroeconomic lever, the overall level of demand in the economy, these problems could be remedied without seriously disrupting the balance between public and private power in the economy. As late as 1959, Sir Robert Hall (who served as the government's economic advisor from 1947 to 1961) observed that in the British government "there is still a tendency to speak in magical rather than scientific terms of the use of interest rates and monetary controls generally."[35]

The overriding goal of the Treasury after World War II was to reestablish an international economic order. This system was to rest on fixed exchange rates and the free movement of currencies. Sterling, supported by its privileged position in the Commonwealth and overseas sterling area, would serve as the primary international reserve and transaction currency. A further goal of many officials lay in linking Britain's domestic economic management to the international economy. The level of domestic economic activity would be regulated as automatically as possible by the international economy. When the pound was strong in the world economy, domestic economic activity would be stimulated; when the pound weakened, the level of domestic activity would be cut back. A system quite this automatic was never established, although it was seriously discussed in the early 1950s. This discussion was characterized by Angus Maddison as "another case of wishful hankering after the will-of-the-wisp of automatic devices, which springs from a desire to abandon the heavy responsibility of formulating policy."[36] Britain's domestic economic policy options were severely limited by several internationally oriented commitments. The first of these was the basic policy commitment to maintain the external strength of sterling as an essential support for Britain's international position. The second was the determination to support sterling internationally by deflating the domestic economy when the pound came under external pressure. Finally, there was the Treasury's deep commitment to more global and automatic techniques of economic management.

To what extent, one can ask, did these policies represent the influence of other groups or interests? Do they indicate, for example, the ability of the Bank of England or the City of London to influence the economic policy-making process? Clearly, the interests of the British financial community were far more closely identified with postwar economic policies than the interests either of British industry or labor. The British financial community tended to be far more interested and involved in external relationships and dealings than with domestic industries, and thus strongly supported all efforts to defend sterling. The Bank of England, of course, has very strong interests in protecting the pound; this has been its primary

---

[35] Sir Robert Hall, *Economic Journal* (December 1959): 648, quoted in Angus Maddison, *Economic Growth in the West* (New York: W.W. Norton Co., 1964), p. 124. See also Opie, pp. 65–67.

[36] Maddison, p. 188.

responsibility and preoccupation. Certainly, the entire financial community favored the Treasury's global, automatic approach to economic policy.

It is difficult, however, to evaluate the actual power of the Bank or the City in economic policy making. Fred Hirsch speaks of the "legendary influence" of the Bank, and Harold Wilson himself describes how the Governor of the Bank of England attempted to force the Prime Minister's back to the wall in November and December of 1964.[37] But it is difficult to accept a view which suggests that the City or even the Bank was able to force its views upon the Treasury or government. Until the very end of the 1950s, there were few differences of opinion on economic policy, domestic or international, and its implementation among major groups in Britain. There were certainly few disagreements on these matters among top political leaders, officials, key industrial figures, and members of the financial community. Later, in 1964 and 1966 (as shall be seen below), what seems most clear is not the capacity of the Governor of the Bank to force the Prime Minister to defend sterling, or even the Prime Minister's fear of the reaction of the City to devaluation, but rather his own deep commitment that sterling should not be devalued.

Too little is known about the role of the Bank or the City in British government. But if the notion of "influence" is used to suggest that governments did something that they would not have otherwise done, or that government policies were somehow subverted or changed from their original intent, it is hard to see that the term is relevant in this context. In a wider sense, the influence of the Bank or the City on governments is very much dependent upon the willingness of the leaders of the government to be influenced. The intrinsic political power of the Bank or the City is extremely limited, and the British government possesses all necessary powers to take steps to diminish or even to eliminate entirely their influence. This is not to say, of course, that governments have not listened to the voice of the financial community or that Chancellors and even Prime Ministers have not feared the wrath of the Governor of the Bank of England. But the explanation here seems, in most cases, to rest upon the particular conception of the objectives and instruments of economic policy held by the political leaders, rather than the power or influence of the financial community.

## III  Political consequence number 1: the defense of the pound

Britain's present economic crisis has its roots in the policy choices made in the early postwar years. A pattern of economic policy was established in the late 1940s and set firmly in the following decade. The rigidities of this pattern were

---

[37] Fred Hirsch, *Money International,* revised edition (London: Penguin, 1969), p. 324. Harold Wilson, *The Labour Government 1964–70: A Personal Record* (London: Penguin, 1970), Chapter 3.

largely self-imposed, but it was strongly linked to many of the nation's most fundamental objectives and self-images and, thus, almost impossible to break down. Symbolically, the keystone of Britain's postwar economic policy was the defense of sterling. This symbol represented the determination of successive governments to maintain a certain role for Britain in the postwar world. Although the image of Britain's international role took a fearful pounding from 1947 onwards, it was twenty years before British governments could accept some of the most basic implications of the country's new international power and status. By then, however, the damage that had been done during the previous twenty years was difficult, almost impossible, to repair, and the neglect of the domestic economy in this period had contributed to new strains and tensions in British society.

In 1955, a new round of economic and financial crises, similar to those of the early postwar years, broke out. From then until the end of the 1960s, Britain was caught in a continuing and worsening round of economic crises which combined growing external weakness with internal stagnation, broken only briefly by periods of more or less controlled expansion.

During this period, relations between government and business and labor became more difficult. There were serious clashes between governments of both parties and the unions and industrial organizations. There was a substantial increase in official and unofficial strikes and increasing concern about the inflationary pressures of rising prices and incomes. The instruments and institutions of economic management were subject to increasing criticism and experimentation. The end of the 1950s was the beginning of the era of greatest institutional instability in British government in modern history. The postwar consensus on the shape of the economy and the goals of economic policy was increasingly questioned.

The growing problems of the economy were blamed inevitably on domestic failings: Britain's outdated industrial structure, backward managers, poor work practices, low investment, high consumption, domestic inflation, falling exports, and, increasingly, the self-interested behavior of organized labor and industrial groups. The growing tension between producer interests and government, and government's apparent vulnerability to pressure from these interests, were viewed increasingly as a primary cause of Britain's unsatisfactory economic performance. It is suggested here, however, that Britain's economic problems were not caused primarily by domestic failings. The breakdown of the consensus on economic policy and the worsening relations between producer groups and government, such as it was, was much less the *cause* than the *effect* of the deteriorating economic situation.

The "failure" of the British economy was due primarily to efforts of successive British governments to maintain an international role which was beyond the nation's capacity. Again and again, British citizens were told by their government that they were living beyond their means and that they would have to accept cutbacks in services, higher taxes, and slower economic growth if the nation were to remain solvent and maintain its international competitiveness. But it was not in its domestic economic life that the country was living beyond its means. It was living beyond its means in trying to support an international life style to which it could no longer be accustomed.[38]

The implications of Britain's international commitments for the domestic economy were largely hidden for a decade after 1949. But the basic patterns of policy which were to affect the domestic economy so seriously and adversely at the end of the 1950s were established much earlier. British economic policies, domestic and international, were dominated from the end of the war by international considerations. Britain emerged in 1945, Susan Strange writes, with "its investing reflexes, as it were, relatively undamaged by war experience."[39] In addition, overseas investment helped keep the members of the Commonwealth, to whom most investment was directed, in line as a cohesive force which supported Britain's international position. Finally, the use of sterling as a primary international currency itself encouraged the British to see the world in terms of investment opportunities. This outflow of capital from Britain to the sterling area was encouraged by the United States, at least after 1947, and it was largely masked by the inflow of Marshall Fund aid to Britain.

Britain's foreign and defense policies show the influence of similar commitments and images. Although the British had been forced to abandon commitments in the Eastern Mediterranean and elsewhere soon after the war, they embarked upon an enormous rearmament program in 1951. This was a program which appears to have been well beyond the capacity of the country. If Britain's international military power seemed to decline drastically, the level of its defense spending remained much higher than any other middle-ranking state, and its strategic perspectives and objectives still remained those of a major power.

Finally, from the earliest postwar years, British governments adopted the policy of restraining domestic investment in order to strengthen the balance of payments, in the hope that capital goods would be exported rather than used by British industry. More generally, reducing the level of domestic demand, it was felt, would lower the flow of imports and ease the pressure of labor shortages on domestic industries. Whenever governments were faced with an adverse balance of payments, and thus with increasing pressure on reserves, they attempted to remedy the situation by cutting back domestic investment. "Like a blind man with a single automatic gesture at his command," Andrew Shonfield wrote, the government "has reached out . . . and taken a smack at investment."[40]

After 1955, the domination of economic policy by international considerations increased still further. In his study of British economic policy since 1945, which was completed early in 1958, Shonfield stated: "There is no doubt that the Government has allowed its domestic policy since 1955 to be determined largely by

---

[38] The analysis in the next pages draws heavily on Strange, Chapters 2, 3, and 9. See also A.R. Conan, *The Problem of Sterling* (London: Macmillan, 1966). Shonfield's *British Economic Policy Since the War* is an earlier but enormously valuable examination of these issues.

[39] Strange, p. 135.

[40] Shonfield, *British Economic Policy Since the War,* p. 49; Pollard, pp. 442–43.

the movement of international confidence in the pound sterling. It is the thesis of this book that such a situation is both tragic and absurd, and that a means of escape from it must be devised."[41] But Shonfield remained a voice in the wilderness.

The balance-of-payments crisis in the Summer of 1955 came as a violent shock to those in government who assumed that monetary policy alone provided the master key in the management of the economy. The government responded to the crisis by restricting credit, bank advances, and hire purchase. The immediate crisis passed. But Britain's economic position remained basically unstable, especially in the wake of the Suez crisis. In the Summer of 1957, the pound came under the heaviest attack yet, and the government's response was the most severe deflationary package that had been applied to the postwar economy.

These events have been described elsewhere and the story need not be told again. For these purposes, only a few matters should be underlined. In first place is the role of producer groups in undermining the government's efforts to slow down rising prices and wages. Second is the content of government policy and the balance within it between domestic and international considerations.

Faced with renewed balance-of-payments difficulties in 1955, the government ruled out the use of direct controls as well as any alteration in the exchange rate. Instead, it attempted to battle inflation on two separate fronts. It continued to intensify restrictions on demand while, at the same time, it called for voluntary restraint in prices and wages. Two attempts were made, in the Fall of 1955 and Spring of 1956, to construct a general restraint bargain similar to that which Cripps had worked out in 1948. Neither attempt was successful, and the government's relations worsened not only with the trade unions but with the industrial organizations as well.

The model of the 1948 restraint bargain was no longer relevant in the mid-1950s. The sense of national unity that had provided the essential foundation for Cripps' efforts no longer existed. Given the government's priorities since 1951, those of freeing the economy and permitting market forces to operate unfettered, its exhortations for voluntary restraint made little sense. Besides, the British people had just begun, in the past two or three years, to feel in their own lives the effects of postwar economic recovery and growth. Finally, the network of consultative ties which had linked the two sides of industry and government since the late 1930s had been permitted to deteriorate, and easy communication was no longer possible.

Both the Federation of British Industries (FBI) and the Trades Union Congress (TUC) opposed a voluntary restraint of wages and dividends. While they disagreed on their diagnosis of the economic situation, both agreed that the government, and not the private sector, should be held accountable for Britain's economic difficulties. Both resented efforts by the government to shift the blame to them.[42] The FBI and the TUC did attempt, during this period, to bargain their

---

[41] Shonfield, *British Economic Policy Since the War*, p. 218. See also J.C.R. Dow, *The Management of the British Economy 1945–60* (Cambridge: Cambridge University Press, 1974), p. 91.

[42] Blank, pp. 133–34.

support of some sort of restraint for a change in government policies. Though the industrial organizations appeared to be more successful in winning a commitment from the government to hold down prices in the public sector, it is hard to see that these efforts were taken very seriously.

The Conservative government, faced with serious external financial problems, was unable to put into effect policies to strengthen the domestic economy (by stabilizing prices and wages) because of the opposition of the great producer organizations, led by the FBI and TUC. Isn't this, then, an example of "pluralistic stagnation"? It can be strongly argued that it isn't. First, although Mr. Butler and Mr. Macmillan said that they opposed efforts to defend sterling by restraining domestic demand (and indeed no doubt meant what they said), the impact of government policy during this period was to attack the major sources of economic growth in the domestic economy. The net effect of Butler's budget in the Fall of 1955 and Macmillan's "little budget" early in 1956 was substantially deflationary—far more, it appears, than was recognized at the time. The budgets attacked domestic investment, raised taxes on a wide range of household goods, and cut subsidies on such items as bread and milk. It was thus ensured that industry and the trade unions would each be antagonized.[43]

Second, although the government (at least Butler and Macmillan) also talked about a restraint bargain, it was unwilling to take an active role in the area of prices and incomes. The government sought merely to act as a broker, to arrange a bargain between the FBI and the TUC. This was the only role it could adopt that was consistent both with its general view of public-private sector relations and with its deep inhibitions about involving itself directly in collective bargaining and the determination of prices, wages, and the conditions of work.[44]

This is not a situation in which government policy was effectively blocked by the actions of private groups. Rather, the government itself was unwilling to accept responsibility for dealing with the ongoing problem of the upward pressure of prices and incomes in the new conditions of the postwar economy. It tried instead to persuade the central industrial and union organizations to accept responsibility for temporarily stabilizing prices and incomes. The government failed, not at making a policy or at making a policy stick, but at persuading other groups to make that policy. Given the economic conditions of the mid-1950s, what Butler and Macmillan proposed had dubious economic utility and would have very likely served mainly to undermine FBI and TUC leaders in their own organizations.

The government, during these years, persisted in using external confidence in sterling as the primary regulator for the domestic economy; as J.C.R. Dow observes, "the successive hoistings and lowerings of Bank rate were dictated almost entirely by external considerations."[45] At the same time, it remained convinced

---

[43] Samuel Brittan, *The Treasury Under the Tories* (London: Penguin, 1964), pp. 182–83; Dow, pp. 90–91.

[44] See (Lady) Barbara Wootton, *The Social Foundation of Wage Policy* (London: Unwin University Books, 1955), Chapter 4.

[45] Dow, p. 91.

that the source of the pound's continuing weakness lay in the domestic economy. Thus, the government was driven to take more and more drastic deflationary measures, further restricting the domestic economy and restraining the forces which would produce economic growth. The severe deflationary package of September 1957 is the clearest example of this situation. After Suez, in the Spring of 1957, a long anticipated strike in the engineering and shipbuilding industries had finally broken out and Britain was faced with its greatest labor stoppage since 1926. The strike was quickly, and surprisingly, settled as a result of apparent government pressure.[46] When a new sterling crisis erupted in the Summer of 1957, the government acted as if it were the direct result of the wage settlements of the previous Spring.

The government's response to the sterling crisis in the Summer of 1957 seemed to indicate that it was determined to eradicate the sources of inflation within the economy at all costs. Professor Beer, for example, speaks of the "shift of priorities . . . toward the deflationary alternative."[47] The Chancellor emphasized his determination to subject the domestic economy to the harsh discipline of external realities. In a speech in the midst of the crisis, he stated, "If inflationary pressures grow inside the economy, other things may alter, other aspects of policy may have to be adjusted, but the strain will not be placed on the value of the pound sterling."[48]

Yet, Britain's domestic economic situation in the Summer of 1957 was not unsatisfactory, and the sterling crisis seems to have been entirely one of confidence which had grown out of unfavorable capital movements and speculation against the pound. G.D.N. Worswick writes that, "Inasmuch as the Government believed the crisis of 1957 was *caused* by wage increases in the Spring of that year they were probably wrong, and to the extent that they acted on this belief the domestic measures taken in September were certainly wrong."[49] The roots of the 1957 sterling crisis are complex, but Worswick concludes that "The 1957 crisis was the first sign of the major difficulties created by the freeing of capital movements in the framework of a world with inadequate international liquidity."[50]

By the end of the 1950s, Britain's weakened international economic position was becoming apparent. Although the balance-of-payments position during the previous decade had seemed to be fairly satisfactory, reserves remained small and, as evidenced in 1957, especially vulnerable to short-term pressure on sterling. Large capital outflows, including outgoing overseas investment, but particularly government spending and lending abroad, were masked by continuing inflows of US aid.

---

[46] See H.A. Clegg and R. Adams, *The Employers' Challenge: A Study of the National Shipbuilding and Engineering Disputes of 1957* (Oxford: Basil Blackwell, 1957), especially Chapter 7.
[47] Beer, p. 367.
[48] Peter Thorneycroft, speech September 24, 1957, quoted in Brittan, p. 187.
[49] G.D.N. Worswick, "The British Economy 1950–1959," in Worswick and Ady, *The British Economy in the Nineteen Fifties,* pp. 49–50.
[50] Worswick, "The British Economy 1950–1959," p. 51.

Once sterling became convertible in 1958, however, pressures increased substantially and the balance-of-payments position worsened sharply. Susan Strange has described four related developments which were responsible for this deterioration:

> First, there was the outflow of British capital especially to the sterling area, which reflected a pronounced predisposition in the British economy towards overseas investment. This predisposition began to exert its maximum demands for foreign exchange just at the time when the political dissolution of empire began to work to a climax. This was the second development: it swelled the foreign exchange costs of British government spending on defense and Commonwealth aid. Thirdly, this dissolution produced a change in Britain's monetary relations, giving former British colonies a new freedom to break out of the strict reserve requirements and free-transfer rules of the old imperial sterling system. Inevitably, this gave rise to widespread concern about the inadequacy of British reserves compared with the 'overhang' of the OSA sterling balances. Fourthly and lastly, there was the coincidence that the reopening of London as a financial marketplace opened wide doors to volatile short-term capital movements—movements which became all the more volatile whenever this overhang was threatened with the slightest hint of a deficit in current payments.[51]

As the position of sterling weakened, financial crises were touched off by British balance-of-payments deficits on current account. In each case, although the crisis consisted essentially of speculation against the pound and of short-term monetary movements, government response was to defend the sterling exchange rate by further deflating the domestic economy.[52] The economy was "cooled off" (whether or not it was actually "overheated") by restricting spending through increases in taxes, a squeeze on credit and controls on hire purchase, and by cutting back investment through increases in rates of interest and altered tax benefits. These restrictive measures were frequently combined with reductions or delays in public investment as well.

Government's aim in deflating the economy was to restore "confidence" in sterling by reducing demand in the economy, and thereby decreasing imports and improving the trade balance, and by raising interest rates to attract short-term capital back into London. In addition, it was hoped (although increasingly disputed) that these measures would "squeeze out" of the economy additional exports and excess employment.

Major deflationary packages were imposed in 1957, 1961, and 1966, but from 1965 onwards, for the duration of the Labour government, the economy was in a state of almost continuous retrenchment. Economists differ on the exact nature and extent of the impact of these deflationary measures on the domestic economy, but their effect, direct and indirect, is undeniable. The most obvious effect, of course, was on Britain's rate of economic growth. Edward Denison has

[51] Strange, pp. 129–30.
[52] Manser, pp. 85–86, and Strange, pp. 300–01.

suggested that three main factors have contributed to faster growth rates in France and Germany than in Britain. The most important of these, the existence of a large pool of labor from agriculture and self-employment, was not available to the British who had long ago integrated the great bulk of agricultural workers into the industrial labor force. Of the other factors, over which Britain had some control, France grew more rapidly because of its higher "residual efficiency," that is, the application of technological and managerial knowledge to production. Germany grew faster because of a higher rate of capital investment.[53]

Restrictive economic policies severely affected both of these factors in Britain. Investment was cut or held back by direct government action and indirectly influenced by high interest rates, credit restrictions, and cuts in investment allowances.[54] The continuous round of stop-go cycles deeply depressed business expectations, limited efforts to expand output and to raise productivity, and made existing investment less productive than it should have been. Here, the contrast with France could not be clearer. In France, one of the primary goals of postwar economic policy had been to raise the expectations of businessmen, "to dispel the gloomy fatalism that had marked French business thinking since the depression. . ."[55] The French were remarkably successful in this effort and it seems that France's ability to achieve dramatic increases in productivity of capital and labor were closely related to this. The impact of government economic policy on British business expectations was, however, quite the reverse. After 1961 and 1965, few businessmen in Britain were willing to take a chance again on national economic growth. Continued domestic deflation aggravated the structural problems of the British economy. Investment remained low. Frequent deflation and continual uncertainty reinforced traditional tendencies toward restrictive practices. Finally, the low level of economic activity inhibited opportunities for more aggressive managerial practices. The resulting low rate of economic growth was insufficient to support improvements in the welfare state and in standards of living demanded by the British population.

## IV  Political consequence number 2: the failure to devise new policy instruments

The deflationary measures taken in September 1957 seemed to signal a major shift in British economic policy; in fact, the signals were uncertain and the continuity of the government's economic policies remained unbroken. The government continued to run a frantic catch-up race. It applied pressure on the brake,

---

[53] Edward Denison, "Economic Growth," in *Britain's Economic Prospects,* cited (fn. 10), pp. 263–78.
[54] Pollard, pp. 442–43.
[55] J.H. McArthur and B. Scott, *Industrial Planning in France* (Cambridge: Graduate School of Business Administration, Harvard University, 1969), p. 483.

then the accelerator, and then the brake once again, trying to adjust the level of the domestic economy to the rises and falls in international confidence in the pound. In 1958, Britain suffered through the worst recession since the war. Industrial production had stagnated since 1955, and excess capacity and unemployment had increased sharply. It began to be suggested, even within industry, that the government's deflationary policies were the primary cause of increasing costs and prices. They achieved this by checking the efficiency of supply, reducing the utilization of capital equipment, and encouraging restrictive practices. The government stepped on the accelerator in 1959 (when Mr. Macmillan campaigned in the general election on the platform "you've never had it so good"). But the brakes were applied again early in 1960.

During this period, between 1958 and 1960, there was a fundamental reassessment of industrial attitudes in Britain. (This was, of course, just one dimension of a wider movement of self-evaluation which produced Koestler's volume, *Suicide of a Nation?*, a flood of red-covered Penguin "What's Wrong with . . ." books, *Beyond the Fringe,* and *Private Eye.*)[56] Industrialists, the TUC, academics, and the media, even high-ranking civil servants, all pointed to "stop-go" economic policies as the major cause of the stagnation which seemed to grip the British economy. The attention of these groups and individuals was captured, at the same time, by the impressive economic growth rates of the members of the newly formed European Economic Community. In comparison with them, and especially with France, Britain's performance seemed all the worse.

By the end of 1960, many were convinced that government priorities had to be altered. Sterling could be protected only by increasing the rate of domestic growth. Growth had to come first, not sterling. It is widely agreed that industry took a leading role in this reappraisal, and these new priorities emerged most clearly in public at a conference sponsored by the Federation of British Industries in November 1960. Heathcoate Amory, the Chancellor of the Exchequer, put forward the traditional priorities in his opening address to the meeting. First, sterling must be kept strong and respected. Second, it was important to have reasonable price stability. Third, it was necessary to expand production. Growth, he observed, was placed last because it was contingent on the others. But the leaders of the Federation went out of their way to disagree with the Chancellor. The other aims of policy, they said, could be achieved only if there were a more rapid rate of economic growth. More rapid growth would make the other objectives attainable, not vice versa.[57]

It is important to underline that the industrialists still kept their attention focused on the domestic economy. Although they were prepared to reverse official priorities with regard to the domestic economy, they did not appear to see that the

---

[56] See D.E. Butler and Anthony King, *The British General Election of 1964* (London: Macmillan and Co., 1965), Chapter 2.

[57] FBI, *The Next Five Years: Report of an F.B.I. Conference at Brighton on 24–26 November 1960* (London, January 1961), pp. 6–7. See *The Financial Times* (London), 28 November 1960.

new priorities they put forward might well be contingent upon new international economic priorities and policies. The industrialists at the Brighton Conference did not disagree with the government's international commitments. They argued that these commitments could be better met by concentrating more directly on domestic economic growth. But at what point would the domestic and international priorities come into conflict? How far could government press for more rapid domestic growth before it ran into the constraints imposed by its external commitments?

In the Summer of 1961, in a series of events which has been described in detail elsewhere, an experiment in economic planning was launched in Britain. [58] The aim of the experiment, first as defined by the Conservatives and then, after 1964, as elaborated by Mr. Wilson's Labour government, was to create an alternative to stop-go economic policies which would emphasize economic growth. A more rapid rate of domestic economic growth would provide the cure for Britain's ailments, just as it had cured those of France.

The experiment, however, cured little. It is widely evaluated as a total and resounding flop. The planning experience has been well criticized, but not all of the criticisms are relevant to this essay. Those of interest here deal with the nature of the planning mechanism established in the early 1960s and, in particular, with the attitudes toward public-private sector relations the mechanism embodied. Hagen and White, for example, argue that, because of its attitudes toward private associations:

> It was almost inevitable that when the British government approached employers' and trade union associations with proposals for the establishment of economic planning machinery, it would do so, not as a representative of the public interest seeking the recommendations of groups with special interests before it exercised its authority, but as one association approaching two other associations to ask them what they would be willing to do. [59]

Shonfield, in the discussion surrounding the formation of the National Economic Development Council (or "Neddy") in *Modern Capitalism,* says that the government claimed no special status. "It behaved as if it were an interest group arguing its case with equal partners who were expected to have other interests." [60] Dorfman concludes simply that Neddy was "the institutionalized re-creation of pluralistic stagnation." [61]

---

[58] For a broad overview of the planning experiment, see Hayward and Watson; John and Anne-Marie Hackett, *The British Economy: Problems and Prospects* (London: Unwin University Books, 1967), Chapter 5 and 6; and Samuel Brittan, "Inquest on Planning in Britain," *Planning* Vol. 33, No. 499 (January 1967).

[59] Everett E. Hagen and Stephanie F.T. White, *Great Britain: Quiet Revolution in Planning* (Syracuse: Syracuse University Press, 1966), p. 124.

[60] Shonfield, *Modern Capitalism,* pp. 151–52.

[61] Dorfman, p. 98.

These views are difficult to accept. The formation of Neddy was a government initiative, or, at least, an initiative by the Chancellor, Selwyn Lloyd, backed by the Prime Minister, Harold Macmillan. Neddy was very much Lloyd's creation. He had a particular conception of the organization and he enlisted the support of the FBI and TUC to help him press his view among his colleagues in the Cabinet, many of whom opposed the idea. He was willing to discuss the structure of the new organization with these groups and, at times, even to accept their recommendations. But the main issue was not tripartite organization. The real issue was Neddy's role in the making of economic policy. Lloyd, the FBI, and the TUC all wanted Neddy to have an authoritative voice in the policy-making process and to serve as a counterweight to the Treasury. The Treasury and other members of the Cabinet preferred it to be outside of the policy-making process, more like a traditional independent advisory body. The critical issue was, thus, Neddy's access to the making of economic policy decisions and whether it would speak with authority or only in an advisory capacity. Lloyd, Macmillan, the FBI, and the TUC all agreed that it should have clout, in opposition to other members of the government.

To be sure, Neddy was conscientiously tripartite. It took as one of its first and most vital tasks to win the confidence of industry and the trade unions. Given the instruments of economic management available at this time as well as the values of British political culture about the role of government, it is difficult to see how Neddy could have done otherwise. This is the point at which I would disagree with Shonfield. Voluntary action remained the most effective vehicle for creating and putting into effect an economic plan. There were many critical differences between the French Commissariat du Plan and Neddy. Most important was the wider political and economic policy environment in which the two organizations existed. The French had both a well-stocked armory of instruments for direct and specific intervention in the economy and industry and a lengthy tradition of such intervention. Second, the responsibility of the first French plan was limited to six "basic sectors" of the economy, much of which was already in the public sector. Neddy was to have responsibility for improving the performance of the entire economy. The Commissariat had the ability to influence the allocation of investment funds and, thus, had some ability to realize its own projections, while Neddy had no such resources. Finally, the French were able, in the early years of the plan, largely to ignore the trade unions.

Yet, despite all of these differences, one cannot fail to be impressed with the extent to which Monnet and the Commissariat pursued the goal of winning industry's confidence and of developing close cooperative and voluntary ties with industrialists throughout the economy. At the same time, like Neddy, Monnet and the French planners sought to avoid too close an association with the French government. Like Neddy, they sought to be *in* the government and yet *outside* of it. Thus, the resemblance between Neddy and the Commissariat du Plan at the equivalent stage of its development, particularly in terms of their broad political strategies to win widespread support in industry and in the economy at large, is very clear.

Neddy faced many problems. Despite Lloyd's intentions, it remained cut off from the government and without access to information on the economy. Because of its uncertain status in government, it experienced difficulty recruiting and retaining staff. More important was the shift in the Cabinet's emphasis, in the Spring and Summer of 1962, toward taking immediate action on wages. Neddy's inability to serve as a vehicle for winning union agreement on wage restraint reduced the government's interest in it and led to the formation of another institution, the National Incomes Commission (NIC). Finally, in 1964, Neddy became entangled in pre-election politics, and discussions on most issues had to be adjourned in the months preceding the election.

But there is no evidence that the representatives of industry or the unions sought to weaken Neddy or to turn it to their own immediate advantage. Indeed, in the view of their constituents, the industrial and trade union leaders on the Neddy Council tended to move too quickly and to be too little concerned with protecting established interests. The government's view of Neddy remained divided. Some members of the Cabinet and officials sought to minimize its influence. Some, like Maudling, who replaced Lloyd at the Treasury, wanted to use it to achieve an immediate bargain on wages. But the members of Neddy continued to view it as a "pressure group for growth" within government and, although they disagreed on many specific issues, they remained united on this point.

Even in its limited lifetime, there was an impressive process of mutual education on the Neddy Council. The Neddy atmosphere contributed to a rapid movement of ideas which encouraged its members to exercise a remarkable degree of leadership within their organizations. The agreements worked out in Neddy were scarcely unimpressive. They included the initial commitment on the growth model, the first industrial inquiry, the formation of the Economic Development Committees (the "Little Neddies") and, finally, the beginning of serious consideration of a prices and incomes policy. Indeed, these discussions and the formation of NIC, as awkward as this was, marked the highly significant step by the government of assuming direct responsibility for the creation of a prices and incomes policy. These developments, of course, provided the critical foundations for the prices and incomes policy formulated by the Labour government after 1964. Neddy exerted a good deal of influence on the participating organizations, too, and stimulated efforts to strengthen the authority of the FBI and TUC over their members. It does not appear that in its first two years Neddy was unsuccessful, all things considered. By 1963–64, its impact was beginning to be felt widely and, with the Labour victory, some of the major defects in the organization of economic planning in Britain seemed to have been overcome.

The reasons for the ultimate collapse of the planning experiment are not to be found in the organization of Neddy or the planning machinery of the Labour government, although there were many defects. Nor do they lie in the commitment to voluntary participation, although industry and the unions were frequently reluctant to follow the leadership of the Neddy Council. They are likewise not found in the failure of government to take a more active and energizing role in the planning process, which, by and large, both Conservative and Labour governments did. The primary reasons for the failure of the enterprise are to be found in the government's macroeconomic policies. The obvious gap in both the Neddy plan and the National plan was the balance of payments. Both plans assumed that exports would somehow expand in the initial running-up period to a higher growth rate and that a favorable balance of payments would be maintained. It was clearly recognized, however, that moving up to a more rapid rate of growth was much more likely to result in increased pressure on the balance of payments as exports were diverted to home use and as additional imports were drawn into the economy.

The critical issue was what government would do in this situation. If it was not prepared to devalue or to take other extraordinary measures to maintain the balance of payments, the growth strategy was flawed at the start, no matter what kind of planning organization was devised. The events of 1964 and 1965 illustrated this fatal defect. By the Summer of 1965, it was clear that official priorities had not changed, at least insofar as sterling was concerned, and that the Wilson government was prepared once again to deflate the economy to save the exchange rate even if this meant giving up its growth commitments. Whether or not the planning experiment would have been successful—indeed, whether it would have been successful even if the balance-of-payments constraint had been eliminated (for this, while a necessary condition for success, was certainly not a sufficient condition)—is really not at issue. What is really at issue are the decisions made by Harold Wilson and his immediate colleagues and advisors in 1964, 1965, and 1966 which ensured the failure of the planning experiment.[62]

Why were these decisions made as they were? It is tempting to search for forces or pressures which influenced the deliberations in the Cabinet and the decisions made by the government. As suggested earlier in this essay, however, it is difficult to accept an analysis which suggests that outside interests or groups *forced* their views upon government in the economic policy-making process or were even able to exercise substantial influence within the process. The decisions of the Wilson government in 1964 and 1966 with regard to sterling appear to confirm this opinion.

Wilson has written of his dealings, for example, with the Governor of the Bank of England in the midst of the economic crisis which broke out in the Fall of 1964. He says that it was the duty of the Governor of the Bank "to represent to the Chancellor and the Prime Minister the things that were being said abroad or in the City; to indicate to the Government the issues on which, in the City's view, it was necessary to win confidence if a disastrous hemorrhage were to be avoided."[63] But

---

[62] Samuel Brittan, *Steering the Economy,* revised edition (London: Penguin, 1971), pp. 291–310; Fred Hirsch, *The Pound Sterling* (London: Gollancz, 1965); Wilfred Beckerman, "Objectives and Performance, an Overall View," in *The Labour Government's Economic Record 1964–1970,* W. Beckerman, ed. (London: Duckworth, 1972), pp. 48–52. This, of course, oversimplifies these events. The Labour government did attempt—at least while George Brown's influence was strongly felt—to protect the balance of payment through physical controls. But within a few months, this effort to find a third way between devaluation and deflation had collapsed, See Opie, pp. 61–63.

[63] Wilson, p. 61.

it is by no means the duty of the Prime Minister, the Chancellor, or the government to rely upon his opinion alone on these matters, nor to follow his advice once it is given. If, in 1964 for example, the influence of the Bank appears to be so potent, it was because of prior policy choices made by Wilson and his government. Because the Prime Minister had rejected alternative policies, such as devaluation, and had severely limited his government's economic policy opinions, the Bank played a major role in working out economic policy at that time. But if Wilson and his government had chosen differently, the role of the Bank would have been much less.

The point is that there was no effective opposition within the government or outside of it to maintaining the same network of international commitments that had bound earlier governments. This was particularly true of those commitments which were bound up in the defense of sterling. In the 1964 electoral campaign, Wilson had talked about the "white-hot" technological revolution which a Labour government would sponsor, and his modern scientific image had won many points over Sir Alec's matchstick economics. But, while Wilson was all for technology and growth, he was even more for the pound. His views should have been no surprise, however. Paul Foot charges that: "Planned expansion and growth took priority over all other aspects of Harold Wilson's socialism, except one: the parity of the pound sterling. Throughout the period (1954–1964), Wilson defended the strength of sterling with all the enthusiasm of his Tory adversaries."[64] No one doubts how the new Labour government's initial decision on sterling was made. Henry Brandon describes the first meeting of the new government:

> Wilson came to the meeting with his mind made up. He was against devaluation. . . . The decision was finally taken, and it was Wilson who took it with impressive firmness. He said that from now on everybody must shut up talking about this subject, and it became known as "The Unmentionable" thereafter.[65]

There are any number of explanations for Wilson's decision. Brandon suggests that Wilson feared the political consequences, that another devaluation "would stamp the Labour Party as the 'devaluation party'. . . ." Others suggest that the Prime Minister believed that devaluation would lead to an uncontrollable run on the pound and new economic disasters.[66] But for whatever reason his decision was taken, it was not taken against the wishes of the majority of the new government or of the leadership of the Labour Party. Few criticized Wilson for failing to devalue, at least at the time. Who supported devaluation in 1964? Probably several members of Wilson's government favored devaluation; certainly, some of his economic

---

[64] Paul Foot, *The Politics of Harold Wilson* (London: Penguin, 1968), p. 138.
[65] Henry Brandon, *In the Red; The Struggle for Sterling* (London: Andre Deutsch, 1966), p. 43.
[66] Brandon, p. 44; Marcia Williams (now Lady Falklander), *Inside Number 10* (New York: Coward, McCann & Geoghegan, Inc., 1972), p. 32.

advisors did. A small group of industrialists was prepared to tolerate devaluation as a means of maintaining a growth policy. But devaluation was not supported by any significant group in British politics in 1964, or even in 1966. Paul Foot writes that as late as March 1966, just before the General Election:

> The vast majority of MPs and rank and file Party members of the Left and Right believed that [Wilson's] stewardship during the seventeen months [of the first Labour Government] had been almost impeccable. Hardly a Member of Parliament had publicly argued for devaluation in that period. . . . The few advocates of devaluation were locked in the silence of Whitehall. Only later were they to emerge to proclaim that devaluation should have come immedi- ately after the election. . . .[67]

The government's views on the pound emerged even more vividly after the March 1966 election. Now, there were far fewer political inhibitions against devaluation. Indeed, in July 1966, a substantial segment of the Cabinet seemed to favor devaluation, at least briefly. At this moment, therefore, the personal commitments of Wilson and his Chancellor, James Callaghan, were most critical. The two top leaders of the government remained deeply opposed to the policy of devaluation. They were convinced that it was a "feather bed" approach to strengthening the economy.[68]

The initial decision not to devalue in 1964 (and again in 1966) had implica- tions which further limited the options of the Prime Minister. Beckerman notes that, "Having made this decision, it was necessary to minimize the threat to the pound by increasingly categorical assertions that the pound would never be deval- ued, and even on the charitable assumption that these assertions were intended primarily for overseas consumption they had the effect of making the leaders of the Party feel publicly committed never to devalue the pound."[69] Roger Opie suggests that the decision not to devalue greatly strengthened the hands of the officials in the Treasury. Once the government had eliminated its room for more drastic maneuvering, nothing else was left but to play out the same old tune, with the officials marking the beat.[70] But, once again, the appropriate scenario for this situation is not one in which governments are influenced by outside groups or see their policies undermined or overturned, but one in which government itself established priorities and then is bound by those priorities.

Rather than searching for the influence of one department, the City, or the Bank, it is more useful and accurate to think in terms of an "overseas" or "sterling" lobby within the government and administration. This lobby shared the belief that Britain's international position and responsibilities constituted the primary policy

[67] Foot, pp. 168–69.
[68] Foot, p. 192; see also Peter Jenkins, *The Guardian* (Manchester), 5 July 1971 on Mr. Callaghan's commitments.
[69] Beckerman, p. 61.
[70] Opie, pp. 61–63.

objectives and that the international role of sterling was vital to this position. They also agreed that Britain's international situation should provide the essential regulator for the domestic economy.

One outsider who served as an "irregular" in the Wilson government observes that:

> It is remarkable how few are the departments primarily concerned to put forward the interests of *this* country, rather than those of our allies and trading partners. . . . There are a great many departments which approach economic problems primarily from the point of view of international negotiations. The Foreign Office has special responsibility for EFTA; the C.R.O. and Colonial Office for the Commonwealth; the Board of Trade for our general relations with our trading partners and for organisations such as GATT; the Treasury is concerned with international financial negotiations and institutions; and the D.E.A. had in its heyday a strong section concerned with overseas relations. This is all very necessary, worthy and proper, but there is a danger that the interests of the British economy suffer by default.[71]

But, in these terms, the "overseas" or "sterling" lobby ceases to be an interest within the larger group. It *is* the larger group. If the sterling lobby or the Treasury dominated policy making, it was because there was no serious opposition to the policies they put forward, not because the Treasury, the City, or the Bank forced their views upon the policy makers.

The perceptions of Britain's international role, and the commitments and policies which led on from them, seemed clearly to represent the attitudes, beliefs, and values of the great majority of the political leadership in Britain after World War II. Given these commitments, the government had no other lever with which to respond to external pressures on sterling but to deflate the domestic economy. This accounts, of course, for the frequently perverse timing of the restrictive measures. Restrictive measures were a response, not to the condition of the domestic economy itself but to the external state of sterling, of external confidence in sterling. As such, these measures were frequently unrelated to domestic developments and often took effect after the economy had already peaked and the level of economic activity had begun to decline.[72]

Yet it is not only a question of there being no other available policy or instrument of economic control. British leaders were convinced that this was the *best* policy available, and that it was *right and necessary* for domestic economic

---

[71] Samuel Brittan, "The Irregulars," reprinted in *Policy-Making in Britain*, Richard Rose, ed. (London: Macmillan, 1969), p. 338; see also Opie, pp. 59–62.

[72] On the government's efforts at "fine tuning," see Dow, and the three (very different) versions of Samuel Brittan's *The Treasury Under the Tories*—1964, 1969, and 1971. See also the articles on fiscal and monetary policy by Richard and Peggy Musgrave and John Kareken in Caves and Associates, *Britain's Economic Prospects,* and by R.C.O. Matthews and G.D.N. Worswick in Cairncross, ed., *Britain's Economic Prospects Reconsidered.*

policy to function in this fashion. Fred Hirsch notes that it was taken for granted by government that:

> The freedom toward which it was driving [in removing all financial controls on sterling] was the natural order of things, to which other facets of the national economy must, equally naturally, adjust themselves. In this simple view, any payments difficulties suffered in these circumstances must be a result of some distortion in domestic economic management—above all, excessive wage increases or excessive public expenditure. . . .[73]

Sam Brittan writes that "the position of sterling as an international currency, with all the risks to which it exposed Britain, was regarded as desirable in itself, like a prisoner kissing the rod with which he is being beaten."[74]

What all of this shows quite clearly is the power of the British government—and of the Prime Minister and a few senior colleagues—to adhere to a policy even when, as in 1967, they were the last ones in the government to do so. The failure of international economic policy between 1964 and 1967, William Wallace writes, "was in the inability of official advisers and Cabinet critics to force the discussion of a major issue of policy at the highest level—because, at the highest level, the Prime Minister and the Chancellor were unwilling to consider it."[75] Sterling was still a symbol of Britain's "international virility," and devaluation until the last moment remained inconceivable.

## V  *Political consequence number 3: conflict with the unions*

Devaluation, when it finally took place in 1967, solved none of Britain's economic problems. It came too late. As Wilfrid Beckerman, who served as an Economic Adviser in the Wilson government, observes: "Failure to devalue earlier meant that both the deficit that had to be eliminated and the surplus that had to be aimed at in order to pay off accumulated debt were much greater than would otherwise have been the case."[76] Instead of freeing the economy from external constraints, the 1967 devaluation forced economic policy makers to squeeze the economy still further and to keep their attention focused even more rigidly on external confidence in the pound. This legacy of British economic policy choices made in the 1950s and early 1960s was to greatly narrow the range of options for policy makers thereafter. Policy choices were limited in other dimensions as well. A new generation of workers and trade union leaders was increasingly unwilling to accede to the government's demands for restraint in the face of rising unemployment and stagnating standards of living. Rising conflict with the unions thus

[73] Hirsch, *The Pound Sterling*, p. 46.
[74] Brittan, *Steering the Economy*, p. 138.
[75] Wallace, *The Foreign Policy Process in Britain*, p. 175.
[76] Beckerman, p. 63.

imposed still another constraint on government economic policy. Devaluation notwithstanding, there were some positive policy developments under the Labour government. But the possibility that these policy developments might lead to improvements in domestic economic performance was limited by the continuation of the external constraint and by increasing conflict with the trade unions.

By the mid-1960s, some significant changes in government policy were taking place. Wilson's government had not been prepared to give way on the exchange rate—the "Great Unmentionable"—in 1964 or even 1966. But other commitments, particularly in the international area, were altered. Overseas investment was brought under greater control and military commitments abroad were scaled down.[77] By the beginning of 1968, once devaluation had finally taken place, Britain's economic prospects seemed brighter. Samuel Brittan writes that "For the first time since it came to office the government had a rational strategy which at least had a chance of working. ... The illusions about Britain's financial and military role in the world—of which Mr. Wilson had originally been the foremost exponent, and which had held the country back for so long—were at long last jettisoned."[78]

The achievements of the Labour government went well beyond this. It had accepted a wide range of responsibilities to encourage more efficient industrial structure and to improve labor training and mobility. It approached its economic and industrial goals increasingly on an industry-by-industry basis, overturning traditional attitudes on globalism and government "neutrality." The number of economists and other specialists within the government was substantially increased, and efforts were made to bring specialists from industry and the universities into the government on short-term assignments. Old barriers and inhibitions had been broken down and new institutions created with responsibility for these policy areas.[79]

Of perhaps greater importance was the government's effort to institutionalize a prices and incomes policy as an integral element of its economic strategy. Building on earlier progress in Neddy, the government finally accepted the responsibility for creating a long-term policy whose basic aim was to reconcile full employment and price stability in a democratic society.[80]

Yet the period between 1968 and 1975 was even more of an economic—and political—disaster than the previous decade. The economy staggered between deep recession and unguided expansion, and suffered the worst of both for much of the

---

[77] Strange, pp. 154–61. Strange suggests that in the early 1970s "British overseas investment will have built up the same sort of self-financing pool that it had before 1914," which will significantly alter the balance of payments on the capital and investment income account (p. 328).

[78] Brittan, *Steering the Economy*, p. 379.

[79] Stephen Young with A.V. Lowe, *Intervention in the Mixed Economy* (London: Croom Helm, 1974), Chapter 2, passim.

[80] On the Prices and Incomes Board, see Allen Fels, *The British Prices and Incomes Board* (Cambridge: Cambridge University Press, 1972); Joan Mitchell, *The National Board for Prices and Incomes* (London: Secker & Warburg, 1972); and Aubrey Jones, *The New Inflation: The Politics of Prices and Incomes* (London: Penguin, 1973).

period. Inflation and unemployment were far greater than at any time since the war. Government economic and industrial policies swung wildly between increased intervention in the economy and withdrawal, and Britain's economic performance continued to decline.

The economic situation during this period, and especially after 1973, was influenced certainly as much, and probably more, by international economic and financial developments as by internal problems. But Britain's economic difficulties seemed significantly worse than those of other industrial nations in this period, and Britain seemed less capable of managing the domestic impact of external events than others. Britain's trade unions were increasingly blamed for these additional difficulties. Relations between the unions and both Labour and Conservative governments between 1968 and 1974 were much worse than ever before in the postwar era. In the number and severity of strikes, as well as in the intensity of feeling on both sides, the scene resembled the worst days after 1918. By 1974, Britain seemed, for the first time since the years immediately following the war, to be at the very edge of economic chaos and, for the first time since 1931, at the doorway of political crisis.

Strains in Britain's industrial relations system were already apparent in the 1950s. A decade later, the system was at the point of explosion. On the one side, the effect of government economic policy had been to retard Britain's economic growth rate. Levels of unemployment had increased in each successive stop-go trough. Growth of real income declined sharply in the 1960s. This occurred partly because of the freeze and severe restraint of incomes in 1961 and again after 1966, and partly because rising levels of wages pushed more and more workers into taxable income levels. Indeed, research done by H.A. Turner and Frank Wilkinson suggests that "Any group of wage earners whose rate of pay between 1965 and 1969 lagged much more than 1 percent behind the annual national average increase in earnings, probably experienced an actual fall in real living standards."[81]

On the other side, the character of Britain's work force had changed significantly by the 1960s. Britain's working population was now made up, to a great extent, of individuals whose outlook and attitudes were shaped by twenty years of full employment and rising standards of living and who were too young to recall the hard times of the interwar years. Their expectations of the rightful rewards for their labor were much higher than their fathers', and they were far more willing to take independent action on the shop floor to maintain these expectations. They were more willing to utilize the leverage which Britain's industrial relations system provided them, increasingly uninhibited about strikes, and less loyal to the national leaders of their unions.[82]

---

[81] H.A. Turner and Frank Wilkinson, "Real Net Incomes and the Pay Explosion," *New Society* (25 February 1971): 309–10; see also Dudley Jackson, H.A. Turner, and Frank Wilkinson, *Do Trade Unions Cause Inflation?*, University of Cambridge, Department of Applied Economics, Occasional Paper 39 (Cambridge: Cambridge University Press, 1972), Chapter 3.

[82] See several recent articles by E.H. Phelps Brown: "New Wine in Old Bottles: Reflections on the Changed Working of Collective Bargaining in Great Britain," *British Journal of Industrial*

The trade unions had strongly supported the Labour government in 1964 and had given their backing, even if with increasing reluctance, to its prices and incomes policy. Even in 1966, as Lewis Minkin observes, most trade union leaders "exhibited a remarkable loyalty" to the government.[83] But the effect of the long-delayed devaluation, and the massive squeeze on the economy which the government put into force after devaluation finally strained this loyalty to the breaking point. The economy was still more drastically deflated, public expenditure was cut, and unemployment permitted to rise to its highest level since 1940. Prices rose and real disposable income fell for many workers. Even after devaluation, the government's attention remained rigidly focused on Britain's external financial situation, and the Chancellor declared that demands for reflation and for a higher rate of economic growth were "nearly insane."[84]

After 1966, the paths of the unions and the government diverged sharply. There was a strong trend toward the left in many unions, and union-government cooperation declined significantly. Strikes increased as workers sought to force higher wage settlements to keep pace with inflation and to maintain their living standards. That a Labour government was in power and demanding still greater sacrifices of higher levels of unemployment, declining standards of living, and reduced social welfare programs, substantially heightened the alienation of the unions.

The increasing wave of strikes and rising conflict with the unions finally drove an angered and frustrated Labour government to break radically with party tradition and directly confront the unions by reviving the old notion of legal restraints on union activities.[85] Regardless of the ultimate justification for some such control over the unions, it would be difficult to deny that the government's timing and approach could not have been more unfortunate. Its action called into question the legal status of the unions and the freedom (already infringed by incomes policy) of collective bargaining. It completed the mobilization of the union movement against the government, increased the power of radical union leaders, and rendered impossible a constructive dialogue on incomes policy or the reform of industrial relations. The collapse of the government proposals was followed by the virtual termination of its prices and incomes policy and by an explosion of worker militancy in which strikes, wages, and prices all increased rapidly.

The breakdown of institutional restraint and a growing readiness of workers to fight for what they believed was their due thus collided with an economy less and less capable of meeting the demands made upon it. Locked into this situation largely by choices it had made in the past, Wilson's government aggravated the

*Relations* Vol. 11, No. 3 (November 1973); "A Non-Monetarist View of the Pay Explosion," *The Three Banks Review* No. 105 (March 1975); and "Labour Policies: Productivity, Industrial Relations, Cost Inflation," in *Britain's Economic Prospects Reconsidered,* Sir Alec Cairncross, ed. (London: George Allen and Unwin, 1971).
[83] Minkin, p. 26.
[84] Ibid., p. 27.
[85] See Peter Jenkins, *The Battle of Downing Street* (London: Charles Knight, 1970).

situation still further by its decision to confront the unions on the most sensitive possible issue. The result was a growing political crisis which further worsened Britain's economic problems.

These trends were accentuated under Mr. Heath's Conservative government, which took power in June 1970. Changes in the government's economic policies and techniques were even more abrupt and violent, relations with the unions more hostile and the number of strikes still higher, inflation far worse, and the impact of external events less manageable than ever before.

The Conservative "new style of government" was meant to be a radical break with the "consensus politics" of the postwar period.[86] Heath promised to reduce the role of government in the economy, to disengage the public from the private sector, and to encourage competitive forces. The neo-liberalist outlook and objectives of the Conservative government in 1970 were similar to those of the Conservative government in the 1950s, but its style was much more aggressive. Rather than emphasizing continuities with the previous Labour government, as Churchill had done, the Heath government emphasized radical change. The government stressed the need "to revive British capitalism: to make it more competitive and efficient, to restore its self-confidence."[87] It rejected tripartite planning which both industrial associations and trade unions supported. It was totally opposed to incomes policy and disbanded the Prices and Incomes Board. It abolished the IRC and throttled back the Ministry of Technology's interventionist approach to industrial policy. The new government was determined to confront the unions: it promised to put heavy pressure on public and private sector employers to resist wage increases and it introduced a new industrial relations act.[88]

By 1974, however, the government's policies were in a shambles. The overall record on economic growth was no better than its predecessor's. The balance of payments remained a severe problem. Inflation, particularly in the wake of the 1973 oil crisis, had intensified dramatically. The government had been forced to reverse some of its most important commitments. It had not been able to permit competitive forces to reign in the market when faced with collapse of a major producer like Rolls-Royce. It had turned back to the same tripartite approach to economic policy making and, most seriously of all, it had introduced, in the Fall of 1972, the most stringent wage and price controls in Britain peacetime history.[89] It had been unable to reform Britain's industrial relations system and had been totally unable to reduce the number of strikes. Indeed, in 1972 Britain lost more workdays through strikes than in any year since 1926, the year of the General Strike.

---

[86] On the Heath Government's economic policies, see J. Bruce-Gardyne, *Whatever Happened to the Quiet Revolution?* (London: Charles Knight, 1974), Chapters 1, 2, 3, 6, 7; and Andrew Gamble, *The Conservative Nation* (London: Routledge and Kegan, 1974), Chapters 6 and 7. See also Minkin, pp. 30–33.

[87] Anthony King, "The Election That Everyone Lost," in *Britain at the Polls; The Parliamentary Election of 1974,* Howard R. Penniman, ed. (Washington: American Enterprise Institute, 1974), p. 6.

[88] Gamble, pp. 122–23 and 143–58; Bruce-Gardyne, pp. 22–25.

[89] King, in Penniman, ed., pp. 11–12.

The Labour Party's 1973 manifesto seemed to illustrate the power of the unions, and particularly of the most radical union leaders, to push the Party's program and policies far to the left. The election of February 1974 took place in the midst of a violent clash between the miners' union and the Conservative government. Mr. Wilson returned to power, although the Labour Party had won only 37 percent of the vote. Both major political parties seemed to have been repudiated at the polls, as their vote declined from almost 90 percent of the total vote in 1970 to just about 75 percent in 1974. The trade unions appeared to control much of the new government's legislative program and to dominate its decision making. In the Summer of 1974, the columns of *The Times* carried articles weighing the possibility of a military coup d'état in Britain.[90]

The relationship between the unions and government in Britain seemed to have undergone enormous change. In some respects, in the antagonism expressed, the relationship resembled that of the 1920s more than the 1940s or 1950s. Unions were far more aggressive, particularly in their efforts to win higher wage settlements. But this mood was also evident in political confrontations with governments, both Labour and Conservative, over proposed legislation dealing with the legal status of unions and with collective bargaining, strikes, and other union activities.

Yet, even with these changes, there were many continuities with the postwar past. Union responses were still largely defensive and conservative. The unions attempted to keep wages ahead of inflation—to keep real net income from falling and to maintain the rising standards of living to which their members had become accustomed in the previous twenty years. They sought to maintain income differentials among different labor (and professional) groups and to preserve their traditional legal status and the freedom of collective bargaining. Thus, although a new cadre of radical labor leaders who rose to power during this period of continuing turmoil put forward much wider demands, British unions still struggled primarily to retain the status quo of the previous postwar years.[91]

One of the most vital dimensions in trade union-government relations in the past decade was the growing crisis *within* the trade unions. Many national union leaders attempted to contain conflict with government to limited areas of disagreement and to avoid wider political controversies, especially within the Labour Party. But they were less and less able to maintain control over their unions or to resist the challenge of individuals who had no such inhibitions. The greatest radicalization of the unions occurred, not so much at the national level, but among individual employees. Peter Jenkins has written about the situation in 1969–70:

The leaders of the trade union movement were not blind to the need for

---

[90] See *The Times* (London), 5 August 1974.

[91] Lewis Minkin, "New Left Unionism and the Tensions of British Labour Politics," paper delivered at a conference on "The European Left " (New York: City University of New York, November 1976), pp. 14–24.

change. They realized the considerable impotence of their position as they conducted, on the one hand, high diplomacy with the Government on behalf of the whole trade union movement while, on the other hand, they struggled with constituents over whom they had little control. They purported to be the authoritative representatives of the unions but they knew that they were seldom in a position to enter into a firm bargain on their behalf.[92]

Even on the shop floor, however, goals remained essentially defensive. Workers were pressed harder and harder to maintain standards of living in the face of continuously rising prices and the impact of higher levels of taxation. As Professor Phelps Brown has observed, "The argument that it was the pay rises that raised the cost of living did not carry conviction in the experience of the individual worker, for almost all the rises in prices that he had to pay came upon him from sectors unaffected by his own pay."[93] They demanded that unions protect their standards of living and supported militant shop floor leaders who fought to do this when national leaders would not. But there was little indication of support on the shop floor for more drastic political change.[94]

Generational changes in the composition of the work force and changes in workers' attitudes were bound to heighten tensions in Britain over the allocation of the national income, the organization of labor, the operations of the social welfare system, and so on—as they did throughout Europe in the late 1960s. The relationship between labor and government in Britain characteristic of the 1945–1965 period had been shaped, in large measure, by attitudes and commitments formed during the depression and world war, and the rise of a new generation of workers and union leaders was bound to create new tensions.

The crisis was made much more severe by the impact of domestic economic policy of the previous decade, as well as by the more immediate effects of the 1967 devaluation. Commitments made by British governments in the 1950s and early 1960s locked the country into a low-growth situation and made it impossible to meet rising expectations of the British population. They led, after 1967, to economic policies which resulted in higher unemployment, a decline in the growth of real net income, and, indeed, to an actual fall in real net income for many.

Tension was further escalated by the decision of the Labour and Conservative governments to confront the unions on issues of great sensitivity to them and of dubious economic utility to the nation. The confrontation with the unions strengthened the hands of the radical union leaders, politicized union demands, and gravely undercut the fragile foundations for an effective prices and incomes policy. It contributed to the further weakening of the authority of the TUC over its

---

[92] Jenkins, pp. 52–53. There were similar decentralizing tendencies within the industrial associations as well. See Blank, pp. 233–34, and W.P. Grant and D. Marsh, "The Politics of the CBI: 1974 and After," *Government and Opposition* Vol. 10, No. 1 (Winter 1975).

[93] Phelps-Brown, "A Non-Monetarist View of the Pay Explosion," p. 18.

[94] Richter, *Epilogue;* Minkin, "New Left Unionism," pp. 14–24.

members. Finally, the confrontation with the unions heightened the level of social conflict in British society, and contributed to the breakdown of the basic consensus in which individual demands have been moderated by a sense of the general welfare.

The breakdown of the consensus was accentuated by the remarkable failure of governments of both parties to comprehend the necessary foundations of institutional development. The new patterns of economic policy which began to emerge in the 1960s involved (and necessitated) substantial changes in the fabric of Britain's political economy. These included changes in the perceptions, attitudes, and behavior of groups and individuals throughout society. The development of these new policies, such as economic planning and a prices and incomes policy, and of institutions which could carry them out would have to be a lengthy, gradual, and delicate process. This was particularly the case in Britain where the traditional framework of policies and values dealing with government's role in the economy was so heavily weighted on the side of non-intervention.

Achievements in institution building were not negligible. The development of Neddy from 1961 to 1965 and the experiments with the Prices and Incomes Board remain impressive. But their longer term impact was small. Successive governments, dominated by a short-term mentality, persisted in seeing each new initiative or institution as an immediate remedy for Britain's continuing economic crisis. The wisdom of Jean Monnet emerges very clearly at this point. Monnet sought, above all, to keep the Planning Commission out of day-to-day politics in France and to concentrate instead on a series of medium and longer range objectives. He did this even if it meant, as in the years after the first plan, that the Plan and the Planning Commission seemed almost to have ceased to exist.[95] But the British had no such opportunity; each new agency was created in a flare of publicity, rushed to the front, and thrust into the thick of battle. As each was bloodied in turn, enthusiasm and political support evaporated. Little thought was given to the needs of long-term institution building or to the relationship among these various institutions or to the coordination of overall economic policy. Instead of a process of gradual institutional development, there was a parade of tentative and partially organized vehicles. The result was to degrade the policies, demoralize the participants, and, in the end, strengthen the hands of those institutions, particularly the Treasury, which traditionally were responsible for the conduct of economic policy and those policies with which they were identified.[96]

Worse still, the new policies and institutions became the meat of party politics. It was deeply ironic that, while there had been little serious debate between the parties on such issues as the international role of sterling, fixed

---

[95] See Jack Hayward, *The One and Indivisible French Republic* (New York: Norton, 1973), pp. 167–69.

[96] See Trevor Smith, "Britain" and "Industrial Planning in Britain," in Hayward and Watson, eds., and Austin Albu, "Lessons of the Labour Government: Economic Policies and Methods," *Political Quarterly* Vol. 41, No. 2 (April 1970).

exchange rates, or overseas investment, now economic planning and prices and incomes policy became matters of hot political controversy. Heath's government was determined to wipe the entire board clean and, to the surprise of the Whitehall machine, it uprooted almost every institution created by the Labour government. Yet, within a year and a half, almost every one had been reestablished, although under a new name. These were again largely demolished by the new Labour government early in 1974, but most have reappeared in a new form. Thus, the credibility of these policies and of government's economic strategy as a whole declined disastrously. The result here, too, was to heighten the sense of fragmentation, conflict, and frustration in British society which is one of the foundations of the present economic crisis.

## VI Conclusion

The objective of this essay has been to discuss the political and economic impacts of certain policy choices made by British governments after World War II, particularly policy choices which involved efforts to restore Britain's role as a major world power. The essay is meant to be a response to those who claim that the fundamental causes of Britain's unsatisfactory economic performance in the postwar period are to be found primarily in the attitudes of British workers and managers, in its labor and industrial organizations, and in the failure or inability of British government to exert its will more forcefully over the economic decision-making process.

The attempt has been made in particular to assess the responsibility of interest groups for the problems of the British economy since 1945. The conclusion reached here is that the responsibility of organized industrial and labor groups, while not negligible, is far from substantial. The responsibility for Britain's economic difficulties, insofar as these were within Britain's capacity to control, lies mainly with successive British governments and with the policies they adopted. Britain's economic problems have risen less from the subversion of government policy by powerful agencies or groups, either in the bureaucracy or in the private sector, than from the impact of the attitudes, commitments, and politics of Britain's top political leaders.

Throughout the essay, it has been suggested that the concept of "pluralistic stagnation" is not very useful in promoting a better understanding of the problems of the British economy in the postwar era. By and large, producer groups in Britain consistently sought to maintain the voluntaristic, consensual system which had developed during the wartime and immediate postwar experience. They rarely attempted actively to oppose government policy, and when they did, almost inevitably limited their opposition to very narrow fronts. Only when the government appeared to be trying to alter this system, and thus to jeopardize the internal interests of the organizations, was resistance likely. Even so, the TUC (and even the unions in general) as well as the major industrial associations remained, in Peter

Nettle's terms, "vulnerable to the pressures of consensus emanating from Whitehall."[97]

The pattern of economic policy which began to take shape in the early 1960s and which centered on .the creation of the National Economic Development Council rested upon the continuation and further institutionalization of this relationship. It was hoped that, through it, substantial changes in the structure of British industry, the organization and operation of the trade unions, and the determination of prices and incomes could be accomplished. It has been argued here that the failure of this voluntaristic approach is more the responsibility of government than of the producer groups.

It is not the intention of this essay to suggest that all of the economic problems that Britain faces today grow out of a set of foreign policy choices and decisions made in the years which followed 1945. A wide range of serious defects of industrial structure, labor organization, and work and management practices would have to have been confronted and solved if Briatin's economic situation were to have been improved. But the pattern of policy which characterized the postwar era severely limited the options of policy makers in dealing with these issues. The result of the government's commitment to maintain Britain's international position was continuing domestic economic stagnation and a failure to develop new techniques and institutions to cope with the structural problems of the economy. This, as has been seen, made it much more difficult for the British to deal with new challenges when they arose at the end of the 1960s.

The argument of Britain's long-term economic decline does not take into sufficient account the impressive gains Britain enjoyed in technological and managerial development from the end of the 1930s through the war years, nor the remarkable recovery of the British economy after the war. It must also be remembered that the "margins of failure" of the British economy, at least through the 1960s, were narrow indeed. The balance-of-payments crises of 1955, 1957, 1961, and even 1964 represented quite small adverse movements against the pound when compared, for example, to the yearly or even quarterly totals of British trade. The impact of government's response to these crises was far more damaging to the British economy than were the problems represented by the balance-of-payments difficulties. There were several points at which the direction of Britain's economic development might have been altered during this period. This is where the failures of perception and policy are most vivid.

Perhaps the greatest failure was the lack of attention given to the problems of the domestic economy in the first postwar years. Yet it is easy to see how Britain's very success blinded its leaders to this need for a full-scale attack on the structural inadequacies of the economy. Britain's military, political, and economic achievements during the war and in the first postwar years were remarkable. Defeat forced the French to confront head-on the underlying defects of their economy; the

---

[97] J.P. Nettle, "Consensus and Elite Domination: The Case of Business," *Political Studies* Vol. 13, No. 1 (January 1965): 23.

achievements of the British economy were so substantial that it was all too easy to overlook its fundamental problems. The war divided the French and held up their weakness for everyone to see; the war united the British and disguised their weaknesses. The failure of the war economy forced the French to reexamine their national economic and industrial policies; the British successes encouraged them to believe that existing policies and techniques were sufficient for peacetime purposes.[98]

In time, Britain's failure to support the European movement may be judged a still greater failure. If Britain had thrown its weight behind the movement in its earliest days, perhaps the entire history of the postwar era would be different. But it is impossible, of course, to say what would have happened. In any case, from the British standpoint, one cannot really blame them for their reluctance to accept this involvement. As late as 1957, they were able to believe, with some justice, that participation in the European movement would merely bring Britain's strength to Europe's weakness.

British failures at the end of the 1950s to recognize the realities of the economic situation and to respond more effectively are less forgivable. Between 1957 and 1959, the writing on the wall became entirely clear. Yet, as Susan Strange has described so well, the British government was unable and unwilling to reduce its international obligations or to concentrate its attention upon the problems of the domestic economy. Macmillan's election campaign in 1959 was patently false. The Tories claimed, "You've never had it so good." (Soon, Labour would say, "You've never been had so good.") But two years later, Macmillan did press for the formation of some sort of economic planning program and declared his intention to take Britain into the Common Market. Yet the government was unsuccessful in both directions, and it is not stretching the argument to say that it was unsuccessful because it was unwilling to abandon its perceptions of Britain as a world power.

The most tragic failure to change the direction of British economic policy was Mr. Wilson's. It is not so much a question of devaluation, which was a necessary but by no means sufficient step to revive the domestic economy. The real failure was Wilson's inability—unwillingness—to utilize the resources which were available to him to reverse the course of British economic development. From the late 1950s, a new consensus had begun to emerge within British leadership. This consensus focused on the need to energize Britain's economy, to modernize its industry, and to overcome the deeply ingrained inhibitions in British society which limited economic growth. Among leading industrialists, in particular, who were deeply disturbed about the damage that stop-go policies were doing to business expecta-

---

[98] The Development Councils provide the best example of this. The reasons for the creation of the Development Councils in Britain were exactly the same as those for the creation of the Modernization Commissions in France. Indeed, it is said that the French followed the British example. What was different in Britain was that there was no interest in the Councils. No one—not even the government leaders responsible—supported them seriously.

tions, the nucleus of a group similar to that which surrounded Jean Monnet had begun to form. They were excited by Wilson's promises of radical (which is to be distinguished from, although not necessarily opposed to, Socialist) leadership and were prepared, I believe, to take on significant new responsibilities in his administration. The government's failure to exploit this resource and, indeed, its alarming capacity for making the most conservative choices at critical moments destroyed this movement and undermined what remained of business confidence. Increasing fatalism and aggressiveness characterized business response to government after 1966.

What can be said of Britain's options at the present time? This essay has attempted to describe the antecedents of Britain's current situation—to set the stage for present decisions—but it is somewhat beyond its focus to deal with these options in substantial detail. The complications of the international economic environment increased dramatically in the early 1970s and further limited policy choices, particularly in relatively weaker economies like Britain's. Indeed, the British seem frequently these days to be the last man in a global game of crack the whip!

The essay has not dealt with the question of British membership in the European Community. Until 1961, Britain remained uninterested in the European movement. Macmillan's decision, in the Summer of 1961, to seek membership in the Common Market was representative neither of a widespread popular commitment to join Europe nor of the attitudes of economic and political elites. Although many industrial leaders were deeply in favor of British membership in the Common Market, a completely convincing case that the economic benefits of membership would exceed its costs was never made. Indeed, professional economists seemed significantly less enthusiastic about membership than industrialists whose views were more intuitive than scientific. Throughout the 1960s, there was never an overwhelming commitment in Britain for Common Market membership; frequently, fewer than half of the population seemed to favor entry. The Conservative Party's leadership on the issue was far more indicative of Mr. Heath's personal feelings than of the views of the party members or leaders.

Thus, for most of the period with which this essay is concerned, involvement in the Common Market was not central to the issues it deals with. By the time Britain did join, the Common Market had lost most of its vitality and was widely understood to be a useful, but not critical, factor in the economic lives and well-being of its members. Common Market membership has not, it would appear, affected Britain's economic prospects or performance in any radical fashion. It has not provided the "cold bath" of increased competition which many business leaders had hoped for, nor has the British economy been undermined by membership as opponents feared. The calculus of benefits and costs remains complex and the overall outcome uncertain.

Britain's fundamental economic problem remains a lack of investment. There have been significant improvements in productivity in many industries, but the growth of new investment, and particularly investment in the most productive areas, has been too slow. The failure to invest has meant a failure to grow, and the failure to grow has exacerbated many of the country's most urgent social and political problems. It has been impossible to maintain rising living standards, welfare programs, and a stable balance of payments with an annual growth rate which is only about 2.5 percent.

Perhaps Britain has now come to the end of the slow slide down. There are certain grounds for optimism, at least cautious optimism. Nine years after the devaluation of November 1967, the liquidation of the pound as an international reserve currency is finally taking place. Devaluation did not provide any greater flexibility in dealing with sterling. The sterling balances increased in the late 1960s and soared after the 1973 oil crisis. The British government welcomed increased foreign holdings of pounds as a way of meeting its current balance-of-payments deficits. Once again, it utilized the device of high domestic interest rates to attract hot money, while punishing domestic investment. The growing instability of the international monetary and financial situation enormously increased the unreliability of this resource, however. Once again, the fate of the domestic economy was too closely linked to the magical notion of "international confidence." It was not, however, only a question of the confidence of foreign holders of sterling in the future of the pound but of the confidence of a few Arab shieks in the economic prospects of Europe and of the United States and the dollar. The dramatic fall in the value of the pound during the past two years has been due to movements out of sterling which have been based only indirectly on the state of the British economy per se. The impact of these movements on the British economy has, nonetheless, been enormous.

Second, there is North Sea oil. This year, North Sea production should cover 15 or 20 percent of Britain's internal needs and, by 1980, North Sea production should cover all domestic needs and provide considerable relief for Britain's balance of payments.[99] Yet there are many hurdles still to come before these gains can be realized: the rising tide of Scottish nationalism is one and the substantial foreign debts incurred in the development of the North Sea fields is another. In any case, while North Sea oil will wipe out the effects on Britain of the increased world price of oil, it is not likely to cushion a significant shortfall in the non-oil balance of payments. North Sea oil will provide a breathing space, not a panacea.

Finally, there is the role of the trade union leaders in recent months. The social contract has been impressively successful. Strikes declined drastically in 1975 and even more so in 1976, and there was clear evidence of a loss of support among the labor rank and file in several key unions for more radical leaders. The unions themselves have provided, as in the past, sturdy support for the Labour government's massive deflationary policies. Finally, there are even signs of deep changes in labor attitudes. A *New York Times* labor specialist wrote, in mid-1976, that "labor-management relations, long regarded as the achilles' heel of Britain's battered economy, are proving a key source of strength in the budding British

---

[99] See "North Sea Countdown," *The Economist* (1 November 1975): 68–69.

recovery."[100] The Confederation of British Industry (CBI), too, has played a significant role in supporting government policies and accepting new responsibilities for representing industrial views in discussions with the government. Indeed, despite the continued protests from all three groups—labor, industry, and government—that the tripartite arrangements of the early 1960s would not be reconstituted, especially with regard to incomes policy, there appears to have been a significant movement in this direction.

These positive elements in Britain's current situation, as welcome as they are, are likely to be insufficient in themselves to reverse the trend of British economic development. The economic policies of the current government constitute a holding operation and not a strategy which will lead to a radical increase in output, productivity, and the rate of economic growth. Things are not getting worse at the moment, but they are not getting better either.

There are limits, too, to the length of time a holding operation can be carried on. Strains are especially likely to appear in the near future in the social contract. Unemployment rates are now pressing up to levels—toward 6 percent—far in excess of anything since the Great Depression, and prices are advancing now considerably faster than wages. Two years of extreme restraint on the part of the working people of Britain have produced, it appears, only rising unemployment and falling standards of living. It is said that the workers and, more particularly, the union leaders have been "educated" now. They are said to realize that inflation is the worse enemy, that inflation produces unemployment, and that the continuation of severe restraint is the only way in which inflation can be overcome. Besides, if the unions do not give their support to the present government, a new Tory regime is likely to be even tougher. Still, I think that it is increasingly difficult for many people to understand that putting more and more people out of work will reduce unemployment. I also think that it is not unlikely that unless some clear benefits in return for these sacrifices can be seen soon, there will be a new explosion of militancy. The British workers have a strong belief in the notion of a *quid pro quo,* and there has been a great deal of *quid* and not much *quo* in the past two years.

Business confidence remains low and is reflected in continuing low rates of investment. A stagnant economy is a low profit economy, and low profitability inhibits investment. Just as it is not at all clear that a policy of trying to shift domestic resources into exports by restraining domestic demand is going to be successful (although it was endlessly attempted in the 1950s and 1960s), it is by no means certain that investment will be stimulated by deflationary economic policies.

The point is that, for all of its ability to hold the fort and despite a number of significant policy developments, the present government has not convinced anyone in Britain that it has a firm sense of direction and that it can move the economy forward. Anthony Howard, the editor of *The New Statesman,* wrote at the end of 1976 that it has been Mr. Callaghan's "misfortune to preside over a Government

[100] A.H. Raskin in *The New York Times.* July 9, 1976.

that has appeared to be without any bearings, let alone a sense of direction. With its economic policy in ruins, it has seemed in fact to be darting about all over the place, playing an increasingly ludicrous game of blindman's bluff with an elusive element called 'international confidence.'[101]

Second, even if Howard's assessment is incorrect and the Callaghan government is able to fit the pieces of its economic policies into a coherent national strategy and even if it is to maintain the confidence of labor and win back that of industry, Britain's now enormous vulnerability to international economic developments means that it cannot climb out of the hole it is in on its own. Britain's economic fortunes depend greatly at the present time on the willingness of the stronger industrial nations, Germany, Japan, and the United States, to reflate their economies considerably more rapidly than they have shown an inclination to do. The recovery from the worst postwar recession has not yet been strong enough to exert much pull on the weaker economies, and, if the frail recovery falters, economies like Britain's will suffer the most, no matter what their governments do.

Finally, the political impact of Britain's economic problems grows more and more evident and serious. In a recent paper, Robert Lieber wrote that "one of the most striking phenomena of the contemporary British situation is that despite all its problems, the essential legitimacy of the British political system has not been called into queson."[102] But if its "essential legitimacy" remains unquestioned, rarely has confidence in government policies, in the political parties, and Britain's political leaders been so low. Confidence in the economy and, much more, in the capacity of governments to deal effectively with economic problems provides the essential foundation for the consensual, voluntaristic system which seems to be Britain's best resource for managing its economy. Ultimately, the peak associations of labor and industry must assume an active and responsible role in the economic policy-making process if it is ever going to be possible to reconcile full employment and stable prices. These organizations will have to accept responsibility for the development of a new wage negotiation system, for the creation of an incomes policy based on self-regulation and control.

Although there has been some degree of centralization within the peak associations during the past two years, this is by no means likely to be permanent. The primary effect of the continued failure to improve economic performance is to heighten the centrifugal tendencies within these organizations, especially with regard to wage settlements.[103] Thus, it may well be that, even if the international crisis eases, the central producer organizations, which have never had much authority

[101] Anthony Howard, "Angry Wage Earners, Floundering Politicians," *New York Times Magazine,* December 26, 1976, p. 36.
[102] Robert J. Lieber, "Labour in Power: Problems of Political Economy" (unpublished paper, November 1976), p. 38.
[103] See, for example, H.A. Turner, "Collective Bargaining and the Eclipse of Incomes Policy: Retrospect, Prospect and Possibilities," *British Journal of Industrial Relations* Vol. 8, No. 2 (March 1970).

over their members, may be too fragmented to share responsibility for economic management in the future. [104] If this is the case, the only remaining options will be a return to a more traditional liberal economic order, as interpreted by monetarism, in which full employment is no longer taken as a base line for economic policy, or a far more interventionist system, in which government takes on a far greater direct role in the operation of the economy. The political impact of either of these choices would be extensive, divisive, and dangerous.

[104] See Samuel Beer, "Paradoxes of Economic Power," in Blank, p. xii. See also Peter Jenkins, "Britain's Troubles," *Trialogue* No. 12 (Fall 1976): 2–4.

# 5
# Japanese Foreign Economic Policy: The Domestic Bases for International Behavior

*T. J. Pempel*

By many criteria, Japan is weak internationally. As a consequence one would expect its foreign economic policy to have been marked by limited choice, weakness, and constant vacillation in the face of external pressures. The domestic political structures of the country, however, have for most of the period since World War II permitted wide choice, strength, and consistency. A corporatist coalition of finance, major industry, trading companies, and the upper levels of the national bureaucracy, coupled with the consistent rule of the conservative Liberal Democratic Party, the systematic exclusion of organized labor from formal policy-making channels, and the lack of social overhead spending, has permitted the Japanese state to function as official doorman determining what, and under what conditions, capital, technology, and manufactured products enter and leave Japan. The strengths acquired from such past policies make it likely that the Japanese state will remain capable of dealing with the increasing domestic and international threats to its capacity to make relatively autonomous choices about Japan's international economic behavior.

If the state is dead elsewhere, it is vital and strong in the generation and implementation of Japanese foreign economic policy. The politics of distribution may have become less central internationally in the face of a seemingly uniform trend among industrial democracies to establish massive social welfare systems, but Japan stands out as a striking counter-example. If such border-defying economic forces as the multinational corporation, transnational organizations, OPEC, and the International Labor Organization (ILO), among others, have been uniformly eroding the ability

T.J. Pempel is a member of the Department of Government at Cornell University. In addition to the contributions made by the various participants in the Conference on Domestic Structures and the Foreign Economic Policy of Advanced Industrial States, helpful suggestions were made on earlier versions of this paper by Haruhiro Fukui, Edward L. Morse, Alan G. Rix, and William Tetreault.

of most governments to choose and implement autonomous goals in their foreign economic policies, the Japanese government has demonstrated a high degree of independence from such seemingly universal impacts.

A good deal of attention has been devoted to the vulnerability of the nation-state to international forces. During the 1950s, much of this concern focused on the purported inability of nation-states to cope with the pervasive threat of nuclear attack or to avoid being dragged unwittingly into the conflicts of the superpowers. More recently, the stress has been on the vulnerability of the state to broad external economic forces. The cumulative impact of works dealing with this latter problem has been to stress the erosion of the analytic salience and the political capabilities of the nation-state.[1]

Valid as such trends may be, it is a mistake to lump all states, or even all industrial states, together without sufficient sensitivity to differences among them. The widely divergent foreign economic policies of the different industrial states, despite common international stimuli, suggest the importance of variations in domestic political structures.[2]

Though the power and will to do so differs from one state to another, national governments exercise key controls over their own territories and can determine, to a large extent, the conditions under which access to that territory will be granted.[3] Moreover, through control over the legality of actions of domestic political actors, governments can exert a strong influence over the capabilities of these actors in the international area. Some governments will use such controls foolishly or corruptly; however, when states use them wisely to further their own objectives, they can hardly be accused of forfeiting their sovereignty.[4]

Japan is one state which exemplifies this fact. Many aspects of Japan's international position have made it seem exceptionally vulnerable to international stimuli and could have seriously reduced the state's ability to carry out policies of

---

[1] This is surely an oversimplification of many diverse works; however, among the works which have moved generally in this direction are: Ernst B. Haas, *Beyond the Nation-State* (Stanford: Stanford University Press, 1964); Karl W. Deutsch, *Nerves of Government* (New York: Free Press, 1966); *The Analysis of International Relations* (Englewood Cliffs, N.J.: Prentice-Hall, 1968); Charles Kindleberger, ed., *The International Corporation* (Cambridge: MIT Press, 1970); Raymond Vernon, *Sovereignty at Bay* (New York: Basic Books, 1971); Edward L. Morse, *Foreign Policy and Interdependence in Gaullist France* (Princeton: Princeton University Press, 1973); "The Politics of Interdependence," *International Organization* Vol. 23 (Spring 1969): 311–26; Richard N. Cooper, *The Economics of Interdependence* (New York: McGraw-Hill, 1968); Robert O. Keohane and Joseph S. Nye, Jr., *Transnational Relations and World Politics* (Cambridge: Harvard University Press, 1970); Richard Rosecrance and Arthur Stein, *Interdependence in World Politics* (forthcoming). The Keohane and Nye book includes a particularly useful bibliography on the subject of transnational relations, and the journal *International Organization* has published a number of significant articles on the problem.

[2] See in particular Peter J. Katzenstein, "International Relations and Domestic Structures: Foreign Economic Policies of Advanced Industrial States," *International Organization* Vol. 30, No. 1 (Winter 1976):1–45.

[3] Samuel P. Huntington, "Transnational Organizations in World Politics," *World Politics* Vol. 25 (April 1973):333–68.

[4] Ibid., p. 364.

its own choosing. In fact, the Japanese government has shown an unmistakable capacity to do just the opposite. Japan's foreign economic policy, for the bulk of the period following World War II, pivoted around clearly defined and rather consistently executed objectives. Its commercial policy rested on an export strategy demanding reasonably free access to world markets. At the core of this export strategy, Japan's monetary policy hinged on a fixed and undervalued exchange rate for the yen. Foreign capital, managerial control, and "overly competitive" imports were kept out of Japan while foreign technology was actively and successfully acquired. Finally, until it was possible to export it without an adverse impact on the balance of payments, domestic capital was kept within national boundaries. Consequently, Japan has utilized foreign economic policy to bolster its overall economic growth with more autonomy, sovereignty, coherence, and macro-level success than any other major industrial power.

Such a policy, it will be argued, has been possible largely because of the confluence of domestic political structures in Japan. The distributional question, if it has been resolved in the general direction of equity in other industrial societies (a point surely subject to debate), has been dealt with differently in Japan. There, a conservative network of technologically advanced industry, finance, and the state bureaucracy has been able to exploit the political exclusion of the left and organized labor to generate a foreign economic policy combining resistance to unwanted international stimuli and creative domestic resource extraction.

This point demands some qualification, however. Dichotomizing between "domestic" and "international" forces masks the fact that international forces are frequently congruent with domestic political aims and vice versa. There is no automatic tension between that which is "domestic" and that which is "international." Yet insufficient attention has often been given to the equally likely possibility that many such international influences are welcomed and actively fostered by either the state as a whole or by key segments of domestic ruling groups. Certainly in the instance of Japan, many cases of international "penetration" have been quite congruent with actions that would have been taken for domestic political reasons and have been more than unwanted external stimuli.

Furthermore, assessing the relative significance of domestic and international forces demands a sensitivity to the nature of different issues, even within the narrow categorization of foreign economic policy.[5] While certain nation-states may

---

[5] The classic statement of this possibility comes from Theodore J. Lowi, "American Business, Public Policy, Case Studies and Political Theory," *World Politics* Vol. 16 (July 1964): 677–715. See William Zimmerman, "Issue Area and Foreign Policy Process: A Research Note in Search of a General Theory," *American Political Science Review* Vol. 67 (December 1973):1204–12 for an application to foreign policy problems. An application to Japanese politics can be found in T.J. Pempel, "Patterns of Policymaking: Higher Education," in T.J. Pempel, ed., *Policymaking in Contemporary Japan* (Ithaca: Cornell University Press, 1977). Haruhiro Fukui has done a great deal of work on the problem in the area of Japanese foreign policy. See particularly his "Studies in Policymaking: A Review of the Literature," and "Tanaka Goes to Peking: A Case Study in Foreign Policymaking," in ibid.

be particularly vulnerable to unwanted international pressures on energy or mone-tary policy, for example, they may be virtually immune to such influences on commercial policy, capital investment, or technology transfer. This is particularly important in assessing Japanese foreign economic policy where the significance of domestic structures and the relative autonomy of the ruling conservative coalition has not been absolute across all component issues. Strength and autonomy in commercial and monetary policy, for example, have not been mirrored in raw materials policy.

Finally, changing domestic and international conditions may have begun to erode the capacity of the Japanese government to continue the policy directions of the past with comparable success. Yet even so, domestic political structures are likely to continue to be a key component of whatever policy directions are taken in Japan.

This, then, is the central argument of the paper: the definition and implemen-tation of foreign economic policy in Japan rests essentially on the domestic political structures of the country, particularly the strength of the state and its network of conservative support. As a prelude to the development of this argument, however, it is necessary to examine the conditions that would seem to make Japan so vulnerable to international pressures.

## *I Confining international conditions*

As is true of all major states, Japan's international position is extremely complex. Yet, along several distinct dimensions, Japanese foreign economic policy should have emerged as highly vulnerable to international pressures, and major checks should have been imposed upon Japanese sovereignty and policy-making autonomy. Japan's international geographic position is weak. Its domestic natural resource capabilities are virtually nil. It has an extremely high strategic dependence on a single country, the United States. Finally, it is well integrated into a number of multilateral economic organizations. These four constraints should have posed major problems for the definition and implementation of a successful and autono-mous foreign economic policy.

Geographically, Japan is situated in an area which has been at the center of major international controversies during the past quarter century. It is in the North Pacific that the generally conceded strategic interests of the USSR, the PRC, and the US come most directly into conflict. During the Cold War, both of the former were ideologically antagonistic to the Japanese government. The Korean War, which was the only major shooting war of the period, found armies allied with these major powers engaged only miles from the Japanese archipelago. The war in Indochina took place further away, but was still closer to Japan than to any other advanced industrial society, including of course the US. Bases in Okinawa played a major role in US military activities there, as did the broader intelligence and shipping facilities maintained by the US on the Japanese mainland.

Furthermore, classical geopolitical theory would suggest that Japan find its major potential market in China, its major potential supplier of raw materials in the Soviet Union, and its major potential customer in the US. All three countries have consistently used their foreign economic policies as tools of foreign policy, and all, of course, have been hostile to one another for most of the period examined here.

Japan is also geographically isolated from major industrial markets and from industrial allies. In this respect, it is quite different from the other major industrial democracies. With the single exception of Israel, those which are not completely surrounded by friendly powers, close allies, and trading partners (e.g., West Germany) at least have such friendly neighbors on one or more borders. With the rise in international transportation and communications and the major changes in weaponry, there has been a decreasing importance of proximity in international politics. Still, Japan's unique geographic position should certainly have made it vulnerable to a wide range of international pressures.

Second, many have suggested that the gods who distribute economic resources have been generous to Japan.[6] Although a host of factors favorable to economic strength can be cited, few of these actually take the form of purely natural endowments. Most are simply the result of past political, economic, and social successes. While Japan has 2.8 percent of the world's population, it has only 0.2 percent of the world land area; roughly half the population of the US is crowded into an area slightly smaller than the state of Montana. Moreover, only about 16 percent of this mountainous total is cultivable.[7] And though the land is flecked with various minerals, few are present in quantities sufficient to make them commercially mineable. Hence, Japan is heavily dependent on the import of critical raw materials.[8] The country lacks any significant domestic supplies of petroleum, iron ore, bauxite, nickel, manganese, phosphorous ore, copper, and chrome, and in most cases is the number one OECD importer of each.[9] In a wide variety of other materials critical to an industrial economy for which there are no ready substitutes, Japan is not much better endowed. The obvious consequence was a considerable dependence on imports of such products as a prerequisite to industrial growth; and as overall industrial activity and raw materials needs have expanded, Japan's dependence on them has continually increased.

[6] Kanamori Hisao, "Sekai Keizai no naka no Nihon," in *Gendai no Nihon Keizai*, Okuma Ichirō and Tsujimura Eitarō, eds. (Tokyo: Nihon Keizai Shimbunsha, 1975), p. 125.

[7] Ibid., p. 132.

[8] One of the earliest and more significant articles to make this point was Ōkita Saburō, "Shigen Yunyūkoku Nihon o Jikaku seyo," *Chūō Kōron* 963 (December 1967). For a more recent version of his thinking, see Ōkita, "Natural Resource Dependency and Japanese Foreign Policy," *Foreign Affairs* Vol. 52 (July 1974):714–24.

[9] See Kanamori Hisao, *Seminā: Nihon Keizai no Jōshiki* (Tokyo: Nihon Hyōronsha, 1976), pp. 16–18; Hayashi Shintarō and Watanabe Fukutarō, *Kokusai Keizai Kyōshitsu* (Tokyo: Yūhikaku, 1973), p. 55.

Since the end of World War II, Japan has been dependent on imports for about 10 percent of its GNP and, with the exception of the US, its imports as a percent of GNP are the lowest in the industrial world.[10] Yet, the reliance on foreign countries for the materials to fuel the domestic economic machine is greater for Japan than for any other major industrial power and has had an undeniable and unavoidable impact on virtually all aspects of Japan's foreign economic policy. This dependence could certainly have put Japan at the mercy of raw materials producers for most of the period in question. Assuredly, the combination of geographical location and the absence of raw materials severely limited the possibilities for Japanese foreign economic policy at the end of World War II.

A third dimension of international vulnerability concerns Japan's strategic dependence on the US. Occupied by US armies following the war, Japan emerged from the Occupation with its overall foreign policy firmly resting on friendly relations with the US while its defense policy pivoted around US willingness to aid Japan militarily in the event of external attack. This alliance was by no means a purely "international" factor. Japan lacks internal political unity on its basic foreign and military policies in ways dramatically different from the consensus that prevails in the US and in most European countries. The ruling conservatives have taken a strong pro-US position with its consequent anti-Communist orientation. The major opposition parties, on the other hand, have long called for varying degrees of separation of Japan's foreign and defense policies from those of the US. Opposition proposals have ranged from complete neutrality to some form of affiliation with the Soviet Union, China, or both. Thus, Japan's American alliance and dependence, though backed by some segments of Japanese society, is vehemently opposed by others, giving it a conspicuously domestic base.

In contrast, for example, to NATO members, Japan lacks similar multilateral alliances with the other industrial powers. The strong bilateral treaty system forges closer military links between the two powers than is true of most other relations among advanced industrial states. These links are bolstered by a close economic relationship. From the early 1950s until the early 1970s, upwards of 30 percent of Japan's total exports were sent to the US, whose goods accounted for approximately the same percent of Japan's imports. No other country has occupied as significant a place in Japan's trade and no other trade relationship of a bilateral nature, with the exception of that between Canada and the US, has been of comparable scale. The entire EEC, for example, took well below 10 percent of Japan's exports during this period.

Japan's overall relationship with the US is, hence, rather unique internationally. The European nations are linked to one another through NATO, the EEC, EURATOM, and the like. Canada, in addition to its ties with the US, has its special relationship with the Commonwealth. Probably the only other industrialized nation-state with a comparably concentrated dependency is Israel, which is similarly linked to the US. Thus, it could certainly be expected that when either is perceived by US officials as central to US policy, American support would be made quickly available. Alternatively, when either deviates too far, the power of the US to insure a measure of conformity would be difficult to check.

Finally, it is important to note that Japan has not been isolationist. It is an active member of the International Monetary Fund (IMF), the Organization for Economic Co-Operation and Development (OECD), the Asian Development Bank (ADB), the Development Assistance Committee (DAC), the World Bank, and a host of other multinational organizations of industrial states which seek to institutionalize the market system on an international scale and to coordinate the international economic behavior of its member states in such areas as monetary, trade, capital, and technology transfer and aid policies. Particularly in light of Japan's great interest in proving itself a loyal and trustworthy member of the "international community" and erasing the negative images left by World War II, these organizational links might have been expected to constrain the autonomy and independence of Japanese foreign economic policy.

In summary, in at least four important dimensions, Japan should have been highly susceptible to international pressures. From such pressures, it would be logical to predict for Japan a passive foreign economic policy. This sort of policy would be dominated by reaction to international stimuli and by sharp constraints on the exercise of policy, rather than by definitional autonomy and implementational initiative. International forces operating beyond the control of the Japanese state should have consistently overridden state sovereignty. Largely because of peculiarities in Japan's domestic political structures, this was not actually the case.

## II Domestic political structures

Contemporary Japanese politics has been dominated by a close alliance among key sectors which have shown a consistent ability to define the national political agenda and to set political priorities for the country. This ability has been particularly well demonstrated within the area of foreign economic policy. Most prominent in this closed coalition are the organs of the national bureaucracy, the peak federations and trade associations of big business, the major financial institutions, particularly the government-dominated banks, and finally, the ruling conservative political party, the Liberal Democratic Party (LDP). Significant in the coalition, but irrelevant to foreign economic policy except in matters concerning the liberalization of agricultural imports, are the peak agricultural cooperatives. Meanwhile, most significantly excluded from this coalition have been organized labor and the political parties it has supported.

Though it is traditional in political analysis to distinguish among state, society, and the structural linkages between them, it would be a mistake in analyzing Japanese politics to presume too sharp a distinction among the three. Peak business and financial institutions have always shown a high degree of penetration of the Japanese organs of state. Definition of the official policy-making agenda of the country typically involves a high degree of public-private intercommunication with neither side dominating the process. Mobility from public life to segments of the private sector is high. Informal mechanisms for public-private policy coordination and implementation are widespread.[11] The state, in turn, has been closely involved in the setting of private policy. Sometimes this occurs directly; sometimes through the issuance of unofficial but nonetheless effective "guidance." Since the LDP has monopolized control of government for more than twenty years, it is difficult to treat it as merely a "link" between populace and government. Practically speaking, it is the government.[12] More central to analysis than a distinction between state, linkages, and society is, therefore, a sensitivity to the mutuality of interests, overlap, and penetration that exists among these key sectors of Japan's governing coalition.

Since the latter part of the nineteenth century, Japan has been characterized by a strong state controlling a relatively homogeneous nation. During its modern period, the country has seen virtually none of the religious, ethnic, linguistic, or geographical clashes that have divided other nations. With only comparatively minor exceptions, the geographical borders of what is contemporary Japan were set by that time, and internal regional struggles have been almost nonexistent. Drawing heavily on the German governmental and constitutional experience and determined to cope with the threat posed to Japanese sovereignty by imperialistic Western powers, the Japanese political leadership of that time established a strong central state machinery. Major powers of policy formation and societal control were given to a well-trained bureaucratic class. The powers of parliament and political parties were left conspicuously and deliberately weak. Local governmental units were under close central scrutiny. Citizens' social and political rights were given far less constitutional and practical standing than their duties and obligations toward one another and toward the state. Conflict and compromise were treated not as the logical outgrowths of social complexities and legitimately competing interests, but as selfish and intolerable threats to the social harmony seen as essential to national sovereignty, development, and well-being. Japan reflected the mystical unity of state

---

[11] E.H. Norman, *Japan's Emergence as a Modern State,* John Dower, ed., *Origins of the Modern Japanese State: Selected Writings of E.H. Norman* (New York: Pantheon, 1975); William W. Lockwood, *The Economic Development of Japan* (Princeton: Princeton University Press, 1954); Lockwood, ed., *The State and Economic Enterprise in Japan* (Princeton: Princeton University Press, 1965); Chitoshi Yanaga, *Big Business in Japanese Politics* (New Haven: Yale University Press, 1968); T.J. Pempel, "The Bureaucratization of Policymaking in Postwar Japan," *American Journal of Political Science* Vol. 18 (November 1974):647–64; Ehud Harari, "Japanese Politics of Advice in Comparative Perspective: A Framework for Analysis and a Case Study," *Public Policy* Vol. 22 (Fall 1974):537–77; Chalmers Johnson, "The Reemployment of Retired Government Bureaucrats in Japanese Big Business," *Asian Survey* Vol. 14 (November 1974):953–65, inter alia.

[12] Nathaniel B. Thayer, *How the Conservatives Rule Japan* (Princeton: Princeton University Press, 1969); Haruhiro Fukui, *Party in Power* (Canberra: Australian National University Press, 1970).

and society integral to Calvin or Rousseau, rather than the model of overlapping checks and balances called for by Locke, Montesquieu, or Madison.

With the defeat of Japan in World War II and the subsequent US Occupation, a number of steps were initially taken to reduce the relative power of the state. A new Constitution embodied the principle of popular sovereignty. A list of citizens' rights and civil liberties was enumerated. The parliament was designated the "highest organ of state power" and its powers were strengthened. State bureaucrats ceased to be the servants of the emperor and the state and became instead "servants of the whole community." Yet despite such changes, no major effort was made to reduce the phenomenal powers of the state bureaucracy through which the Occupation forces were compelled to operate.[13] Then, with the establishment of a Communist government in China and the outbreak of the Cold War, America's aims shifted from the "democratization and demilitarization" of Japan to the creation of a strong anti-Communist ally. Enthusiasm waned for the initial efforts to reduce the powers of the national government and its financial and commercial allies. Instead, numerous checks were reinstated on the powers of organized labor, the left-wing parties it supported, local governments, and other competing centers of power. Though in some respects not as great as they had been in the 1930s, the powers of the state bureaucracy to define and implement national goals emerged as probably stronger than those in any other major industrial state with a parliamentary system.

Meanwhile, since 1955, the LDP has retained absolute majorities within both Houses of the Diet and, consequently, total control over appointments to all Cabinet posts. Before that time, with only one brief exception, the party's conservative forebears held similar control. As a result, the LDP, somewhat like the Italian Christian Democrats, has come to be the "party of government" with close cooperation between itself and the organs of the state bureaucracy. This includes considerable reliance on the bureaucracy for its party policy proposals, a high degree of interlocking among functional committees, a high degree of movement from the upper echelons of the bureaucracy into the party, LDP control over major civil service promotions, and the like.[14] Thus, the two sectors have become inextricably entwined.

It is worth noting, however, that as regards public policy, the balance between party and bureaucracy is particularly favorable to the latter. Only two party officials, the minister and the parliamentary vice-minister, are at the top of each bureaucratic agency. This is in contrast, for example, to the US with its multiple upper layers of presidential loyalists. Two officials alone to steer organizations composed of talented lifetime bureaucrats would normally be expected to

---

[13] Tsuji Kiyoaki, *Nihon Kanryōsei no Kenkyū* (Tokyo: Tōkyō Daigaku Shuppan, 1969); Ide Yoshinori, "Sengo Kaikaku to Nihon Kanryōsei," in *Sengo Kaikaku*, Vol. 3, *Seiji Katei*, Tōkyō Daigaku Shakai Kagaku Kenkyūjo, ed. (Tokyo: Tōkyō Daigaku Shuppan, 1974), pp. 143–229.
[14] Fukui, *Party in Power;* Thayer; Pempel, "Bureaucratization of Policymaking"; Chalmers Johnson, "Japan: Who Governs? An Essay on Official Bureaucracy," *The Journal of Japanese Studies* Vol. 2 (Autumn 1975):1–28, inter alia.

face difficulties in carrying out drastic policy revisions or detailed day-to-day supervision of policy. Further constraints on party control are set by the fact that, largely as a result of the internal factionalism of the LDP, these officials rarely retain office for more than a single year. With a few notable exceptions, a minister and his parliamentary vice-minister are barely learning the responsibilities and problems of the ministry they allegedly control when they are rotated out to be replaced by novices. Thus, a policy line once decided in Japan tends to be followed without major interruptions. There is no change in the ruling party to bring about redirection, and the capabilities and interests of individual cabinet members to force changes in the directions being taken by the state bureaucracy are significantly circumscribed.

The Japanese bureaucracy obviously does not operate in flagrant disregard of LDP interests and dictates. A close harmony of interests and attitudes between the two is surely more notable.[15] However, Japanese policy, certainly on questions involving the international economy, tends as a consequence to be characterized far more by the continuity and consistency associated with bureaucratic generation and maintenance than with the more erratic and occasionally popularly motivated policies that are often made at the direction of a new cabinet or a new chief executive in other industrialized societies. Characteristic of the latter category would be Prime Minister Wilson's initial opposition and subsequent support for devaluation of the pound, President Nixon's decision to restrict textile imports as a mechanism to appease the contributors to his successful "Southern electoral strategy," or Willy Brandt's intensifying of West Germany commercial relations with the East.

In this regard, Japanese economic policy has been notable for its continuity and internal consistency. The most central concern of the Japanese state, both prewar and postwar, has been economic development. In the Meiji Period, this meant rapid, catch-up industrialization. Immediately after World War II, it meant economic recovery and the redevelopment and improvement of the prewar industrial machine. By the 1960s, it meant large-scale economic growth based on high technology industries.[16] In all instances, policy implementation has required a meshing of domestic and foreign economic policies.

Throughout modern Japanese history, the government bureaucracy has played a key role in economic policy, though only in the earliest periods did it become involved in the direct management of key industries.[17] Typically, it has

---

[15] Pempel, "Bureaucratization of Policymaking," takes up the reasons for some of the harmony.
[16] Thomas C. Smith, *Political Change and Industrial Development in Japan: Government Enterprise, 1868–1880* (Stanford: Stanford University Press, 1955); Norman; Lockwood, *Economic Development of Japan;* Lockwood, ed., *State and Economic Enterprise;* Hugh T. Patrick, "The Phoenix Risen from the Ashes: Postwar Japan," in *Modern East Asia: Essays in Interpretation,* James B. Crowley, ed. (New York: Harcourt, Brace and World, 1970): pp. 298–335, inter alia.
[17] Smith; K. Bieda, "Economic Planning in Japan," *Economic Record* Vol. 45 (June

relied on a close coordination of actions with big industry and big finance to insure the implementation of policies beneficial to the latter, and by extension in the eyes of government, to the nation as a whole. Once a conservative accommodation was reached between large landowners and urban industrialists at the end of the nineteenth century, the conservative political parties came to play a comfortable brokerage role among these key sectors and big agriculture. This broker's role has been continued by the presently ruling LDP. Like the Italian CD, the LDP draws the bulk of its electoral support from rural sectors while its financial support comes from big business and big finance. Because of its controlling position in government, the LDP can provide public policies directed at meeting the demands of both sectors.

As a consequence, though Japan is distinctly pluralistic, there has been a consistently close relationship between the state bureaucracy, ruling politicians, and big business. Japan never developed the strong laissez-faire traditions of England and the United States. Its period of early industrialization did not witness anything comparable to the autonomous American, British, or German industrialists forging paths fundamentally independent of their respective states or dragging hesitant anti-industrial and agriculturally oriented governments behind them. Nor was its industrial development hampered, as in the French Third and Fourth Republics, by a retarded business sector dominated by small and medium-sized firms able to rely on the state in their efforts to resist plant and scale improvements that would bring them up to a more internationally competitive scale of production. Instead, the Japanese government has always been a conspicuous and active presence, moving the nation's industrialization forward, consistently aware of the country's comparative international position, ever desirous of retaining or improving on it. Japan thus went directly from an agrarian feudal economy to a moderately planned industrial economy without being impeded by the constraining facade of a "free market" industrial economy. Businessmen in Japan, as elsewhere, frequently complain of undue government interference in what are seen to be private matters. They frequently seek to enlist political party allies in minimizing government direction. Moreover, the business sector has long held a position of tremendous influence vis-à-vis both parties and government agencies. Despite those factors, the relationship between these sectors has been based more on mutual dependence and common interest than on an antagonism born of radically different orientations.[18]

Japan is frequently characterized as having an economy with a dual structure. But "dualism" in Japan does not refer to the gap between an agrarian, single-product hinterland and a more commercialized urban sector. It refers rather to the fact

---

1969):181–205; Kozo Yamamura, *Economic Policy in Postwar Japan* (Berkeley: University of California Press, 1967); Haruhiro Fukui, "Economic Planning in Postwar Japan: A Case Study in Policy Making," *Asian Survey* Vol. 12 (April 1972):327–48.

[18] Yanaga; Gerald L. Curtis, "Big Business and Political Influence," in *Modern Japanese Organization and Decision-Making,* Ezra Vogel, ed., (Berkeley: University of California Press, 1975), pp. 33–70.

that Japanese business is composed of two sectors. The first is large-scale in capitalization, highly technology intensive, and managerially efficient. Most typically, it includes the several dozen Japanese firms in Fortune's International 500 and their imitators. The second sector is numerically larger and is composed of smaller, less efficient, labor-intensive firms that employ the bulk of the Japanese private labor force.

Such a wide range of industrial structures is by no means unique to Japan and the percentage of employees in Japanese manufacturing enterprises of fewer than 100 employees is only slightly higher than in Italy and France. It is, however, considerably higher than in the US, the UK, or West Germany.[19]

What is more interesting in the Japanese case is that both types of firms coexist within the same industrial sectors with wide wage differentials separating the two.[20] The smaller and medium-sized firms account for over 70 percent of Japan's total output in light industries and over 50 percent of the country's total output,[21] figures higher than is often assumed. Yet while many of these firms produce finished products for limited and local markets, far more are subcontractors with close and rather permanent affiliations with the much larger firms, particularly firms employing over 1,000. These larger companies, even though they constitute only 0.1 percent of the total number of firms, employ 16 percent of the nonagricultural labor force and account for 27.5 percent of the total output.[22]

Most of Japan's largest 100 firms own at least 10 percent of the capital in from 11 to 200 other firms with a startling increase in such ownership during the decade of the 1960s.[23] Hence, "business" is not a unified sector in Japan (if ever it is elsewhere). While Japanese business certainly manifests competition among different industries, a more central distinction in business orientation and influence is firm size. The general pattern of industrial organization and firm interrelationships in Japan involves a broad base of many small satellite firms linked collectively and hierarchically to a limited number of vastly larger parent firms. The lines of political influence run in the opposite direction: the small number of larger parent firms is central in the shaping of Japanese economic policy while the larger number of small firms is often forced to bear the major burdens of any economic dislocations caused by these policies.[24]

---

[19] Yano Tsuneta Kinenkai, ed., *Nihon Kokusei Zue 1976* (Tokyo: Kokuseisha, 1976), p. 326 (hereafter *Zue*).

[20] Shimura Takao, *Nihon Keizai no Kōzō Hendō* (Tokyo: Mineruba Shobō, 1973), pp. 40–42. See also Andrea Boltho, *Japan: Economic Survey, 1953–1973* (London: Oxford University Press, 1975), p. 28; *The Industrial Policy of Japan* (Paris: OECD, 1972), esp. Chapter 4.

[21] Ibid., p. 70.

[22] *Zue*, p. 324.

[23] Kozo Yamamura, "Structure is Behavior: An Appraisal of Japanese Economic Behavior, 1960 to 1972," *The Japanese Economy in International Perspective*, Isaiah Frank, ed. (Baltimore: Johns Hopkins Press, 1975), p. 70. See also Shimura, pp. 29–39. Okuma and Tsujimura, Chapter 7.

[24] One example of this can be found in technology usage and diffusion; see Saito Masamu, "Diffusion Mechanisms of Technology and Industrial Transformation: Case of Small Scale

Industries in Japan, as elsewhere, are linked through trade associations. The more than 600 product-specific trade associations in chemicals, steel, textiles, electronics, heavy machinery, shipbuilding, insurance, and the like are central to industry's official contacts with government agencies. Dominated for the most part by their larger member firms, such associations gather a wide range of data and provide technical information and market development strategies for their memberships. In addition, they serve to consolidate membership opinion in matters of relevant government policy and function as a two-way pipe line between their memberships and governmental agencies.

Approximately 100 of the major trade associations and about 750 of the major public and private corporations in Japan are organized into the national peak association of industry, the Federation of Economic Organizations (FEO), which maintains a substantial staff in Tokyo and close liaison with the key sectors of business. It engages in a wide range of contacts with government officials on macroeconomic policy. A host of functional committees meets on an almost constant basis with various government officials and agencies at all levels.[25] Also extremely influential in the shaping of macro-level economic policy are the Japan Committee for Economic Development (JCED) and the Federation of Employers Associations (FEA), the latter also acting as business's major organizational bulwark against organized labor.

These trade and peak business associations provide a wide range of services for their memberships and a variety of inputs to government. But in addition to pushing membership opinions up to the government level, they also are conduits to insure industrial compliance with government policy. This has been particularly important for insuring such broad business conformity and harmony with government direction as has occurred.

Special mention should also be given to an additional, uniquely Japanese element of the business sector: the trading company. Only a few parallel institutions exist in the world, none in major industrial states.[26] Though there are over 6,000 trading companies in Japan, ten majors dominate the picture with Mitsubishi Shoji, Mitsui Bussan, Marubeni, and C. Itoh perhaps the most well-known internationally. As a term, "trading company" is something of a misnomer, suggesting that such a concern performs no more than a brokering function. Instead, the major Japanese trading companies have worldwide networks providing a wide range of services. These include research and development, export-import financing, transportation, domestic commercial transactions, joint ventures organization, third party trade, major overseas construction, and information gathering.

---

Industries in Japan," in *Transfer of Technology for Small Industries* (Paris: OECD, 1974).

[25] Gerald L. Curtis, in Vogel, p. 55.

[26] On the trading companies elsewhere, see K. Bieda, *The Structure and Operation of the Japanese Economy* (New York: Wiley, 1970), p. 203. The only exceptions he notes are United Africa and Swiss Trading Corporations, both in South Africa, and Société Général in Belgium.

The top ten handle 50 percent of Japan's exports, 60 percent of the country's imports, and about 20 percent of domestic wholesale transactions. The total value of their operations is twice the national budget and about 30 percent of GNP. Obviously, they are in a position to play a key role in both domestic and foreign economic policy.[27] Mitsui Bussan's 350,000 kilometer communications network, for example, is more extensive than that of the US State Department, the Japanese Foreign Ministry, or any major news service. It is topped only by that of the US CIA. As a result, Mitsui has information about a wide variety of international political conditions, business opportunities, technological developments, changes in monetary movements, and so forth, often on an instantaneous basis. Because of their ability to satisfy on an international basis the needs of both, the trading companies also play an important role in minimizing the tensions between industries which are primarily export-oriented and those which are primarily import-oriented. Most trading companies, like other big firms, are tied to a single major bank and form part of the integrative pattern of Japanese banking and commerce. Thus, these firms are in a position to play a central role in advancing Japan's trade interests, technological development, and overseas investment opportunities.

The final major conservative camp actors of significance to Japanese foreign economic policy are the financial institutions. The Japanese banking system is among the most centralized and controllable in the world. At the top of the hierarchy stands the Bank of Japan, which is 55 percent government-owned and has close ties to the Ministry of Finance.[28] It is occasionally referred to disparagingly as no more than a single section in one of Finance's several bureaus. Given the high liquidity of the Japanese economy as a result of the extremely limited amount of negotiable debt and the virtual absence of a private capital market, the Bank of Japan has become the single tap through which virtually the entire Japanese monetary and credit supply must flow. Indeed, the Bank of Japan can be characterized as virtually the sole lender in Japan, rather than the "lender of last resort" as in the case of central banks in many other systems.[29] At the same time, borrowing from the Bank of Japan is a privilege, not a right. The Bank of Japan controls almost the entire credit supply by a variety of techniques including reserve use, lending, and alteration of the discount rate. In order to guarantee future borrowing capabilities, most banks must therefore remain consistently sensitive to the Bank of Japan's overt and indirect policy preferences.

Below the Bank of Japan in size and prestige are the slightly more than a

---

[27] Kikuiri Ryūsuke, "*Shōsha:* Organizers of the World Economy," Frank Baldwin, trans., *The Japan Interpreter* Vol. 8 (Autumn 1973):354. On Japanese trading companies see also "Trading Houses in Japan," *The Oriental Economist* Vol. 38 (January 1970):37–38; Morihisa Emori, "The Japanese General Trading Company," in C. Fred Bergsten, ed., *Toward a New World Trade Policy: The Maidenhead Papers* (Boston: Lexington, 1975), pp. 127–35.

[28] Dan Fenno Henderson, *Foreign Enterprise in Japan* (Chapel Hill: University of North Carolina Press, 1973), p. 135. On the Bank and its role, see also Gardner Ackley and Hiromitsu Ishi, "Fiscal, Monetary and Related Policies," in *Asia's New Giant,* Hugh Patrick and Henry Rosovsky, eds. (Washington: Brookings Institution, 1976), pp. 153–247.

[29] Boltho, p. 120.

dozen city or commercial banks. Well below these are the local and trust banks. It is the city banks which provide the bulk of the major loans to corporations. Most of the money loaned comes from the Bank of Japan, and all city banks are permanently in its debt. Hence, they are well-tuned and receptive instruments in the overall orchestration of governmental policy.

Though most corporations attempt to develop and maintain relations with more than one city bank, there is almost inevitably a major imbalance in their distribution of business. Most of a corporation's commercial transactions are handled through one city bank as are most of its borrowings, and the individual city banks, as a result, form the core institutions in many of the commercial-financial linkages known as *keiretsu*. These links tend to insure credit for firms only in accordance with broader policies of the Bank of Japan and the government. Since there is no firm line of credit on the US pattern, business firms, like the banks themselves, can only get the monies they desire in accordance with their willingness to act in conjunction with official directions.[30]

Because of the extremely high debt-equity ratio in Japan, the entire economy can be shifted drastically in a short time by a slight change in the monetary policies of the Bank of Japan. Monetary policy has thus been a key tool of economic policy in Japan. A modest alteration of the discount rate, for example, which might take months to be felt in other countries, has an almost instant effect in Japan. Such changes are passed from the Bank of Japan through the city banks and on to key corporations with a startling swiftness. The banks thus play a central economic role, albeit one of significantly less autonomy and independence from government than their German counterparts.

Labor has been the most fundamentally excluded sector from this dynamic coalition of government, the conservative parties, big business, and big finance. From its first appearance just after the turn of the century, the labor movement has been embued with a doctrine of class conflict; and the strength it began to gain during the late 1930s contributed significantly to the country's overall move toward the right. The labor movement and the political left were effectively suppressed under the wartime Imperial Rule Assistance Association, and labor's claim to political legitimacy was unrecognized. However, suppression failed to resolve the essential division between capital and labor.

The problems between the two sectors reemerged under the Occupation, which initially encouraged the widespread formation of unions and the legitimization of the union movement. But the Occupation's subsequent policy shift against the left and toward the conservatives was coupled with efforts to weaken the labor movement.[31] Nonetheless, organized labor had gained considerable strength in a

[30] Henry C. Wallich and Mable I. Wallich, "Banking and Finance," in Patrick and Rosovsky, pp. 293–98, deals with the formation of *keiretsu*.

[31] Ōkōchi Kazuo, *Sengo Nihon no Rōdō Undō* (Tokyo: Iwanami Shoten, 1955); Ōkōchi Kazuo and Matsuo Hiroshi, *Nihon Rōdō Kumiai Monogatari: Shōwa* (Tokyo: Chikuma Shobō, 1965).

few short years and has since come to play an undeniably active role in Japanese politics. Still, it has never returned to the position of power and legitimacy it enjoyed during the first few years in the Occupation.

Japanese labor is organized into several major national federations. Union membership is approximately 35 percent of the work force which is comparable to West Germany (37 percent) and higher than the US (30 percent). Despite this, Japanese labor plays nothing like the role of its counterparts in these less polarized industrial states. The national labor federations have been oriented toward ideological and national level political issues while the individual member unions, especially the private sector unions, have been dominated by bread and butter concerns and a high level of company loyalty. Linkages between the two levels of union organization are weak. As a result, it is difficult for the national federations to guarantee cooperation from member unions on federation policy. The major unions, in turn, cannot rely on strong federation support to prevent management-led efforts to replace them with counter unions more conservative politically and more loyal to the company's economic interests.[32] Thus, the pattern of labor organization contrasts with that of business. Business is dominated by close links between small and large firms who cooperate in a relationship of greatest benefit to the larger firms. In the case of labor, the general links are weaker, with each level pursuing different goals: ideology and high politics for the federations, bread and butter concerns for the member unions. Ultimately, both patterns of organization benefit the larger business firms. Small businesses provide indirect and cheaper labor supplies plus a safety valve during economic downturns. Unions in the factories of large firms can be counted on to follow an economic, rather than a political, strategy of bargaining and to retain a high stake in the ultimate economic success of the firm.

Throughout the postwar period, the national federations have consistently supported leftist political parties, most notably the Japan Socialist Party, Japan's largest opposition party. But although the party has rather consistently drawn in the neighborhood of one-third of the total vote, it has been completely shut out of formal power. As a result, Japan, during the entire period since 1947, has never had a government which has included political parties receiving substantial support from organized labor. Even in France and Italy where political cleavages bear some similarities to the Left-Right, labor-capital divisions of Japan, certain portions of the labor movements have supported parties included in the government. In Japan, by way of contrast, organized labor and the parties of the left have failed to gain the combination of legitimacy and formal governmental participation that has characterized their counterparts in all other major industrial societies.

---

[32] See the case study in Robert E. Cole, *Japanese Blue Collar* (Berkeley: University of California Press, 1971). On unions more generally see also Alice Cook, *An Introduction to Japanese Trade Unionism* (Ithaca: Cornell University Press, 1966); K. Okochi et al., *Workers and Employers in Japan* (Princeton and Tokyo: Princeton University Press and Tokyo University Press, 1974). See also M.Y. Yoshino, *Japan's Managerial System: Tradition and Innovation* (Cambridge: MIT Press, 1968).

It would be totally erroneous to imply that the Japanese labor movement or the political left in the country are without power or influence. Through confrontation tactics, they have checked many government activities to which they have been opposed. Through personal intervention and quiet compromise, they have influenced many government decisions, often without acquiring public credit for such influence.[33] Still, as constant "outs," they have far less leverage in the formal halls of policy making than is true of organized labor or leftist parties in other parliamentary democracies.

The picture that emerges of Japanese domestic politics, therefore, is one of two antagonistic "camps," each relatively strongly united internally and simultaneously strongly opposed to the other. True and significant as this is, it is important to note that elements of Japanese policy making and Japanese politics, including foreign economic policy, reflect more than simply the division between organized labor and organized capital. Fundamental as this division is to policy content, other lines of conflict appear on a variety of component issues. In addition to the broad link between big business, big finance, and the state bureaucracy, for example, there are a number of subsidiary links and divisions. The Finance Ministry, for instance, is particularly closely tied to the Japanese banking groups, while the Ministry of International Trade and Industry (MITI) is much more intimately linked to the major enterprises, trade associations, and the peak associations of big business. The Ministry of Agriculture and Forestry is closely linked to the peak farm cooperatives, the Ministry of Transportation to the shipping and auto industries. Within these individual ministries as well, particularly strong links are often formed between functional agencies and specific private sectors, such as those between the Ships Division of the Ministry of Transportation, the private Japan Motor Boat Racing Association, the trade association for the shipbuilding industry, and the related transportation committees of the Diet and the LDP. Meanwhile, the Foreign Ministry, which of course plays a variety of important roles in foreign economic policy, has quite different and usually much weaker constituencies on the domestic front. So too does the Fair Trade Commission (FTC) which, while not at all central to foreign economic policy per se, has responsibilities in overseeing monopoly prevention and cartel creation. These functions, in turn, have been central to foreign economic policy.

Frequently, such alignments have led to conflicts over policy specifics reflecting particularistic interests within the broader consensus. Not infrequently, one ministry and its allies are pitted against another and its allies. This has been particularly the case in battles between MITI and the Finance Ministry over tax incentives to businesses engaged in exports or between MITI and the Foreign Ministry over concessions to offer in trade, aid, and capital import policies. Other conflicts have occurred between the FTC and "the economic ministries" over

---

[33] This point is developed in T.J. Pempel, "The Dilemma of Parliamentary Opposition in Japan," *Polity* Vol. 8 (Fall 1975):63–79.

industrial rationalization and cartelization and between the Finance Ministry and the Ministry of Agriculture and Forestry over food imports, to cite only some of the more prominent examples.

Serious as certain of these inter-ministerial struggles have been in many cases, they have often been highly fortuitous and integrative in many aspects of overall policy. For example, the Foreign Ministry's orientation toward the improvement of Japan's relations with other industrial states has made it something of an advocate of a more open economy. MITI's links with big industry work to insure that such advocacy does not damage domestic industrial interests. The Finance Ministry, because of its conservative fiscal concerns and links to banking, seeks to guarantee that a balance be struck between the internationally or domestically desirable and the fiscally feasible.

Thus, an emphasis on internal consensus and broad agreement, particularly within the conservative coalition, should not obliterate the importance of many of the divisions that also occur among members of that coalition. The Japanese conservative camp is composed of multiple actors with their own particularistic interests and perspectives, many of which are not readily reconcilable. And it is a self-serving mistake of the first order to contend in a simplistic fashion that some unified automaton called "Japan, Inc." runs the country, devoid of division and seeking only the monomaniacal expansion of its own undeviating view of the world. Detailed case studies of almost any two randomly selected elements of Japanese foreign economic policy reveal different alliances and divisions within the conservative camp. In turn, however, such divisions, significant as they may be on any particular case, still occur within a broad consensus and the policies which the government has followed have been sufficiently coherent and consistent to suggest that this consensus is more significant than the divisions which exist within it. The old slogan of Gōto Shōjiro remains relevant to intra-conservative tensions: *Daidō Shōi*, differences on small things; agreement on large things. Most of the intra-conservative differences on foreign economic policy have been subordinated to broader agreements and there has been a general consensus among its key sectors in forging integrated policy among component issues.

Consequently, most aspects of foreign policy, economic policy, and foreign economic policy have been characterized by a pro-business conservatism that has been largely untempered for the bulk of the period since the end of the Occupation by either the pro-left or social welfare policies sought by labor and the opposition parties. The Japanese government, moreover, has not taken on the role of government as referee between disputes among forces in the private sector in anything like the manner of governments in the US or England. In neither the prewar nor postwar periods did it function in the capacity of a liberal state in Lowi's sense of that term.[34] Rather, it demonstrated an unmitigated, albeit varying, confidence in the need for state authority, providing itself with an impressive armory of weapons

---

[34] Theodore J. Lowi, *The End of Liberalism* (New York: Norton, 1969).

for intervention in the economy to promote its conservative, pro-business conception of the national interest. Neither industry, finance, nor the conservative political parties have seriously challenged the legitimacy or the use of these powers; bargaining and cooperation among all has been the norm. This feature has significantly shaped Japan's foreign economic policy in virtually all areas including commerce, monetary policy, overseas aid, technology importation, and capital transfers. It has also provided the basis for a foreign economic policy which has fused these component policies in a manner more coherent and resilient to pressures from international bodies and other states than those in perhaps any other major industrial nation-state during the same period.

## III Foreign economic policy

Faced with a combination of international weaknesses and a serious ideologically-based threat to its own domestic hegemony, the conservative coalition responded with highly creative policies integrating foreign and domestic economic policies designed for its own benefit. It did this through a policy of rapid economic growth based on a strategy of selective development of "key sectors." This policy relied on the importation of technology and raw materials and the export of high quality manufactured products. Throughout, the policies depended on labor's minimal ability to claim a full share of any economic successes achieved and the absence of any political need to make major governmental contributions to improved social overhead and social welfare. This policy has been possible because the state bureaucracy could restrict both access to Japan from outside, and the access of domestic political actors to the outside world. The government has thus served as a doorman between domestic Japanese society and the international arena, determining what could enter or leave Japan and on what conditions. While such control assuredly did not insulate Japan fully from international developments, it filtered their impact through the Japanese state. This gave the state a considerable degree of control over the way in which external impacts were felt.

Macro-level economic growth has been the central political goal to which virtually all other Japanese policies have been subordinated during the postwar period. Foreign economic policies have been integral to this overall growth. As such, Japanese foreign economic policy has been neither isolated from, nor contradictory to, domestic economic policies. Nor has it been directed more fundamentally at achieving security, military, or other external political and noneconomic aims.[35] Whatever visions Japanese conservatives may have had of a grandeur long since lost or of international laurels still to be gained, any such realization was to be preconditioned by economic growth. Grandstand gestures, ideological interventions, and imperial pretentions of such economic impracticality as flights to the

---

[35] K. Bieda, *The Structure and Operation of the Japanese Economy.*

moon, economic blockades, or a *force de frappe* were avoided.[36] International glory was domesticated and treated as measurable through increases in GNP.

Such circumspect policies were, of course, rooted in domestic practicalities. Even though Japan now has the seventh largest conventional military force in the world, a significant body of organized opinion in Japan, especially as articulated by organized labor and the political left, holds such forces to be unconstitutional. There is a substantial inclination on the part of the public toward one or another variant of pacifism, with strong constraints on the development of, say, a nuclear capability or the dispatch of military forces overseas. Moreover, the Japanese economy was devastated by the end of World War II. Capital was depleted and the industrial infrastructure was almost totally destroyed. Labor productivity and technological advancement were low. Nearly one-half of the work force was in agriculture. Hence, imperial gestures were highly impractical then and are only slightly more so now. As a result, any explicitly "foreign" component of Japan's foreign economic policy has been quite limited and has almost always been directed toward activities that would contribute in one capacity or another to the overall advancement of the domestic economy.

The economic nightmare that faced Japan at the end of the war continued until the US Occupation shifted its aims toward the promotion of Japanese economic growth and recovery and instituted the major fiscal and monetary stringencies which came to be known as the Dodge Line. Stimulated by the economic demands of the Korean War and aided by a relaxation of US controls toward the end of the Occupation, the Japanese government began to move toward the two related economic goals that continued to dominate official thinking at least until 1971: economic growth and the transformation of the industrial structure.

As early as 1951, the government demonstrated an unwillingness to accept short-term economic logic. It refused to concede the country's limited natural resources and inadequate capital supply and take advantage of its ample, well-trained labor supply to concentrate on the production of toys, textiles, and Christmas tree ornaments. Nor was there any inclination at high governmental levels among big finance or industry toward the "open market" or "free trade." As Kindleberger has noted, these concepts imply little more than protection for the established exporter, yet "the headstart is regarded as a divine right, and [protection] to let a foreign industry gather strength to meet import competition as an offense against morality."[37] Instead, through a combination of policies, the government sought to restructure the economy sector by sector in the interest of creating capital and technology intensive industries which would insure long-term benefits and would provide the potential for continued economic expansion.

---

[36] See, inter alia, Robert Gilpin, *U.S. Power and the Multinational Corporation* (New York: Basic Books, 1975); Robert Gilpin, *France in the Age of the Scientific State* (Princeton: Princeton University Press, 1968); Stephen Blank, "Britain: The Politics of Foreign Economic Policy, the Domestic Economy, and the Problem of Pluralistic Stagnation," in this volume.
[37] Charles P. Kindleberger, *Power and Money* (New York: Basic Books, 1970), p. 120.

Though by no means the sole motivation for the rationalization, oligopolization, and cartelization that became an integral part of the sectoral development policy, the initial justification was to allow the country to take advantage of economies of scale in the purchase of raw materials and overseas technology. In this way, Japan could reduce its international vulnerabilities and, simultaneously, insure the highest degree of international competitiveness for the exports to be produced by the modernized sectors. The policy thus clearly aimed at benefitting the larger sectors of the economy first. The ultimate justification of such an imbalanced approach was the trickle-down theory whereby benefits achieved initially by leading sectors would somehow eventually benefit all others in Japan. Yet, until the trickle reached bottom, gratification would have to be deferred.

The policy of economic and industrial transformation involved a complex meshing of a variety of domestic and foreign economic policies. The results were much like a multi-colored ball of wax. The influence and presence of single hues are discernible; but, more often, colors blur into one another creating combinations that deny the isolability of any one. Central to the overall policy was the selective development of particular key industries and economic sectors. In the earliest stages, this involved such basic items as steel, electric power, coal, shipbuilding, and chemicals, as well as such quality exports as binoculars, electronic equipment, and motorcycles. Gradually, as the technology for these products was improved and their markets were secured, interest and resources were redirected toward automobiles, heavy machinery, aircraft, and on to atomic power and computers. With key industries leading the way, attention was focused on attaining high levels of economic growth, particularly through the mechanisms of indicative planning.[38]

In 1950, the government issued its first economic plan aimed at the modernization of industrial plants, the promotion of foreign trade, and the reduction of dependence on foreign imports. One year later, the government began laying plans for the reorganization of key industries to be aided by large infusions of public capital.[39] A series of industrial reorganizations and similarly oriented economic plans followed. The best-known internationally was the "Plan to Double the National Income," issued in 1960. And while there have been multiple twists in the path, it has been these goals of economic growth and industrial transformation that the government and organized big business have followed into the 1970s.

Organized along functional lines comparable to those of major industrial sectors, the Ministry of International Trade and Industry was a key mover in these reorganizations. It set numerical goals for output and reductions of unit costs. In conjunction with the Ministry of Finance, it provided financial assistance through low-interest government loans, aid in securing private loans, accelerated depreciation, and tax-free reserves. In addition, by sustaining an on-going system of formal

[38] On Japanese economic planning see, inter alia, Bieda, "Economic Policy in Japan"; Fukui, "Economic Planning in Postwar Japan"; Tsunehiko Watanabe, "National Planning and Economic Growth in Japan," in *Quantitative Planning of Economic Policy,* Bert Hickman, ed. (Washington: Brookings Institution, 1965), pp. 233–51.
[39] Ibid.

and informal committees, both ministries facilitated the constant exchange of opinion among government, big business, and finance.[40] Moreover, selected firms were given preference in the procurement of scarce raw materials. They were also aided in acquiring necessary overseas technology, duty free equipment imports, tax subsidies, and certain exceptions from anti-monopoly regulations. As noted, there was an increasing sophistication in the industries so chosen, though at the time each was selected, it was considered to be a key developing sector in the national and world economies.

MITI's efforts at rationalizing industrial sectors rested heavily on monopolization and cartelization in order to take advantage of economies of scale in production and division of domestic and world market shares in sales. Although monopolies had been banned under the early policies of the US Occupation, these policies were reversed by the Americans and the most salient features of early anti-monopoly policies were eliminated.[41] With the creation of the Export and Import Trading Act of August 1952, the Japanese government explicitly permitted exporters to enter agreements on price, quantity, quality, design, or other matters in relation to products for export. All that was necessary was post hoc notification of MITI which, in turn, was to notify the Fair Trade Commission.

Thereafter, cartels were formed under a variety of laws authorizing them in specific fields such as electronics, machine tools, fertilizers, marine products, and the like. In conjunction with these efforts, a host of major mergers was carried out, largely under MITI's auspices. The objective was to rationalize particular fields such as automobiles, steel, and computers.[42] During the 1960s, upwards of 500 major and minor mergers occurred each year; by the end of the 1960s and the beginning of the 1970s, they were taking place at the rate of 1,000 plus annually.[43] In 1960, 93 percent of Japan's companies had been capitalized at less than ¥ 500,000. By 1974, this figure had dropped to 76 percent. At the same time, the number of corporations capitalized at over ¥ 1 billion more than quadrupled.[44] The overall movement toward concentration was virtually unswerving. By 1974, five corporations or fewer controlled 90 percent or more of the steel, beer, nylon, acryl, aluminum ore, auto, and pane glass industries.[45]

[40] On MITI see Noguchi Yūichirō, *Nihon no Keizai Nashonarizumu* (Tokyo: Diyamondo-sha, 1976), esp. Chapter 1; Honda Yasuharu, *Nihon Neokanryō-ron* (Tokyo: Kōdansha, 1974), Chapter 1; Kusayanagi Daizō, *Kanryō Ōkokuron* (Tokyo: Bungei Shungū, 1975), pp. 251–77. See also the forthcoming essay by Chalmers Johnson on MITI in Robert Scalapino, *The Foreign Policy of Modern Japan* (Berkeley and Los Angeles: University of California Press, forthcoming).
[41] Eleanor Hadley, *Antitrust in Japan* (Princeton: Princeton University Press, 1970). Also Kozo Yamamura, *Economic Policy in Postwar Japan.*
[42] Eugene J. Kaplan, *Japan: The Government-Business Relationship* (Washington: US Government Printing Office, 1972), pp. 77–158.
[43] Kōsei Torihiki Iinkai, *Kōsei Torihiki Iinkai Nenji Hōkoku* (Tokyo: Ōkurashō Insatsu Kyoku, 1975), p. 177.
[44] *Zue*, p. 414.
[45] Ibid., p. 416.

MITI was the prime orchestrator of these policies, retaining throughout a high degree of control over industrial activity through its broad powers "to license and approve" a wide variety of industrial activities. This control was such that any new petroleum refining plant, new dock, or new ship over a certain size required specific MITI authorization.[46]

The success of this domestic sectoral development policy also hinged very much on the ability of the Japanese government to manipulate the interrelationship between the domestic Japanese economy and the broader international market. The government found that it was able to control both what Japan took from the international arena and the conditions under which these items entered Japan. This control also extended to the conditions under which Japanese products found their way into the international marketplace. The government was the well-controlled revolving door providing sole entrance to and exit from Japan.

Central to the overall economic development policy was controlled access to raw materials. Technology, too, had to be acquired, and without its usually automatic accompaniments, foreign capital and managerial control. Since major expenditures were to be made for raw materials and technology, considerable effort had to be devoted to the promotion of exports in order to reduce the deficit in Japan's balance of payments. Finally, to complete the circle, a drastic overhaul of Japan's domestic industry was critical for exports to be internationally competitive. This required new capital, raw materials, technology, and protection. Hence, achievement of the desired economic changes necessitated a good deal of state direction and coordination among related policies, domestic and foreign.

On the basic problem of importing raw materials, the combination of government priority-setting and controls, plus private sector support, is clear. Formally until 1961 and informally for long thereafter, the government maintained strict controls over Japanese imports. This was achieved largely through import licenses and quotas on specific items. Consumer products were tightly restricted and given low priority while raw materials and the machinery for industrial development were emphasized. Because of Japan's weak foreign exchange position until the late 1960s, direct investments overseas were officially discouraged in almost all areas except raw materials extraction. Even so, most of the items Japan needed were acquired on the world market. Trading companies complemented government information agencies in searching for the most attractive world prices, and government funding policies and foreign exchange quotas were directed toward acquiring only essential items. Raw materials that entered Japan were subject to the strictest of government controls to insure that they were distributed in conjunction with established sectoral priorities. In 1962, a list of items which could be imported and whose import was to be encouraged was eliminated in favor of a negative list of restricted products. Nonetheless, close cooperation continued to prevail between

---

[46]Ryutaro Komiya, "Japan and the World Economy," in Bergsten, *Toward a New World Trade Policy*, p. 191.

government and private industry in securing products central to rapid industrial growth and technological transformation.

Parallel to the need to import raw materials was the need to bring in high level technology aimed at improving the level and sophistication of production within selected sectors of Japanese industry. Here, too, the government, in conjunction particularly with the trade associations, exercised tight controls. These included a wide range of directives on the types of technologies most wanted by Japanese firms.[47] The government also sought to insure that only needed technologies entered and that they went to the firms best able to use them. There was a case-by-case screening of all technology agreements until 1968, even though such controls were by then difficult to justify simply in terms of the balance of payments. Japan was the only OECD country to retain controls until that date, and only in 1974 were restrictions lifted on certain other key technology imports.[48] One report indicated that the now famous Sony Corporation had to wait almost two years during the early 1950s to get government approval to import transistor technology because a MITI official had concluded that Sony would be incapable of wisely utilizing this knowledge.[49] When Texas Instruments finally concluded an agreement on semi-conductors, the government, in conjunction with electronics trade associations, insisted that no single Japanese firm be able to monopolize the technology and that the major electronics firms be granted roughly equal access.[50] Moreover, MITI participated directly in many "private" negotiations on royalty rights and territorial sales restrictions in an effort to get the best deals for Japanese industry. It also sought to insure that technology licensing would quickly lead to Japanese absorption of the new information and would allow the Japanese partner to take over complete production at the earliest possible date.

Nevertheless, between 1950 and 1974, over 15,000 type A technology import agreements were reached. They resulted in a major influx of foreign technology critical to a variety of industries.[51] Between 1950 and 1970, Japan spent about $3 billion in technology acquisition.[52] The comparative significance of this mechanism can be seen from Table 1.

In addition to aiding in the development of domestic Japanese industries,

---

[47] Peter Drysdale, ed., *Direct Foreign Investment in Asia and the Pacific* (Sydney: Australian National University Press, 1972); Terutomo Ozawa, *Japan's Technological Challenge to the West, 1950–1974* (Cambridge: MIT Press, 1974), esp. Chapter 2; Merton J. Peck and Shūji Tamura, "Technology," in Patrick and Rosovsky, pp. 525–85.

[48] It was then, for example, that the ban was lifted on computers.

[49] Philip H. Trezise and Yukio Suzuki, "Politics, Government, and Economic Growth in Japan," in Patrick and Rosovsky, p. 798.

[50] Texas Instrument's *Annual Report*; see also *Business Week*, 27 January 1968, p. 132.

[51] G.R. Hall and R.E. Johnson, "Transfers of United States Aerospace Technology to Japan," in *The Technology Factor in International Trade*, Raymond Vernon, ed. (New York: Columbia University Press, 1970), pp. 305–58, provides a detailed assessment of the role within this one area. See also Henderson, p. 229, which notes that 30 percent of Japanese industry operates on foreign technology.

[52] Ibid., p. 87.

Table I  Average annual growth rate in payments for technology

|  | 1961–64 | 1964–67 | 1967–70 |
|---|---|---|---|
| Japan | 11.2 | 15.4 | 21.9 |
| France | 22.1 | 6.4 | 15.0 |
| UK | n.a. | 12.7 | 13.3 |
| US | 16.7 | 10.4 | 9.9 |
| West Germany | n.a. | 7.8 | 16.9 |

Source: Adapted from Merton J. Peck with the collaboration of Shuji Tamura, "Technology," in *Asia's New Giant*, Hugh Patrick and Henry Rosovsky, eds., (Washington, D.C.: Brookings Institution, 1976), p. 532.

licensing arrangements for foreign technology helped to keep down direct imports other than raw materials. A broad range of more direct import restrictions were, however, also widely employed, Cash deposits were required for import licenses to be granted. This provided a serious deterrent in Japan's cash-short economy and was a device particularly suited to the bureaucracy's close control over banks and monetary policy. Tariffs on most manufactured products, particularly consumer goods, were significantly higher than in most other industrial countries during the 1950s and 1960s; even after the Kennedy Round, their general range was still somewhat higher than those of the US, the UK, or the EEC.[53] In addition, the government maintained a wide range of import quotas, quantitative restrictions, and other non-tariff barriers. Many were for the protection of retarded industries and the politically important agricultural sector, but the more central focus was on those infant industries where the Japanese government was seeking to develop international competitiveness. A myriad of bureaucratic regulations accompanied this process. In 1964, the Temporary Commission on Administrative Reform found that there was a combination of over 700 cabinet ordinances, ministerial ordinances, and official notifications concerning these matters.[54]

Because the importation of raw materials was inevitable, most import restrictions applied to consumer and manufacturing products. The result is that Japan has one of the most skewed import-export balances in the industrial world, in terms of commodities. A larger percentage of Japan's total imports is in raw materials than for any other country, while a larger percentage of the total exports is in manufactured goods. This can be seen from Table 2.[55]

[53] Leon Hollerman, "Foreign Trade in Japan's Economic Transition," in Frank, p. 191; Haruko Fukuda, *Japan and World Trade: The Years Ahead* (Westmead: Saxon House, 1973), pp. 77–81; Hayashi and Watanabe, pp. 83–86.

[54] Rinji Gyōsei Chōsakai, *Kyōkan Kyōgōhan Bōeki Kankei Kyoninka Jimu no uchi Kakushōcho ni wataru mono 'Kyōkan Kyōgō' ni kan suri Kaizenan*, Part I (June 1964), passim.

[55] See also Nikkei Bunko, ed., *Bōeki no Chishiki* (Tokyo: Nihon Keizai Shimbunsha, 1973), p. 175, for earlier figures; pp. 165–77, for an analysis.

## Table II  Distribution of exports and imports by commodity

|         | EXPORTS          |                     | IMPORTS          |                     |
|---------|------------------|---------------------|------------------|---------------------|
|         | Percent primary  | Percent manufactured | Percent primary  | Percent manufactured |
| Japan   | 4.3              | 94.6                | 69.0             | 30.6                |
| US      | 32.5             | 64.9                | 32.2             | 65.2                |
| W. Ger. | 8.9              | 89.9                | 39.1             | 58.7                |
| France  | 25.8             | 73.4                | 34.3             | 65.7                |
| England | 13.3             | 84.1                | 42.0             | 57.0                |
| Italy   | 15.9             | 83.9                | 49.3             | 50.5                |

Source: Adapted from *Nihon Kokusei Zue 1976* (Tokyo: Yano Hisashiro Kinenkai, 1976), pp. 180–81.

While it is frequently alleged that Japan's import restrictions were outdone only by its restrictions on the import of foreign capital, in fact, Japan has not been completely reluctant to utilize foreign monies. It took a loan from the World Bank for $40 million to develop electric power as early as 1953, and by 1960, it had borrowed upwards of $150 million from that source.[56] And the Japan Productivity Center was established with $300 million in overseas capital.[57] But the form of such loans simply reinforces the point about the reluctance to allow into the country funds over which the government could not exercise control. These funds, coming as they did essentially on a government-to-government basis, only reinforced the Japanese government's strong control over the nation's economy. In contrast to such funds, which were welcomed, the government was extremely strict in refusing to allow in private funds which could lead to loss of national control over key sectors of the economy such as happened during the Occupation with the oil industry.[58]

There was fear, too, of disruption of both the domestic marketing arrangements and the labor patterns so beneficial to big business. Government and organized business were both reluctant to complicate their close working relationship by the inclusion of major foreign producers. The advantages of foreign, most notably American, firms in technology, capital, and/or marketing could have posed key problems of competition for Japanese industry generally, and they might easily have prevented the entire development of the industries targeted for key economic roles in the future.

A number of severe restrictions on such investment were imposed during the period in question. These ranged from the Foreign Exchange Trade Control Law of

---

[56] Iida Seietsurō, "Nihon Keizai no Kikō to Kōdo Seichō no Shikumi," in *Shōwa no Sengoshi* IV, Ienaga Saburō et al., eds. (Tokyo: Sekibunsha, 1976), pp. 23–29.

[57] Ibid., p. 30.

[58] For an excellent discussion of this problem see Yoshi Tsurumi, "Japan," *Daedalus,* Special Issue: *The Oil Crisis in Perspective* Vol. 104 (Fall 1975): 113–27.

1949 and the Foreign Investment Law through tightly controlled foreign exchange banks. Other restrictions included permission of only yen-based companies (until Japan joined OECD in 1963) and the virtual ban on purely foreign companies until 1967. Subsequently, a combination of technical liberalization plus bureaucratic restrictions and delays was utilized to prevent undesired investments, particularly in the critical sectors of the economy.[59] Thus, by 1968, there were only 51 significant foreign-controlled firms in Japan (50 percent of ownership; ¥ 100 million in capital).[60] Despite the importance of foreign capital for some aspects of Japan's development, the bulk of it came in the form of government-to-government loans or portfolio purchases which lacked managerial control capabilities. Thus, of about $18 billion in total foreign investment in Japan between 1950 and 1971, only about 6 percent involved direct investment which included foreign managerial controls.[61]

It is clear that virtually all of the foreign capital which entered Japan did so in ways that were subject to close scrutiny and regulation by the government. The latter was thus able to develop the industries it deemed critical without the problems of foreign or multinational dominance so prevalent in key sectors of European industry. Meanwhile, available monies were allocated largely in accordance with priorities set by government and organized big business. The Bank of Japan and the related city banks, meanwhile, played the key role both in the distribution of funds, at least as seed money designed to influence credit availability at lower levels, and in the administration of many of the government's foreign exchange and borrowing regulations.

If the government was strict in controlling what came into Japan, it was equally strict in directing what left the country and under what conditions. If the success of its controls over imports of raw materials, technology, capital, and manufactured goods depended heavily on cooperation among government, industry, finance, and the trading companies, the same pattern can be found in controls over exports and capital investment. The government provided a wide range of direct and indirect financial incentives for Japanese exports. Before entering GATT, Japan exempted certain portions of total corporate income based on the firm's export performance. In addition, a "link system" tying import licenses to export performance was begun in 1952.[62] Subsequently, a host of measures involving depreciation, tax deferments, cheap short-term credit, and other indirect subsidies were introduced.[63] In most respects, government assistance in promoting exports

---

[59] Henderson, passim.
[60] Ibid., p. 17.
[61] Ibid.
[62] G.C. Allen, "Japan's Place in Trade Strategy," in *Trade Strategy and the Asia-Pacific Region*, Hugh Colbert, ed. (London: Allen and Unwin, 1970), p. 65. Yoichi Okita, "Japan's Fiscal Incentives for Exports," in Frank, pp. 207–30.
[63] Ibid. The cost of these incentives in terms of lost tax revenues is calculated by the Ministry of Finance annually and from 1962 through 1971 they came to well over $40 billion. Okita, "Japan's Fiscal Incentives . . .," p. 219; my calculations.

took forms parallel to those used in France and Italy. In addition, however, an Export Conference (later renamed the Trade Council) composed of the Prime Minister, relevant ministers, the head of the Bank of Japan, and business leaders, but excluding organized labor, met regularly to examine the best methods of export promotion and to set key goals and directions. The major trading companies, meanwhile, remained in close contact on a daily basis with government officials over major transactions, and administrative guidance on specifics was regularly given.

This variety of assistance made it possible for Japanese export prices to remain virtually stable during the entire postwar period. The country was thus given a strong advantage in price competition and a strong contribution was made to the international success of its exports. Moreover, though Japan's economic growth could not be labeled "export-led," the country was certainly "export conscious," and exports played a central role in domestic economic success. This included an ability to utilize exports to retain production levels in export-oriented firms during domestic slowdowns. This ability was particularly important in helping Japan to pull quickly out of slumps in 1958, 1962, and 1965. In this regard, Japanese policy resembled that of West Germany. Export promotion was also essential to overall economic development in helping Japan to limit its balance of payments deficits which otherwise could have been enormous given the need to import technology and raw materials.

Nowhere can the close cooperation between government and the private financial and commercial sectors, or the coherence of potentially separate elements of the country's foreign economic policies, be better seen than in Japan's "aid" ventures. Japanese overseas aid began with war reparations agreements made with several Southeast Asian countries during the 1950s. Though such reparations were justified as governmental restitution to these countries for damages suffered as a result of World War II, specific details of the payments were developed largely at the initiative of big business.[64] As a result, they proved to be profitable both in gaining access to needed raw materials in Southeast Asia and in providing export markets for Japanese products at a time when the economy was just beginning its subsequent takeoff. "Reparations" came in the form of export credits, tied loans, plant exports, and long-term investment projects. These were not only of direct and immediate benefit to Japanese business at the time but also to a variety of individual businessmen and politicians on both sides of the reparations negotiations. They clearly aided Japan in regaining economic access to Southeast Asia.[65] Businessmen and politicians developed personal ties and communications networks that led to a vast increase in Japanese extraction of raw materials from the area and the

[64] Yanaga, pp. 205 ff.; Jon Halliday and Gavan McCormack, *Japanese Imperialism Today* (Middlesex: Penguin, 1973), pp. 20–23.
[65] Ogawa Kunihiko, *Kuroi Keizai Kyōryoku* (Tokyo: Shimpō Shinsho, 1974), goes into some of the more sordid arrangements involving former prime ministers' benefits from various reparations, for example, based on records of the National Diet. Lawrence Olson, *Japan in Postwar Asia* (New York: Praeger, 1968), also provides some insightful examples of the same.

development of a major export market for Japanese products, plants, and subsequently export capital.[66]

This pattern was followed in subsequent "aid" arrangements throughout the region and later in Latin America. Japan provided various forms of assistance in exchange for the rights to import a specified quota of the country's primary goods and to sell various products. In 1962, for example, 15 percent of the iron ore, 30 percent of the copper ore, 16 percent of the bauxite, and 7 percent of the petroleum which Japan imported were linked to Japan's technical assistance in the production of these resources in less developed countries.[67] Until 1972, "aid" was similarly tied to the purchase of Japanese goods. Less than one-third of the total flow of Japanese aid consisted of pure grants, technical assistance, and contributions to multinational agencies; more than two-thirds was of a purely commercial nature.[68] The only real "aid," namely government assistance, represented a low 0.25 percent of Japan's GNP. This figure stands in contrast to the Development Assistance Committee (DAC) goal of 0.7 percent and is well below that of all other major industrial states with the exception of the US.[69] Mixing commercial interests and "aid" is common to other industrial countries, but Japan's terms have been uniformly recognized as more overtly commercial and its terms for loans more stringent than those of any other industrial state.[70]

Similarly, Japan, though a latecomer to direct overseas investment, managed effectively to integrate this component of policy into its broader aims of gaining access to raw materials, balancing payments, and insuring the success of its exports. The policy-making process also involved an integration of public and private sector activities and an element of domestic political strategy. Balance of payments fears led to strict legal restrictions on most investment activity prior to 1968. Until that time, the value of overseas investments was small and confined mostly to the extractive industries; later some import substitution investments were made in manufacturing. All investment activities were legally to be promotive of exports, non-competitive with domestic firms, and congruent with monetary policy. As

[66] Nishikawa Jun, *Shigen Nashonarizumu* (Tokyo: Diyamondo-sha, 1974), pp. 3–38; Ogawa, passim. In 1975, 37 percent of Japan's exports and 49 percent of its imports came from Asia, *Zue*, p. 147. One-quarter of its direct overseas investments were in South Asia; see Tsūshō Sangyōshō Sangyō Seisakukyoku, *Wagakuni Kigyō no Kaigai Jigyō Katsudō* (Tokyo: Ōkurashō Insatsukyoku, 1975), p. 234.

[67] Robert S. Ozaki, "Japan's Role in Asian Economic Development," *Asian Survey* Vol. 7 (April 1967), p. 241.

[68] Sukehiro Hasegawa, *Japanese Foreign Aid: Policy and Practice* (New York: Praeger, 1975), p. 25.

[69] Ibid.; Hayashi and Watanabe, pp. 244–48: Gaimushō, *Kokusai Kyōryoku Handobukku* (Tokyo: Kokusai Kyōryoku Kenkyūkai, 1975), pp. 624–32; *Kaigai Keizai Kyōryoku Binran 1975–76* (Tokyo: Kaigai Keizai Kyōryoku Kikin Chōsa Kaihatsubu, 1975), pp. 316–63; Tsūshō Sangyōshō Tsūshō Seisakukyoku, *Keizai Kyōryoku no Genjō to Mondaiten* (Tokyo: Okurashō Insatsukyoku, 1975), inter alia.

[70] My thanks to Alan G. Rix for a number of conversations on his on-going research into this area and for several unpublished drafts of papers in which he amply demonstrates this point.

Japan's balance of payments improved, however, and as the supply and cost of labor became less favorable to business, offshore production facilities were set up with government encouragement, largely in Asia and Latin America. Since 1968, overseas investment growth has been staggering. Ventures have been particularly conspicuous in the extractive industries, especially petroleum and copper, again reflecting the overriding concern with raw materials.[71] Yet, particularly since the yen revaluation of 1971, there has been an increased investment in manufacturing industries as Japan, like West Germany, seeks to offset a suddenly "too favorable" balance of trade and to retain sales markets gained earlier. MITI, the Ministry of Finance, and the government generally have explicitly encouraged this sort of investment with such policies as a rise in the rate of tax-deductible loss reserves. Not surprisingly, Japan's direct overseas investments have almost exclusively involved private investment in countries ideologically compatible with Japan's ruling conservatives.[72] In addition, many of Japan's more conspicuous polluters have been moving production facilities abroad with government assistance as the Japanese populace develops an increased sensitivity to some of the more odious accompaniments of the rapid earlier industrialization.

Achievement of the overall success of Japanese foreign economic policy would have been impossible, particularly with the same degree of speed, uniformity, and harmony that occurred, had it not been for the central position of the Japanese state and its close working relationship with the banking system, the trading companies, and the trade associations. To take only a few examples, the rationalization process and the formation of export cartels required a unique blend of governmental direction in setting a wide range of goals and providing a diversity of incentives. Also important were the ability of both government and banking to provide the necessary funds and a willingness on the part of key industrial sectors to accept conditions for all trade members and to insure compliance with trade association practices. It also required that MITI be able to bypass the FTC on problems of cartelization. Given the conservative orientation of the entire government and the broad array of political and financial assets that could be mustered by MITI, FTC opposition to cartels was rarely a genuine problem.

Similarly, technology importation policies also required a strong state and a cooperative business community. The vast international information network of the major trading companies, as well as that of MITI itself, insured that the "right" technology was easier to find. The strong state system made it possible to acquire such technology on terms far better for Japan than similar technology commanded in Europe. Overseas aid, including war reparations and subsequently direct foreign investment, was typically negotiated on a government-to-government basis. It was

[71] Dodwell Marketing Consultants, *Japanese Companies' Overseas Investments* (Tokyo: Dodwell, 1974), p. 6; M.Y. Yoshino, "Japanese Foreign Direct Investment," in Frank, p. 251; *Kaigai Keizai Kyōryoku Binran 1975–76*, pp. 432–33.

[72] Among the most noteworthy are Indonesia, South Korea, and the Philippines. Taiwan does not receive "aid," yet it is the recipient of many generous commercial packages which would appear to be tied to the common conservative and anti-Communist orientations of the leaders of Taiwan and Japan.

always done, however, with a sensitivity to the interests of the particular private firms most likely to be affected.[73]

The results for Japan's economic growth and transformation are generally well-known, but one or two statistics may dramatize them more vividly. Japan's GNP rose approximately six and one-half times between 1952 and 1974, a figure unmatched by any other major industrial democracy.[74] Moreover, the Japanese growth rate was consistently among the highest in the world. In terms of the absolute size of the GNP, during this period Japan moved from being one of the smallest of the medium-sized economies to being the third largest in the world, lagging behind only the US and the USSR.

Within the country, a major transformation took place. In 1950, nearly one-half of the work force was employed in the primary sector; by 1975, this figure was below 13 percent.[75] Between 1955 and 1970, the value share of food and textiles, clothing and leather industries fell from 56 percent of Japan's total industrial production to 34 percent while heavy industry and chemicals rose from 44 percent to 66 percent.[76] During 1961–68 alone, there was a 39 percent structural change in the Japanese economy in favor of heavy and chemical industries. This was over twice as great as that of the next highest OECD member, France, and nearly four times greater than that for the group of OECD countries as a whole.[77]

By the early 1970s, Japan led the world in the production of a wide range of sophisticated products such as ships, radios, cameras, transistorized televisions, commercial motor vehicles, and motorcycles, to name only a few. In exports as well, Japan's development is equally marked. In 1955, it held approximately 2 percent of the total share of world exports. By 1974, the figure had more than tripled to 6.2 percent,[78] putting Japan third, behind only the US and West Germany. During the decade 1960–70 alone, the compound annual growth rate of Japanese exports was 16.9 percent, far above the 9.3 percent world average and well over double the US rate of 7.6 percent. In 1950, seven of Japan's top ten exports were in apparels, toys, staple fabrics and similar items. By 1975, the top ten included only one such item, namely synthetic fibers and fabrics, while steel, shipbuilding, automobiles, and radios headed the list.[79]

---

[73] It is perhaps interesting to note, for example, that a project now under discussion between the Ministry of Transport and the Indonesian government to provide navigation equipment in the Malacca Straits involves equipment that is produced only by Japan's Fujitsū.

[74] My calculations from "Zuhyō ni miru Sengo Sanjūnenkan no Senshin Rokkakoku Keizai no Suii," *Ekonomisuto* 1 March 1976, p. 80.

[75] *Zue*, pp. 96–98.

[76] Christian Sautter, *Japon: Le Prix de la Puissance* (Paris: Editions du Seuil, 1973), translated into Japanese as *Japon: Sono Keizairyōku wa Honmono ka?* (Tokyo: Sangyō Nōritsu Tanki Daigaku Shuppan, 1974), p. 60.

[77] Isoda Keiichirō, *Nihon Bōeki no Mirai* (Tokyo: Tōyō Keizai Shimpōsha, 1972), p. 92.

[78] *Zue*, p. 117.

[79] Tsūshō Sangyōshō, *Tsūshō Hakusho 1975*. See also Lawrence Krause and Sueo Sekiguchi, "Japan and the World Economy," in Patrick and Rosovsky, p. 409, for a more technical assessment of the changing nature of Japanese exports.

## IV  The other Japan

Important as a wide assortment of technical and economic factors might have been in Japan's overall economic success, it is equally true that the government's policies depended heavily on the exclusion of the political Left and organized labor from both official policy making and the ruling coalition. As Robert Gilpin has noted in the world context:

> Although the economic and technical substructure partially determines and interacts with the political superstructure . . . politics determines the framework of economic activity and channels it in directions which tend to serve the political objectives of dominant groups and organizations. Throughout history each successive hegemonic power has organized economic space in terms of its own interests and purposes.[80]

The explanation is as true internationally as it is for the relative distribution of economic costs and benefits within the Japanese political context. Japanese foreign economic policy has been carried out in a context in which the political exclusion of the Japanese Left and organized labor has allowed the Japanese government to avoid the redistribution of social benefits that has taken place, at least to some extent, in societies with a higher degree of corporatist inclusion of the labor sector. Virtually all key aspects of Japanese foreign economic policy would have been impossible in other industrial societies where organized labor plays a regular, or at least a periodic, role in the formal governmental and policy-making processes.

Compared to those of other advanced industrial states, total expenditures by the Japanese national government have been extremely low. With virtually no exceptions since the early 1950s, Japanese government expenditures have represented a rather consistent 20 percent of the country's GNP. In contrast, at least since 1965, the other major industrial states of North America and Western Europe have tended to expend about 25 percent, with most in the 30–35 percent range and a few, such as Denmark, Sweden, and Norway, over 40 percent. Moreover, there has been an almost universal increase in this figure for other states whereas in Japan it has been virtually unchanging.[81]  A major factor in this low level and consistency has been the minimal governmental contribution to social welfare and social overhead. Table 3 illustrates this fact. Government expenditures for direct consumption or indirect transfers to private individuals or organizations have been consistently and considerably below those of other major industrialized states, while investment as a percentage of GNP has been one and one-half times higher. In brief, the government has avoided the social overhead expenditures that have been

---

[80] Robert Gilpin, "The Politics of Transnational Economic Relations," in Keohane and Nye, p. 53.
[81] OECD, *Statistiques de Recettes Publiques de Pays Membres de l'OECD 1965–72* (Paris: OECD, 1975), p. 24.

## Table III Share of government expenditure in GNP[1]

| | Total | of which: | | |
|---|---|---|---|---|
| | | CONSUMPTION | INVESTMENT[2] | TRANSFERS[3] |
| Average 1953–55 | | | | |
| Japan | 17.8 | 8.9 | 4.6 | 3.7 |
| Five majors[4] | 23.6 | 8.6 | 2.9 | 8.5 |
| Average 1970–72 | | | | |
| Japan | 19.6 | 7.9 | 6.0 | 4.5 |
| Five majors[4] | 32.7 | 12.4 | 3.6 | 12.4 |

1. excluding expenditures for military
2. excluding nationalized corporations and public corporations
3. to households and private non-profit institutions
4. unweighted average of ratios for France, US, UK, West Germany, and Italy

Source: Andrea Boltho, *Japan: An Economic Survey, 1953–1973* (London: Oxford University Press, 1975), p. 124.

considered politically essential in other states. Rather, it has concentrated its resources on measures of direct benefit to the corporate sector of the economy.

The result is that on a wide range of social indicators, Japan is at or near the bottom of any ranking of industrialized states.[82] Absolute medical care benefits per capita are well below those of any other major industrial nation while medical care benefits as a percent of GNP are lower than in almost any other advanced country.[83] The ratio of Japanese social security expenditures to GNP varies between one-half and one-third of the sums paid in other developed countries.[84] In higher education, the Japanese government contributes a dramatically lower percentage of both total costs and costs as a percentage of GNP than any other major state.[85] On a wide spectrum of other indicators, Japan also ranks at or near the bottom. A recent comparative study by Wilensky showed that total public expendi-

[82] See Patrick and Rosovsky, pp. 36–37; S. Prakash Sethi, *Japanese Business and Social Conflict* (Cambridge: Ballinger, 1975), p. 10; Saitō Seiichirō, "Atarashii Kokumin Seikatsu no Kōzu," in *Sekai no naka no Nihon Keizai,* Shimano Takuji, ed. (Tokyo: Gakuyō Shobō, 1975), pp. 62–63.
[83] Shigeyoshi Jinushi, "Social Security System in Transition," *Developing Economies* Vol. 10 (December 1972):501.
[84] Ibid., pp. 501–12.
[85] Ministry of Education, *Educational Standards in Japan, 1970* (Tokyo: Ministry of Education, 1971), pp. 145–46; T.J. Pempel, "The Politics of Enrollment Expansion in Japanese Universities," *Journal of Asian Studies* Vol. 33 (November 1973):67–86.

tures in Japan for social welfare as a percent of GNP were the lowest in the industrialized world.[86]

By choosing not to expend funds on social benefits, the government has provided a two-fold stimulus to capital formation. On the one hand, monies not spent for social welfare could be allocated to industrial development. But beyond this, the absence of a developed social welfare system and the lack of a developed system of personal credit spurred Japanese citizens to save, particularly through government-controlled postal savings accounts, at rates unparalleled in the world. Only by doing so could they make capital purchases, provide higher education for their children, and prepare for the potentially disastrous "rainy days" of either poor health or retirement. Japan's savings ratio of approximately 25 percent is far higher than that of the next closest countries (Germany, the Netherlands, and Finland with about 20 percent) and two and one-half times higher than savings rates in the US or the UK. Even more impressive are the figures as a percentage of disposable income. There, Japan is first with 16.5 percent, while Germany's rate is 13.5 percent, and the US is a comparatively low 6.0 percent.[87] This high savings rate has provided the Japanese government, Japanese banks, and, in turn, Japanese industry with a very large reservoir of usable capital.

Viewed from another perspective, the general bias of policy is the same. The relative shares of capital and labor in Japanese national income have shifted dramatically, with capital's percentage tripling between 1953 and 1972 to just under 30 percent.[88] Meanwhile, labor productivity far outstripped rises in real wages. From 1955 to 1970, it rose approximately 3.6 times while real wages rose only about 2.3 times.[89] Only in the late 1960s did increases in real wages begin to parallel or exceed gains in labor productivity.[90] The consumer price index (which tends to reflect real living costs to the bulk of the populace) rose far faster than either real wages or the wholesale price index (which tends to reflect the costs to business and industry).[91] While there is no question but that labor and the consumer tend to receive a disproportionately low share of real rises in productivity within all capitalist economies, the gap in Japan remains significantly larger than that for most of its counterparts. Table 4 gives data measuring the relative gap between the consumer price index and the wholesale price index for a variety of industrialized

[86] Harold L. Wilensky, *The Welfare State and Equality* (Berkeley: University of California Press, 1975), pp. 30–31.

[87] Boltho, pp. 84–93; T. Blumenthal, *Saving in Postwar Japan* (Cambridge: Harvard University Press, 1970); Toshiyuki Mizoguchi, *Personal Savings and Consumption in Postwar Japan* (Tokyo: Kinokuniya, 1970), inter alia.

[88] Boltho, p. 181.

[89] My calculations from *Japan Statistical Index*, various years.

[90] Andō Yoshio, *Kindai Nihon Keizaishi Yōran* (Tokyo: Tōkyō Daigaku Shuppan, 1975), pp. 10–12, 180.

[91] On the different measures, see inter alia, Bieda, *The Structure and Operation of the Japanese Economy*, p. 41.

Table IV  Consumer price index as a proportion of wholesale price index

|              | *1960–65* | *1965–71* | *1950–71* |
|--------------|-----------|-----------|-----------|
| Japan        | 1.323     | 1.257     | 1.580     |
| Italy        | 1.114     | 1.037     | 1.464     |
| UK           | 1.062     | 1.075     | 1.286     |
| Sweden       | 0.995     | 1.116     | 1.273     |
| US           | 1.047     | 1.088     | 1.209     |
| West Germany | 1.076     | 1.110     | 1.175     |
| France       | 1.060     | 1.071     | 1.067     |

Source: Hiroshi Kawaguchi, "Nature and Causes of Contemporary Inflation," *The Developing Economies* Vol. 10 (December 1972): 411.

countries. It demonstrates clearly that the gap in Japan has been far wider than in other capitalist countries.

Other data also support this interpretation. A study of Japanese firms with more than ten employees shows that labor's relative share of gross value added was 39.1 percent in 1965. In American firms of more than one employee, it was 51.5 percent in 1964. In all English firms, the figure was 53.0 percent in 1963. In Swedish firms of more than five employees, it was 55.3 percent in 1964.[92] Whether the simple point that labor does not get its "fair share" under capitalist systems is true or not, it is irrelevant in a comparison between Japan and other capitalist systems. What is significant is that Japan has lagged consistently behind the other major capitalist economies in the benefits accorded to consumers and labor and that comparable social and economic benefits have failed to be garnered by these sectors within Japan.

Such imbalance might logically have been expected to lead to constant and dramatic protest, if not to revolution, given the size of Japan's industrial labor force. There has, of course, been real growth in Japanese incomes. Furthermore, a rapidly expanding economy, even if not equitable in its pattern of distribution, is difficult to oppose. Color televisions, telephones, automobiles, air conditioners, refrigerators, and other consumer durables have become increasingly diffused throughout Japan, often at rates exceeding those of many other industrial countries. Nonetheless, although there has been protest in Japan on economic issues, hours lost to strikes have been comparatively low and labor has been unsuccessful in forcing major action by the government to improve social conditions within the country or to make fundamental adjustments in the pattern of distribution of economic costs and benefits. Certain peculiarities of labor organization within the country help to explain why this was the case.

Individual Japanese firms frequently provide a wide array of fringe benefits for their employees. Medical and health facilities, housing, transportation al-

[92] Robert E. Cole, "Japanese Workers, Unions and the Marxist Appeal," *The Japan Interpreter* Vol. 6 (Summer 1970):118–19.

lowances, recreational facilities, scholarships for employee children, and a host of other benefits are often granted over and above a worker's salary.[93] Such benefits provided by companies obviously reduce the likelihood that collective labor pressures will be brought to bear on the government for these same benefits. One might argue that such benefits are comparable, whether provided by the public or the private sector. Yet countries which have government programs of social security, medical assistance, family allowances, and the like have usually adopted these programs in large part because of pressure from organized labor which has justified them in terms of its members' needs. And social benefit programs, once instituted, have been beneficial to much broader segments of society than organized labor alone. The point, therefore, is not that some segments of Japanese society receive good salaries and substantial benefits through their companies. They obviously do, and, in many cases, the absolute benefit levels are equivalent to those provided by governments in other countries. More important is the fact that such benefits, typically, are given voluntarily and can be withdrawn at the firm's discretion. Moreover, only the largest Japanese firms which contain the bulk of organized labor tend to provide such benefits. Because of the lack of nationwide programs based on universalistic criteria, comparable benefits are denied to workers in most small and medium-sized firms as well as to the bulk of the general populace. Hence, the paternalism of a relatively limited number of the largest firms in providing job security and privatized benefits to the best-organized elements of Japanese labor tends to vitiate the likelihood that those same sectors will feel any necessity to take the lead in securing such benefits for the populace as a whole.

Beyond this, it is the small and medium-sized firms in Japan that also bear the brunt of business downturns. For some firms this means bankruptcy; more often it means that their workers will be forced to take up any "slack" in the country's economy. Since workers in such small and medium-sized firms are largely unorganized, it is they who suffer in the form of shortened hours, unpaid bonuses, "voluntary" early retirements, or actual loss of jobs.

The broad contribution to the success of foreign economic policy that this provides is complemented by a number of other more explicitly firm-related factors. Because organized workers in the largest firms are relatively assured of jobs and must thus be treated as a fixed cost, in times of slowdowns, Japanese firms, like those in West Germany, tend to export in hopes of retaining productivity rather than contracting domestic production to cut costs. The result is highly salutary to government policy in its contribution to the overall expansion of exports. Moreover, although they do not necessarily rise in direct proportion to labor productivity, salaries and bonuses within the firm clearly improve with the firm's overall success. Consequently, the firm's workers and their union federations have little economic incentive to protest when and if the firm's products are exported at prices designed to make them more easy to purchase abroad than at home.

[93] See inter alia, Naomichi Funahashi, "The Industrial Reward System: Rewards and Benefits," in Okochi et al., eds., *Workers and Employers in Japan*, pp. 383–89.

Labor's organization along enterprise union lines also diffuses tensions over other aspects of Japan's foreign economic policy that have occasioned complaints from organized labor elsewhere. Virtually all (organized) workers are guaranteed jobs; and, over the bulk of the postwar period, Japan's unemployment rate has been consistently among the lowest in the world.[94] Thus, there is less union concern about the possible negative influence of job-reducing technological improvements. Moreover, most technologically displaced workers are retrained for new jobs in the firm rather than discharged. Overseas "aid" in the form of plant exports is seen as benefitting the firm, not as costing jobs. Capital transfers and direct investments are seen as similarly beneficial by unions. As a consequence, unions and the political parties of the Left have been conspicuously silent on most aspects of Japanese foreign economic policy despite their intense interest in domestic economic policy. The link between domestic economic policy and foreign economic policy seems not to have been made in their policy positions.

Meanwhile, the ultimate success of the small and medium-sized firms is linked to the success of the industrial leaders, reducing the likelihood that individual firms left out of the first order benefits will organize to oppose this distribution collectively.

Consequently, even though the overall picture of Japanese foreign economic policy reflects a strong state successfully coordinating a variety of component policies in conjunction with big business and finance, the economic dependency of small and medium-sized firms, plus the system of enterprise unions, tends to minimize the political reactions to the policy's overall political biases. Their links to the success of the largest firms work to reduce the likelihood that sub-contractors or enterprise unions will press at the national governmental level for a fundamental redistribution of economic benefits. In this way foreign economic policy is able to retain its generally "pro-big, anti-small" basis.

## V Domestic versus international forces

Above and beyond the purely domestic contributions to the success of Japan's foreign economic policy, it is important to recognize that elements in this success developed out of the relationship between domestic and international forces. Not all of the potentially deleterious international conditions faced by Japan's conservative coalition proved to have quite their anticipated results. In some cases, international pressures coincided with the policy directions pursued by domestic Japanese actors in the conservative coalition. In other instances, domestic political forces proved capable of explicitly resisting unwanted international pressures or of at least creatively manipulating such pressures. In still other cases, possibly negative international conditions proved to have unexpectedly fortuitous consequences.

[94] *Ekonomisuto,* 1 March 1976, p. 83.

Most significant in this regard was Japan's relationship with the United States. Japan's entire foreign policy was predicated on a close military and commercial alliance with the US. The inherent dependency that arose was increased by the absence of at least parallel, if not countervailing, alliances with other states. Moreover, the US during the 1950s and 1960s was the preeminent military and economic power among the industrial democracies, providing it with the potential to exercise rigid external controls over the foreign and economic policies of all its allies. It was the "maker" of the international system, while others were at best "breakers" of the system's rules or at worst "takers" of all that was dished out. Yet, as regards Japan at least, the abstract potential for despotism was often mitigated by benevolence in practice: the United States, though it clearly pushed the Japanese government to take actions the latter might not have taken if left completely to itself, did not exploit its unilaterally powerful position in an untempered fashion. Instead, in an effort to insure the continued economic success and political stability of the pro-American, anti-Communist regime in Tokyo, successive US governments, at least through the decade of the 1960s, took positions strikingly favorable to Japanese foreign economic policy.

The US took its pound of flesh in many early negotiations with Japan, particularly in air and fishing treaties.[95] It also exerted explicit pressure not to engage in economic dealings with Communist countries, particularly the Soviet Union and China. The US was successful in a few instances where private US-based companies exerted an economic stranglehold over key sectors of Japan, such as when the oil majors resisted Japanese purchases of Soviet oil in the early 1960s.[96] Furthermore, as the US began in the late 1960s and early 1970s to suffer from inflation, balance of payments problems, slow growth, inefficient domestic industries, and unemployment, Japan, at times, seemed a convenient scapegoat. As a result, the US was willing to attack a number of features of Japanese foreign economic policy.

Yet on balance, the relationship with the US was greatly beneficial to Japanese foreign economic policy. Under the Occupation, the Americans helped to stabilize the economy. They even went so far as to provide advice on export markets to help the Japanese to build up foreign reserves. Subsequently, the US limited its own tariff barriers to Japanese goods, despite Congressional and business pressures to do otherwise. In addition, while not vehemently opposing restrictions on Japanese imports and capital investment, it implicitly encouraged Japanese exports and gave Japan favorable access to US capital markets by exempting Japan

---

[95] Noguchi, Chapter 1.
[96] Savitri Vishwanathan, *Normalization of Japanese-Soviet Relations, 1945–1970* (Tallahassee: Diplomatic Press, 1973), pp. 101 ff; Warren Hunsberger, *Japan and the United States in World Trade* (New York: Harper and Row, 1964), pp. 213–14.

from the interest equalization tax until 1965.[97] Prior to 1971, the US exerted little pressure to revalue what came to be a clearly undervalued yen. It refrained from pressuring Japan despite a major bilateral trade imbalance which began in 1965 and reached a $3 billion surplus in Japan's favor by 1972.[98]

Moreover, US assistance was critical both in gaining the World Bank loans needed for Japan's rapid reindustrialization and in promoting Japan's entry into a wide variety of multinational economic organizations in the face of opposition from the European and Oceanic states.[99] Without US assistance, it is unlikely that Japan would have secured membership so early. In addition to granting Japan "international respect" and recognition as an "advanced industrial state," these memberships eventually led to the collective reduction of a vast array of barriers that had been erected against Japanese goods, particularly in Europe, making possible much of the export success that Japan achieved.

Although they were possibly an insult to national sovereignty, US military bases in Japan provided a good deal of capital to the Japanese economy in the 1950s, while the Korean and Indochina Wars, despite their adverse human consequences, were positive boons to the Japanese economy. Japan fulfilled major textile orders for US forces in Korea as well as a bevy of profitable support activities. As a result, the Korean War is generally conceded in both Japanese private and government circles to have been one of the best things that happened to the Japanese economy in the first fifteen years after surrender. Meanwhile, the war in Indochina provided a similar impetus during the mid- and late-1960s.[100] Krauss and Sekiguchi calculate that a total of at least $1 billion was added to Japanese exports by 1971 due to the war.[101]

It is clear, therefore, that in many areas, conscious and unconscious help by the United States proved to be an essential international contribution to the success of Japanese foreign economic policy. Yet it must be realized that most such help was aimed at, and contingent upon, the continuance in power of the conservative coalition. The apparent international munificence of the United States was a consequence of the congruence of policy aims between its government and that of Japan. It certainly seems safe to conclude that US assistance would have been far less likely had Japan been governed by a drastically more leftist coalition.

It is important to remember as well that, in many instances, Japan made extremely creative use of US assistance and was more than passively propped up

[97] I.M. Destler et al., "The Textile Wrangle: Conflict in Japanese-American Relations 1969–71" (1976, processed manuscript).
[98] Based on the US-Japan Trade Council, *United States Exports to Japan* and *United States Imports from Japan* (various dates).
[99] Gilpin, *U.S. Power and the Multinational Corporation*, pp. 109–11; F. C. Langdon, *Japan's Foreign Policy* (Vancouver: University of British Columbia Press, 1974); Gardner Patterson, *Discrimination in International Trade: The Policy Issue, 1945–1965* (Princeton: Princeton University Press, 1966), pp. 272–307, inter alia.
[100] Halliday and McCormack, pp. 11–12.
[101] Krause and Sekiguchi, in Patrick and Rosovsky, p. 419.

through international support. The US, anxious to bolster all of its military allies, provided a good deal of the technology that Japan imported on particularly, favorable terms. But Japan adapted much of this military technology to commercial use. The braking system on Japan's super express trains came from the F-104 fighter jet. The oil hydraulic technology of the F-86F was used in fire truck hoses. Japan Aviation Electronics Industry Ltd. adapted a gyroscope to bowling alley equipment, horse racing starting gates, and seismographs, while Nissan Motors used a version of the F-86F engine for shock resistance testing in autos and resistance measurement for skyscrapers.[102]

Finally, Japan demonstrated, in a number of cases, an anxiousness and a clear ability to act independently of, and at times in direct conflict with, pressures brought to bear by the US, either individually, or as the leader of various international coalitions aimed at redirecting aspects of Japanese foreign economic policy. A number of areas demonstrate this capacity most explicitly. They include trade with Communist countries and pressures to increase and liberalize the conditions for overseas aid. Equally important have been pressures to liberalize imports and the conditions for capital investment in Japan as well as to restrict Japanese exports of certain products to specific countries. What is most striking when all these are considered is the extent to which Japan, given its strong state and close links with business and finance, was capable, for the most part, of resisting and dealing independently with unwanted foreign pressures.

Given its overall strategic orientation, it is not surprising that the United States continually sought to integrate Japan into its strategic policy of anti-Communism and economic isolation of the Soviet Union and China. Under the US Occupation, Japan was bound by the trade embargo of the US and its allies. However, while official Japanese policy was supportive of US policy toward China until the 1970s, as early as 1952 trade between Japan and China began under a series of privately negotiated "unofficial" agreements. These were the result largely of pressures emanating from Japanese big business groups, many of which had collectively or individually been involved in trade with China and the development of Manchuria during the pre-war period. By 1956, Japanese exports to China exceeded the value of those to Taiwan, largely as a result of actions by private sector groups in Japan.[103] Although there was a slight turnabout under the extremely conservative Prime Minister Kishi in the late 1950s, under Prime Minister Ikeda, the Japanese government initiated a policy of "separating politics from economics." The result was that from then on private commercial agreements between the two countries were encouraged. The peak business federations were central to such policies initially. To meet Chinese demands that companies involved in mainland trade not deal simultaneously with Taiwan, for example, private enterprises in Japan, with government encouragement, established a number of "dummy corporations" to handle the China trade. By 1970, Japan was using

[102] Ozawa, pp. 74–75; *The Japan Economic Journal*, 10 October 1972.
[103] Fukui, *Party in Power*, p. 229.

Export-Import funds to extend credit to China and was clearly moving independently of the US on the commercial front.[104] When Nixon shocked Japan by announcing his visit to Peking, independence in relations with China became the Japanese watchword. By September 1972, Japan had extended formal recognition to the government in Peking while the US continued to advocate a more "cautious" attitude in dealings between the two countries.[105]

A similar independence from US policy preferences can be seen in economic relations with the Soviet Union. As noted earlier, Idemitsu Kōsan had tried to develop petroleum imports from the USSR in 1958 only to have Japan back down in the face of a US threat to refuse to purchase jet fuel from the company if the imports continued. By the late 1960s, however, Japan was more capable of carrying out independent economic negotiations with the USSR; and, in 1968, Japan signed a $160 million lumber agreement as the first Russo-Japanese venture in the economic development of Siberia. By 1971, Japan had overtaken the UK as the largest capitalist trading partner of the USSR.[106] Particularly interesting in relations between the two countries was a project which would involve joint Japanese-Russian development of the Tyumen oil fields and the construction of a major pipeline from the oil field to the east coast of Siberia from whence oil could be transported to Japan.[107] Again negotiations were carried out through the Japanese private sector, most notably the FEO and the Japan Chamber of Commerce, though the Japanese government became peripherally involved through the need for Export-Import bank financing of the project.[108] Throughout the negotiations, close cooperation was maintained between Japanese government and business, even though the government continued to avoid direct involvement. Significant for the purposes of this analysis is not only the persistence and importance of business-government cooperation, but also the fact that the Japanese government was willing to encourage such negotiations in spite of US reluctance. Only after negotiations had proceeded to Japan's satisfaction did the government begin attempting to include the US in the project and then on terms suitable to Japan.

A number of broader controversies arose between Japanese domestic inclinations and international pressures. At times, these "international" pressures were an outgrowth of US-led pressures on Japan, aimed at finding a scapegoat for US domestic economic problems and the decline in overall US strategic, military, and economic influence throughout the world. Most frequently, the pressures came in the form of requests that Japan play a "more responsible" role in international

---

[104] Langdon, p. 178.
[105] Haruhiro Fukui, "Tanaka Goes to Peking," in Pempel, *Policymaking in Contemporary Japan.*
[106] Halliday and McCormack, p. 232.
[107] On Tyumen, see Gerald L. Curtis, "The Tyumen Oil Project and Japanese Foreign Policy," paper presented at the Research Conference on Japanese Foreign Policy, Kauai, Hawaii, 14–18 January 1974; David Hitchcock, Jr., "Joint Development of Siberia: Decision-Making in Japanese Foreign Relations," *Asian Survey* Vol. 11 (March 1971):279–300.
[108] Curtis, "The Tyumen Oil Project and Japanese Foreign Policy."

political and economic affairs. In most cases, Japan showed a capacity to determine such "responsibilities" for itself.[109]

To start with the easiest case, pressure from groups such as ASEAN, UNCTAD, DAC, etc., for Japan to increase its aid and to liberalize the terms of such aid, it is clear that domestic political considerations were predominant. Although Japanese aid rose to become second only to that of the US, it remained quite low in absolute and relative terms and the conditions under which it was given remained strict. Only in 1972 did Japan untie its loans from the need to use all or portions of them to "buy Japanese" and only in 1973 did total Japanese aid exceed 1 percent of GNP. More telling is the fact that government aid remained at 0.25 percent of GNP, well below demands of both Third World countries and DAC standards and demands, and that the bulk of Japanese aid involved private business transactions of high profitability. Further, when faced with the economic recession of 1973–74, Japan quickly reversed the direction of even the limited rise in its aid that had been taking place. In 1974, total aid fell to 0.65 percent of GNP. According to DAC figures, official aid as a percent of GNP dropped for only two countries in 1975, Italy and Japan.[110] Clearly, then, aid has been one area of foreign economic policy where Japan has followed domestic commercial and political instincts rather than international pressures.

On the question of commercial and investment policy, the OECD countries, including the US, exerted constant pressure on Japan during the 1960s and into the 1970s to liberalize conditions. These pressures were clearly related to the expansion of Japanese exports to the major industrialized states. While Japan did, in fact, issue formal plans to liberalize as early as 1960 and while a series of moves to do so took place during that decade, it is difficult to conclude that these occurred at the expense of domestic development and economic demand. More impressive is the fact that through a combination of formal "liberalizations" and back door restrictions, the conservative coalition succeeded in holding off much of the competition from abroad in the areas most sensitive to the government's industrial policy. Even though, for example, the import of automobiles was liberalized in 1965, high luxury taxes and a complex inspection system (combined with roads not readily negotiable by a Ford Pinto let alone a Lincoln Continental) served effectively to restrict most foreign automobile imports while Japan's own auto industry continued to gain strength. In other areas, MITI oversight served similarly. For direct investment, the story was the same.

---

[109] It should be noted that most of these pressures which did conflict with Japanese domestic political thrusts had their own domestic motivations. Most notably, pressures against Japan to reduce exports came as a consequence of organized economic groups within the relevant states. Correspondingly, pressures for liberalization of capital movements and imports came from businesses most likely to take advantage of these changes. Nothing surprising should be found in this observation; it is simply a reaffirmation of the domestic sources of much of international behavior.

[110] *Zue*, p. 201.

On the question of exports, the importance of Japanese domestic political structures is again great. Japan was quick to point out to its critics the inconsistency between their demands that Japan liberalize its own economy in the name of free trade and an open world economy and simultaneously restrict its own exports. But at the same time it was able, through its close control over the domestic capital market and through the strength of its trade associations, to enter into a series of "voluntary export restrictions" for particular products.[111] These effectively served to diffuse much of the hostility against Japanese products. Such restrictions, usually negotiated on a single product with a single country, meant that Japan could maintain general solidarity between business and government at home while "dividing and conquering" overseas. First used in the textile area, the "voluntary restrictions" depended for their effectiveness on the strength of the trade associations within the industry in question and on the ability of association leadership to allocate market shares and enforce quotas on individual members. Most were able to do so because of the assistance they received from banks and the government. This system went a long way toward preventing the establishment of even more odious international barriers to Japanese goods in the form of general import quotas and tariff rescheduling. It also provided a face-saving device for foreign governments not willing to renounce their formal adherence to the principles of free trade but under domestic pressure to "do something" about Japanese goods seen as threatening politically significant local markets.

Finally, it is necessary to realize the purely fortuitous element involved in certain aspects of Japan's "weak" international position. Several possible weaknesses contained elements which proved to be blessings in disguise for Japan.

Consider first the problem of Japan's domestic terrain, geographical position, and its need for raw materials. While presenting numerous problems, this combination. also had ironically beneficial consequences for the development of Japanese foreign economic policy. To begin with, it was particularly significant in pushing Japanese government and business officials to concentrate major resources on the development of a technologically sophisticated shipbuilding industry and the integrated siting of key industries and ports. As a result, Japan pioneered in the development of supertankers and came to dominate the international shipping industry. Moreover, this shipping success bolstered its abilities in overseas commerce. Finally, its industrial location policy, while catastrophic for the environment, was extremely cost effective, particularly in reducing domestic transportation costs.

Similarly, while in the abstract a shortage of raw materials might be bad, Japan, drawing as it could on the facilities of its trading companies, turned the shortage into an advantage. Rather than having to rely on domestic sources of raw

---

[111] On voluntary restrictions, see Patterson, pp. 307–17; John Lynch, *Toward an Orderly Market: An Intensive Study of Japan's Voluntary Quota on Cotton Textile Exports* (Tokyo: Sophia University, 1968), passim; C. Fred Bergsten, "On the Non-Equivalence of Import Quotas and Voluntary Export Restraints," in Bergsten, *New World Trade Policy*, pp. 239–71.

materials with their potentially serious political consequences,[112] Japan could buy what it needed at the best world prices from anyone willing to sell. Moreover, it thus became possible for the government to control virtually the entire national supply of key materials through its import licensing. For most of the postwar period, this proved to be exceptionally advantageous.

A similar blessing in disguise can be found in the fact that by the late 1960s Japan's GNP was about twice as large as the combined GNPs of all states in East and Southeast Asia (China through Indonesia). As an economic giant in an area of Liliputians, Japan faced many problems, but it was also in a particularly favorable position to bargain for needed raw materials through direct purchase, extractive investments, and "aid" related ventures. With Europe's pullback from the area, local anti-Communist governments were faced with severe capital shortages that they believed could be filled only by the US or Japan. For many, Japan was a welcome counterweight to the overwhelming presence of the US. Moreover, particularly in Indonesia, Taiwan, and South Korea, many government officials had close personal ties with Japanese business and political leaders which dated from the prewar period. And while many of the aid and investment projects in the area have their sordid aspects, a rich Japan and a poor Asia were a compatible economic match, serving the overall anti-Communist orientations of the various governments.

At least one final benefit emerged from the apparent weakness of Japan's international position, namely the impetus to internal unity that comes from the perception of an external threat. Japan's international weaknesses, real and imagined, served as a boon to its internal consensus.[113] Most particularly, individual elements in the conservative coalition were induced to cooperate with one another by the fear that failure to do so would result in Japan's inability to deal effectively in the international arena, most probably to the detriment of every element of that coalition. More broadly, the government could utilize this same perception of international weakness as the justification for the sacrifices it demanded of the general Japanese citizenry. Nothing was so effective for internal Japanese unity as an external bogey man, be it international Communism, the threat to continued supplies of natural resources, or the collective wrath of the other industrial powers. The appearance of weakness may itself have been one of Japan's greatest strengths.

Thus, it is clear that there is no explicit or automatic trade-off between domestic and international stimuli in the generation of Japanese foreign economic policy. In a number of instances, international pressures were congruent with those

---

[112] Consider only the major problems posed for the Japanese budget by government support for rice prices to meet the political demands of farmers. See Michael W. Donnelly, "Setting the Price of Rice: A Study in Political Decision-Making," in Pempel, *Policymaking in Contemporary Japan.*

[113] The comments of Joseph S. Nye, Jr., and Stephen D. Cohen at the Conference on Foreign Economic Policy of Advanced Industrial States were particularly helpful in developing this point. More generally, see Georg Simmel, *Conflict and the Web of Group-Affiliations* (New York: Free Press, 1955) and Lewis Coser, *The Functions of Social Conflict* (New York: Free Press, 1956), passim.

operating domestically and certain aspects of Japan's foreign economic policy necessitated the close harmonization of the two. In others, domestic political conditions allowed for resistance to unwanted external stimuli. In still others, seemingly negative international conditions proved to have highly beneficial consequences.

As a result of the analysis in this and preceding sections, therefore, it makes little sense to deal with purported international pressures without adequate sensitivity to at least three things. First, one must consider the overall importance of domestic political factors in the generation of foreign economic policy, at least in Japan. Second, it should be recognized that a perception which dichotomizes international and domestic pressures as antithetic is inadequate. Third, it is important to be sensitive to the way in which different combinations of domestic political structures and the nature of the issue involved will influence the relative significance and impact of international forces.

## VI Toward the future—a reversal of the past?

The basic argument posed in this paper has been that a conservative coalition linking key elements of Japanese government, big business, and big finance has carried out a foreign economic policy aimed at maximizing that coalition's interpretation of the Japanese national interest. Policy choices have been made at the expense of organized labor, smaller businesses, and consumers. Moreover, domestic political factors have been relatively more important in the shaping of that policy than international factors. Yet the closer one gets to the present, the more evidence there seems to be on the surface that the pattern is changing. The prior dominance of the conservative coalition seems on the wane, while the neo-mercantilist policies of Japan seem incapable of being continued in the face of new trends in world politics and international economics.

To begin with, the anti-labor, anti-consumer bias of policy has not been as consistent or all-embracing in recent years as it was during the decade 1955–65. As the LDP's electoral majority has continued to shrink, as left-of-center coalitions have come to control virtually all of Japan's major cities, as pollution has choked the country's citizens, as the overall economy has continued to grow, and as disillusionment with the costs of economic success has begun to set in among intellectuals, businessmen, bureaucrats, and workers alike, the extremes of past policies have been tempered. National labor federations, sensitive to the difficulties of effecting national-level changes through plant-level bargaining over bread-and-butter issues, instituted the "spring offensive" aimed at insuring major increases in workers' salaries and benefits. Their actions included street demonstrations and national-level strikes led by unions in high growth sectors. These tactics began to generate substantial rises in real wages; and in the early 1970s increases in salaries began to overtake increases in productivity for the first time.[114] Moreover, consumer pressure, local elections, and the courts have all begun to play a role in Japanese policy making unknown in the 1950s or 1960s. In doing so, they have forced changes in industrial location policies, pollution control, pricing policies and the like.[115] As the Japanese economic pie continues to grow and as the LDP majority in charge of dividing it continues to evaporate, it is increasingly unlikely that economic policy can continue to be as negligent of large segments of Japanese society as it has been in the past. The blind concern with expansion at all costs is being strongly questioned, even by elements of the conservative coalition. Increased emphasis on the quality of life, the redistribution of benefits and greater government investment in social overhead policies is bound to generate policy changes in areas such as capital export, monopolization, import of consumer goods, monetary policy, and technology importation.[116]

Real changes are taking place within the political structures and value orientations of Japan which should not be minimized. Still, there is little to suggest that a truly monumental reversal of the policies of the past is likely. Following the economic gains of labor in the late 1960s and early 1970s, for example, the world recession saw Japanese annual wage increases fall from a national average of 32 percent in 1974 to 13 percent in 1975 to 8.5 percent in 1976.[117] Clearly, labor is by no means forcing a fundamental redistribution of income within the country; most of its gains have come only with an expanding economic pie and still remain the first targets of cutbacks. Moreover, the two major parties of the Left, the Japan Socialist Party (JSP) and the Japan Communist Party (JCP), have not been the major beneficiaries of popular disenchantment with the LDP. JSP seats in the Lower House of the Diet were last above one-third following the 1958 elections. Since then they have rather consistently declined until now the party holds less than one-quarter of the seats. The JCP, after a brief flurry of success in the 1969 and 1972 elections which made them the second largest opposition party (with only 8 percent of the seats), fell off sharply in the 1976 election. Meanwhile, small parties and proto-parties of the center-Right remain sufficiently strong to ensure continued LDP rule in the immediate future through a coalition with one or more of them. Should this occur, it would require certain policy changes mitigating some of the past extremes in elements of policy affecting foreign economics, but it would be unlikely to reverse directions fundamentally. Certainly, such a coalition would not drastically affect the structure of the state bureaucracy or the major financial and monetary institutions of the country which are now so crucial to the definition and implementation of foreign economic policy. Finally, it is worth remembering

---

[114] *Zue*, p. 102.

[115] Margaret McKean, "Pollution and Policymaking," in Pempel, *Policymaking in Contemporary Japan*.

[116] See, as examples: Economic Planning Agency, *Basic Economic and Social Plan: 1973–1977* (Tokyo: Government Printing Office, 1973); Sangyō Kōzō Shingikai, *Sangyō Kōzō no Chōki Bijon* (Tokyo: Tsūshō Sangyō Chōsakai, 1975).

[117] *The Economist*, 4 December 1976, p. 104.

that whatever changes do come about will occur with the overall level of Japanese production and potential growth vastly greater and, hence, vastly more capable of incorporating them into existing policy preferences than would have been possible had they come ten or twenty years earlier.

On the question of domestic versus international influences, certain trends in international economics and politics might be pointed to as evidence that the opportunities for the continuation of Japanese neo-mercantilism are coming to an end. Détente, the decline in US capacity for police activities in Asia, plus the domestic economic problems of the US, all suggest that past US benevolence toward Japanese foreign economic policies is not likely to continue. The trends in international commercial and monetary policies appear clearly toward cooperation and integration, with a consequent reduction in the ability of any single state to operate with complete impunity. The success of OPEC portends to many the rise of Third World cartels capable of collective action to cut off supplies or at least to raise dramatically the prices of raw materials critical to all the industrialized states of the North, including Japan.[118] In this context, recent Japanese trade and capital liberalization, continued dependence on a more protectionist US, revaluation of the yen, and impotence during the oil crisis suggest an increase, rather than a decrease, in Japanese vulnerability and responsiveness to international forces.

Japan's reduction of restrictions on imports and capital investments might well be the easiest case with which to deal. There can be no doubt that Japan has, in response to international pressures, significantly liberalized conditions for both. By many formal criteria, capital investment and trade barriers are increasingly comparable to those of the United States and Western Europe. The Japanese economy, however, is now internationally competitive in most areas. Japanese policy makers have clearly and consciously chosen to liberalize from a position of strength, anticipating the generally full integration of Japan into international trade and capital markets. They themselves are moving away from the neo-mercantilism of the past.[119] Japan, however, will participate in such markets as a strong, active, and relatively autonomous actor; it will by no means be the passive respondent to internationally-generated stimuli. Moreover, individual products, particularly in agriculture and high technology areas, have been and will continue to be subject to serious evaluation and restrictions before barriers are reduced. Japanese policy makers are certainly unlikely ever to be convinced that total liberalization of all trade and capital flows and the actual encouragement of more multinational

[118] See especially C. Fred Bergsten, "The Threat from the Third World," "The Threat Is Real," and "The Response to the Third World," *Foreign Policy* Vols. 11, 14, 17 (Summer 1973; Spring 1974; Winter 1974–75).

[119] See the sources cited in fn. 116 plus Japan External Trade Organization, *Japan: Into the Multinationalization Era* (Tokyo: Press International, 1973), and *Japan as an Export Market* (Tokyo: JETRO, n.d., probably 1972); Tsūshō Sangyōshō Sangyō Seisakukyoku, *Wagakuni Kigyō no Kaigai Jigyō Katsudō*; Tsūshō Sangyōshō Tsūshō Seisakukyoku, *Keizai Kyōryoku no Genjō to Mondaiten*, Chapter 2; Tsūshō Sangyōshō, *Tsūshō Hakusho 1975*, passim, but esp. Part I, Chapter 2 and Part II, Chapters 2 and 3, inter alia.

investment in high technology ventures in Japan will provide them with "international hostages" so linked to Japanese economic success that they will in fact become genuine advocates of Japanese interest.[120] Rather, state bureaucrats and key business leaders seem more convinced that unfettered liberalization would do no more than make Japan a captive of the economic power of its potential "hostages." Consequently, state control and decision-making powers in the area of commercial policy and capital investment within Japan have not been, and are unlikely in the future to be, surrendered to "economic interpenetration" and the ephemera of "the international free market." Power has always abhorred a truly free market and Japan has become powerful. Though Japanese policy makers will surely follow a more "internationalist" course of action in commercial policy and capital movements than in the past, it will be largely because it is both in their self-defined best interests and within their ability to do so. Domestically defined priorities will continue to predominate in Japan. Nor does it appear that Japan is content to remain (if ever it was) no more than a US-sponsored flash in the pan, constantly dependent on the conditions of sales in the American market. As the US economy has faltered and protectionist sentiments, directed particularly against Japan, have become stronger, the government has moved consciously to reduce Japan's trade dependence on the US.

Japan appears to have been somewhat more vulnerable on the questions of yen revaluation and the oil crisis. With regard to the yen, the Japanese government, particularly the Ministry of Finance, took the position that the exchange rate of ¥360 to the dollar was inviolable from the time it was established in 1949. Maintenance of this single exchange rate was a significant factor in Japan's international trading success. As Japan's balance of payments became favorable, and as foreign exchange holdings mushroomed, however, international pressures for revaluation became intense. The Japanese government resisted strongly and, as late as June 1971, it adopted a plan entitled "Eight Items of Urgent Policy Measures to Avoid Yen Revaluation." This plan included reduction of quantitative restraints, capital export, tariff cuts, reductions in non-tariff barriers, economic cooperation, export restrictions and the like. There was a clear willingness to sacrifice a great deal to retain the value of the yen. Then in August came the announcement that the US would allow the dollar to float, with the expectation that this would inevitably mean a revaluation of the yen. Not until December was the yen revalued, during which time, according to one calculation, a total of $2.5 billion was lost to the Japanese economy.[121] A number of factors surrounding this case seem to suggest that Japanese foreign economic policy is vulnerable to international, particularly US, pressures: the long time taken in revaluation, the major efforts to

[120] My thinking on this point has been helped considerably by discussions with Richard Rosecrance. A more optimistic perception of the role to be played by new international forces, particularly the multinational corporation, can be found in John Diebold, "Multinational Corporations: Why Be Scared of Them?" *Foreign Policy* Vol. 12 (Fall 1973): 79–95.

[121] Toshio Shishido, "The Framework of Decision-Making in Japanese Economic Policies," in *Perspectives on U.S.-Japan Economic Relations*, Allen Taylor, ed. (Cambridge: Ballinger, 1973), p. 205.

avoid revaluation just prior to the Nixon announcement, and the fact that the yen was finally revalued not once but twice, causing it to appreciate by about one-third in eighteen months.

This apparent vulnerability is, of course, partly real. Under the present international monetary system, all advanced capitalist countries are mutually dependent on the actions of one another. Furthermore, as Japan has become more and more of a success story, following a policy based on claims of poverty and economic weakness has become less feasible. Hence, international pressures for an increased sensitivity of the yen to changes in other currencies have been stronger than in the past and are unlikely to abate in the future. Japan, as an increasingly important member of the integrated capitalist economic system, will continue to be pressured to make adjustments in accord with that significance. Yen revaluation was but one instance of that broader trend.

Nevertheless, it would certainly be a mistake to attribute the slowness in Japan's revaluation to a simple case of domestic reluctance to face international facts. There were strong pressures within Japan for a revaluation, particularly from corporations grown so successful that they sought increased opportunities for the overseas investment which a revalued yen would provide. To these interests, US pressures and actions provided precisely the external stimuli needed to overcome the reluctance to unpeg the yen from its 1949 values.

Assuredly, it is also a drastic mistake to conclude that the slowness in Japanese official action was the result of official timidity, bureaucratic incompetence, or the inability of Japanese officialdom to realize the changed realities. One author suggests that "$800 million was lost by the Bank of Japan during the first ten days after the announcement [by Nixon], buying $4 billion at the old rate of 360 yen, because no one took the initiative to close the Tokyo Foreign Exchange."[122] Admittedly, Japan was slow to react, but the government's lack of speed can be interpreted far more logically when one considers the close relationship between Japanese government and business. Japanese firms had billions of dollars out in multiple arrangements throughout the world when the Nixon announcement was made; trading companies were particularly vulnerable and would have taken severe losses had the Japanese government allowed the yen to float immediately. Waiting several months until revaluation provided them with an opportunity to liquidate their holdings of what were clearly going to be revalued currencies, with the Japanese government and the Bank of Japan paying most of the bill. In short, the close relationship between the state and business necessitated state action to prevent intolerable business losses.

Since the rapid revaluation in 1971–73, the Japanese government has also shown an increased capacity to resist international pressures on the yen. The Ministry of Finance and the Bank of Japan have followed a "dirty float" policy, intervening to protect the value of the yen at a value only about 16 percent above

---

[122] Ibid.

the pre-1971 level. Japan now has one of the strongest world currencies. Its exports have continued to thrive and it was one of the first countries out of the international recession. The yen clearly remains vulnerable under the present international monetary system, and unchecked neo-mercantilism through an overvalued yen is unlikely to be as internationally tolerated in the 1970s as it might have been in the mid-to-late 1960s. Nevertheless, Japan has shown a definite capacity for self-interested autonomy of action in its monetary policies during the last few years that negates any assessment of the country as any more internationally vulnerable than its European and North American counterparts.

Finally, there is the oil crisis. This crisis was a distinct and severe blow to the Japanese economy which went against any political impulses that could be identified domestically and which provided a clear case of international forces countering domestic. Of course the entire industrial world was affected, but Japan more so than others. Japan relies on oil for 70 percent of its energy needs and when the oil shock came, Japan was dependent on imports for 99 percent of its petroleum. Roughly 80 percent came from the Middle East and Near East.[123] Such dependency was completely out of proportion to most other countries; only Italy and Denmark were close. Moreover, though somewhat successful in reducing their control over retailing operations, Japan was still a country heavily dominated by the oil majors.

Panic ensued following OPEC's across-the-board reduction of crude exports in October 1973. Within the government there was ministerial confusion and disagreement over responses to this completely unexpected event. There was a major division over how far both to "tilt" in favor of the Arab countries and to abandon Japan's close following of US policy of support for Israel. By late November, opinion among MITI and FEO business leaders was strongly in favor of a pro-Arab stance regardless of US pressures to the contrary. A statement was issued on the 22nd that made a marked turn-about in Japan's policy. It represented what one writer calls "the first open break with American foreign policy in post-war diplomatic history that Japan had dared to make."[124] The statement was followed by a grant of $5 million to aid Palestinian refugees. In December, Miki Takeo was dispatched as a special ambassador to the Middle East to improve relations through aid and technology arrangements. His visit and a subsequent one by Nakasone Yasuhiro led to major increases in bilateral aid arrangements between Japan and the oil exporting nations. In the following three years, a number of projects in the area, especially in petroleum extraction, were initiated with Japanese assistance. A tilt had occurred, one that required balancing off a variety of domestic and international pressures, and one that illustrated the ability of international events to disrupt Japanese foreign economic policy. Japan's vulnerability on raw materials

[123] Japan Transport Economics Research Center, *Illustrated Transport Economy of Japan, 1974* (Tokyo: Japan Transport Economics Research Center, 1974), pp. 40–41.
[124] Tsurumi, p. 124. On the oil shock and its domestic political consequences, see also Kenneth I. Juster, "Japanese Foreign Policy Making During the Oil Crisis " (unpublished honors thesis, Department of Government, Harvard University, March 1976).

and energy had forced significant changes in policy. At the same time, it would be a mistake to overestimate the degree to which Japan was more willing to bend than other industrial nations, to overstress the extent of the Japanese shift, or to read into the peculiarities of the situation unwarranted implications for the future.

By 1974, Japan had signed the International Energy Program Agreement and returned to a policy of coordinating its actions with those of the OECD nations, including the US. In addition to the search for international cooperation among industrial countries in dealing with the oil producers, the Japanese government has taken numerous steps to reduce the country's overall dependence on Middle Eastern oil as controlled through the oil majors. These steps have ranged from MITI's major investment in the development of an electric car through oil exploration measures in the coastal waters of the Pacific and increased investigation and reliance on alternative energy sources. In this sense, it is clear that the Japanese government, in conjunction with private industry, has been searching for a combination of domestic remedies to its international dependence on raw materials. At the same time, it is undeniable that the threat of combined action by raw materials producers from the South poses a genuine threat to the North: will they be able to continue following previous practices of dividing and conquering, playing off the interests of competing producers of raw materials? Japan, with its high dependence on a variety of raw materials available largely from the less developed areas of the world, is even more vulnerable than most. But it would be a mistake to overestimate the ease with which other raw materials producers could act collectively to intimidate Japan and/or the other industrialized states. A wide range of impediments, political, economic, and cultural, stands in the way of collective action by timber, bauxite, copper, phosphate rock, or tin producers. Their ability to imitate OPEC and thereby recalibrate the North-South balance is vastly overrated.[125]

Consequently, even though the domestic and international conditions facing Japan have changed drastically over the past few years and even though Japanese policy has become more internationalist and less neo-mercantilist, the changes occurring do not seem to be of a magnitude sufficient to suggest that any fundamental overhaul is forthcoming in Japanese foreign economic policy. Alterations are likely and changes are inevitable, but no fundamental reorientation in the significance of domestic versus international forces appears to be in the offing. Japanese dependence on raw materials is clear and unmistakable, making it highly vulnerable to such collective pressures as can be exerted over access to them. Japanese monetary and commercial activities are significantly intertwined with the actions of other states. The conservative coalition in Japan now lacks the command-

---

[125] See inter alia Bension Varon and Kenji Takeuchi, "Developing Countries and Non-Fuel Minerals," *Foreign Affairs* Vol. 52 (April 1974):497–510; Theodore H. Moran, "New Deal or Raw Deal in Raw Materials," *Foreign Policy* Vol. 5 (Winter 1971–72):119–34; Stephen D. Krasner, "Oil is the Exception," *Foreign Policy* Vol. 14 (Spring 1974):68–84; Franklin B. Weinstein, "Multinational Corporations and the Third World: The Case of Japan and Southeast Asia," *International Organization* Vol. 30, No. 3 (Summer 1976):373–404.

ing control it once exercised and domestic pressures for economic reorientations are more marked than ever before. Yet the overall significance of the Japanese economy within the world context is also greater than ever before, and the bargaining resources available to business, financial, and government leaders in Japan are vastly greater than in the past.

Interdependence and the new international economic order have their distinct and unmistakable limits. To the extent that the same basic structures are likely to dominate within Japan, the definition and pursuit of "Japanese national interests" will remain internally generated, and the general direction of future policies is likely to resemble that of the past. If and when these interests come into conflict with "international" pressures and interests, it is the former that are most likely to prevail. Under any foreseeable circumstances, the domestic context of Japanese politics will remain critical to any assessment of Japanese international and foreign economic behavior.

# 6
# West Germany:
# The Dynamics of Expansion

*Michael Kreile*

During more than two decades, West German foreign economic policy has served a strategy of export-oriented growth. The success of this strategy is based on a number of factors, such as Germany's industrial structure, a favorable international environment, a pro-investment domestic economic policy and the constructive role of labor in postwar economic development. Decision making in foreign economic policy is characterized by the dominance of the export sector. The strategy of export expansion met with obstacles in two areas. In Eastern trade policy export interests clashed with the imperatives of "high politics" during the Cold War era. In monetary policy, the chronic undervaluation of the Deutsche Mark, a crucial factor of export competitiveness, collided with the goal of price stability. Both cases highlight the limits of export sector dominance. In recent years, the internationalization of German industry and the process of structural change have created problems that suggest that the German economy is reaching the limits of export-oriented growth. These pose new challenges to economic policy makers.

When Chancellor Helmut Schmidt's Social Democratic Party based its 1976 election campaign on the theme of West Germany's outstanding economic performance, the reactions of foreign observers ranged from praise and admiration to envy and concern. The Federal Republic looked like an island of stability compared to other West European countries which were saddled with two-digit inflation rates and threatened by the advance of Communist parties or the specter of international bankruptcy. Rising from wartime defeat and destruction, West Germany, within

Michael Kreile is a member of the Institut für Politische Wissenschaft at the University of Heidelberg.

barely three decades, has in fact become what might be called, in Francois Perroux's terms, the "économie dominante" in Western Europe. The key to this success story can be found in the German strategy of export expansion.

Export-oriented growth created full employment and prosperity which, in turn, guaranteed popular support for the market economy and the system of democratic institutions. On the other hand, political and social stability became an economic asset of critical importance for the international competitiveness of West German industry. The dynamism of export expansion is illustrated by the following figures. During 1950–53, German exports accounted for 4.6 percent of world exports. In 1970–73, with this share climbing to 11.2 percent, West Germany had become the world's second largest trading nation behind the United States.[1] The ratio of exports to GNP rose from 8.5 percent in 1950 to 15.9 percent in 1960. It had reached the level of 23.1 percent in 1974 when merchandise exports hit the record mark of 230.6 billion DM. As a result of these developments, in 1975 one out of five jobs depended on exports.[2]

Although the postwar take-off was largely propelled by the needs of reconstruction and a pent-up demand for consumer goods,[3] exports became a major contributor to economic growth over the years, since they speeded up investment, stimulated productivity, and ensured full employment.[4] Export demand also proved to be decisive in pulling the economy out of recessions.[5] However, in 1975, the slump in export demand contributed to the deepest recession of the postwar era and revealed the vulnerability which comes with high levels of economic interdependence.

Export-oriented growth followed the logic of industrial structure, but it was also a product of deliberate policy. In the aftermath of World War II, West Germany found itself "with the same well-rounded industrial structure that it had before the war."[6] With almost two-thirds of prewar capacity in heavy industry and producer goods industries located in the Western zones, partition reinforced the concentration on basic and capital goods industries.[7] This structure meshed almost

---

[1] Figures from Werner Glastetter, *Außenwirtschaftspolitik* (Cologne: Bund-Verlag, 1975), p. 20.

[2] See DIW (Deutsches Institut für Wirtschaftsforschung), Wochenbericht 22/1976, p. 224, and Kurzmitteilung, "Zur Internationalisierung der westdeutschen Wirtschaft," *WSI-Mitteilungen* 4/1976, pp. 230–34.

[3] See Wolfram Fischer, "Bergbau, Industrie und Handwerk 1914–1970," in *Handbuch der deutschen Wirtschafts-und Sozialgeschichte,* Hermann Aubin and Wolfgang Zorn, eds., Vol. 2: *Das 19. und 20. Jahrhundert* (Stuttgart: Ernst Klett Verlag, 1976), pp. 796–843, p. 838.

[4] See Wolfgang Michalski, *Export und Wirtschaftswachstum* (Hamburg: Verlag Weltarchiv, 1970).

[5] See Wolfgang Kasper, "Stabilization Policies in a Dependent Economy: Some Lessons From the West German Experience of the 1960s," in *Stabilization Policies in Interdependent Economies,* Emil Claassen and Pascal Stalin, eds. (Amsterdam and London: North-Holland Publishing Co., 1972), pp. 270–86, p. 272.

[6] Henry C. Wallich, *Mainsprings of the German Revival* (New Haven: Yale University Press, 1955), p. 7.

[7] See Marianne Welteke, *Theorie und Praxis der Sozialen Marktwirtschaft* (Frankfurt and New York: Campus Verlag, 1976), pp. 18–19.

perfectly with the postwar patterns of world demand. Reconstruction at home and abroad, the priority accorded to economic growth by the main partner countries, and, subsequently, the industrialization drive of Eastern bloc and Third World countries resulted in a booming demand for capital equipment. Rising standards of living abroad also stimulated the export of consumer durables.

West German competitiveness in international markets benefited from an abundant supply of labor. This was provided at first by the enormous inflow of refugees from Eastern territories and the German Democratic Republic (GDR)— over 10 million by 1953—and later by the massive recruiting of foreign workers. Their numbers rose from 167,000 in 1959 to 2.24 million in 1971 when they accounted for 10.3 percent of the total labor force.[8] Until late in the 1960s, labor unions exercised remarkable restraint, if not docility, in their wage policy. This attitude reflected a high degree of "inflation-consciousness" as well as a concern for export performance. Class conflict was suspended in exchange for the dividends of growth.

Although there is certainly some truth to Kindleberger's argument that it was the "force des choses" (i.e., structural economic and social factors) rather than policy which produced the German results,[9] economic policy was definitely an important ingredient of the magic potion. Tax policy was designed to encourage capital formation and throughout the 1950s enabled business to engage in large-scale self-financing.[10] This did not fail to produce a very skewed distribution of income and property.

A deliberate policy of deflation combined with "income policy from below" (Kindleberger) kept inflation rates down and domestic demand checked, so that the drive for export markets was doubly stimulated.[11] Foreign economic policy in particular has been consistent in its design to develop and expand export markets for German industry. It was accompanied by an "export mystique" which no relevant social group called into question. Politicians, industrialists, and union leaders alike adhered to the principle that German competitiveness in world markets had to be maintained and strengthened. As one observer put it, "the specter of lost international competitiveness continually haunts German policy making."[12] Price stability and export competitiveness thus became the overriding objectives of monetary policy.

In spite of rising export surpluses caused by a chronic undervaluation of the Deutsche Mark, parity maintenance was dogma. Parity changes were only resorted to

---

[8] Figures from OECD, *Manpower Policy in Germany* (Paris: OECD, 1974), p. 151.

[9] Charles P. Kindleberger, "Germany's Persistent Balance-of-Payments Disequilibrium," in Robert E. Baldwin, et al., *Trade, Growth and the Balance of Payments, Essays in Honor of Gottfried Haberler* (Chicago, Amsterdam 1965), pp. 230–48, p. 248.

[10] Wallich, p. 300; Welteke, pp. 70–71.

[11] See the instructive data on the components of global demand in Werner Glastetter, "Die Entwicklung der außenwirtschaftlichen Verflechtung der Bundesrepublik Deutschland im Zeitraum 1950 bis 1975," *WSI-Mitteilungen* 5/1976 (May 1976), pp. 237–45, p. 240.

[12] William P. Wadbrook, *West German Balance-of-Payments Policy*, Praeger Special Studies in International Economics and Development (New York: Praeger Publishers, 1972), p. 63.

as an "ultimate ratio" when imported inflation gravely imperiled price stability. For about fifteen years, exchange rate policy was probably more important than any other specific measure of export promotion. Tax subsidies of a more mercantilistic nature had been abolished in 1955, when the Export Promotion Act (*Ausfuhrförderungsgesetz*) was repealed despite clamorous protests from industry.[13] The present armory of export policy instruments includes export credit guarantees, the remission of the value-added tax on exports, and interest rate subsidies for a small volume of export credits. Yet it probably remains below the level of mercantilism practised by other OECD nations. The commitment to import liberalization implicit in the German choice of the world market is due as much to the pressure from trading partners as to the precepts of neo-liberalism. Nevertheless protectionist sectors have successfully managed to defend a hard core of quantitative restrictions and relatively high levels of tariff protection.

The liberal philosophy which characterizes foreign economic policy in general has also been extended to the treatment of direct foreign investment in both directions. Foreign capital has been allowed to dominate certain strategic sectors. For example, 80 percent of the oil industry is controlled by international oil companies.[14] On the other hand, the process of internationalization of the German economy has been greatly accelerated since the late 1960s. Direct investment abroad has increased at a rapid pace. In 1975, it reached the level of 42 billion DM, which corresponds roughly to the amount of direct foreign investment in the Federal Republic of Germany (FRG).[15] Capital export was strongly encouraged by the government to offset, at least partly, the surpluses in the trade balance (for details see section IV).

The structural economic importance of the export sector has been effectively translated into political power.[16] The dominance of the export sector, therefore, represents the most salient feature of foreign economic policy making. The axis of the policy network is a close cooperative relationship linking the ministerial bureaucracy to interest groups in industry, trade, and banking. The style of policy making represents a middle course between the active interventionism of the French state bureaucracy and an outright colonization of government departments by interest groups as in Italy. As industry performed brilliantly on its own, the

[13] See Heinz Müller, *Die Exportförderung der Bundesrepublik Deutschland in kritischer Sicht* (Dissertation, Marburg, 1961), p. 38.

[14] See Monopolkommission, *Hauptgutachten 1973/1975: Mehr Wettbewerb ist möglich* (Baden-Baden: Nomos Verlagsgesellschaft, 1976), p. 308; and "Ausländische Beteiligungen an Unternehmen in der Bundesrepublik," *Monatsberichte der Deutschen Bundesbank* 26. Jg. Nr. 11 (November 1974), p. 28. According to Monopolkommission, pp. 164–65, the 21 majority-owned affiliates of foreign enterprises that ranked among the 100 largest German enterprises in 1974 accounted for 19 percent of total sales of the 100 largest.

[15] See Karl Heinrich Herchenröder, "Investitionen im Ausland," *Handelsblatt* (Düsseldorf), 14–15 May 1976, p. 3.

[16] See also Wadbrook, p. 80 and Kasper, p. 283.

government was usually neither asked nor tempted to mingle in commercial transactions. The nuclear deal with Brazil provides an exception to this rule.[17]

Although the West German political system is frequently referred to as a "Chancellor's democracy" or "party democracy," these labels have little explanatory value with regard to foreign economic policy making. Parties and parliament find themselves on the periphery of the policy network. Their role is to ratify decisions rather than to formulate policy. There is no doubt that Chancellors have made some crucial decisions in the area of foreign economic policy, and it is certainly no accident that Chancellor Schmidt takes pride in his reputation for effective economic crisis management and a solid grasp of international economic problems. But under the German cabinet system, the commanding heights of foreign economic policy are occupied by the Ministry of Economics. Monetary policy, which has been crucial in creating an atmosphere of "trust" for business expansion, is dominated by the Bundesbank.

Organized labor is largely frozen out of the policy-making process. One reason for this may be that labor unions were in basic agreement with the strategy of export expansion even if they did not like all of its implications. But organized labor is likely to seek a more active role in the future if capital export and structural change should result in (or be perceived as causing) higher levels of unemployment. For there is a growing feeling, as the ongoing debate on *Strukturpolitik* indicates, that the West German economy may be entering the stage of self-exhaustion with regard to export-oriented growth. The very success of the export strategy seems to have undermined some of the foundations upon which it was built. Economic strength has increasingly become a source of vulnerability.

## *I The international setting of West German foreign economic policy*

An inquiry into the international determinants of West German foreign economic policy cannot fail to stress the overwhelming importance of international developments which have shaped West Germany's economic and political institutions. The establishment of a liberal capitalist system after the fall of Fascism was largely predetermined by the front lines of the Cold War. "The Federal Republic was an offspring of bipolarity, conceived and nurtured by the strategic imperatives of the West."[18]

During its formative years, the FRG represented the almost ideal type of a "penetrated system." American hegemony and the Marshall Plan crucially conditioned its integration into regional and global regimes of liberalized trade and payments. This "choice," however, was not merely imposed by Allied fiat. It was

---

[17] See Peter Hermes, "Außenpolitik und Außenwirtschaftsinteressen," *Aussenpolitik* 3/76, pp. 247–55, p. 250.

[18] Josef Joffe, "The Foreign Policy of the German Federal Republic," in *Foreign Policy in World Politics,* Roy C. Macridis, ed., 5th ed. (Englewood Cliffs, N.J.: Prentice-Hall, Inc., 1976), p. 121.

also in line with the ideological preferences of West Germany's political and economic leaders who, for this very reason, enjoyed the patronage of American planners. Besides, there was clearly a lack of attractive alternatives. Partition had amputated Prussia's industrial zones from their agricultural hinterland and trade with Eastern Europe had dried up as a result of Stalinist bloc integration and Western economic warfare. By financing imports of desperately needed foodstuffs and raw materials, the Marshall Plan provided the resources to sustain an embryonic recovery of industrial production.[19] It was thus instrumental in the successful transfer of the "politics of productivity" (Charles Maier). Industry was reorganized in accordance with American antitrust philosophy. Decartelization and free enterprise prevailed over the British preference for the socialization of basic industries. The constitution of "free and democratically organized labor unions" was encouraged.[20] Economics became the prime preoccupation of a people who had suffered want and were alienated from politics.

The Pax Americana provided a congenial environment for German export expansion, as world trade flourished under the rules set by GATT and the Bretton Woods system. Until the beginning of the 1960s, American military protection even represented a positive item in the German balance of payments, for the maintenance costs of American forces in Germany were borne by the US. It was only in November 1961, when the German reserve position had reached a very comfortable level, that an offset agreement was negotiated providing for weapons purchases in the US as well as other measures of burden sharing.

With the gradual decline of American hegemony, the Federal Republic's external monetary policy became increasingly a function of Germany's dependence on the US for its security. German reliance on American nuclear and conventional protection "produced a docility and compliance with American wishes which was the more remarkable as German economic strength continued to grow and to be acknowledged. . . . The basis of the alliance obviously was primarily military, but the pay-off was primarily monetary."[21] Various devices designed to shore up the US balance of payments position, like the Roosa Bonds and the creation of Standard Drawing Rights (SDRs), were dependent on West German cooperation. Since the Bundesbank refrained from converting dollars into gold, a commitment laid down in the famous Blessing letter of 1967, West Germany prolonged the viability of the Bretton Woods system. This approach was in striking contrast to French policy which challenged US hegemony by systematically exchanging dollar reserves for gold. German readiness to cooperate with the US was, however, limited by the need to establish a delicate balance between loyalty to the US and EEC solidarity.

[19] See Knut Borchardt, "Wachstum und Wechsellagen 1914–1970," in Aubin and Zorn, p. 721.
[20] See Hans-Hermann Hartwich, *Sozialstaatspostulat und gesellschaftlicher status quo* (Cologne and Opladen: Westdeutscher Verlag, 1970), p. 69, passim.
[21] Andrew Shonfield, gen. ed., *International Economic Relations of the Western World 1959–1971* (London: Oxford University Press, 1976), Vol 2: *International Monetary Relations*, by Susan Strange, pp. 46–47.

The EEC was part of the favorable international environment in which the German export offensive developed. Originally, European integration had several key functions for the West German state. It symbolized the break with a disastrous tradition of nationalism and helped the FRG to gain international legitimacy. At the same time, like NATO, it served as a framework which made the FRG a more predictable factor for its partners. Economically, the EEC rested on a Franco-German "entente" which opened French markets to German industry in exchange for German subsidies to French agriculture. With the adoption of a common commercial policy, the member states of the European Community have given up national control over one traditional component of foreign economic policy. Since 1970, commercial and tariff agreements are concluded by the Community.[22] The partial de-nationalization of foreign economic policy has contributed to the emergence of complex patterns of interaction between national and supranational bureaucracies.

Yet, the achievements of "negative integration" (i.e., the elimination of barriers to the free flow of goods, services, and labor and the establishment of a common external tariff) have failed to produce the impetus for the "positive integration" anticipated by the founding fathers. Prospects for economic and monetary union are dim indeed. Regional and industrial policies worthy of this name have not materialized. Even worse, the Community lacks a coherent raw materials and energy policy. Foreign policy coordination in the framework of "European Political Cooperation" (Davignon Committee) is fairly limited in scope. This state of affairs explains why member states are highly reluctant to hand over to the Community the instruments of foreign economic policy that still remain under their jurisdiction (e.g., export credit policy and industrial cooperation agreements).

These instruments have assumed growing importance in West Germany's economic relations with the East which have experienced a spectacular upswing in the wake of Chancellor Brandt's *Ostpolitik*. Yet, the development of economic cooperation has not been accompanied by concomitant progress in the security field. As a result of *Ostpolitik,* the Federal Republic has ceased to be a revisionist power. West German diplomacy has gained considerably in freedom of maneuver. In some quarters, this has revived the specter of a *Schaukelpolitik* in the Rapallo tradition. But as long as Central Europe remains the theater where two antagonistic alliances confront each other armed to the teeth and as long as the European Community proves unable to develop an "integrated" defense policy, the large majority of West Germans will continue to rely upon American military protection as the ultimate guarantee of their security. While détente has tended to de-emphasize problems of military security, the crises rocking the international economy have placed issues of economic security at the top of the agenda of German policy makers. The breakdown of the Bretton Woods system, the Arab boycott,

---

[22]With state-trading countries, member states were allowed to conclude two-year agreements until the end of 1972.

and the worldwide recession have signaled the end of a *belle époque*.[23] Because of its export dependence, the Federal Republic has an overriding interest in the preservation of an open and liberal world economy. That is why German leaders display an almost missionary zeal in their efforts to stem the rising tide of *dirigisme* in international economic relations. Hence also their preoccupation with domestic conditions in other West European nations which sometimes expresses itself in ill-considered declarations and admonitions. Yet, behind a façade of arrogance of power looms the fear of paradise lost.

## II  Institutions and interests

Government:

Weighing the balance of public and private power, one finds that the West German state has always been stronger than the popular conception of *Soziale Markwirtschaft* would suggest. This notion implied a clear-cut separation of powers in the economic sphere: the economic process was essentially to be left to the self-regulating mechanisms of the market. The state had to lay down the rules of the game (via *Ordnungspolitik*) and to assume some responsibility for growth in general.[24] Shonfield has rightly emphasized the gap between liberalist doctrine and interventionist practice. This gap even characterized the period when Ludwig Erhard, the architect of the Currency Reform of 1948 and Minister of Economics from 1949 to 1963, occupied the commanding seat of economic policy. Yet, as far as foreign economic policy is concerned, the most important function of the Ministry of Economics during the formative years was undoubtedly that it acted as the steering agency of *"Ordnungspolitik."* As such, it became the driving force behind the installation of a liberal regime of foreign trade.

Trade liberalization, it was felt, would speed up economic recovery by exposing West German industry to the competitive pressure of the world market.[25] Foreign economic policy had to break completely with the nefarious practices of exchange controls, autarky, *Großraumwirtschaft,* and close government supervision of foreign trade which had been prevalent under the Third Reich. Moreover, pressure to expand liberalization brought to bear upon Germany by the Organization for European Economic Cooperation (OEEC) was probably instrumental in overcoming protectionist resistance which articulated itself through the Federation of German Industry (BDI) and the Christian Democrat (CDU) parliamentary group. Ironically enough, Erhard, in questions of tariff policy, often enjoyed fuller support from the

---

[23] See Wolfgang Hager, "Europe's Economic Security," *The Atlantic Papers* 3/1975, p. 11.
[24] See Hans-Joachim Arndt, *West Germany: Politics of Non-Planning* (Syracuse: Syracuse University Press, 1966), p. 13.
[25] Wallich, pp. 229–35.

Social Democrats (SPD) than from his own party, including Chancellor Adenauer.[26]

The initial hegemony enjoyed by the Economics Ministry in the field of foreign economic policy was reduced to some degree after the Foreign Office was set up in 1951. When the Federal Republic acceded to sovereignty in 1955, a jurisdictional conflict arose between the Economics Ministry and the Foreign Office over the question of which department would primarily control foreign economic policy. The Foreign Office claimed that foreign economic policy was an instrument of foreign policy, the efficacy of which should not be sacrificed to free trade ideology. The Ministry of Economics, for its part, argued that trade policy was inseparable from general economic policy and that it was an integral element of a coherent economic philosophy. According to this view, liberalization made the use of foreign economic policy, for other than economic purposes, obsolete. The conflict was resolved by a compromise. The Foreign Office was entrusted with the external representation of the Federal Republic in matters of foreign economic policy (e.g., negotiation of trade agreements and protocols). The Ministry of Economics continued to be in charge of relations with domestic actors.[27]

When Schiller entered office as Minister of Economics in 1966, he fathered a new conception of economic policy which was embodied in the Act for the Promotion of Stability and Growth of 1967. It formulated the objectives of and provided the tools for a Keynesian policy of managing macroeconomic demand *(Globalsteuerung)* designed to overcome the recession of 1966–67. The act obliged the Federal and state governments to pursue policies "that contribute, in the framework of a market economy, simultaneously to achieving price-level stability, a high degree of employment and external equilibrium, together with steady and adequate economic growth."[28] During the following years, however, the goal of external equilibrium was often treated with "benign neglect." During Schiller's tenure, the Economics Ministry also embarked on an active policy of concentration in sectors heavily subsidized by the government or dependent upon the state as a major buyer (e.g., coal, aeronautics, computers, nuclear energy). In most cases, the rationale was to build up national champions able to compete effectively in international markets.[29] Nevertheless, the Ministry has remained an institutional stronghold of free market philosophy. Orthodox liberalism coupled with budgetary considerations is at the root of its vigorous opposition to Third World demands for a New International Economic Order (NIEO).

Besides having virtual veto power over commitment of funds, the Ministry

---

[26] Wallich, p., 238. See also Gerard Braunthal, *The Federation of German Industry in Politics* (Ithaca: Cornell University Press, 1965), pp. 327–28.

[27] See Kurt P. Tudyka, "Ökonomische Dimensionen auswärtiger Beziehungen," *Atomzeitalter* 1968, pp. 341–42; and Oskar Baier, "Um die Führung in der Handelspolitik," *Gewerkschaftliche Monatshefte* (December 1955), pp. 752–54.

[28] Georg H. Kuster, "Germany," in *Big Business and the State in Western Europe,* Raymond Vernon, ed. (Cambridge, Massachusetts: Harvard University Press, 1974), p. 69.

[29] Ibid., pp. 74–76.

of Finance is in charge of monetary and credit policy. Consequently, it represents the Federal Republic in the International Monetary Fund (IMF) and other bodies dealing with international monetary reform, usually together with representatives of the Bundesbank. The Ministry for Economic Cooperation handles capital aid to developing countries. The Ministry of Food and Agriculture participates in the formulation of the European Community's common agricultural policy.

How is coordination between ministries achieved? As Mayntz and Scharpf have pointed out, "The cabinet has not developed into a collective decision-making body that is in effective control of government policy."[30] In the area of foreign economic policy, coordination is mainly the affair of interministerial committees which have proliferated over the years. There are interministerial committees for imports, trade policy, export guarantees, and investment guarantees which meet under the chairmanship of the Economics Ministry. The Committee of State Secretaries for European Affairs, the main coordinating body for EC policy, is chaired by the Parliamentary State Secretary in the Foreign Office.[31] Normally, the ministries are represented at committee meetings by senior civil servants. Their role in the formulation and execution of foreign economic policy can hardly be overestimated. Although officials tend to consider themselves as servants of the "public good," and not as agents of particular interests, a symbiotic relationship exists between the ministerial bureaucracy and interest group staffs.[32] Under the rules and procedures of the government, the main interest groups are entitled to be heard and consulted during the drafting stage of legislation when their interests are affected. This means, in practice, that interest group functionaries participate in the legislative process at a stage when draft projects are still kept secret from Bundestag deputies. Interest group representatives are also involved in the drawing up of commodity lists and sit on interministerial committees in an advisory capacity.

Parliament is more or less eclipsed by the direct cooperation between interest groups and the ministerial bureaucracy. Of 286 petitions filed by the BDI between 1952 and 1964 on subjects related to foreign economic policy, only eight were addressed to the Bundestag. The Bundestag Foreign Trade Committee (1949–1965) was often bypassed or presented with *faits accomplis* to be enacted. During the deliberations on a new tariff regime in 1950–51, the government cleared its tariff proposals in advance with the relevant industry and trade associations. Referring to the consensus reached, it usually obtained swift approval by the committee.[33] The modest role of the Bundestag also stems from the fact that foreign economic policy is largely conducted by decree and hence does not require legislative action.

---

[30] Renate Mayntz and Fritz W. Scharpf, *Policy-Making in the German Federal Bureaucracy* (Amsterdam: Elsevier, 1975), p. 42.

[31] See Hans-Peter Schwarz, "Die Bundesregierung und die auswärtigen Beziehungen," in *Handbuch der deutschen Außenpolitik*, Hans-Peter Schwarz, ed. (Munich: Piper Verlag, 1975), pp. 72–73.

[32] See also Mayntz and Scharpf, p. 60.

[33] On the role of parliament in foreign economic policy making, see Tudyka, "Ökonomische

## Industry, trade, and labor

By virtue of its size, the export sector has considerable clout in the process of foreign economic policy making. Its dominance is anchored in the amazing export dependence of key industries. This dependence is converted into political influence through a network of well-organized and articulate business associations. The following figures may provide an idea of what exports mean for some branches of industry. In 1975, the aggregate (direct plus indirect) export dependence of the investment goods industries which accounted for more than 55 percent of all industrial exports amounted to 47.4 percent. In the machine-building industry, it came to 56 percent; in the automobile industry, to 52 percent. The figures for the iron-producing industry and for the chemical industry are 67 and 48.5 percent respectively.[34] In 1974, the export share in total sales was 47 percent for the automobile industry, 44 percent for machine-building, and 36 percent for the chemical industry. Daimler-Benz in 1975 had an export share of 39 percent. Hoechst, Mannesmann, and Thyssen exports amounted to 32, 50, and 34 percent of total sales, respectively.[35]

West German industry is not only highly concentrated but also remarkably well organized. Branch industrial and national peak associations function as efficient agents of interest aggregation. Branch associations in some cases assume functions which go far beyond traditional interest group activities. The Iron and Steel Association, for instance, has features of an industry-wide planning institution, as it collects and distributes information on planned sales, production capacities, and investment plans.[36] The national branch associations, like the Association of the Chemical Industry or the German Machine Builders Association (VDMA), are grouped together in the powerful Federation of German Industry (BDI). Conflicts of interest between different branch associations make sometimes for a lengthy and laborious bargaining process within the BDI. On matters of foreign trade policy, tensions usually arise between export-oriented branches like VDMA or the chemical industry, on the one hand, and protectionist sectors on the other. The national peak industrial associations of the EC nations have joined in the Union of Industries of the European Communities (UNICE). Other relevant peak associations are the German Diet of Industry and Commerce (Deutscher Industrie-und Handelstag–DIHT), the top-level organization of 81 local and district chambers of industry and commerce,[37] the Federation of Wholesale and Foreign Trade (BGA), and the Federation of German Banks. BGA and DIHT act as champions of liberalism on

---

Dimensionen auswärtiger Beziehungen," and Kurt P. Tudyka, "Der Außenhandelsausschuss des Deutschen Bundestags," in *Tradition und Reform in der deutschen Politik. Gedenkschrift für Waldemar Besson*, Gotthard Jasper, ed. (München: Piper Verlag, 1976), pp. 441–80.

[34] DIW-Wochenbericht 22/76, p. 221.

[35] See Kurzmitteilung, "Zur Internationalisierung der westdeutschen Wirtschaft," p. 232; *Le Monde* (Paris), 9 December 1976, p. 27.

[36] Arndt, p. 73.

[37] See Braunthal, p. 26.

questions of foreign economic policy. The peak associations of industry, trade, and banking have established liaison institutions, such as the Working Group on Foreign Trade *(Arbeitsgemeinschaft Außenhandel)* and the Working Group on Developing Countries.

As pointed out earlier, the close contacts between the government bureaucracy and interest groups provide the main channel for organized business to exert influence on policy making. Public and private bureaucracies work hand in hand. Conflicts among interest groups occasionally confer a broker function to the ministerial bureaucracy. Other channels are direct access to the Chancellor or membership in his economic kitchen cabinet. Large enterprises do not have to rely on their association to find attentive listeners in the Bonn ministries. Interest group influence is institutionalized in the numerous ministerial advisory councils, the most important with respect to foreign economic policy being the Foreign Trade Advisory Council of the Ministry of Economics. In 1975, it was composed of 41 members. Seventeen of these were directors of export-oriented industrial corporations. Five were bankers, including one director of the labor union-owned *Bank für Gemeinwirtschaft.* Six members came from protectionist branches and two were labor union experts.

Labor unions have been part of the "grand coalition" that has supported export expansion. Their role in the shaping of foreign economic policy, however, has been extremely limited, bordering on exclusion. In the 1950s, labor unions generally backed Erhard's drive for import liberalization, "arguing that increased imports would provide more choices to consumers, and charging that certain business quarters were not prepared to agree to this for fear of what would happen to their profits at home, while they planned to exploit the export market."[38] Export surpluses were seen as a consequence of import restrictions and lagging domestic consumption and were designated as the main source of inflation.[39] Nevertheless, labor unions largely accepted the export mystique. Export orders contributed to full employment and thereby strengthened labor's position on collective bargaining. Real wages (net) rose on average by 4.9 percent per year between 1950 and 1972. This roughly corresponded to the annual productivity increase of 5 percent over the same period.[40] The IG Metall, the powerful metal workers union (membership in 1973: 2.4 million; total DGB membership: 7.16 million), has its centers of strength in export-intensive branches. The tangible results of export-oriented growth outweighed by far "macroeconomic" concerns about imported inflation and the real transfer of goods in favor of Germany's trade partners that export surpluses entailed. Labor's relative passivity in the area of foreign economic policy can therefore be explained by two factors. First, labor

[38] Ibid., p. 331.

[39] See Herbert Ehrenberg, "Gewerkschaftliche Lohnpolitik in der Hochkonjunktur," *Gewerkschaftliche Monatshefte* 3/1962, pp. 154–59; and, Walter Hesselbach, "Löhne und Preise in einer wachsenden Wirtschaft," *Gewerkschaftliche Monatshefte* 6/1962, pp. 321–27.

[40] Joachim Bergmann et al., *Gewerkschaften in der Bundesrepublik* (Frankfurt and Cologne: Europäische Verlagsanstalt, 1975), pp. 108–09.

reaped the dividends of growth (without necessarily trying to maximize them). Second, at the branch level, the interests of labor and capital converged.

## Protectionist sectors or compensating the losers

Producers' alliances have become particularly visible in recent years when employers and union leaders of the textile and clothing industries unanimously called for protection against "import dumping" from Eastern Europe and the Far East. However, the case of protectionism is quite complex. Export orientation of a branch does not equal renunciation of protection. There are strongly export-oriented branches, such as the nonferrous metal industry, iron and steel production, or the chemical industry, that have managed to maintain high levels of tariff or quota protection for certain product groups. Even though the overall trend of West German foreign economic policy has been in the direction of import liberalization, protectionist sectors did, in fact, win some battles. Protectionist branches frequently make their demands through the BDI. As a result, DIHT and BGA have become the most vocal advocates of further import liberalization. If we use as an indicator of protectionism an effective protection level of 15 percent or above (vis-à-vis non-EEC countries) in 1970, we obtain the following list of highly protected branches.[41] These branches are raw materials- and labor-intensive. They accounted for 22 percent of total industrial sales in 1970. Included are the cellulose and pulp producing industry, nonferrous metals, paper processing, textiles, clothing, iron and steel production, fine ceramics, iron and steel foundries, leather processing, and wood processing. If one takes the criterion of overall effective protection, the last three branches in the list of ten highly protected branches have to be replaced by petroleum refining, mining, and aeronautics.

Agriculture is a protectionist sector par excellence and farmers have probably been one of the most successful interest groups. When negotiations on the Common Market agricultural price system failed to produce the level of grain prices farmers had asked for, the Farmers Association obtained generous compensation from the government through indirect income subsidies and other measures. When the DM revaluation of 1969 threatened to reduce agricultural income under the existing CAP pegged-exchange-rate system, the Farmers Association successfully pressured the government to introduce a compensation scheme.[42] The case of agriculture forcefully suggests that the political influence a sector wields is not necessarily commensurate with its structural economic strength.

---

[41] Jürgen B. Donges et al., *Protektion und Branchenstruktur der westdeutschen Wirtschaft* (Tübingen: J.C.B. Mohr [Paul Siebeck], 1973), p. 97. Nominal protection affects import prices; effective protection, domestic production costs. Effective protection is higher than nominal if protection increases with the processing level. Overall effective protection includes tariffs, quotas, and non-tariff barriers. See ibid., p. 16.

[42] Dieter Piel, "Die außenpolitische Rolle der Wirtschaftsverbände," in Schwarz, *Handbuch der deutschen Außenpolitik*, p. 214.

*III Export interests and "high politics"—the case of Eastern trade policy*

West German trade policy towards Eastern Europe and the Soviet Union has been largely determined by the political climate of East-West relations. At first sight, it seems to be a showcase for the subordination of economic motives and private interests to the primacy of foreign policy. Yet, a closer analysis reveals that the export sector was relatively successful, as the process of détente gained momentum, in overcoming government resistance to the removal of politically motivated restrictions on trade. The case of Eastern trade policy, therefore, not only provides some insights into the making of foreign economic policy but also shows how export interests fared under the changing conditions of "high politics." From its inception until the middle of the 1960s, West German *Ostpolitik* was dominated by the endeavor to achieve reunification. Trade policy was to serve as an instrument in the pursuit of this basic objective. Consequently, trade with the East developed in a climate of political and psychological tension from the very beginning. Export interests and foreign policy objectives often clashed, and business was suspected of putting profits above patriotism. Under the Adenauer administration, trade relations with the Soviet bloc were consciously neglected. The inertia which then characterized *Ostpolitik*, in general, and trade policy, in particular, not only symbolized the refusal to deal with the enemies of German unity but also served to demonstrate Bonn's "unswerving allegiance to the West."[43] The Federal Republic had no diplomatic relations with Communist countries until 1955 when Adenauer negotiated the establishment of diplomatic relations with the Soviet Union in exchange for the release of German prisoners of war. Consequently, prior to 1955, formal trade agreements could not be concluded. Industry stepped in to fill the vacuum. With government approval, the "Eastern Committee of the German Economy" (*Ostausschuß der deutschen Wirtschaft*) was set up in 1952 as the sole representative organ of the peak associations of industry, trade, and banking. Its tasks were to advise the government on questions of East-West trade and to prepare documents for official trade negotiations. In the absence of diplomatic relations, it was authorized to conduct trade talks on its own. Its executive office was established at BDI headquarters in Cologne. The *Ostausschuß* was not an institutional innovation. It rather appears as a successor to the "Russia Committee" which, from the late 1920s on, coordinated trade relations with the Soviet Union. De facto, on behalf of the German government, the Ostausschuß concluded the first commercial agreements with Rumania in 1953 and with the People's Republic of China in 1957. While the Ostausschuß leadership sought to improve trade relations with the East, the BDI leadership did not display much enthusiasm for *Osthandel.* BDI

---

[43] Frederick F. McGoldrick, *The Politics of West German Foreign Economic Policy Toward the Communist States of Eastern Europe 1955–1968* (Ph.D. dissertation, The American University, 1973), p. 505.

President Berg unconditionally supported Adenauer's foreign policy and did not object to the restrictive policy followed by the government with respect to import liberalization and the granting of government-guaranteed long-term export credits to Comecon countries. Criticism from industry mounted, however, when the government, in December 1962, denied export licenses to three of the largest steel producers for steel pipes ordered by the Soviet Union. This decision was taken on the grounds of a secret NATO Council resolution calling for a ban on the export of large-diameter steel pipes to the Soviet bloc. German compliance with the resolution was considered a test case for alliance solidarity and the Bundestag members representing the steel industry (Birrenbach of Thyssen and Dichgans, the deputy chairman of the Iron and Steel Industry Association) conformed to the government line. The embargo decision almost provoked a coalition crisis. The Free Democrats (FDP), junior partner of the Bonn coalition, rallied to the SPD in its opposition to the government. A government defeat in the Bundestag was only avoided because the CDU/CSU decided to boycott the vote and thus prevented the necessary quorum.[44]

The steel industry was outraged and viewed the embargo as causing enormous damage to trade relations with the Soviet Union. Moreover, the export sector became increasingly concerned about its "terms of competition" when Great Britain and Italy started a credit race by granting long-term credits covered by government insurance for the export of capital equipment to the Soviet Union. This violated the terms of the Berne Union agreement which prohibited credit terms for deliveries of capital equipment exceeding five years. Italy, Britain, and France had adopted a more pragmatic approach to East-West trade in general and were eager to reap the commercial benefits of détente. The efforts undertaken by the Federal Government to achieve coordination of credit terms under NATO or EEC auspices met with failure as West Germany's partner-rivals could pointedly refer to the West German lead in Eastern markets. The restrictive trade and credit policy had not prevented an almost continuous expansion of West German trade with Eastern Europe up to then. This was due to a long-standing tradition of commercial relations and the critical importance of imports of capital equipment for the industrialization process of the Comecon countries. Nonetheless, industrialists became alarmed at the prospect of losing Eastern markets to Western competitors. Spokesmen for the Ostausschuß therefore advocated a "de-politicization" of Eastern trade.[45] The gradual relaxation of credit restrictions was finally brought about by insistent pressure from the export sector in 1964–65. This was a time when, in political circles, it was increasingly recognized that the manipulation of trade was unlikely to yield significant concessions from the Soviet Union.

[44] See Robert W. Dean, *West German Trade with the East: The Political Dimension,* Praeger Special Studies in International Politics and Government (New York: Praeger Publishers, 1974), pp. 127–40.
[45] See Michael Kreile, "Ostpolitik und ökonomische Interessen," in *Die Ostpolitik der BRD,* Egbert Jahn and Volker Rittberger, eds. (Opladen: Westdeutscher Verlag, 1974), p. 74.

The export sector was also the driving force behind the liberalization of imports from state-trading nations which became a necessity as Eastern trade deficits grew. In 1965, the Ostausschuß submitted detailed proposals for liberalization to the Ministry of Economics. They represented a compromise between the conflicting interests of import-sensitive branches, on the one hand, and the interests of import trade federations and export industry on the other. The new import regulations promulgated by the Economics Ministry in May 1966 closely followed the Ostausschuß recommendations.

Once the strategic decisions regarding the course of trade policy had been taken by the government, the Ostausschuß proved to be very influential in shaping the content of this policy. Its striking effectiveness stems from several factors. Having the monopoly over representation at the level of national peak associations, it functions as a clearing-house, seeking to reach "quasi-unanimity" by in-house negotiations. It is thereby enabled to confront the government bureaucracy with a carefully hammered out common position. Its president, Otto Wolff von Amerongen, excels in dynamic leadership. The Ostausschuß staff has accumulated remarkable expertise, and many of the Rhine and Ruhr top managers who count sit on the executive committee. It is doubtful, however, whether the export sector would have succeeded, as it did, in bringing the government to reverse its trade policy had this not been in line with the change to a more flexible "policy of movement" towards Eastern Europe initiated by Foreign Minister Schröder in the early 1960s and continued under the Grand Coalition.

By eliminating political and psychological barriers to trade expansion and long-term economic cooperation with the East, the *Ostpolitik* conducted by the SPD-FDP coalition since 1969 has opened a new phase in foreign economic policy towards Comecon countries. The Federal Republic's economic potential makes it an attractive or even privileged partner for the Soviet Union. Economic motives have undoubtedly influenced the Soviet decision to normalize relations with West Germany. This is indicated by the huge compensation deal concluded in February 1970.

The Soviet Union ordered 1.2 million tons of large-diameter steel pipes from Mannesmann. (The 1962 embargo had been lifted in the Autumn of 1966 by NATO at the request of the German government at a time when the German steel industry was in crisis.) Payment was to be made through deliveries of Soviet natural gas to the Ruhrgas AG starting in 1973. The deal required a long-term credit of 1.2 billion DM which was granted to the USSR by a consortium of four banks led by the Deutsche Bank. The interest rate of 6.25 percent was called a preferential rate at the time, market rates being 1.5 to 2 percent above this level. But it is widely assumed that the banks, which owned a substantial part of Mannesmann shares, recovered their "concession" through Mannesmann's selling price. The natural gas "component" of the deal had been the object of an intense controversy. "German" natural gas producers, among them ESSO and SHELL which also controlled Dutch natural gas exports to the FRG, worried about price competition. They petitioned the Economics Ministry to prevent an agreement on Soviet natural gas deliveries.

Ruhrgas AG, the largest German natural gas distributor, however, wanted to be able to offer natural gas at competitive prices in Bavaria (transport costs from the Czechoslovakian border being lower than those from Holland) and to exert pressure on Dutch pricing policy. The opponents of natural gas imports from the Soviet Union received support from CDU politicians who argued against energy dependence on the USSR on national security grounds. Economics Minister Schiller approved the deal in order to improve competition and to diversify energy supplies. Since then, economic diplomacy has assumed a growing importance. Closer economic cooperation with the East is intended to create links of functional interdependence generating vested interests in the development of détente.

The main economic goals sought by the Federal Republic can be summarized as follows: diversification of export markets, development of new sources of raw materials and energy, and, if possible, the relocation of raw material and labor-intensive production lines. These objectives obviously reflect changes in economic structure and factor endowments and indicate the lessons learned from the "energy crisis." To promote trade and industrial cooperation, the government deployed a wide range of instruments. It took further measures of import liberalization, set up joint commissions for economic and technical cooperation composed of government officials and businessmen, and raised significantly the ceiling for export credit guarantees. The Federal Republic's trade surplus in Eastern trade rose from 0.7 billion DM in 1970 to almost 8 billion DM in 1975. Exports tripled between 1971 and 1975. Cumulative indebtedness of East European countries (including the USSR) vis-à-vis the FRG amounted to 20 billion DM in 1975.[46] The import-sensitive or so called "neuralgic" branches (textiles and clothing, fine ceramics, etc.) which protested strongly against further liberalization of imports from Eastern Europe received some compensation with the tightening-up of the "anti-dumping" price review procedure.

In 1973–74, a controversy developed over whether or not the government should subsidize interest rates for long-term export credits as the Soviet Union had suggested. This offered an interesting perspective on the distribution of power within the foreign economic policy network. Interministerial conflict seems to have arisen between the Foreign Office and the Chancellor's Office, on the one hand, and the Ministries of Economics and Finance on the other. Whereas the former favored the idea for foreign policy reasons, the latter argued that the measure was totally inappropriate given the huge surplus in trade with the East. Moreover, the Economics Ministry raised objections related to *Ordnungspolitik* and the Minister of Finance opposed the move on budgetary grounds. The Ostausschuß and the DIHT spoke out against export subsidies that discriminated among trade partners. The machine-building industry federation (VDMA), on the contrary, asked to be put on an equal footing with Western competitors who benefited from government

---

[46] Figures from Alex Möller, "Probleme und Perspektiven der wirtschaftlichen Verflechtung zwischen der Bundesrepublik Deutschland und den Staatshandelsländern," *WSI-Mitteilungen* 5/1976, p. 288; and *Monatsberichte der Deutschen Bundesbank*, July 1976, p. 14.

subsidized export credits. With interest groups and government divided, the status quo option prevailed.

However, when export demand slackened under the impact of the worldwide recession, the DIHT seized the opportunity to propose a general revision of export finance and credit guarantee terms. Referring to the failure of harmonization efforts among the main exporting nations, the DIHT suggested that credit terms had become an increasingly important factor of competitiveness. The DIHT asked, therefore, for an at least partial adaptation of German conditions to those enjoyed by other West European exporters. Within three months of the publication of the DIHT proposals, the government followed suit. The competent interministerial committee decided upon a revision of guarantee conditions. This last example demonstrates, once again, that Eastern trade policy, though closely related to the overall strategy of *Ostpolitik,* has been much more open to interest group influence than *Ostpolitik* narrowly conceived. *Ostpolitik* stands out as an area of "high politics" par excellence. It was essentially formulated both by the relevant government departments (Chancellor's Office and Foreign Office) and by the foreign policy establishment of the Bundestag parties. Business hardly ever dared to intervene in this sensitive core area of foreign policy.

## *IV  Monetary policy: the dilemmas of stability*

Monetary policy, it was argued earlier, played a crucial role in the strategy of export expansion. It did so because it kept inflation rates low and thus provided an essential condition for export competitiveness. This favorable export position was further enhanced by the undervaluation of the DM. However, undervaluation produced growing export surpluses which were bound to undermine stability. How this contradiction crystalized into political conflicts will be examined in a case study on exchange rate policy. Before considering this problem, it is necessary to give a broad outline of the monetary policy network.

*The Bundesbank:* West German monetary policy is marked by the hegemony of the Bundesbank. Institutionally, the Bundesbank is a part of the executive branch. Its governing bodies, Directorate and Central Bank Council, have the status of a central federal office (Oberste Bundesbehörde). The Bundesbank is, however, independent of the Federal Government in its fulfillment of the function legally defined as "regulating the money circulation and the supply of credit to the economy with the aim of safeguarding the currency." At the same time, the Bundesbank is bound to support the government's overall economic policy as long as this is consistent with its mandate.[47] Functionally, it has developed into "a kind of macroeconomic super-institution" (Arndt). It can decide, as Hankel suggests,

---

[47] See Helmut Schlesinger and Horst Bockelmann, "Monetary Policy in the Federal Republic of Germany," in *Monetary Policy in Twelve Industrial Countries,* Karel Holbik, ed. (Boston: Federal Reserve Bank of Boston, 1973), p. 169.

"with almost complete autonomy, de facto and de jure, how much economic growth, how much employment, and how much social protection should be granted the nation."

Even if this may slightly overstate the degree of Bundesbank autonomy, it indeed dramatizes the old problem of "responsibility without parliamentary accountability."[48] Bundesbank autonomy, it is true, has increased with the collapse of the Bretton Woods system. Under the regime of fixed exchange rates, the bank's freedom of maneuver was severely restricted by the fact that the authority to make parity changes and to close foreign exchange markets resided with the government. With the emergence of a system of floating exchange rates, the balance of power in monetary policy has shifted in favor of the Bundesbank. (This does not apply to the European currency "snake" where parity changes are still decided by the Finance Minister. The management of the snake, however, is a matter of an extremely close day-to-day cooperation among central banks.)

The essence of Bundesbank philosophy has been succinctly stated by Wadbrook: "Powerfully influenced in its institutional shape and through its personnel by memories of Germany's two great inflations, the Bundesbank has consistently seen defense of the DM's domestic value and international parity as the primary goal, not only of its own, but of all economic policy."[49] Full employment had to be sacrificed to price stability, if necessary. This was demonstrated by the recession of 1966–67 which was caused, to a large extent, by an overly restrictive Bundesbank policy. In this context, it is worthwhile to note that Otmar Emminger, the current President of the Bundesbank and a towering figure in West German monetary policy, liked to refer to Lord Beveridge's concept of full employment according to which a jobless rate of 3 percent corresponded to full employment. The average unemployment rate of 0.8 percent during the years 1961–1966 was considered a situation of excessive employment and, hence, a dangerous source of inflation. No wonder, then, that the Bundesbank, together with large sectors of the business community, tended to view the recession as a necessary purge which restored labor discipline as well as confidence in the currency.[50] Yet not only price stability, but also the exchange rate parity, were held to be sacrosanct for more than a decade.[51] This resulted in an almost chronic undervaluation of the DM which gave rise to increasing export surpluses. These, in turn, fueled inflation. The burden of adjustment was to be shouldered by deficit countries which had deviated from the path of monetary discipline. West Germany assumed the task of exporting stability to its partners.[52]

---

[48] Arndt, p. 94; Wilhelm Hankel, "A New Order for American-European Monetary Policy," in *The Euro-American System,* Ernst-Otto Czempiel and Dankwart A. Rustow, eds. (Frankfurt and Boulder, Colorado: Campus Verlag, 1976), p. 53.

[49] Wadbrook, p. 90.

[50] See Otmar Emminger, *Zwanzig Jahre deutsche Geldpolitik* (1968), pp. 11, 16; Wadbrook, p. 57.

[51] Hugo M. Kaufmann, "A Debate over Germany's Revaluation 1961: A Chapter in Political Economy," *Weltwirtschaftliches Archiv* Vol. 103 (1969 II), pp. 181–212, p. 191.

[52] Wadbrook, p. 251.

This rather ideological approach to exchange rate policy has, in recent years, been replaced by a more rational one. But a concern for price stability continues to determine the stand German monetary authorities take on questions of exchange rate policy and international monetary reform. From this derives their preference for the system of floating currencies and their opposition to an increase in unconditional international credit facilities.[53]

The relations between the Bundesbank and the government seem to have been governed by close consultation and cooperation, although occasional clashes have occurred.[54] The law, it is true, "makes no real provision against prolonged conflict"[55] if a government policy of expansion and full employment should collide with a deflationary course taken by the Bundesbank. It would be difficult for the government to influence decisively the composition of the Central Bank Council (the supreme executive organ, composed of the President and Vice-President of the Bank, the members of the Directorate and the Presidents of the state central banks) because the members appointed by the government (President, Vice-President, and Directorate) have a term of office of eight years. Moreover, the Presidents of the state central banks, appointed by the Bundesrat upon the virtually binding suggestion of the respective state governments, enjoy a majority over the members appointed by the Federal Government. Yet, in the long run, the Bundesbank cannot afford to conduct a policy diametrically opposed to that of the government. This might provoke a revision of the Bundesbank Act, a possibility hanging like Damocles' sword over the heads of the central bankers. However, such a move would probably expose the government to the reproach that it was embarking on an unbridled policy of inflation.

The macroeconomic tasks of the Bundesbank are based, of course, on the traditional function of the central bank. Its role is to be the "banker's bank," the "lender of last resort."[56] The Bundesbank is in permanent close contact with the banking system. In general, it has shared the conservative philosophy of the financial community. Even though there is a close affinity between the Bundesbank and the financial community created by recruitment, experience, and ideology, it would be misleading to consider the Bundesbank merely as a bridgehead or an extension of the private sector. Borrowing a Marxist term, one might say that the Bundesbank participates in the functions of the state as "ideal collective capitalist (*ideeller Gesamtkapitalist*)." The countercyclical management of liquidity supply as well as the supervisory functions of the central bank vis-à-vis the state central banks are, therefore, bound to produce tensions between the Bundesbank and the banking community.

*The banks:* Banks have traditionally occupied a strategic position in the German economy. The German banking system is largely one of "universal" banks,

[53] See Hans-Eckart Scharrer, "Währungspolitische Perspektiven für die Bundesrepublik Deutschland in der Post-Bretton-Woods Ära," *WSI-Mitteilungen* 5/1976, p. 302.

[54] See Arndt, p. 95; Wadbrook, p. 90.

[55] Wadbrook, p. 89.

[56] See Schlesinger and Bockelmann, p. 171.

i.e., specialization is low. One can roughly distinguish three categories. The first is composed of the commercial banks. Most prominent among them are the "Big Three": Deutsche Bank, Dresdner Bank, and Commerzbank. The second category includes the savings banks and the central giro institutions. These are banks under public statute. Finally, there are the cooperative banks.

In terms of business volume (total liabilities plus certain items "below the line"), the public banks account for about 40 percent, the private commercial banks for approximately 25 percent, and the cooperative sector for 14 percent, the rest being accounted for by mortgage banks and other categories of specialized credit institutions.[57] The "power of the banks" is a term which commonly refers to the large private banks. It is founded on several factors which, taken together, add up to an impressive potential of control and influence over key sectors of the economy. (The secretiveness of the big banks, however, makes it difficult to get a satisfactory data base on this count, as the Monopoly Commission, an independent body of experts comparable to the Royal Commission, recently found out to its disappointment.[58])

The "Big Three" own substantial stock in a number of large corporations. Banks hold more than 25 percent of voting capital in 28 of the 100 largest enterprises.[59] Banks exercise the proxy votes in company meetings for the shareholders who have deposited their shares with the bank, if mandated by them. Bank directors sit on the supervisory boards (*Aufsichtsrat*) of numerous corporations. At the end of 1974, 641 of the 2036 joint-stock companies (*Aktiengesellschaften*) had 986 bank representatives on their supervisory boards. These representatives accounted for 28 percent of all board members.[60] The Monopoly Commission has concluded that the exercise of stockholders' rights, the information obtained through board membership, and decisions on the financing of investment projects confer management functions on the banks and represent a threat to competition.[61]

The Commission has, therefore, recommended a 5 percent limit on bank participation in non-banks. Bankers tend to argue that influence over management decisions is essentially limited to finance questions.[62] They further insist that denial of credit is not an effective weapon. As competition in the credit sector has tended to increase in recent years, public banks have engaged more and more in large-scale industrial financing.[63] "Coordination by banker" (Shonfield), the pro-

[57] Ibid., p. 164; Irene Moesch and Diethard B. Simmert, *Banken. Strukturen, Macht, Reformen* (Köln: Bund Verlag, 1976), p. 23.

[58] Monopolkommission, pp. 199, 247.

[59] Ibid., p. 195; see also p. 258.

[60] Ibid., p. 270.

[61] Ibid., p. 46.

[62] E.g., Franz Ulrich, "Großbanken heute," in *Neuzeitliche Bankpolitik-Analysen und Meinungen aus der deutschen Kreditwirtschaft*, R. Wittgen, ed. (Frankfurt: Fritz Knapp Verlag, 1974), p. 75.

[63] Moesch and Simmert, pp. 68–70; Burkhart Röpker, ed., *Wettbewerbsprobleme in Kreditgewerbe* (Berlin: Duncker und Humblot, 1976).

gramming of investment plans or production capacities in certain sectors of industry, should be the exception rather than the rule. In this respect, the role of branch industrial associations (e.g., the Iron and Steel Association and the association of the cement industry)[64] seems to be much more important.

The close links between private banks and the export sector have established a community of interest in the area of foreign economic policy. This is especially true with respect to exchange rate policy (see below). The banking community participates in the formulation and implementation of export credit and capital export policy. It is represented in the interministerial committees for export credit guarantees and foreign investment insurance in an advisory capacity. The banking community is also represented in the supervisory councils or boards of public institutions like the Kreditanstalt für Wiederaufbau, an agency in charge of long-term financing of exports and development projects through capital aid to the Third World.[65]

Another example of the semipublic functions of the banking system is the Central Capital Market Committee, a club of the chief issue banks, founded in 1957 in agreement with the Economics Ministry. It controls access to the capital market and coordinates the issue projects of public and private non-banks, "at times using its powers to reduce foreign demand in Germany's market."[66] Given the narrowness of the German capital market, the role of the Committee is considerable.

As indicated earlier, the relationship between the Bundesbank and the banking system is at times a conflictual one. This has been brought out by the recent debate over whether or not the banks are able to thwart the monetary policy of the Bundesbank.

Given the "open external flank" under the system of fixed exchange rates, imported liquidity enabled the banks to pursue credit expansion in spite of monetary restrictions. Even after the March 1973 decision to float the DM, the banks continued on a risky course of credit expansion. It required urgent appeals and draconian measures by the Bundesbank to compel the banks to stop credit expansion.[67] When the Bundesbank switched to a policy of expansion in 1975, the banks were blamed for not passing on easier credit conditions to their clients rapidly enough. Bankers argue, however, that the banks can only support official monetary policy if competition forces them to adapt themselves to market trends working in the same direction.[68] Yet as the Bundesbank and Monopoly Commission have suggested, the issue is precisely whether competition in the banking sector is working satisfactorily.

[64] See Röpker, p. 261.

[65] Hans-Eckart Scharrer, "Die Rolle der Banken," in Schwarz, ed., *Handbuch der deutschen Außenpolitik,* pp. 219–24.

[66] Wadbrook, p. 28; Helmut Schlesinger, "Geldpolitik in der Phase des Wiederaufbaus (1950–1958)," in Deutsche Bundesbank, *Wirtschaft und Währung in Deutschland 1876–1975* (Frankfurt: Fritz Knapp Verlag, 1976), p. 600. A Bundesbank representative attends the meetings with the status of "guest."

[67] Moesch and Simmert, pp. 70–71.

[68] Helmut Geiger, *Bankpolitik* (Stuttgart: Kohlhammer, 1975), p. 111.

Exchange rate policy—the political economy of DM revaluation

Under the system of fixed exchange rates and free capital movements, parity maintenance was bound to conflict with domestic stabilization. Anti-inflation policy proved to be self-defeating as it induced capital inflows which aggravated the balance-of-payments surplus and countered efforts to bring liquidity under control. Parity changes, however, were likely to hurt powerful domestic interests. DM revaluations, the *coups de théâtre* of monetary policy, therefore became episodes that were characterized by embittered controversy and dramatic action. The 1961 and 1969 cases are particularly instructive as they show the extent, as well as the limits, of export sector dominance in the process of economic policy making.

At the end of the period of reconstruction and monetary reintegration, the rapid expansion of German exports and the parallel build-up of reserves permitted the full liberalization of capital transactions and the introduction of full convertibility in 1958. Rising export surpluses and long-term capital imports called for a monetary policy oriented towards external equilibrium. In 1958, Bundesbank policy in foreign exchange markets sought, in fact, to encourage the export of funds.[69] However, in the Autumn of 1959, when the economy reached a boom phase, the Bundesbank responded by gradually raising the discount rate and by a series of other restrictive measures. Thereby, it was confronted for the first time with the dilemma "that external equilibrium and domestic stability may, in certain circumstances, call for diametrically opposite monetary policy measures." This was a dilemma "which was to be an almost constant feature of the following decade," according to two Bundesbank officials.[70] The instruments deployed by the Bundesbank to ward off the growing inflow of liquid funds proved to be ineffective. The majority of the Central Bank Council was not prepared to revalue the DM, although the United States and Britain put pressure on Germany to take measures to reduce its balance-of-payments surplus. Revaluation was excluded on the grounds that the surplus position did not reflect a fundamental disequilibrium but derived from factors that were only temporarily operative. Consequently, the Bundesbank reversed its policy. It lowered the discount rate from 5 to 4 percent and eased liquidity restrictions. This change in credit policy during a domestic boom (a "dramatic reappraisal," according to Emminger) "had a highly sobering effect in economic policy circles."[71] Eventually, it led to the revaluation of 1961.

Imported inflation had been a theme of monetary policy discussion since the Summer of 1956.[72] In April 1957, the economists forming the *Wissenschaftliche Beirat beim Bundeswirtschaftsministerium* (Council of Scholarly Advisors at the

---

[69] Schlesinger and Bockelmann, p. 183. Our discussion of the 1961 revaluation is largely based on the excellent case study by Kaufmann (fn. 51) and the Schlesinger/Bockelmann article.

[70] Schlesinger and Bockelmann, p. 184.

[71] Ibid., p. 187.

[72] Emminger, "Zwanzig Jahre deutsche Geldpolitik," p. 19; Emminger, "Deutsche Geld-und Währungspolitik im Spannungsfeld zwischen innerem und äusserem Gleichgewicht (1948–1975)," in Deutsche Bundesbank, *Wirtschaft und Währung in Deutschland*, p. 495.

Ministry of Economics) had analyzed the problem of export surpluses and pointed to the vicious circle in which monetary policy was trapped.[73] They proposed a general realignment of exchange rates but suggested that Germany might be compelled to resort to unilateral revaluation if debtor countries were not ready for joint action or refused to devalue individually.[74] Erhard, the Economics Minister, and Finance Minister Etzel were in favor of revaluation.[75] Adenauer, influenced by his advisors from industry and banking, rejected the idea. During the 1960–61 debate, economists of the Freiburg school pleaded for revaluation. Organized labor and the Social Democrats called for the lowering of tariffs and the elimination of quotas in order to fight imported inflation. The SPD also spoke out in favor of Erhard's fiscal plans which amounted to a de facto revaluation.[76] It was, however, opposed to a de jure revaluation because of the risks involved. Revaluation was strongly advocated by the *Sparkassen- und Giroverband,* the organization of savings institutions. The opposite camp united commercial banks and industry. Abs (Deutsche Bank) argued that revaluation would reduce Germany's export share and "its capacity to assist underdeveloped countries"(!).[77] He advocated an increase in capital exports as a solution to the surplus problem. BDI President Berg warned Erhard that "an open or concealed revaluation of the mark could result in a catastrophe for the entire economy."[78]

Adenauer followed Berg's "advice" and vetoed Erhard's fiscal plans. Industry developed its own anti-inflation and balance-of-payments program. It included:

> a call for price discipline, the commitment of subscribing to a development loan in the amount of DM 1 billion, in order to reduce the excess liquidity in the economy, the promotion of capital exports, a freezing of part of its investment capital at the central bank, and a gentleman's agreement between the public sector and the building industry whereby the construction of nonessential buildings would be postponed.[79]

The proposed development loan, however, was likely to induce a return flow of export orders from the Third World. The Bundesbank and the Economics Ministry were careful to point out that the loan was not a guarantee against revaluation. The Central Bank Council also recommended the export of capital. In 1961, a total of 4 billion DM was thus mobilized for development aid. The surplus position of 1960 can therefore be viewed, according to Emminger, as one of the triggers of a

---

[73] Wissenschaftlicher Beirat beim Bundeswirtschaftsministerium, *Gutachten* (30 April 1957), p. 25.
[74] Ibid., p. 31.
[75] Emminger, "Deutsche Geld-und Währungspolitik im Spannungsfeld zwischen innerem und äusserem Gleichgewicht (1948–1975)," p. 495.
[76] Kaufmann, p. 199.
[77] Ibid., p. 203.
[78] Ibid., p. 205.
[79] Ibid., p. 206.

systematic policy of development assistance.[80] When Bundesbank action to defend the parity of the DM intensified inflationary pressures, the government finally decided, in March 1961, to revalue the DM by 5 percent. Berg felt betrayed by Adenauer and reacted by suspending payment of a monthly contribution of 100,000 DM to the CDU treasury.[81] IG Metall called revaluation a "necessary experiment to restore international and domestic equilibrium."[82] The *Sparkassenverband* sent a cable to Adenauer expressing "thanks and congratulations in the name of all savers."[83] At first sight, the decision to revalue may appear as a defeat of the export sector. But the modest rate of 5 percent suggests that the measure represented "a compromise of opposing financial and political interests."[84]

The recession of 1966–67 was at the root of an unprecedented export offensive. While imports stagnated, export surpluses shot up. Cost and price levels remained relatively stable during the recovery in 1968. Current account surpluses were perpetuated. Following the May 1968 crisis in France, speculation against the franc in October precipitated speculation concerning DM revaluation. Internal discussion on revaluation had begun in the Spring of 1968. At that time, it was the Bundesbank and members of the Council of Experts who recommended revaluation. Schiller opposed such a move. When the November crisis led to a Group of Ten meeting in Bonn, most of the participants expected that West Germany would revalue. Although the Central Bank Council reaffirmed its position that this was imperative and despite strong international pressure, the Grand Coalition government remained inflexible.[85] As a substitute for revaluation, it introduced a special export tax of 4 percent and a corresponding tax rebate on imports.[86]

Debate over revaluation flared up again in the Spring of 1969 after De Gaulle resigned, and speculation mounted anew. The controversy became increasingly more heated until the September elections. Two coalitions which resembled those of 1961 opposed each other. This time, however, the Bundesbank sided with the advocates of revaluation.[87] The most critical difference from 1961 was that the question divided a grand coalition and became a major issue in the election campaign. Schiller had changed his previous stand and had become the main protagonist of the revaluationist camp. When he proposed a 7 percent revaluation in a cabinet meeting on May 5, he suffered a defeat. His CDU colleagues did not wish to grant him a victory which could be advertised to the voters. Chancellor Kiesinger

---

[80] Emminger, "Deutsche Geld-und Währungspolitik im Spannungsfeld zwischen innerem und äusserem Gleichgewicht (1948–1975)," p. 505.

[81] Kaufmann, p. 208.

[82] *Der Gewerkschafter* 3/1961, p. 3.

[83] Kaufmann, p. 208.

[84] *The Times* (London), 6 March 1961, quoted from Kaufmann, p. 209.

[85] Emminger, "Deutsche Geld-und Währungspolitik im Spannungsfeld zwischen innerem und äusserem Gleichgewicht (1948–1975)," p. 518.

[86] See Strange, p. 326.

[87] See Franz-Ulrich Willeke et al., "Die Aufwertungsdebatte in der BRD in den Jahren 1968 und 1969," *Hamburger Jahrbuch für Wirtschafts- und Gesellschaftspolitik* 16 (1971), pp. 287–316.

pledged "that revaluation was ruled out 'immer und ewig,' for all eternity."[88] A practically inescapable decision was thus delayed by the dynamics of party politics until October 1969, when the SPD-FDP coalition that emerged from the elections revalued the DM by 9.3 percent. The efforts deployed by the export sector to prevent "a parity-induced cut of its boom profits" were based, as Wolfgang Kasper has pointed out, "on the illusion that the 1969 profit situation would not be deteriorated by a subsequent wage explosion." The wage explosion which, in fact, occurred in 1969–70 had, however, the effect "that industry's resistance against an early revaluation ironically produced a wage-push-cum-revaluation compression of profits."[89] Although the outcomes of the 1961 and the 1969 revaluation battles are somewhat ambiguous, both cases suggest that sectoral interests do not prevail when they conflict sharply with the requirements of macroeconomic equilibrium as defined by the authorities in charge of economic and monetary policy.

## The dilemma transformed

Disorder in international money markets continued to be the major source of inflation for the German economy during the early 1970s. The Bundesbank lost control over liquidity supply. Monetary policy was periodically overwhelmed by the "spring tides" of speculative money inflows.[90] It was only the transition to a regime of generalized floating in March 1973 which finally enabled the Bundesbank to conduct, once again, an effective stabilization policy. The sealing of the "open external flank" represented a turning point in monetary policy, as it permitted a decoupling of the Federal Republic from the international inflation trend.[91] Between the beginning of 1972 and mid-1974, the DM appreciated by 17 percent vis-à-vis the average of all currencies.[92] Yet, ironically, this did not prevent rising export surpluses which, in 1974, hit the all-time record mark of 51 billion DM.

In order to provide an explanation for these developments, one can do no better than to refer to the OECD diagnosis:

> The impact of revaluations on Germany's external competitive position is difficult to quantify. Up to 1973, there was little doubt that the major effect was to raise export prices relative to those of important trading partners, but with buoyant world demand and easier supply conditions in Germany than in other industrialized countries, the impact on export volume was rather small and the net effect therefore "perverse." Since 1974, with inflation running well below the OECD average, the price gap began to close again. However,

---

[88] Strange, p. 327.
[89] Kasper, pp. 283–84.
[90] Emminger, "Deutsche Geld-und Währungspolitik im Spannungsfeld zwischen innerem und äusserem Gleichgewicht (1948–1975)," p. 522.
[91] Ibid., p. 487. For a discussion of the limits of protection through "floating," see ibid. pp. 534–36.
[92] Ibid.

much of this appears to have been at the expense of profit margins, as labor costs continued to rise relative to those of its trading partners, whereas relative export unit values were on the whole falling (Table I). During 1974, the sharp loss in German market shares abroad must, however, also be viewed against the large gains of the two preceding years.[93]

Table I Cost and price developments in manufacturing

1970 = 100

|  | 1972 | | 1973 | | 1974 | | 1975 | |
|---|---|---|---|---|---|---|---|---|
|  | 1st half | 2nd half | 1st half | 2nd half | 1st half | 2nd half | 1st half | 2nd half |
| Unit labour costs in industry, DM | 121 | 128 | 136 | 144 | 153 | 167 | 173 | 179[2] |
| Unit values of manufactured goods exports, DM | 103 | 104 | 104 | 107 | 117 | 125 | 131 | 131 |
| Relative[1] unit labour costs in industry | 107 | 108 | 118 | 132 | 128 | 129 | 130 | 123[2] |
| Relative[1] export prices of manufactures | 103 | 103 | 106 | 110 | 105 | 104 | 107 | 102[2] |

[1] German unit labour costs and export unit value indices expressed in $US, relative to a trade-weighted average of nine other major trading countries' unit labour costs and export unit value dollar-based indices. The other countries considered are Canada, USA, Japan, France, Italy, UK, Belgium, Netherlands, Norway.
[2] Third quarter 1975 only.
Sources: Bundesbank and OECD.

## V The export of capital and the challenge of structural changes

Since the late 1960s, the internationalization of West German industry has progressed rapidly. Direct investment abroad which in 1965 amounted to 8.3 billion DM reached the level of 21.2 billion DM in 1970. By 1975, it had doubled to 42 billion DM. These figures underestimate the stock of German direct foreign investment by at least 20 percent because German statistics do not include reinvested earnings. In comparison, the book value of US direct foreign investment came to 257.4 billion DM in 1973; that of British investment, to 71.2 billion DM.[94]

As direct foreign investment in the FRG amounted to 42.4 billion DM in 1975, the case of West Germany actually shows a roughly balanced pattern of cross-investment. West Germany may even have crossed the threshold towards

[93] OECD Economic Surveys, Germany (Paris: OECD, May 1976), pp. 12–13.
[94] Data from Henry Krägenau, Internationale Direktinvestitionen 1950–1973 (Hamburg: Verlag Weltarchiv, 1975), pp. 32, 139; and Herchenröder in Handelsblatt 14–15 May 1976. The comparability of foreign investment statistics is discussed in Krägenau, pp. 30–35.

becoming a net exporter of productive capital. In the recession year of 1975, there was a capital outflow of 5.23 billion DM. This was only slightly below the record figure of 5.64 billion DM in 1973. Inflows for 1975 came to only 2.53 billion DM.[95] German capital exports had lagged far behind those of Britain and the US, due to the expropriation of foreign assets during World War II, and to the strategy of undervaluation favoring exports as well as to labor market conditions. However, West Germany, very much like Japan, is now catching up, to some extent, with the US and Britain. Although in some branches foreign production increasingly tends to replace the servicing of foreign markets through exports, the volume of foreign production still remains far below that of exports. "From 1971 to 1973, enterprises of the FRG produced an average of 36 percent of the value of their exports abroad, and those of Japan 48 percent. The figures for the United States and the United Kingdom are 380 percent and 202 percent, respectively."[96]

The regional distribution of German direct foreign investment is characterized by a marked concentration on industrialized countries. In 1974, these countries accounted for 70.4 percent of all industrial investment with 29.6 percent going to developing countries. Among host countries, France, Switzerland, and the US ranked on top with a share of about 10 percent each. Looking at the sectoral distribution, one finds that the chemical industry leads with 19.5 percent, followed by the electrotechnical industry with 10.6 percent, iron and steel with 7.9 percent, automobiles with 7.2 percent, and machine-building with 7.3 percent.[97] These branches are also highly export-intensive. The largest enterprises in branches exposed to the pressure of import competition have also resolutely chosen the strategy of foreign investment. The giants of the textiles and clothing industry had foreign production shares (in total sales) of 22.5 percent (Freudenberg Group), 25.8 percent (Schulte und Dieckhoff), and 41.5 percent (Triumph) in 1971.[98]

Available studies on investment behavior indicate that the prime motive of German enterprises going abroad is to take advantage of market opportunities by serving a foreign market through local production rather than through exports.[99] This holds particularly when foreign competitors have established themselves in the country in question or when market access is rendered difficult by trade barriers

[95] Herchenröder in *Handelsblatt*. See also Rainer Jonas, "Auswirkungen des weltwirtschaftlichen Strukturwandels auf die Arbeitsmarktentwicklung in der Bundesrepublik," in *Wirtschaftsstruktur und Beschäftigung*, Horst Heidermann, ed. (Bonn-Bad Godesberg: Verlag Neue Gesellschaft, 1976), pp. 9–28, 22.

[96] Bernard Mennis and Karl P. Sauvant, *Emerging Forms of Transnational Community: Transnational Business Enterprises and Regional Integration* (Lexington, Massachusetts: Lexington Books, 1976), p. 15.

[97] Data from Jonas, pp. 23–24. The figures given on sectoral distribution refer to percentage shares of total direct foreign investment. Industrial investment accounts for 76.3 percent, investment in the service sectors for 21.2 percent of the total.

[98] R. Jungnickel et al., *Die Deutschen Multinationalen Unternehmen*, M. Holthus, ed. (Frankfurt: Athenäum Verlag, 1974), p. 116.

[99] For a concise treatment of the main theories on foreign investment see Robert Gilpin, *U.S. Power and the Multinational Corporation: The Political Economy of Foreign Direct Investment* (New York: Basic Books, 1975), Chapter 5.

and import substitution policies. Wage differentials were, according to a study published in 1974, a rather secondary motive, except for highly labor-intensive branches.[100] During the last few years, however, rising wage levels combined with successive DM revaluations seem to have stimulated the relocation of production facilities. These same factors may explain the decline in foreign investment in the Federal Republic.[101] This line of argument is stressed by bankers, industrialists, and the business press. Wages certainly did rise considerably or, according to some, even "exploded." Unit labor costs have developed as follows (1960 = 100): 1969: 129.3; 1970: 142.1; 1971: 155.9; 1972: 165.0; 1973: 177.5; 1974: 193.2.[102] But as the data presented above demonstrate, the export competitiveness of German industry has not markedly suffered.

Capital exports have been encouraged by the government since 1959 in order to offset surpluses in the trade balance and to increase "private" development assistance.[103] Actually, the government favors capital export as an alternative to "labor import" because the number of foreign workers is perceived as having reached a level that exceeds the integrative capacity of West German society. Moreover, the "export" of labor-intensive production lines to developing countries is expected to stimulate structural change in the West German economy and to improve the international division of labor.[104] Another rationale for the promotion of direct investment is the interest in securing raw materials supplies. Direct promotion of capital exports through various kinds of government subsidies has been limited mainly to investment in developing countries,[105] the most important promotion scheme undoubtedly being the Development Aid Tax Law (*Entwicklungshilfesteuergesetz*). It was so effectively shaped by the "capital export lobby" that it subsidized, inter alia, investment in hotel towers on the Costa Brava.[106] As for investment in industrialized countries, tax legislation was revised in 1969 and 1972 in order to remove existing tax discrimination against foreign investment and to improve the "competitiveness" of German enterprises with respect to tax treatment.[107] Investment promotion agreements with Third World countries, in-

---

[100] Jungnickel et al., p. 158.

[101] See Herchenröder in *Handelsblatt*, and *Handelsblatt*, 10 June 1976, p. 6.

[102] Sachverständigenrat, *Jahresgutachten 1975*, Bundestags-Drucksache 7/4326, Tabelle 17, p. 233.

[103] See Henry Krägenau, "Entwicklung und Förderung der deutschen Direktinvestitionen," in *Förderung privater Direktinvestitionen*, Hans-Eckart Scharrer, ed. (Hamburg: Verlag Weltarchiv, 1972), pp. 492–597.

[104] Herbert Ehrenberg, "Strukturpolitik-zentrale wirtschaftspolitische Aufgabe der neuen Legislaturperiode," *WSI-Mitteilungen* 11/1976, p. 664. This article was published shortly before its author became the new Minister of Labor in the second Schmidt government.

[105] Krägenau, in Scharrer, pp. 492–97.

[106] The law was replaced in 1974 by the "Entwicklungsländersteuergesetz" which favors especially investment in least developed countries. Tourism investment no longer qualifies for tax privileges. See Heinrich Jüttner, *Förderung und Schutz deutscher Direktinvestitionen in Entwicklungsländern* (Baden-Baden: Nomos Verlagsgesellschaft, 1975), pp. 116–19.

[107] See Rolf Knieper, *Weltmarkt, Wirtschaftsrecht und Nationalstaat* (Frankfurt: Suhrkamp Verlag, 1976), pp. 189–96.

vestment insurance, and double taxation agreements should also be mentioned. It is not clear, however, to what extent investment decisions have been influenced by these instruments.[108] They obviously have created a favorable climate for capital export. But, as Rolf Knieper suggests, legislative action may have simply followed the economic process.[109]

Organized labor does not object to capital export on principle.[110] However, in the labor-intensive branches hurt by imports from low-wage countries, the displacement of jobs through foreign investment results in a partial breakup of producers' alliances. IG Textil (the textile and clothing workers union), for example, proposed, in 1974, a special tax penalizing the export of capital to low-wage countries and the repeal of all government guarantees and subsidies for investment in the Third World.[111] This proposal was not taken too seriously and there is nothing comparable to the American "export of jobs" debate in West Germany. But if domestic investment remains low and unemployment high, labor is likely to become more critical of foreign investment.

Yet the export of capital is only one element in a larger process of structural change which critically affects employment conditions. *Strukturpolitik* is defined by its proponents as an active, anticipatory structural policy designed to facilitate the adaptation of the economy to changing patterns within the international division of labor. The debate which currently surrounds this policy has been rendered all the more topical by the fact that the 1974–75 recession has resulted in the highest level of unemployment West Germany has known since 1955 (4.7 percent in 1975). And it is widely assumed that, even with a reduction of cyclical unemployment, a relatively high level of unemployment is likely to persist.[112] On the other hand, the *Strukturpolitik* discussion is fraught with uncertainties precisely because it is difficult to sort out the cyclical and structural aspects of the current economic situation. According to some observers, the structural crisis thesis will even "melt like snow in the sun" (Schiller) once the recession is over.[113] The most articulate advocates of *Strukturpolitik* are to be found among the progressive technocrats of the Social Democratic Party who are able to draw on studies undertaken by economic think tanks like Prognos AG Basel and the Kiel Institut für Weltwirtschaft. Since *Strukturpolitik* proposals reflect a traditional social democratic concern with full employment, they are viewed favorably in the labor union camp where dissatisfaction with the limited results of global demand management is mounting.

---

[108] See Jüttner, p. 139.

[109] Knieper, p. 184.

[110] Labor union experts in 1969 criticized proposals to encourage capital export through tax privileges. See Manfred Hölzel, "Keine Förderung deutscher Direktinvestitionen im Ausland," and Rolf Seitenzahl, "Zahlungsbilanz, Kapitalexport and Auslandsinvestitionen," both in *Gewerkschaftliche Monatshefte*, June 1969, pp. 349–56.

[111] *Handelsblatt*, 8–9 November 1974, pp. 1 and 3.

[112] OECD Economic Surveys, *Germany*, p. 10, p. 34.

[113] Jonas, p. 13.

The diagnosis of structural change runs roughly as follows.[114] Since 1970, the industrial sector has shrunk by 1.4 million employees or 11 percent of its labor force. The service sector has grown and now accounts for 47 percent of the labor force. However, between 1970 and 1975, total employment decreased by 1.4 million. This is only partly due to cyclical factors. To some extent, this trend represents the nemesis of undervaluation. The extended undervaluation of the DM not only artificially increased export competitiveness. Through higher import prices, it also shielded domestic industries (especially consumer goods) from competition and kept marginal producers in business. This effect was reinforced by a conservation-oriented structural and regional policy. In addition, a liberal labor market policy which provided a continuous supply of foreign workers allowed artificially high levels of labor intensity and relieved entrepreneurs from the need to adapt themselves to changing conditions of production. A general slowdown of industrial growth has been accompanied by saturation tendencies in some consumer durables markets.

Moreover, developing countries are becoming aggressive exporters of labor-intensive consumer goods, and traditional exporters of raw materials increasingly seek to export their commodities in a processed form. Competitive pressure on domestic producers is bound to increase if the government effects its commitment to open the German market to Third World imports by gradually removing tariff and quota restrictions. It is estimated that in the leather-processing, textiles and clothing and shoe industries, between 280,000 and 480,000 jobs will be lost during the period 1972–1985 depending on the degree of import liberalization.[115] On the domestic side, the need for environmental protection limits industrial growth along traditional lines. The problems related to the integration of "guest labor" into German society are another limiting factor. The recruitment ban on foreign workers from non-EEC countries issued in 1973, therefore, represents more than a cyclical measure. As foreign workers and their families constitute a population of over four million, there exists, de facto, an immigration situation.[116] If youth unemployment in general remains at much higher than average levels, the second generation of immigrants could become a potentially anomic subproletariat.

The recipe for coping with some of these problems is a strategy of selective competitiveness.[117] The advocates of *Strukturpolitik* propose a specialization of

[114] See Klaus-Werner Schatz, "Zum sektoralen und regionalen Strukturwandel in der Bundesrepublik Deutschland," *WSI-Mitteilungen* 11/1976, pp. 653–60; Klaus-Werner Schatz, *Wachstum und Strukturwandel der westdeutschen Wirtschaft im internationalen Verbund* (Tübingen: J.C.B. Mohr [Paul Siebeck], 1974), pp. 198–252; Hans Bülow, "Entwicklungstendenzen der internationalen Arbeitsteilung und Rückwirkungen auf die Industriestruktur der Bundesrepublik Deutschland," *WSI-Mitteilungen* 5/1976, pp. 254–67.
[115] Hugo Dicke et al., *Beschäftigungswirkungen einer verstärkten Arbeitsteilung zwischen der Bundesrepublik und den Entwicklungsländern* (Tübingen: J.C.B. Mohr [Paul Siebeck], 1976), pp. 34, 97, 146.
[116] See Ursula Mehrländer, "Zur politischen Konzeption der Ausländerbeschäftigung," in Heidermann, ed., *Wirtschaftsstruktur und Beschäftigung*, p. 101.
[117] See Schatz, "Zum sektoralen und regionalen Strukturwandel in der Bundesrepublik Deutschland," p. 659.

German industry in highly competitive branches like the machine-building and chemical and pharmaceutical industries, and in key technologies, like data processing and electronic components. Research and technology policy is assigned the task of stimulating the development of new products and technologies, e.g., in the areas of environmental protection and public transport.[118]   New jobs should be created by an expansion of the service sector. According to a more radical formulation, West Germany is "overindustrialized" and will have to switch from the export of goods to the export of capital, services, and know-how.[119]   However, a highly qualified labor force combined with an active technology policy will probably guarantee competitiveness at high wage levels even in some labor-intensive branches. *Strukturpolitik*, in this view, is imperative because the current level of real wages and the structure of production are incompatible with full employment.[120]   Not surprisingly, the BDI argues, in this context, the basic problem lies in high wages and low profits. This requires wage restraint and tax reductions in order to improve profit expectations. The Economics Ministry concurs to the extent that it acknowledges the need for wage restraint to close the investment gap. The Ministry believes that a ratio of exports to GNP of 25 percent will remain necessary in the future.[121]   It cautions against the temptations of sectoral policies which might lead to investment cartels and investment controls. That is, indeed, where the bone of contention lies. Although there is a broad consensus as to the necessity of some kind of *Strukturpolitik*, the content and instruments of this policy are controversial. Whereas some advocates of *Strukturpolitik* favor certain forms of investment control and sectoral fine-tuning in economic policy, the adherents of economic liberalism believe that this would violate the basic principles upon which a market economy is built.[122]   The debate over *Strukturpolitik* is therefore one over the limits of state intervention in a market economy.

## VI   Conclusion: stabilizing the international milieu

As the recession of 1975 has shown, the bastion of stability has an open flank. If the trends just outlined should render the unions more militant and thereby escalate the struggle for the national product, domestic strains would also help to scratch the image of Croesus. West Germany then might appear more like a "normal" country. But even in this hypothetical case, the Federal Republic is

---

[118] See Volker Hauff and Fritz W. Scharpf, *Modernisierung der Volkswirtschaft: Technologiepolitik als Strukturpolitik* (Frankfurt and Cologne: Europäische Verlagsanstalt, 1975); and Volker Hauff, "Sichere Arbeitsplätze durch Modernisierung der Volkswirtschaft," *Neue Gesellschaft*, 6/1976, pp. 457–67.

[119] Peter Rogge of Prognos AG, according to *Handelsblatt*, 6 May 1976, p. 4.

[120] Ibid. For a different view of the dynamics of structural change see *Handelsblatt*, 7 April 1976, the report on a study of DIW Berlin.

[121] See *Handelsblatt*, 6 May 1976, pp. 4–5.

[122] See for example Sachverständigenrat, *Jahresgutachten 1975*, pp. 125–27.

unlikely to follow the British or Italian "example." For the time being, its economic strength remains an object of hopes and fears. West Germany's seemingly irresistible ascension has reached a point, where, as Evans and Novak recently noted, "the continuing growth of . . . West German economic power is clearly beginning to worry all the rest of Europe."[123]

How much is there to worry about? To begin with, consider the most conspicuous symbol of international status: the hoard of foreign exchange reserves. In 1975, these amounted to the equivalent of $31 billion. They clearly represent an instrument of political and economic leverage. At the same time, these reserves have given rise to inflated expectations regarding Germany's capacity for economic assistance and created resentment among debtors, actual or potential. Looking at the use to which these reserves are put, one can easily discern that the Bundesbank loan to Italy or the German share of the IMF loan to Britain do not reflect a will to power. Rather, they represent defensive measures intended to stabilize trade partners. They are basically dictated by the insight which François Duchêne has expressed as follows: "if all the major European economies are in trouble, the capacity of Germany to maintain its own health and give a lead to the world economy will be greatly weakened, if not nullified."[124] The disintegration of the European Community into first-, second-, and third-class members due to different levels of economic performance is hardly a source of satisfaction for German policy makers. Low German inflation rates obviously are a problem for other West European countries; witness the fate of the currency snake. Yet an "upward realignment" of the German inflation rate would not solve the difficulties of these countries and would meet with strong political resistance at home. Negative convergence will not improve the prospects for European integration. On the other hand, progress towards economic and monetary union undoubtedly requires a gradual equalization of levels of economic development and depends on a certain convergence of socio-political trends in the main Community nations. Given the uncertainties of French and Italian politics, the new Schmidt government will soon have to seek a constructive *modus vivendi* with Euro-Communism.

In negotiations on international economic reform, the Federal Republic has tended so far to act as a conservative power, preaching the virtues of economic liberalism. The Lomé Convention, however, indicates that the FRG is willing to make limited concessions in order to satisfy Third World demands. West German policy makers will have to overcome the temptation to prescribe to the world at large the recipes that have proven successful at home. West Germany's economic expansion, it should be recalled, took place in an international environment which

---

[123] Evans and Novak, "Bonn's Role in Europe: A Dilemma," *International Herald Tribune* (Paris), 25 November 1976, p. 6. See also the diatribe by Jean-Pierre Vigier, "L'Europe sous une hégémonie germano-américaine?", *Le Monde Diplomatique* (Paris), December 1976, pp. 1, 7.

[124] François Duchêne, "The United States and the European Community", in *America as an Ordinary Country. U.S. Foreign Policy and the Future,* Richard Rosecrance, ed. (Ithaca and London: Cornell University Press, 1976), p. 92.

was governed by rules that harmonized with the domestic economic order. But after the legitimacy of the rules has been called into question, the FRG will have to adjust to the politicization of international economic relations. The cherished principle of the separation of trade from politics is undermined as its area of application shrinks. The spread of "state interventionism and dirigism in international economic relations" (Hermes),[125] the nightmare haunting the architects of German foreign economic policy, is already much more a reality than a distant threat. Vis-à-vis the Third World, stabilization therefore requires that the Federal Republic combine its resources with an imaginative diplomacy in order to create the political conditions of economic security.

[125] See Hermes, p. 251.

# 7
# Italy: Dependence and Political Fragmentation

*Alan R. Posner*

Italy's political economy is characterized by international weakness and internal fragmentation and polarization. Since 1947, Italy's foreign economic policies have been defined by a broadly-based political and social coalition dominated by the Christian Democratic party (DC). This coalition has incorporated or maintained close links with ministerial bureaucracies, the Bank of Italy, state-controlled industrial and commercial enterprises, large corporations, and Catholic trade unions. It has attempted to foster a postwar climate receptive to business interests and to foreign investment; one which would facilitate the maintenance of a stable domestic political and social order. At the same time, the DC coalition is so fragmented by factionalism and personal competition that economic policy making has lacked direction and has been marked by personalism and by improvisation. Italian policy makers operate in a precarious environment in that they must use political and economic weakness in order to mobilize the international assistance needed to maintain the internal social order as well as external economic survival.

Italy's postwar foreign economic policies have been defined by a political and social coalition that has generally attempted to foster an economic climate receptive to business and foreign investment. This coalition, presided over by the Christian Democratic Party (DC), has managed to incorporate or establish close links with ministerial bureaucracies, the Bank of Italy, large corporations, and state-controlled industrial and commercial enterprises. While nothing in Italy's political economy is simple, it is safe to say that Italy has always been export-oriented. Since the Second World War, the DC has been aware of Italy's material weakness and internal

Alan R. Posner is a member of the Political Science Department at the University of Massachusetts at Boston.

fragmentation and despite a mixed attitude toward the private sector, the party has attempted to preside over a neo-Liberal environment. It was hoped that by facilitating exports and foreign investment, such a milieu would lead to the maintenance of a stable domestic political and social order.

While this coalition is unified in seeking electoral advantage, it incorporates so many strains that it is characterized internally more by factionalism and personal competition than by programmatic consensus. The result is that the definition of the objectives of economic policy is often characterized by personalism and improvisation and that economic policy implementation has been hampered by the lack of direction from the DC. This tendency has been reinforced by the lack of a strong bureaucratic tradition of the kind that can be found in France. Although the Foreign Ministry has been explicitly charged with coordinating all external policy, other state agencies have become increasingly active in the economic sector. Similarly, state-controlled enterprises have become as significant in domestic and international economic affairs as the large private corporations. Given the DC's sympathy for the expansion of state-controlled enterprises with their patronage networks, the private sector and the state-controlled enterprises must both tolerate a high degree of coexistence and interaction under the umbrella of the DC coalition.

From 1947, when the basic model of Italy's neo-Liberal political economy was established, until the 1960s, the political Left was excluded from the coalition that defined and implemented foreign economic policy. This group was largely organized around the Communist and Socialist Parties (PCI and PSI) and had close connections with the largest component of organized labor. Its demands received progressively more attention as the DC coalition attempted to broaden its base in the 1960s by means of the "Opening to the Left." But the DC shift in emphasis did not disturb the basic continuity of the neo-Liberal strategy.

Italy's international weakness and its domestic fragmentation and polarization were as apparent in the late 1940s as in the mid-1970s. These international and domestic factors and the nature of its governing coalition help to explain Italy's apparent passivity even in the face of critical structural problems in the political economy and serious trade deficits recently exacerbated by high energy costs. To be sure, Italy's structural problems were present, if less apparent, during the 1950s and early 1960s when export-led growth and low wages helped to foster the famous "economic miracle." But by the late 1960s the situation was already critical. It was aggravated still further by the oil price rises of 1973–1974.

These structural and trade problems have been mutually reinforcing. In the absence of an administration that can govern effectively without the PCI or that can reconcile itself to governing with the PCI, Italy will not be able to attack its internal and external problems. At the same time, in the absence of long-term economic help from outside, it will be difficult to alter conditions inside Italy to the point where structural realignments can take place. However, as will be shown below, international assistance to Italy has almost always had political conditions attached which narrow the range of domestic options for Italian statesmen. At the same time, Italy's internal predicaments make it difficult for statesmen to devote time to matters of foreign economic policy.

But to some extent, Italy's weakness and instability can be perceived as sources of strength or at least as bargaining leverage. Externally, Italy hopes that other Western nations will have to shore up an important industrial partner. Internally, the dominant coalition can make a case that the prevailing domestic political alignment is the only one that Italy's partners abroad will consent to help. From the above, it is clear that Italy's foreign economic policy is the result of the interaction of domestic determinants and elements in the international economic setting. The passive DC coalition operates in (and is virtually coterminous with) a weak state that has to respond to the harsh realities of the international political economy. Italian policy makers operate in an environment characterized by precariousness. They can only use their political and economic weakness as a tool with which to mobilize international assistance in order to maintain internal dominance and external economic survival.

## I   The international context of Italy's foreign economic policy

Italy's recent international economic operations as well as its apparent inability in the face of significant increases in PCI strength to define and create a widely accepted, long-term political alignment have underscored what is by now a fairly commonplace analysis. Italy is described as a political actor characterized by a lack of international autonomy and a high degree of internal fragmentation.[1] Italy's material weakness and historic disappointments as an actor in world politics have led its leaders to make foreign policy coterminous with "fedeltà atlantica" (Atlantic fidelity) and a commitment to the European Community.[2]

The formulation of Italian foreign economic policy since the end of World War II has been closely linked to domestic economic and social policy. After 1945, leaders such as Premier Alcide De Gasperi and Count Carlo Sforza, (a leading Italian Europeanist affiliated with the small Republican Party and Foreign Minister from 1947 to 1951), recognized that their main international priority was to avoid isolation and unilateralism. This was necessary for a variety of reasons. Diplomatically, Italy was to be restored to a position of international legitimacy after the Fascist interlude by stressing the Italian willingness to sacrifice sovereign prerogatives in the interest of European harmony. Economically, Italy would forsake autarky and work for its own recovery by operating in a framework larger than a single state. The resulting international ties and internal recovery would also serve

---

[1] This essay is, in part, based on a larger study of Italy's Atlantic policies which focused on the interaction between Italy's external policy and its domestic politics and political culture. This earlier study included interviews in Rome and in Brussels with parliamentarians, party publicists, diplomats and government functionaries, interest group representatives, journalists, and scholars. Peter Katzenstein's advice and suggestions were invaluable to me in preparing this essay and I am grateful for Peter Lange's comments on an earlier draft.

[2] For references to general Italian foreign policy, see for instance Massimo Bonanni, ed., *La Politica Estera della Republica Italiana,* 3 vols. (Milan: Edizioni di Comunità, 1967), Primo Vannicelli, *Italy, NATO, and the European Community* (Cambridge, Mass.: Harvard University Center for International Affairs, 1974), and F. Roy Willis, *Italy Chooses Europe* (New York: Oxford University Press, 1971).

to reduce domestic social cleavages and political instability. Thus, except for the leftist Communist-Socialist opposition, Italian elites found it relatively easy to support the Marshall Plan with its American and European dimensions. Italian adherence to the European Coal and Steel Community in 1950–1951 also conformed to the designs of De Gasperi and Sforza. They sought to use external economic ties as instruments of domestic economic (and political and social) stabilization. From the early years of Republican Italy's existence, then, the stability of its fragmented and modernizing society was perceived as being highly dependent on external instruments and non-Italian actors.

Since 1949, the national security tie with the United States has been perceived as vital by many Italian leaders. At the same time, a rather pervasive distaste for power politics has fostered a desire to play a somewhat passive and detached role inside the framework of the Atlantic Alliance. Italy's affiliation with the European Community is seen in a more positive and less apologetic light than the Atlantic connection. Nonetheless, interaction with it is perceived as being diplomatic in nature and therefore roughly part of the same configuration as the Atlantic Alliance. Thus, all external policy, including that of an economic nature, is deliberately de-emphasized. Dino Del Bo, an experienced Italian politician and former President of the High Authority of the European Coal and Steel Community (1963–1967), has noted that Italian political parties and public opinion are not interested in foreign economic policy.[3] If anything, this tendency to de-emphasize foreign economic policy has been reinforced of late by the revelations of corruption involving both foreign-controlled multinational corporations in Italy and state-owned corporations such as the Ente Nazionale Idrocarburi (ENI). ENI is the state oil and energy holding company which has long been noted for its overseas activities.[4]

At the same time, these external ties have restricted both Italy's political and economic options. Incipient neutralism has had to swerve in the face of the perceived need, domestic as well as international, for the American security connection.[5] And, as Dino Del Bo has noted, Italy has had to reconcile a desire for expanding markets in Eastern Europe with the wishes of its allies.[6]

Italy's concrete international economic dependence can be quickly illustrated by a variety of data. Foreign trade as a percentage of gross national income rose from 26 percent in 1960 to 33 percent in early 1973. This is a level similar to that of Britain and West Germany.[7] At the same time, in 1974 Italy was dependent on

---

[3] Dino Del Bo, "La Componente Economica," in *Inchiesta sulla Politica Estera Italiana,* Dino Del Bo et al. (Rome: Lerici, 1970), pp. 29–30.

[4] On ENI corruption, see for instance Alberto Statera, "ENI/Che Cosa Trova il Nuovo Presidente: Un Cane con Sei Zampe nel Pantano," *L'Espresso* Vol. 21, No. 31 (3 August 1975): 60–63.

[5] Umberto Segre, "Atlantismo e Neutralismo nella Politica Estera Italiana," in Bonanni, Vol. 2, p. 570.

[6] Del Bo in Del Bo et al., pp. 17–18.

[7] Karl Kaiser, "Le Relazioni Transnazionali," in *Il Caso Italiano,* Fabio Luca Cavazza and Stephen R. Graubard, eds., 2 vols. (Milan: Aldo Garzanti, 1974), Vol. 2, p. 404.

imported fuel for 82 percent of its total fuel requirements. This is a higher percentage than for any industrial country except Japan and Denmark.[8] Further, in 1973 Italy was dependent on oil for almost 79 percent of its primary fuels, compared to 72.5 percent for France, 58.6 percent for West Germany, and 52.1 percent for Britain.[9] Early in 1975, Italy had a foreign debt of \$16.6 billion, much of which was related to energy needs.[10] By mid-1975, the debt was still at \$14.6 billion[11] although the non-oil trade deficit had largely been removed.[12]

Another important dimension of Italy's economic environment since the basic economic strategy was accepted in 1947 has been the receptivity to foreign investment. As Charles Kindleberger has observed, Italians go so far as to interpret the purchase of industry by foreigners as a form of foreign investment.[13] At the same time, the level of foreign investment in Italy is difficult to determine. Statistics published by the Bank of Italy give the following breakdown for 1972:

| | |
|---|---|
| Italian shares held by foreigners | 22 percent |
| Italian shares held by other companies | 45 percent |
| Italian shares held by other private individuals | 30 percent |
| Other shares | 3 percent |

But these figures are problematic. Some so-called foreign capital is in fact illegally expatriated Italian capital which is then reinvested in Italy.[14]

Internally, Italy is confronted by serious political and social problems. These are aggravated by a government that is immobilist and by a pervasive lack of confidence in a government formula that seems obsolete.[15] Increasingly, the only alternative being weighed by Italian elites is the inclusion of the PCI in a coalition with the DC which would provide an enormous parliamentary majority; or at the very least an alliance between the DC and the PCI but with the PCI not included in the actual cabinet. It is suggested that even this latter option will make the government more vigorous in pursuing new economic policies while reassuring workers as to government intentions.

---

[8] *Economist* (London), 31 January 1976, p. 81.
[9] Louis Turner, "The European Community: Factors of Disintegration. Politics of the Energy Crisis," *International Affairs* (London) Vol. 50, No. 3 (July 1974): 408–09.
[10] Cesare Merlini, "Italy in the European Community and the Atlantic Alliance," *The World Today* Vol. 31, No. 4 (April 1975): 164.
[11] "Italian Debt: A Lot of Interest," *Economist* (London), 20 September 1975, pp. 97, 99.
[12] "Political and Economic Developments," *Economic News from Italy* Vol. 30, No. 37 (September 12, 1975): 1–2. See also Marcello De Cecco, "Italy's Payments Crisis: International Responsibilities," *International Affairs* (London) Vol. 51, No. 1 (January 1975): 5, 9.
[13] Charles P. Kindleberger, "Economia al Bivio," in Cavazza and Graubard, pp. 254–55.
[14] John Earle, *Italy in the 1970s* (Newton Abbot, Devon: David Charles, 1975), p. 134.
[15] Italy's preeminent Christian Democratic Party (DC) has provided every Premier and many key economic ministers since 1945. Since 1964 (with one brief exception), Italian governments have been either Center-Left coalitions (DC, the major Socialist party, PSI, Social Democrats, and Republicans) or stopgap governments of the DC and one other party, or a DC minority government which stays in office as the result of PSI (and lately PCI) abstention or support.

Given the above, there is some consensus that Italy requires economic assistance from its Atlantic allies and European partners.[16] These external helpers, in particular the United States and West Germany, want two things from Italy. First, they seek a return to internal political stability and economic equilibrium. The latter is usually defined in the short term as an economic austerity program and an end to Italy's non-oil balance-of-payments deficit. Second, they want the continued exclusion of the PCI from the national government.[17] To the extent that PCI tolerance *might* indeed be a prerequisite to promoting economic stability (for instance, in view of Communist influence in the trade unions), this second goal may contradict the first.[18] The PCI is well aware of foreign attitudes and seems content for the moment to insist on an inclusion in policy determination without direct government participation or ministerial responsibility. In this way its prestige and legitimacy are enhanced while foreign fears are mollified. At the same time, the PCI cannot be blamed if policies fail.

## II  The DC coalition and the politics of passivity

Italian politics has been dominated in the postwar period by the Christian Democratic Party.[19] While this party had an absolute majority in Parliament only during the period 1948–1953, it has been Italy's largest party and has provided every Premier since 1945. Despite some shifts in the political forces comprising the governing coalition, the primacy of the DC in postwar Italian politics is without question. Yet the DC is not always successful in achieving its goals, especially when it tries to do too much. In 1965, for instance, the DC attempted to retain the Presidency of the Republic for the third time in succession, in the face of opposition from its coalition allies. Eventually, these other parties aligned with the PCI to elect the Social Democrat Giuseppe Saragat. The DC's position in this case was weakened by the fact that internal rivalry prevented the party from agreeing on a single candidate. Similarly, a few years ago the DC insisted on supporting an effort to overturn, by referendum, a recently enacted divorce law despite opposition from other parties in the government. Again, a de facto alliance between

[16] See for example Alvin Shuster, "Italy Seeks Help to Bolster Lira," *New York Times,* January 23, 1976, pp. 1, 43.
[17] See "New Ways to Pay for Oil Imports," *Business Week,* September 7, 1974, pp. 22–23, as well as Merlini, pp. 164–65. For an estimate of the benefits that might follow from PCI inclusion, see Peter Lange, "What Is To Be Done—About Italian Communism," *Foreign Policy* No. 21 (Winter 1975–76): 239.
[18] This kind of contradictory politico-economic goal formulation is not unknown to analysts of American foreign policy. For much of the 1950s and 1960s, it was apparent that in observing the development of new and poor countries, American policy makers wanted and expected simultaneous economic progress and political stabilization. See Robert Heilbroner, "Counter-revolutionary America," in *A Dissenter's Guide to Foreign Policy,* Irving Howe, ed. (Garden City: Doubleday Anchor, 1968), pp. 253–59.
[19] This section owes a great deal to the suggestions of Peter Katzenstein and Peter Lange.

supporters of these parties and of the PCI defeated the DC's efforts. One important result was that the DC's position was weakened in a comprehensive manner while that of the PCI was enhanced. Thus, the DC has recently seemed preeminent without being able to exercise effective leadership. From this derives its image of passivity in the face of fragmentation and crisis in the policy-making environment.

As a catch-all party, the DC has been able to represent a variety of interests and clienteles by means of distinct and well-organized factions within the party structure.[20] The traditional components of the DC in the immediate postwar period had an agrarian-Mediterranean orientation. These included Southern landlords, independent peasants, and a clerical right wing interested in having the state maintain the conservative social and political status quo. There was in addition a DC left wing made up of two factions: an "economic Left" with ties to the Resistance and to Catholic workers, and a "political Left" of intellectuals linked to elements in the Vatican.[21] While the latter two factions were socially more progressive, they agreed with the other DC factions on the need to maintain a state religion and the primacy of the DC. Given that party's primacy, much of Italian policy making is the result of the jockeying for position among factions of the DC or among the personalities around whom the factions gravitate. Alan Zuckerman has suggested that Italian coalition politics is one of factional competition inside the DC.[22] Yet while there is internal competition, there has also been external unity on the fundamental issue of maintaining DC primacy and patronage power and on the basic goals of domestic and foreign economic policy.

By the beginning of the 1950s, there had evolved in the DC as a whole a somewhat more technocratic orientation. This tendency encouraged DC interest in urban society and permitted more active state intervention in industrial and commercial affairs. This led to the strengthening of the Istituto per la Ricostruzione Industriale (IRI—state industrial and commercial holding company), first set up by the Fascist government in 1933, and the establishment of the Ente Nazionale Idrocarburi in 1953. While separate from the state bureaucracy, these agencies are staffed in part by patronage appointment. But these shifts in emphasis did not alter the essential consensus inside the DC; that of maintaining party dominance by means of an American connection, the maintenance of at least the approximate social status quo, and the extension of patronage throughout the

---

[20] On DC factions, see also Raphael Zariski, "Intra-Party Conflict in a Dominant Party: The Experience of Italian Christian Democracy," *The Journal of Politics* Vol. 27, No. 1 (February 1965): 19–34. On clientelism in Italy, see for instance Luigi Graziano, "Patron-Client Relationships in Southern Italy," *European Journal of Political Research* 1 (1973): 3–34.

[21] In the late 1940s, these two groups were often called, respectively, "Gronchiani" (after Giovanni Gronchi who later became President of Italy) and "Dossettiani" (after the intellectual, Giuseppe Dossetti). More recently, these factions have been the labor-oriented Forze Nuove and the political Left Base.

[22] Alan Zuckerman, "Political Clienteles in Power: Party Factions and Cabinet Coalitions in Italy," *Sage Professional Papers in Comparative Politics* 5, Series No. 01-055 (Beverly Hills and London: Sage Publications, 1975), pp. 34 ff.

232                                                    *Alan R. Posner*

political and economic system.[23] P.A. Allum notes that the DC has encouraged policies to promote "parasitic intermediary strata."[24] In this connection, Giuseppe Are has observed that these same elites have managed even to integrate European obligations and the maintenance of a clientilistic system of staying in power. For instance, he says that the European Community would want Italy to adopt effective regional policies which would:

> scavalcare ed esautorare i numerosissimi enti piccoli e grandi attraverso i quali la classe politica italiana è avvezza a dispensare il pubblico denaro nella forma di 'provvidenze,' o stanziamenti settoriali o corporativi, poco funzionali forse ai fini dello sviluppo, ma utilissimi per l'amministrazione delle clientele elettorali.[25]

Within the DC consensus discussed here, there were as noted different strains. But these strains could be accommodated inside the DC on grounds that were ideological as well as realistic. The catch-all quality of the DC could be justified in terms of the Catholic social doctrine of reconciling groups in conflict. Also, the DC's preeminence in Italian society has meant that those with demands to make would come to the party with both the most influence and with the ability to reinforce ties by means of patronage. Not only are there close connections between the party organization and government and semi-public agencies, but the Italian *sottogoverno* (literally, under-government) of patronage positions extends into the sectors of industry and commerce.[26]

In spite of some mixed feelings about the private business sector, since the war, the DC has attempted to foster what might be called a "neo-Liberal" economic climate.[27] At the least, it has promoted conditions favorable to Italian and international business interests. Even state-controlled enterprises have manifested a determination to be run according to sound business principles while taking cognizance of party and state interests. Significantly, the early postwar economic climate was set by De Gasperi on the advice of Luigi Einaudi of the Liberal Party (PLI), at one time Governor of the Bank of Italy and Budget Minister and later President of Italy. Einaudi's emphasis was on austerity and stabilization to prevent

[23] Socialist Party (PSI) acceptance of this system of ground rules and rewards was at the heart of the Opening to the Left in the early 1960s when the PSI took a share of national political power.

[24] P.A. Allum, *Italy—Republic Without Government* (New York: Norton, 1973), p. 247.

[25] "overcome and deprive of authority the very numerous small and large agencies through which the Italian political class is accustomed to distribute public funds in the form of sectoral and corporative grants and appropriations that are perhaps not functional in terms of development goals but that are very useful for the administration of electoral clienteles." (Author's translation.) Giuseppe Are, "L'Italia nella Politica Internazionale," reprint from *Il Mulino* (November-December 1973): 18.

[26] On how the public enterprises are part of the DC coalition, see for instance Andrew Shonfield, "L'Impresa Pubblica: Modello Internazionale o Specialità Locale?" in Cavazza and Graubard, Vol. 2, pp. 271–74.

[27] See Michael Watson, "Conclusion," in *Planning, Politics and Public Policy*, Jack Hayward and Michael Watson, eds. (Cambridge, England: Cambridge University Press, 1974), p. 448.

inflation and to stimulate exports and foreign investment in Italy. These policies of the late 1940s laid the groundwork for the economic growth of the 1950s.[28] It was the DC's adoption of Einaudi's policies in 1947 that both helped precipitate the exclusion of the Marxian Left (PCI, PSI) from the Italian government and helped prepare Italy for effective participation in the Marshall Plan. The subsequent national elections in 1948, fought in a climate of controversy over the Cold War and Italy's Marshall Plan orientation, gave the DC its only absolute parliamentary majority. In its campaign, the DC received significant support from the United States and from the Vatican.

All the same, the interaction between the private business sector and the DC has not been without problems. For a time, "big business" in Italy aligned itself with the PLI. This tendency was due especially to the greater propensity of the DC during the 1950s to support the expansion of state-controlled industrial and commercial enterprises such as ENI and IRI. But by the early 1960s the end (with one brief exception) of PLI participation in governing coalitions meant that the business sector had to look to the DC if it hoped to influence government economic policy. In effect, the major components of the private sector have also become part of the DC coalition.

Thus business had to look more to the DC at the very moment when the DC was acquiescing in an expansion of social services, increases in wages, and more state intervention in the economy. This shift in emphasis was motivated by the dual purpose of extending patronage possibilities and creating a climate which would facilitate the Opening to the Left. In a sense, this shift also marked a partial end to the exclusion of non-Catholic labor from the DC-dominated coalition.[29] Recently, however, the more productive parts of the private sector have complained that they are having to bear the cost of helping the less productive segments of society. They charge that there has been no effort on the part of the DC to cut government expenses by reforming the bureaucracy. This reluctance stems, of course, from the DC's unwillingness to interfere with its patronage structure. The upshot has been a continuing liberal thrust in economic orientation but with very high social costs.

These shifts in emphasis on the part of the DC coincided with its decision to share power with the PSI in the early 1960s. It is significant that the PSI accepted, at times grudgingly to be sure, its role as a kind of junior partner in the DC coalition system. Participation in the state and quasi-state patronage system was the PSI's reward for reconciling itself to the DC's economic primacy. At the same time, to facilitate integrating the PSI into the coalition, the DC reconciled itself to giving labor a larger share of the national wealth. But continuity was evident through the

---

[28] On the policies of this period, see Allum, p. 246, Murray Edelman and R. W. Fleming, *The Politics of Wage-Price Decisions: A Four-Country Analysis* (Urbana, Ill.: University of Illinois Press, 1965), p. 65, Kevin Allen and Andrew Stevenson, *An Introduction to the Italian Economy* (London: Martin Robertson, 1974), p. 168, and Charles P. Kindleberger, *Europe's Postwar Growth* (Cambridge, Mass.: Harvard University Press, 1967), p. 40.

[29] To the extent that, especially until the early 1960s, a system of national collective bargaining was the norm in Italy, even labor had to look to the DC-dominated coalition governments for decisions. These relationships will be discussed below.

retention of the essential goals: to maintain both DC primacy and a socially stable environment receptive to international business.

If anything, shifts in emphasis notwithstanding, the Opening to the Left seemed to reinforce the basic structures of Italy's foreign economic policy and policy making. All segments of Italy's internal and international political economy are part of the DC-dominated coalition. The state bureaucracy is politically controlled by cabinet ministers representing factions in the DC and its coalition allies. Italy's state and semi-state enterprises are related to the DC by means of the patronage structure. While somewhat more autonomous, even the Bank of Italy is closely tied to the DC. The Governor is chosen, in part, by the directors of banks owned by IRI, although formal appointment is by presidential decree.[30] The private business sector has no one but the DC to turn to since the only alternative to DC dominance is PCI control; or at the very least a DC-PCI partnership. And labor, even with its long-time exclusion from policy making and with recent changes in collective bargaining procedures, has had to look to the DC-dominated coalition in order to seek redress of grievances. Thus, the DC is dominant but the very broadness of its coalition fosters passivity rather than effective policy making.

## III The Bank of Italy, state enterprises, and the private sector

The pervasiveness and fragmentation of the DC coalition and its essential absorption of the Einaudi-Liberal outlook from 1947 on points inevitably to the central role of the Bank of Italy in coordinating Italy's political economy. In the opinion of P.A. Allum, the reforms of 1947 were the "basis for economic growth and the instrument for imperative coordination of all sectors of the economy by the Bank of Italy."[31] For much of the postwar period, Italian business has perceived the Bank as the real guide to the Italian economy and there has been acceptance of the fact that relations between business leaders and the government were mediated by the Bank.[32]

All the same, if the DC's fragmented coalition means that the Governor of the Bank of Italy has to play a leading role in economic policy making, it is also true that this office is closely tied to the coalition. While the Governor is in theory an advisor to the Ministry of the Treasury and the Interministerial Committee on Credit and Savings, he is also independent of Ministries and of Parliament. And he has wide powers of initiative. He is chosen by the Administrative Council of the Bank and this appointment is confirmed by presidential decree.[33] But the Bank's

---

[30] The first President of the Republic was Einaudi himself (1948–1955). With the exception of the Social Democrat, Saragat, (1965–1972), other Presidents have been Christian Democrats. The Bank of Italy will be discussed further below.

[31] Allum, p. 246.

[32] Ibid., p. 248. A 1962 EEC study said that central banks are especially important in Italy and in France. Cited in Edelman and Fleming, p. 17.

[33] See Raphael Zariski, *Italy: The Politics of Uneven Development* (Hinsdale, Ill.: Dryden Press, 1972), p. 257.

Council is made up of the Governor, twelve members nominated by an assembly representing banks and credit agencies that hold Bank of Italy stock, and three others. Thus, the Governor is responsive to Italian banking interests.[34] However, significant sectors of Italian banking are controlled by IRI which is a part of the DC patronage system. It would seem, then, that the Bank is not so much independent of the political system as it is a crucial (and often successful) competitor within that system. In this respect, the Bank of Italy appears to be less autonomous in the political environment, functionally as well as in a statutory sense, than is the case with the West German Bundesbank.

An important factor in explaining the postwar strength of the Bank of Italy is that Italy has attempted to manage its economy largely by means of monetary policy. As Murray Edelman and R.W. Fleming have noted, Italian fiscal policy "is a resultant of bargaining among party factions. . . ." It is therefore caught up in the immobility of DC (or DC-PSI) coalition politics. Monetary policy, on the other hand, is laid down by the Treasury Ministry and the Interministerial Committee on Credit and Savings. In practice, this has meant that the key actor has been the Bank. This reality derives from the tradition, established in 1947, of strict Bank control over liquidity.[35] Reserve requirements date back to that time when the Bank, headed by Einaudi, worked to limit credit in order to control inflation.[36] Since then, the Bank has had the power either to change the size of required reserves or to permit a change in their composition to free liquidity. This has meant that the Bank of Italy has been able to regulate the "monetary base" of Italian banks. In this way the Italian central bank can control borrowing and lending transactions abroad by Italian banks.[37]

It is clear that in terms of the definition of the objectives of monetary policy and, therefore, of economic policy in general, this system was designed to foster a climate favorable to business and export expansion. The tight credit policies of the late 1940s and the 1950s did not interfere with industry. Edelman and Fleming have pointed out that those hurt most by these policies were the unemployed who tended to support the leftist parties (PCI, PSI).[38] These parties were excluded from the government and from the formulation of economic policy in 1947, roughly when the Einaudi system went into effect. At the same time, actual business involvement in the formulation of these policies in the period from 1947 to the 1960s seems to have been problematic. There were no formal consultations with industry although some ministers on the Bank-dominated Interministerial Committee on Credit and Savings presented the business point of view. Obviously, there was even less labor involvement in the definition of these policies.[39]

[34] Edelman and Fleming, pp. 16–17.
[35] Ibid., pp. 16, 65.
[36] Allen and Stevenson, p. 164.
[37] Ibid., pp. 165–67.
[38] Edelman and Fleming, p. 65.
[39] Ibid, pp. 68–69.

It is apparent that these policies and the policy-making system that developed them had the purpose of favoring business as well as the parallel and equally important purpose of favoring the political position of the DC. In 1960, for example, the DC was interested in obtaining an expansion of liquidity. It was hoped that such a move would encourage PSI support for the Opening to the Left by holding out the prospect of income redistribution. Guido Carli, the new Governor of the Bank of Italy and himself a supporter of the "Opening," acted to loosen controls.[40] This development helped set the stage for the significant wage increases of 1962. The following year, there was a 16 percent increase in wages while the GNP went up only 4.8 percent.[41] These DC-Bank policies were implemented at a time when the labor situation was much closer to one of full employment than was the case during the 1940s and 1950s and when business was already apprehensive over the Opening to the Left. Thus they contributed to higher inflation and by 1963–1964 they were partly responsible for a full-scale economic crisis. The Bank's subsequent attempts to use monetary policy to retrench contributed to the 1963–1965 recession.[42] One must conclude that the Bank operates according to criteria that are political and electoral as well as those that are designed to provide a sound business climate. At the same time, Allen and Stevenson have noted that the 1963–1965 recession showed that Italy's heavy reliance on managing the economy by means of monetary policy has favored the adoption of excessively deflationary policies. The same assessment applies to the 1969–1973 recession, which was also the result of political and labor factors.[43]

It is thus difficult to assess the distribution of benefits of Italy's monetary policies. There is an inclination on the part of politicians to let the Bank make difficult decisions, supposedly on technical, rather than political, grounds. For one thing, the Bank enjoys more respect and trust from foreigners than does the government per se. This respect can be used as an inducement to get foreign help. The end result is that any strategy for resolving Italy's international (and even related internal) economic difficulties emphasizes foreign assistance and especially borrowing from national and international funding sources.[44] As will be seen, the head of the Bank of Italy, Carli, was deeply involved in the important 1974 negotiations to receive a loan from West Germany.[45]

One observer, Marcello De Cecco, has noted a problem in this connection. Economic policy has been "depoliticized," he says, in that it is left to the central banks, thereby "systematizing a highly dangerous form of taxation without representation."[46] In Italy this is part of a larger picture where an acquiescence in the

---

[40] Ibid., pp. 67–68, and Allen and Stevenson, p. 169.

[41] Willis, p. 76.

[42] Allen and Stevenson, pp. 168–70. See also Edelman and Fleming, p. 68.

[43] Allen and Stevenson, p. 171.

[44] Eugenio Scalfari, "Parla Carli: Come Lascio la Lira," *L'Espresso* Vol. 21, No. 32 (10 August 1975): 59.

[45] See, for instance, "Raising the Eurowind," *Economist* (London), 24 August 1975, pp. 51–52.

[46] De Cecco, p. 9.

absence of strong political institutions fosters policy making by technocrats whose influence comes from personal ties to party factions and interest groups.

Within the constraints set by the DC system and the Bank of Italy, Italy's industrial and commercial policy, both domestic and international, is largely the result of decisions made by two strong sets of institutions: state-controlled enterprises and large private corporations. State-controlled enterprises are a key element of the Italian economic system, tied even more closely than the Bank of Italy to the DC coalition. This state level of industry and commerce is dominated by the two giant state holding companies, IRI and ENI, which have important international roles.[47] For instance, ENI deals directly with foreign energy suppliers; IRI has been charged with a special role in the development of the South where many Italians assumed that European Community regional development policies would prove particularly efficacious.

In spite of an early orientation toward fostering a business climate favorable to the Italian private sector and foreign investment, from the early 1950s the preeminent DC has been sympathetic to the expansion of state-controlled enterprises. Especially in the 1950s, businessmen were suspicious of this benign attitude. The DC has favored these institutions for a number of reasons. First, they seem to conform to the traditional Christian Democratic doctrine of de-emphasizing private profit in industry and commerce as part of a strategy of reconciling workers and employers. Secondly, unlike the private sector, these enterprises very quickly became important elements of the DC's patronage system.[48] Finally, many of these enterprises have been headed by dynamic individuals who developed close personal and political ties to politicians and factions inside the DC and other government parties.

There is another element which touches on the relationship between these enterprises and the international dimension of the Italian business climate. The overall receptivity of Italy's economic leaders toward foreign investment has already been discussed. Shonfield has noted, however, that the larger public enterprises maintain that their own expansion helps the long-term national economic interest by keeping foreigners from buying Italian concerns. He also points out that this claim is favorably received in a larger Italian political setting that attributes conspiracies to foreign companies.[49]

The evolving importance of these enterprises is indicated by the increase in the state holding companies' share of industrial investment from 15 percent in the mid-1950s to 40 percent in 1972.[50] These enjoy the advantages of private corporations with fewer disadvantages. They are able to make use of direct market financing: in 1973, for example, Italian public sector institutions borrowed $4,400

---

[47] Details about IRI and ENI may be found in M.V. Posner and S. J. Wolfe, *Italian Public Enterprise* (London: Gerald Duckworth, 1967).
[48] See again Shonfield in Cavazza and Graubard, pp. 271–74.
[49] Ibid., p. 286.
[50] Ibid., p. 270, and OECD, *Economic Surveys: Italy* (Paris: OECD, November 1972), p. 74.

million abroad.[51] But they have in the past also used the direct investment of public funds for short-term ends.[52] They are as likely as the large private corporations to pay only lip service to government economic planning.[53]

All in all, these enterprises enjoy a great deal of autonomy within the overall structure of the DC coalition. They are supposed to be under the joint supervision of the Ministry for State Holdings and, in the international context, of the Foreign Ministry. But the former is small and weak and the two holding companies have long confronted it with *faits accomplis*. The Foreign Ministry is easily bypassed.[54] In fact, there is a tradition, best exemplified by the late head of ENI, Enrico Mattei, for the holding companies to be headed by decisive *condottieri*. This term refers to the adventurous soldiers of fortune of the early Renaissance. Their modern counterparts do not concern themselves with petty and partisan bureaucrats and thrive on intense personal competition.[55] While the emphasis here is on personal power, it is a power reinforced by ties which the *condottiere* develops with particular party factions.

The aggressive attitude of the holding companies is reinforced by the fact that they identify with private industry concentrated in the North and that they feel a certain amount of contempt for the ministerial politicians and bureaucrats who are drawn heavily from the South. While the reputation of the holding companies has been tarnished of late because of corruption and the lateral movement of ENI officials into private corporations,[56] they have a public image of efficiency and favorable ideology. That is, they are perceived as operating with an orientation toward both profit making and public welfare. Private industry, on the other hand, is perceived as selfish, while the orthodox state bureaucracy is considered inefficient, wasteful, and corrupt.[57] Shonfield noted that in Italy there is much less esprit de corps among senior government officials than there is in France.[58]

As of mid-1975, ENI had holdings in or produced the following: oil, gas, chemicals, nuclear production, plastics, synthetic fibers, tankers, foreign subsidiaries, a daily newspaper, and a press agency.[59] ENI and IRI reportedly own 16 percent of the shares of the giant Montedison corporation, now headed by the former director of ENI, Eugenio Cefis.[60] IRI and ENI also have benefited from extensive patronage responsibilities and from close ties to certain influential political factions and individuals, especially those from the left wing of the DC. Thus,

[51] OECD, *Economic Surveys: Italy* (Paris: OECD, January 1975), p. 34.

[52] Shonfield in Cavazza and Graubard, p. 286, and Edelman and Fleming, p. 19.

[53] Gianfranco Pasquino and Umberto Pecchini, "Italy," in Hayward and Watson, pp. 73–74, 85.

[54] See Jack Hayward, "National Aptitudes for Planning in Britain, France, and Italy," *Government and Opposition* Vol. 9, No. 4 (Autumn 1974): 409.

[55] See Andrew Shonfield, *Modern Capitalism* (London: Oxford University Press, 1965), p. 197.

[56] Statera, pp. 60–62.

[57] There is a significant strain of Catholic and Marxian technocracy in Italy that believes that public enterprise is more ethical and just than private.

[58] Shonfield, *Modern Capitalism*, pp. 196–97.

[59] See the unsigned article in *L'Espresso* Vol. 21, No. 31 (3 August 1975): 59.

[60] Leo Sisti, "Giolitti: C'è una Sola Cosa da Fare: Pulizia," in ibid., p. 61.

Mattei was for a long while a close associate of former President Giovanni Gronchi, originally an exponent of the "economic Left" of the DC. The two reinforced each other's preferences for unilateral Italian policies toward Russia and the Middle East. They championed these policies for ideological reasons as well as for the energy advantages that might be gained. In the late 1950s and early 1960s, ENI, a part of the state apparatus, was running a foreign policy that, on East-West relations and the Middle East, differed from that of the governing coalition and was not supervised closely by the Foreign Ministry or even the cabinet.

Mattei tried to arrange a marriage between a daughter of Italy's ex-king and the Shah of Iran to facilitate Italian oil negotiations with Iran. He succeeded in making Italy the first Western customer for Russian crude oil despite opposition from the Vatican and others inside and outside Italy.[61] ENI used its own news-paper, *Il Giorno* of Milan, to publicize its intentions and accomplishments. At times there were clashes between ENI functionaries (often Catholic technocrats) who emphasized Italian unilateralism outside Western Europe and Gaetano Martino, the Foreign Minister. Martino had negotiated the Treaty of Rome and was a leader of the pro-business, pro-European, anti-clerical Liberal Party.

While operating without ENI's and IRI's political advantages, the large enterprises of the private sector such as Fiat, Pirelli, and Olivetti also have a tendency to arrange foreign transactions with only a minimum of prior consultation with the Foreign Ministry or other government agencies. Fiat has acted independently in its relations with Eastern European governments. Italian state agencies were brought in only when negotiations were far advanced.[62] I was told often in Rome that Italy had no real foreign policy. Rather, it has the international operations of Fiat and Montedison.[63] This is clearly an overstatement. All the same, it demonstrates that close corporate ties to the DC coalition notwithstanding, much of Italian foreign economic activity takes place in an environment where there is a minimum of coordination by politically accountable government agencies.

The largest Italian corporations are truly multinational. Fiat, in 1969, had invested 43 percent of its capital outside Italy. Pirelli and Olivetti did 49 percent and 78 percent, respectively, of their business outside the country.[64] Thus, the Foreign Ministry, charged with coordinating the international economic policy for a country whose foreign economic ties are vital, is often bypassed or confronted with *faits accomplis* by the major centers of economic power.

## IV Government machinery and foreign economic policy

Because of its international dependence and internal fragmentation one might

---

[61] Peter Nichols, *Italia, Italia* (Boston: Atlantic Monthly Press, 1973), p. 153.
[62] Kaiser, in Cavazza and Graubard, pp. 410–11.
[63] Interview No. 1.
[64] Kaiser, in Cavazza and Graubard, p. 409.

expect Italy to follow the strategy of, for instance, the Netherlands, Belgium, and Denmark. These countries have sought to maximize national advantage by vigorously working to make the Atlantic and European organs more responsive to their needs. But Italy has not followed this strategy. Rather, the general pattern of Italian external policy, in both the military and economic sectors, has been one of passivity. The most important explanation of this pattern is the nature of the broad DC coalition, which diffuses responsibility and, while inhibiting decisive policy making, encourages competition among its various components.

The diffusion of responsibility for foreign economic relations is extended still further by two fairly unique Italian structures. These in turn are closely related to the Catholic and Marxian subcultural dominance of Italian public life. The Church influences foreign economic relations in general but especially foreign aid. It is common for Italians to count assistance and missionary work by the Italian Church in foreign countries as part of Italian foreign aid.[65] A large portion of other Italian "foreign aid" is actually overseas investment by Italian firms. Bonanni notes that the Foreign Ministry's Commission for Aid to Developing Countries limits itself to examining proposals from Italian private companies for work outside Italy. The Commission does not take planning initiatives and is content to leave Italy's role with the new nations as one involving primarily private concerns.[66]

Further, the PCI plays a role (albeit a largely undocumented one) in supervising and easing economic relations between public and private Italian enterprises and Communist countries. The presumption is that all but the largest Italian enterprises wanting to deal with the Eastern governments must go through the PCI or the Communist-Socialist labor confederation.[67] This naturally increases the prestige and legitimacy of the PCI. It is also assumed that the PCI expects financial inducements and other concessions in return for its help. Thus, anti-Communist businessmen and technocrats have to reward the PCI for making their economic transactions easier. Another irony in this regard is that, according to Del Bo, Italy has traded with Russia by extending credits, a method some characterize as a subsidy to Russia from the Italian government.[68] At the same time, it is assumed that the PCI has received large subsidies from the Russians while trying to gain strength at the expense of government parties.

But it is also true that, in general, the members of the DC-dominated coalition have little interest in foreign affairs or foreign economic policy. This coalition is part of a subculture-dominant political system where statesmen repre-

---

[65] G.S., "L'Aiuto Italiano ai Paesi in Via di Sviluppo," *Affari Esteri* Vol. 2, No. 8 (October 1970): 161, and Centro Studi N. Rezzara of Vicenza, "Il Contributo Italiano ai Paesi in Via di Sviluppo" (Vicenza, ca. 1970, offset), pp. 3–20. The small Italian Radical Party complains that the Church performs too many functions at home as well that should be the responsibility of the state.

[66] Massimo Bonanni, "Nuovi Operatori di Politica Internazionale," in Bonanni, Vol. 3, p. 695.

[67] Kaiser, in Cavazza and Graubard, p. 411, and Norman Kogan, *The Politics of Italian Foreign Policy* (New York: Praeger, 1963), p. 90.

[68] Del Bo in Del Bo et al., pp. 17–18.

senting both of the important subcultures, the Catholic and the Marxian, have shown considerable reluctance to become involved in the problems of foreign relations.[69] At best, there is a tendency to leave foreign policy considerations at the level of innocuous generalities and to avoid discussions of instrumental policy choices.[70] A consequence of this is that Italy's foreign operations are marked by a lack of coherence and assertiveness which leaves Italy's diplomats with little guidance. This has been the case even where important Italian interests are involved.[71]

This lack of coherence is related to the fact that Italy's government has been dominated since the Second World War by parties with no prior governing experience. Furthermore, these parties represent subcultures that are antagonistic toward the kind of instrumental and nationalist foreign policies considered legitimate by other sovereign states. To some extent, this is because these parties (the DC and various Socialist groupings) undertook to govern in the wake of Mussolini's disastrous efforts to carry out a traditional external policy. Equally important, however, Italian Catholics and Marxians are doctrinally uneasy with foreign policies that do not emphasize universalist values such as international reconciliation and anti-militarism, a tradition sometimes described as "irenic."[72]

The upshot is that little political direction is given to government agencies explicitly responsible for external relations. This gives considerable leeway to a variety of state and private agencies, all of which have ties to particular party factions or individuals. Minimizing external policy at the political level also means that pronouncements on foreign policy issues, economic as well as politico-military, often appear to be part of the interparty and interfactional debates that characterize the jockeying for power inside and between Italy's political forces. But these are usually phrased as generalities and are primarily a kind of code for finding points of contact among political forces seeking to establish or preserve a particular domestic alignment.[73] A publicist of the Catholic Left might suggest that, while Italy cannot leave NATO without adversely affecting European equilibrium, the Italian government can still contest militaristic and imperialist decisions by NATO institutions.[74] Presumably, this would help convince the PCI that Italy's Catholic (and at times Socialist) foreign policy spokesmen are amenable to subtle changes in

---

[69] On political culture as "operative ideals," see William T. Bluhm, *Ideologies and Attitudes: Modern Political Culture* (Englewood Cliffs, N.J.: Prentice-Hall, 1974), pp. xi–xii, and Samuel Beer, *British Politics in the Collectivist Age* (New York: Random House-Vintage, 1969), pp. xii–xiii.

[70] Roberto Guidi, "Gli Strumenti," in Del Bo et al., p. 65.

[71] Interviews No. 20, 4, and 14.

[72] Stefano Silvestri, "Il Dibattito sulla NATO in Italia," *Lo Spettatore Internazionale* Vol. 3, No. 1 (January–February 1968): 133–34. In this case, "irenic" refers to an orientation toward peace.

[73] For references to this position, see Stanley Hoffmann's Foreword to Vannicelli, pp. ix–x, and Hoffmann, "Pranzo a Tre sulla Politica Estera Italiana," in Cavazza and Graubard, pp. 393–94.

[74] Emanuele Ranci Ortigosa, "Imperialismo, NATO, e Paesi Europei," *Relazioni Sociali* Vol. 10, Nos. 7–8 (July–August 1970): 478–79, 494.

Italy's international position. The primary aim, in short, is to find points of contact for domestic political purposes.

This kind of extended interparty and interfactional negotiation can be confusing. For one thing, a publicist or a parliamentarian of a particular faction may express serious disagreement with Italian foreign policy. Yet the determination of that policy may be the responsibility of a minister or undersecretary from the same faction. The result seems to be a combination of acquiescence and alienation, often in the same people. This is hardly an atmosphere conducive to coherent policy making.

The diffusion of responsibility in foreign economic policy making is indicated by the large number of government agencies with direct functions in this area. In addition to the Foreign Ministry, there are the three separate strictly economic ministries: Treasury, Finance, and Budget. There are in addition the Ministry of Industry and Commerce and the separate Ministry of Foreign Trade.

But the list continues: in a country where considerable international activity is carried on by state-owned enterprises, the Ministry for State Holdings ("Participations") has important supervisory functions touching on international relations. And in the age of the European agricultural policy, the Ministry of Agriculture has an international role as does the Ministry of Labor, considering the large number of Italians working in other countries. It is also clear that other actors with foreign policy interests, such as corporations, politically affiliated trade unions, and special interest groups with ties to particular DC or Socialist factions, will attempt to use the specialized ministries in their respective sectors to implement their designs.

While in theory the Foreign Ministry is supposed to coordinate Italy's relations with other countries, Italian elites have not interfered with the external activities of other agencies. This fact, however, does not mean that the Foreign Ministry does not attempt jealously to retain preeminence and to insist that it (and especially its Director-General for Economic Affairs) be involved in all international economic undertakings. There is an organ for coordination, an interministerial committee chaired by this functionary. It includes the Directors (or senior career officials) of the Ministries of Finance, the Treasury, the Budget, Agriculture, Industry and Commerce, Foreign Trade, and State Holdings. The consensus is that it does not function well.

The story here is more than one of mere bureaucratic pluralism. It is closely tied to the overriding environment of political fragmentation. In Italy's coalition politics, the portfolios listed above (and the undersecretaryships in these offices) must be distributed carefully, not just among the various parties in the government but also among the factions of these parties. The result is a situation in which a mutual veto is easier to achieve than coordination. This is especially the case when coordination is the responsibility of a weak Foreign Ministry which lacks political direction.

One reason for this is that sympathy on the part of some Catholic and Marxian politicians for a technocratic approach to policy has permitted the specialized agencies to acquire de facto responsibilities in foreign economic policy, especially if they are headed by politicians or bureaucrats with influence or special qualifications.[75] Hence, Emilio Colombo's experience and expertise in European Community affairs led to whatever ministry he headed—whether Treasury, Finance, Foreign Trade, or Industry and Commerce—having effective power in the foreign relations area. The Foreign Ministry has been hesitant to admit its own reduced power by seeking advice or personnel from these and other technical agencies.

Thus, while the Foreign Ministry has been charged with coordinating all external relations including foreign economic policy, it is unable to do so. In part, to be sure, this is the result of poorly prepared personnel. For while the Foreign Ministry claims responsibility for all Italian external policy, it has not organized itself to include personnel trained in technical specialities like defense policy and foreign economic relations. And the unwillingness of the political elites to be concerned with foreign relations operations means that there is little political pressure to reorganize. The Ministry continues to stress traditional methods of recruitment and training with an emphasis on the legal and political sectors. At the same time, it jealously guards its prerogatives to conduct foreign relations in the face of perceived encroachments by various economic ministries.[76]

It follows then that the low priority assigned to foreign policy in general and the disinclination of political elites to appear to be concerned with the real world of diplomacy mean that Italy's international economic machinery is left with little direction or support. One example of the inclination to focus on problems of general orientation may be found in the context of the November 1975 summit meeting of the leading Western industrial nations. The Italian Premier, Aldo Moro, gave special attention to problems of East-West relations rather than to a sector that touched Italy's ongoing economic crisis more directly.[77]

An important consequence of this institutional fragmentation and lack of coordination is that both personalism and improvisation are reinforced. Particularly aggressive and experienced statesmen will often dominate the area of foreign economic policy regardless of the actual office occupied at any given time and with a minimum of direct Foreign Ministry involvement. While this means that expertise will be brought to bear on a problem, it also leads to resentments and to difficulties in developing in any one place the resources and staff that could be used for ongoing policy making.

The upshot is a reliance on improvisation. While Italian improvisations have at times been successful, it is difficult to extract from essentially individualistic experiences a more extended and reliable foreign economic policy capability. There is, then, a certain acquiescence in a personalist rather than an institutionalized orientation. A further instance of institutional weakness is the extremely limited

---

[75] Bonanni in Bonanni, pp. 688–89.
[76] Del Bo in Del Bo et al., pp. 15–16.
[77] See Clyde Farnsworth, "Shaky Europe Looks to the Summit for Aid," *The New York Times,* November 14, 1975, p. 10.

role played by Parliament, especially in the foreign relations area. Important foreign policy decisions are not normally subjected to parliamentary scrutiny.[78]

## V  Outcomes of political economy abroad and at home

In spite of the fact that the European Community is one of the two key poles of Italy's external relations, the passivity and lack of direction engendered by Italy's coalition politics have made it difficult for Italy to benefit from Community membership. This is especially apparent in the area of agriculture. As late as 1967, Italy had 24.1 percent of the labor force employed in that sector, more than any other Community member.[79] After much hard bargaining on Community agricultural matters in the early 1960s when Italy alternated between successes and disappointments, the effects on Italy of the Community's common agricultural policy could be seen by the period 1966–1968. In Willis' words, "The prognosis was not particularly favorable."[80] There was only a slight increase in Italian exports to Community countries. The results in fruits and vegetables were especially disappointing. For instance, Italian citrus exports were hindered by poor quality control and packaging, by poor distribution methods, and by increasing competition from Spain, Israel, and others.[81] In fact, Italians claimed that their partners were ignoring Community preferences and abusing quality controls to block Italian imports.[82]

It is also evident that Italy's problems in the European agricultural sector were derived from internal political and social factors. A lack of agricultural rationalization and an increase in personal consumption helped to maintain a trade imbalance in food. For example, per capita meat consumption increased 100 percent between 1952 and 1968. In 1972–1973, Italian food exports were 7 percent of total exports while food constituted 20 percent of Italian imports.[83] Just as important, DC-dominated governments have been unwilling to modernize agriculture to make it more competitive in the European Community. This could have been done, for instance, by modernizing social security laws and regional development programs. The failure to do so has been the result of an inability to establish a consensus in the fragmented DC coalition on how best to accomplish this modernization without disturbing the clientelistic rural structure and social welfare organizations that have benefited the DC in past elections. One consequence of these political factors has been that while Italy has paid a great deal to

---

[78] The practice of using the Bank of Italy permits further reduction of accountability on the grounds that the Bank is technical and not political.
[79] Zariski, *Italy*, p. 38. France was second with 16.6 percent.
[80] Willis, p. 88.
[81] Ibid., pp. 88, 130.
[82] Ibid., p. 88.
[83] OECD statistics.

the European agricultural fund (FEOGA), it has gotten little in return.[84] Giuseppe Are has noted that Italy's inability to make use of FEOGA funds (much of which came from Italy in the first place) has been due to a lack of adequate plans. [85] From evidence such as this, Willis has concluded that in the 1958–1968 period the financial position of Italian farmers worsened in relation to all other Italian groups.[86]

It must not be forgotten that there is an organizational-diplomatic dimension to Italy's unassertiveness in foreign economic relations. What is to be made of the limited sense of involvement even in international economic cooperation? This is presumably a sector congenial to political elites bent on emphasizing international solidarity and the need to accept limitations on sovereign prerogatives. If Italy is too weak, fragmented, and culturally unwilling to play a unilateral role in international economic affairs, it would seem wise for Italy to devote its energies to coherent and assertive participation in international arrangements. Yet there is considerable testimony that this is not done. Cesare Merlini, a knowledgeable observer and the head of Italy's Institute for International Affairs (IAI), has noted that Italy gets little from the European Community. This, he says, shows Community insensitivity toward Italy. It also demonstrates, however, that the Italian government does not defend Italy's interests in the Community.[87] For instance, it has been argued that Italy's comprehensive economic situation could be improved as the result of real Community assistance for Southern regional development.[88]

One problem with this assumption, however, relates to Italy's difficulty in interacting with multilateral agencies. On one level, this is simply a matter of assigning a low priority to international economic commitments when drastic economic measures are needed at home. There have been many occasions on which Italy has been unresponsive to European Community regulations and directions. For instance, Primo Vannicelli has described how, at the time of its 1963–1964 economic crisis, Italy turned to the United States for help rather than working within the Community; also how Italy was particularly slow in passing legislation needed to implement the Community's value added tax (VAT) system.[89]

On another level, there is a problem with diplomatic representation in the foreign economic field. It is difficult to send the best Italian diplomats to work with multilateral agencies. There are complaints that the work, largely technical, is too demanding and the location of the agencies in places like Brussels and Luxem-

---

[84] Willis, p. 147.
[85] Are, p. 22.
[86] Willis, pp. 88–89.
[87] Merlini, p. 163.
[88] "Italy and Its Partners: A Case Study in International Crisis: Conference Discussion," *International Affairs* (London) Vol. 51, No. 1 (January 1975): 16.
[89] See for instance Vannicelli, pp. 28–29 on how Italy has not been a reliable Community partner. See also Donald J. Puchala, "Domestic Politics and Regional Harmonization in the European Communities," *World Politics* Vol. 27, No. 4 (July 1975): 504–06, 511.

bourg is not desirable.[90] This lack of good Italian diplomats in Brussels, for example, has been noted by European Community functionaries (including some Italians) and by representatives from other countries.[91] According to Dino Del Bo, Italy has been at a disadvantage vis-à-vis other Community members because it did not have a vast empire in which to prepare international leaders and functionaries.[92] One critic of the Foreign Ministry maintains that under Enrico Mattei ENI had a more effective foreign economic policy than the Ministry where, after the Treaty of Rome, lethargy set in.[93] While this may be so, it is also true that ENI under Mattei was not particularly interested in the EEC; it was more oriented toward Eastern Europe and the Third World.[94]

The morale of Italian personnel assigned to multilateral agencies must also be affected by the unwillingness of ambitious politicians/statesmen to serve on European bodies. They feel that, once in Brussels, they will be forgotten. The case of Franco Maria Malfatti is illustrative. A young ally of Amintore Fanfani, he was persuaded to assume the presidency of the European Community Commission when it was Italy's turn in 1970. He arrived in Brussels and indicated that he hoped to be able to spend considerable time in Italy keeping himself visible. He was somewhat miffed when informed that the presidency of the Commission was a full-time job. Shortly thereafter, he resigned when early elections were called in Italy. The result was that Italy forfeited the Commission presidency.[95]

One articulate Italian diplomat in Brussels admitted that his country's representation was poor but maintained that the diplomats did as well as could be expected under the circumstances. They were penalized by the lack of support for their efforts and the lack of coordination and direction from Rome. They were forced, he said, to use the "mezzi di bordo," a nautical term meaning the means at hand (or on board). This was unlike the position of the French, Dutch, and Germans, for example, who had strong support from their home ministries.[96] Italians had to rely on the virtuosity of certain individuals to overcome institutional weaknesses.

This lack of institutional support is a situation that Italian observers have noted repeatedly. Pietro Quaroni, a well-known retired diplomat who served as ambassador in a variety of key posts, has noted that the Ministry of Agriculture has a very difficult time finding the statistics on Italian production necessary to provide support to those negotiating agricultural matters in the European Community.[97]

[90] From Foreign Ministry staff newsletters of 1970.
[91] A member of the American Mission to the European Community found this rather strange since he said that young American Foreign Service officers liked to be assigned to those kinds of missions in that the work seemed more concrete than in traditional diplomatic posts.
[92] Del Bo in Del Bo et al., p. 16.
[93] Luigi Graziano, *La Politica Estera Italiana nel Dopoguerra* (Padova: Marsilio, 1968), p. 41.
[94] Willis, pp. 184, 187.
[95] Nichols, p. 153.
[96] Interview No. 25. Italian diplomats and those from other countries at NATO headquarters reported analogous features. Interviews No. 26, 24, and 45.
[97] Pietro Quaroni, "La Diplomazia," in Del Bo et al., pp. 124–25. Interview No. 20.

This is an area observers return to constantly. In F. Roy Willis' words:

The Italian ministers probably made a major error in policy by assuming that Italy would remain a net exporter of agricultural products, whose interests were similar to those of France, rather than an importer, which it shortly became, whose interests were closer to Germany.[98]

John Newhouse has also addressed this element of Italian policy making:

Italy needed time . . . not only to improve its agriculture but to assemble data that would give a more precise view of the actual scope of its agricultural problems; this information lag . . . has always been a problem for Italy in Community affairs, and particularly agricultural affairs. Rome, in short, was the least willing of any of the parties to agree to a financial regulation of more than one or, at most, two years duration.[99]

Factors like these certainly restrict the effectiveness of Italy's multilateral diplomacy. Diplomats are free to revert to a more traditional stance where the emphasis is on general formulations rather than on specific and technical issues. Given the priorities of Italian political elites and the consequent unlikelihood of any effort to reform the diplomatic machinery, significant shifts will probably not be forthcoming.[100]

At the same time, one must recall that Italians recognized very soon after the Second World War, even before the foundation of the Coal and Steel Community, that there was a need to move toward good "industrial diplomacy."[101] Then why did they move so slowly and so erratically? For one thing, Italy's political fragmentation and cultural biases away from foreign policy left the diplomats alone to act traditionally or emphasized grandiose schemes with little chance of success. Thus, in 1958 the then Premier Amintore Fanfani reshuffled the diplomatic corps with the express purpose of promoting younger men who would institute a more activist diplomacy toward the countries of the Middle East and Africa rather than focusing on problems closer to home such as those of the recently established EEC.[102] Del Bo implies that Italians perceive their international dependence and inferiority as leading to permitting others to take the lead. Thus, in the 1950s, Italy considered itself under French and American patronage. The inclination was to let

---

[98] Willis, p. 79.

[99] John Newhouse, *Collision in Brussels* (New York: Norton, 1967), pp. 69–70. There are some who feel that, all things considered, Italy has not done too badly in European agricultural negotiations. If this is the case, some Italian diplomats believe that it is due to diplomacy by improvisation. In this connection, Pietro Quaroni has noted that "La furberia e l'abilità hanno i loro limiti." (Slyness and ability have their limits.) See Quaroni in Del Bo et al., p. 130.

[100] Peter Lange has suggested that PCI inclusion may make for a more assertive foreign policy. See Lange, p. 239.

[101] Del Bo in Del Bo et al., p. 14.

[102] See for instance ibid., p. 13, and Niccolò Carandini, "Purga a Palazzo Chigi," *Il Mondo* Vol. 10, No. 47 (25 November 1958): 1.

those countries take the initiative.[103] It is reasonable to conclude that, currently at least, the situation in foreign economic policy is analogous. The only difference is that the patrons now are Germany and the United States.

In examining outcomes of foreign economic policy, it is important to consider the role of labor in the Italian foreign economic policy environment. It has already been established that the 1947 Einaudi-DC program for economic stabilization and recovery gave priority to the needs of Italian and international business. Benefits to workers were secondary. In fact, the 1947 program was adopted almost simultaneously with the exclusion from the governing coalition of those parties (PCI and PSI) that most directly represented large numbers of Italian industrial workers. This strategy was facilitated by the labor situation in Italy. As Kindleberger and others have pointed out, Italy had "unlimited supplies of labor" at this time.[104] In addition, the labor force was divided politically along lines set by the sectarian Italian political system and increasingly aggravated by disputes over the Marshall Plan and the Cold War environment in general. The Catholic component was part of the DC coalition and the larger, Marxian-oriented force was closely connected to the PSI and the PCI.[105] By the end of the 1940s, labor unions were split into competing federations along similar sectarian lines.

The result was that at least until the early 1960s, management was able to dominate labor largely because of political factors. Also in this period there was a system of national collective bargaining. Under it, minimum wage standards were set in negotiations between workers and national employers' organizations with direct government (that is to say, DC) involvement.[106] These factors made it difficult for the workers to contribute to cost-push inflation. The economic environment in the postwar period included a low national debt and limited military expenditures. There also were increases in productivity. Since consumer prices rose less rapidly than wages, there was an improvement in workers' living standards.[107] The disruptive capabilities of the PCI- and PSI-led labor unions had been amply demonstrated at the time of the Marshall Plan. In view of this, the governing coalition's political-economic strategy has been described as one of providing "a minimum standard of living that will minimize social and political protest while it makes only minimal demands upon industry."[108]

By the early 1960s, again as the result of political as well as economic factors, the situation began to change. As part of laying the groundwork for the Opening to

---

[103] See for instance Del Bo in Del Bo et al., p. 19.

[104] Kindleberger, *Europe's Postwar Growth*, p. 36. See also Jack Hayward, "Editorial Foreword" to Isidoro Franco Mariani, "Incomes and Employment Policies in Italian Economic Planning," in Hayward and Watson, p. 202.

[105] Zariski, *Italy*, p. 262, and Hayward, "Editorial Foreword," in Hayward and Watson, p. 202.

[106] See for instance Zariski, *Italy*, p. 66, and Hayward, "Editorial Foreword," in Hayward and Watson, p. 202.

[107] Hayward, "Editorial Foreword," in Hayward and Watson, p. 202.

[108] Quoted in ibid.

the Left, the DC-dominated coalition in 1956 consented to the creation of Intersind, a public enterprise employers' organization.[109] Previously, private employers' organizations like Confindustria had also negotiated with public employees. From the founding of Intersind, public enterprise and private sector employees negotiated with different organizations. By the early 1960s, public employees were enjoying large wage increases. This led to demands for increases in the private sector as well. The years 1962–1963 saw a 42 percent increase in wage rates and a significant increase in the percentage of national income constituted by wages. According to Kindleberger, that percentage increased from 50.8 percent in 1950, to 55.1 percent in 1960, to 57.4 percent in 1962, to 62.5 percent in 1963, and to 63.8 percent in 1964.[110]

Also in 1962, there were moves, first toward industry-level (as opposed to national) collective bargaining and then toward plant-level bargaining.[111] This was a period when the DC was attempting to cement the Center-Left by seeming to be more socially and economically progressive. It was not, therefore, unusual to see the Ministry of Labor siding with the unions in order to get their political support and to dampen unrest.[112] But as Kindleberger has noted, the response of Italian workers to wage increases has been different from that of German workers. With increases in wages, Italian workers saved less. With higher wages (and prices), they bought more, including more imported goods. They also borrowed more. The results were higher costs and lower profits. These factors, along with the economic policies of the Center-Left and greater union militancy, led to a capital flow abroad and a worsening of the balance-of-payments situation.[113]

These elements provided the foundation for a structural crisis in the Italian political economy. This crisis has been aggravated since the beginning of the 1970s by a change in the labor market and a decline in productivity. There is no longer a reserve of workers. Labor is now in a seller's market.[114] And the DC-led Center-Left had to work to maintain support by means of further concessions to the workers. The latter have lately been reinforced by a PCI that has established itself as a legitimate party of protest and has increased its strength at the polls. At the same time, the preeminent DC has been perceived as having been in power and led by the same tired men for too long. This picture has been enhanced by the scandals and indications of corruption that have afflicted the DC and its parliamentary allies.

Given Italy's material weakness and the fragmented internal and international political environment in the late 1940s, it is difficult to see how Italy could have developed a different system for defining economic policy or for distributing the

---

[109] Ibid.
[110] Kindleberger, *Europe's Postwar Growth*, p. 41.
[111] Hayward, "Editorial Foreword," in Hayward and Watson, p. 203.
[112] Ibid.
[113] Kindleberger, *Europe's Postwar Growth,* p. 40, and "Economia al Bivio" in Cavazza and Graubard, p. 244.
[114] See Are, p. 21.

fruits of that policy. This is especially true considering the passivity and immobility of the broadly-based DC coalition and its electoral strategy of directing an expanding patronage system toward the middle class or those with middle-class aspirations. The Opening to the Left was less a matter of structural reform than a means of expanding the base for the original strategy by bringing the PSI into the DC-dominated coalition and its patronage system. It seems possible that eventual power-sharing between the DC and the PCI will have results analogous to those of the Opening to the Left in the 1960s. That is, an expansion of the DC coalition will occur, rather than significant changes in the structure of Italy's political economy.

## VI Prospects for the future: Italy after the oil crisis

The above discussion highlights the problems Italy faces as an actor in the international political economy. Not only is Italy dependent on other actors, but its ability to define and implement foreign economic policies has been hampered by the immobility of the DC political and social coalition that has governed Italy since the 1940s. Social and economic strains have been present in Italian society since the Second World War. But they have become especially serious since the "economic miracle" of the 1950s and early 1960s came to an end. The Opening to the Left, which was implemented at roughly the same time as the twilight of this economic phase and which was intended to blunt social resentments, has not fulfilled this expectation. By the early 1970s, Italy's structural crisis had become extreme.

This was the context in which Italy had to confront the oil price increase of late 1973 and early 1974. It is apparent that this crisis has had the effect of both increasing Italy's international dependence and aggravating an already fragmented internal order.

The data in Table I indicate the impact of OPEC price increases. In January–July 1974, two-thirds of Italy's trade deficit was due to the purchase of petroleum products.[115]

These developments showed the extent of Italian dependence on OPEC policies and good will. Arab perceptions of Italy were puzzling to Italians. Italy had tried for a long period to show evenhandedness in connection with the Middle East and significant groups in the Catholic and Marxian subcultures had manifested friendship toward the Palestinians. Further, ENI had worked hard to establish friendly ties with oil-producing countries. It did so largely in the interests of access to oil. But this strategy was also part of an effort to demonstrate that a Catholic-dominated public enterprise would deal more fairly with raw material producers than American or British private companies. Yet while France and Britain were

---

[115] Bank of Rome, "Two Months of Economic Activity in Italy," *Review of the Economic Conditions in Italy* Vol. 29, No. 6 (November 1975): 556. Guido Carli has maintained that the mid-1975 improvement in Italy's balance-of-payments position was due to a reduction of imports which followed from reduced productivity in Italy. See Scalfari, p. 60.

## Table I Balance of trade figures in billions of lire

|      | Imports | Exports | Balance |
|------|---------|---------|---------|
| 1972 | 11,264  | 10,849  | -415    |
| 1973 | 16,224  | 12,969  | -3,255  |
| 1974 | 26,604  | 19,684  | -6,920  |

Source: Bank of Rome, *Review of the Economic Conditions in Italy* Vol. 28, No. 6 (November 1974): 583; and Vol. 29, No. 1 (January 1975): 109.

called "friendly" by the Arabs, Italy was in limbo. It was labeled neither as friendly nor as unfriendly.[116] This brought home to Italians once again that they have very little in the way of international bargaining strength.

But while the price of oil increased, Italy had little problem with supply. For Italy, Britain, France, West Germany, and the Netherlands together, there was a 5 percent reduction in the oil supply between December 1973 and March 1974 as against the same period in 1972–1973. Yet in Italy alone there was 4 percent *more* oil available.[117] At the same time, Italy's energy consumption went up 6 percent at the height of the crisis. Romano Prodi and Alberto Clô suggest that this was due to one of several factors. There was either an inelasticity of energy consumption patterns, a lack of government concern, or a distortion in the distribution cycle. What is apparent is that after the crisis, an interministerial committee approved a plan to strengthen the government's ability to regulate petroleum use. Little, however, was done in the way of follow-up.[118] Another consequence of the crisis was that ENI, after a long period of trying to be independent of the large multinational oil companies, had to reconcile itself to cooperating with these companies, at least in the near future.[119]

Italy's increased balance-of-payments deficit was a consequence of the oil crisis. The internal economy was also affected. Higher fuel prices contributed to inflation and still more wage demands. Eventually, the result was reduced productivity and higher unemployment. This, in turn, increased dissatisfaction with the government's performance.

There was considerable sentiment in Italy that priority be given to internal change. Specifically, the inclusion of the PCI in the cabinet was promoted as a means of providing stability in the factories and confidence among the workers. There were also fears that the international financial community, public and

---

[116] Merlini, p. 164, and Turner, p. 409.

[117] Other figures for individual countries are: Netherlands, -16 percent; Germany, -12 percent; France, -7 percent; Britain, -1 percent. See Romano Prodi and Alberto Clô, "Europe," in "The Oil Crisis: In Perspective," Raymond Vernon et al., *Daedalus* Vol. 104, No. 4 (Fall 1975): 101.

[118] Ibid., pp. 102–04.

[119] Ibid., pp. 96–97.

private, would refuse help and perhaps even work to sabotage the Italian economy in the event of PCI inclusion.[120] The latter was not a universal view and some observers maintained that Western financial interests should welcome a politically and economically stable Italy.[121]

At any rate, the government, fearing bankruptcy, sought international assistance as a first priority. The most important source of assistance was West Germany. After Italy agreed in the context of the European Community to reduce imports and especially the non-oil component of its payments deficit, Germany finally agreed to lend Italy $2 billion[122] with part of Italy's gold reserves as collateral. The provisions of the loan were negotiated in Bonn in August 1974 by Finance Minister Colombo and Bank of Italy head Guido Carli.[123] The final agreement was decided in Bellaggio on August 30–31 by Premier Mariano Rumor and German Chancellor Schmidt.

In actuality, this transaction appeared to be more a swap than a loan. If Italy could not pay Germany back in dollars by 1976, Germany would be able to sell the Italian gold on the free market. If the price of gold were above $120 an ounce, Italy would get the difference. If it were below that figure, Germany would postpone the gold sale.[124] Thus in 1975 Merlini and others felt that the end result of this operation would be a screened gold sale.[125] In fact, however, by early September 1976, Germany had agreed to roll over the loan on the understanding that due to the decline in the price of gold, "Italy would ... draw no more than 1.6 billion dollars."[126]

It is perfectly clear that the 1974 loan was a way of subsidizing Italy's oil costs.[127] Thus, Italy's energy problems have led to a double dependence: dependence for supply (and pricing) on OPEC and dependence on German financing or on a German willingness to purchase Italian gold. The dependence on OPEC has

[120] See the remarks by Joseph La Palombara quoted in Gianni Corbi, "PCI/La Nuova Strategia: Dear Jerry, Carissimo Enrico," *L'Espresso* Vol. 21, No. 34 (24 August 1975): 10–11.

[121] There were left-wing Socialist elements in Italy in the late 1940s who maintained that Italy could be radically Socialist (but not Stalinist or pro-Russian) and would not have to join an American bloc in order to receive American economic assistance. They felt that the United States would be more interested in an Italy that was strong and stable than in fostering a conservative and volatile client state.

[122] "The Communities and the Italian Measures," *European Communities Bulletin* Vol. 7, Nos. 7–8 (July–August 1974): 19, and "EEC Economies: Hanging Separately," *Economist* (London), 10 August 1974, p. 52.

[123] "Raising the Eurowind," p. 51.

[124] "Harold Is Turning into Europe's Invisible Man," *Economist* (London), 7 September 1974, pp. 63–64.

[125] Merlini, p. 164.

[126] "Political and Economic Developments," *Economic News From Italy* Vol. 31, No. 36 (3 September 1976): 1. See also "Gold: Flexible Descent," *Economist* (London), 18 September 1976, p. 77. Another observer has maintained that instead of new collateral, the Germans wanted trade concessions: a decrease in Italian exports to Germany and an increase in German exports to Italy. He noted, however, that the Germans could not press the Italians too hard since they wanted to keep the Italian government stable. See "Italy: Gold is the Snag in Debt Rollover," *Business Week,* September 13, 1976, p. 47.

[127] "New Ways to Pay for Oil Imports," pp. 22–23.

consequences for Italian foreign policy. Italy will have to maneuver, even more carefully than before 1973, between a Middle East policy that is not antagonistic toward the Arabs and the overall Italian need for an American national security connection. The dependence on German financing and, to some extent, on the large loans Italy has received from the IMF has domestic consequences as well. This is because of German and American insistence that the PCI continue to be excluded from a share of national political power.

Merlini notes that, while Secretary of State Kissinger expressed concern over the Italian inflation rate, he was more interested in the political side of the question, keeping the PCI out of power.[128] There is, however, a general problem with this approach. If traditional anti-inflationary methods are used, the result could be even higher unemployment than exists now. This kind of remedy would only serve to aggravate worker antagonism toward the government and would strengthen pressures for PCI inclusion. Apparently, the PCI feels that an austerity plan which might result in additional unemployment could be part of the negotiations leading to a more direct role for the PCI in the government.

In spite of official denials by the Germans that they had any wish to interfere in Italy's internal affairs in 1974, a German official admitted: "You can be sure Germany will not let Italy go down the drain and bring Communists or Fascists to our doorstep."[129] And it has been noted that Italian officials explicitly rejected any possibility of PCI inclusion in the government immediately after the Italo-German loan agreement.[130] It has recently been admitted, albeit ambiguously, that at the Puerto Rican economic summit meeting in June 1976, Italy's industrial allies discussed punitive measures that might be taken against Italy in the event Communist influence became too apparent.[131]

The formulation of the Einaudi-De Gasperi model in 1947 rested on the assumption that Italy was materially weak. It was also based on the assumption that Italy's internal fragmentation would undermine the DC-dominated coalition's power in the absence of external support. Thus, the need for external support and the threats imposed by internal fragmentation are mutually reinforcing. Italy's economic weakness leads to more pressure from the PCI for a share of national political power. In turn, the greater the degree of the internal threat to DC dominance, the more help the governing coalition feels it should be able to expect from Italy's Atlantic and European industrial partners.

Thus, in terms of Italy's interaction with the international political economy in the recent period, one of its main bargaining devices has been that its creditors could not afford to see it go bankrupt.[132] Nevertheless, it is apparent that the

---

[128] Merlini, p. 165.
[129] "New Ways to Pay for Oil Imports," p. 23.
[130] "Italy: The Silent Ones," *Economist* (London), 14 September 1974, p. 46.
[131] "U.S. Concedes It Discussed a Ban on Loans to Italians," *New York Times*, August 5, 1976, p. 7.
[132] De Cecco, p. 10.

efforts of Italy's statesmen to find some way of stabilizing the domestic political and economic situation are hampered by the need to operate according to rules imposed by outsiders. This might be of some comfort to those (and they are numerous) who would, in any event, oppose PCI inclusion in the government. But it does reduce the flexibility of those who might pursue a strategy of attempting to restore Italy's international economic position while working for domestic political and economic rationalization. Yet more by choice perhaps than by inattention, there is little impetus to accomplish this rationalization.

Given the programmatic passivity inherent in the dominance of the DC coalition, Italy's international weakness can, in desperation to be sure, become an element of strength. That is, it can be used as a means of assuring assistance from other industrial states, especially those who are fearful of growing Communist influence. This is more than a variation on the old theme of "Italia povera, povera Italia" (Italy is poor, poor Italy). It comes close to the formula described by Thomas C. Schelling: "The government that cannot control its balance of payments, or collect taxes, or muster the political unity to defend itself, may enjoy assistance that would be denied if it could control its own resources."[133]

At the same time, the DC-dominated coalition can imply that its continued preeminence, and consequently the basic postwar neo-Liberal economic model with its support for a climate conducive to business and foreign investment, is a precondition for external aid for the nation as a whole. Again, there is an equating of the DC with the state. It is an equation that does, after all, rest on the fact that the DC has held the dominant position in Italian politics since 1945. It is interesting that some observers maintain that a share of national political power for the PCI will ensure domestic stability. In this way, they argue, foreign investors and others who would assist the Italian economy would be reassured that their investments were safe. But this argument is somewhat problematic. All the same, Stanley Hoffmann is close to the Italian dilemma/strategy affecting both internal and external operation when he discusses the general mutual vulnerability of current world politics: "I don't know where my power ends and yours begins, since my power is partly your hostage and vice versa, and the more I try to force you to depend on me, the more I depend on you."[134]

Here again, the interaction between Italy's structural shortcomings and its international economic dependence is clear. In the short run, the competing personalities and clienteles of the DC coalition perceive their political and social interests to be based on programmatic passivity and support from outside the country. As a result, Italian foreign economic policy makers will continue to acquiesce in, or see no alternative to, Italy's dependent status.

---

[133] Thomas C. Schelling, *Strategy of Conflict* (New York: Oxford University Press, 1963), p. 23, also p. 37 on "coercive deficiency" and p. 196 on "rocking the boat"; and his *Arms and Influence* (New Haven: Yale University Press, 1966), pp. 100, 118, 121.

[134] Stanley Hoffmann, "Groping Toward a New World Order," *New York Times,* January 11, 1976, Section 4, p. 1.

# 8

# The French State in the International Economy

*John Zysman*

The French state bureaucracy, able partially to shelter itself from Parliament and to influence the industrial sector directly, has been able to protect national interests in an economically interdependent world. It struck a regional bargain that committed agriculture to the European Community and in effect provided a German subsidy to French farmers. It mediated between the national and international market to promote industrial modernization and force a restructuring of critical industrial sectors. It has grown increasingly sophisticated in its dealings with multinational companies. Early efforts to insist on purely French operations have been abandoned, permitting the state to negotiate more effectively with the multinationals and obtain substantive rather than symbolic goods. These policies have cushioned agriculture's transition into an industrial world and helped pressure a previously protected industry to modernize. Finally, the state has played trader, trying directly to market French goods and assure payment for imports in package trade deals. The French have not been able to impose their own rules on monetary and energy matters. Yet their efforts suggest that a nation-state can use administrative or domestic economic resources to reduce its vulnerability to international developments, though it cannot of course escape from the system.

Since the Second World War, the French state has attempted to manage the terms of the nation's economic relationships with other nations, to maintain as best it could French control of the domestic economy, and thus, to control and direct the terms of interdependence. Foreign economic policy has, consequently, been intertwined with a domestic policy of rapid industrial growth, serving both as a prod for the state to jolt recalcitrant businessmen and as a device to sidestep obstacles to

John Zysman is a member of the Department of Political Science at the University of California, Berkeley.

continued industrialization. Indeed, solutions to domestic economic problems have been sought in the international arena. Throughout the period, French industries deemed critical have been nurtured.[1] Agriculture has been subsidized to avoid the political disruptions of an aggrieved peasantry. At the same time, the less vital but politically delicate traditional sectors have been protected and maintained. Broadly put, economic policy, both at home and abroad, has sought to impose acceptable economic and social outcomes by direct state intervention when necessary, not simply to set conditions favorable to growth. The French state has attempted to create social protection against economic disturbance and has placed explicit limits on the operation of the market.

Despite well-publicized failures, such as the Machines Bull incident, these state policies have been remarkably successful and increasingly sophisticated. The outcomes that were achieved would have been unlikely without direct state intervention and political manipulation of domestic and international markets. The French state, it will be argued, effectively mediated the economic relations between France and its trading partners either when the terms of trade could be directly negotiated among nation-states or when access to the French market could be administratively controlled and a domestic capacity to supply home markets could be insured by specific state actions.

Certainly, De Gaulle subordinated purely economic objectives to his unsuccessful political efforts to restructure the world order. The domestic economy was often manipulated, some might say distorted, for foreign policy purposes. Yet his political enterprise required a strong industrial base and a stable economy. Therefore, setting apart extravagant exceptions such as the French effort to undermine the dollar's position as an international reserve currency, political and economic goals generally required the same foreign policy strategies. Consequently, although De Gaulle's international political efforts were often thwarted, he continued and accelerated the transformation of the economy and the reorganization of the state bureaucracy and its relation to the executive begun under the Fourth Republic. His successors, Giscard in particular, have turned the instruments and tactics of his policies to the more modest goal, always a part of De Gaulle's enterprise but not its final purpose, of obtaining the best terms of exchange for France within the existing world order. The organization of the French state, that is, of the executive and the bureaucracy, and its relation to the other institutions of the society make these strategies of direct intervention possible. Put somewhat differently, these factors encourage the state-led effort to improve France's economic position among nations. Indeed, one can argue from the French case that its foreign economic policies are an extension of the domestic strategies of the state to the international scene.

Importantly, the debate over international economic policy in France has

---

[1] Critical industry as used here is a political, not an economic, label, reflecting the state's priorities, not inherent economic values. In an important sense the traditional and modern sectors in French industry are political, not economic, facts, depending on legislative and bureaucratic definitions as much as on any industrial or market logic. For an elaborate analysis of such a phenomenon see Suzanne Berger, "Why Traditional Classes Survive." (unpublished paper, Massachusetts Institute of Technology).

been in an openly political, rather than an economic, idiom. In the political idiom, international trade is conflict in which the rewards go to the stronger and more clever. In an economic idiom, the reallocation of production according to principles of comparative advantage to achieve greater efficiency and welfare is emphasized. The "state" in the French neo-mercantilist political idiom is the agent of the national society. Indeed, the open use of state power at home and abroad to achieve domestic economic ends has been a continuous theme since the war, linking the *dirigisme* of De Gaulle and the supposed liberalism of Giscard. De Gaulle's presidency effectively divides postwar French politics into three eras and provides a setting for the discussion of a separate domestic issue in each period. Moreover, each epoch in French postwar politics corresponds roughly to an episode in the evolution of the international economy. The Fourth Republic, established at the end of the war, lasted until De Gaulle's return to power in the army coup of 1958. It therefore found itself entangled in the postwar efforts to establish economic and security systems among the Western nations. De Gaulle's presidency, which established the Fifth Republic, overlapped the height of American postwar power, the late 1950s and early 1960s. His successors in the Fifth Republic have been confronted with the erosion of American hegemony and of the economic rules that came with that hegemony. Although the vital domestic problems and the international setting have evolved, important continuities in policy initiatives can be identified.

This analysis can be put in the language of the volume. The French state defined policies which were intended fundamentally to support its domestic strategy for growth. In agriculture, for example, this meant finding solutions to domestic problems in international arrangements and extracting the best possible terms and outcomes from international exchange. There has thus been an effort both to construct international economic institutions favorable to French interests and susceptible to French influence and to achieve the best possible deal for France within any particular regime. The individual elements of policy form part of this larger effort. Agriculture has been buffered by the European agricultural policy. Critical sectors of industry have been supported by a mixture of domestic investment and market control over export promotion. Multinational corporations were first approved in particular sectors, then an effort was made to use their own needs to the ends of the French government. The shifting balance between political and economic purposes was clear-cut in monetary policy where efforts to promote exports required an undervalued currency and the attempt to manipulate the monetary order required hefty reserves and a strong currency. These policies were implemented in a coordinated and coherent fashion which linked domestic policies to international policies in an often purposive and directed fashion. The state, in essence, sought to use every trick of the trade to mediate the relationship between France and the international economy.

The particular policies, of course, depended on the continuing effort to promote growth in a constantly shifting international environment. The constant effort to promote particular outcomes as well as favorable conditions by linking elements of domestic and international policy was made possible by the organization of the bureaucracy and its relation to the other economic institutions. A highly centralized bureaucracy with a wide range of highly selective economic instruments could envision coordinating bits of policy toward particular ends. Somewhat insulated from particular pressures, it was able to impose direction in the economy around it.

## I France in an interconnected world

French foreign economic policy has involved the state in negotiating terms of trade for national actors, in directly arranging trade and production, and in mediating between the national and international markets to dictate particular domestic economic outcomes. Specific outcomes have been defined and then pursued by manipulating a range of instruments in monetary and trade policy. (The state's influence in industry, it must be underlined, is not uniform. Extensive direct power is only felt in a range of politically defined critical industries.) Yet increasingly open trade and exchange among private actors has characterized the years since Bretton Woods. The argument here will not be that the French escape from the resulting constraints of international markets, or, rather, of a particular international economic regime. It will claim that they wage a remarkably equal and increasingly sophisticated fight, often turning apparent vulnerability into strength. They were not able to break up a system dominated by a stronger power, the US, but, seemingly, were able to manipulate their position to increase their national take. The influence of the French state within its domestic economy, it is crucial to note, has certainly been greater in the open trade postwar years of the Fourth and Fifth Republics than it was in the more protectionist period of the Third Republic. There is, in fact, a connection, though the case must not be overdrawn. Growing international exchange and competition gives the French state certain powers within the national economy, whether or not that economy is sensitive or vulnerable to outside events.

The French case, and the Japanese one as well, suggest that domestic resources can be mobilized effectively to neutralize or accommodate international constraints. To judge the nation's vulnerability to the international market, one must set the nation-state's capacity to respond to shifts in international market conditions against the scale and variety of the changes that affect its society and economy. The national political and institutional structure affects a government's capacity to evolve instruments that do mobilize domestic resources to counter international shifts. In fact, the capacity of the national government to respond has increased along with domestic sensitivity to the international market. The balance must be continuously assessed, and one must not conclude automatically that increased market interconnections have brought significant changes at home or abroad without first evaluating the domestic capacity to react. Vulnerability, then, depends on the organization of the state and society, not just on the problem or the international setting.

The postwar technological revolution in communications and transportation has indeed shrunk the world and the multinational corporation has linked it together in distinctive ways. National adjustments have been required by this new environment. This is not, of course, the first major shift in the international order and similar changes in the past have had profound impacts on domestic politics. Indeed, the growth of the industrial system, of the system of nation-states, can be viewed as an outcome of economic competition among political units, none of which had the military or economic power needed to establish an empire. Economic interconnections began, according to that argument, with the creation of the world system for the exchange of agricultural products in the sixteenth century. In the view articulated by Immanuel Wallerstein, economic "interdependence" among political units is capitalism.[2] "Interdependence," seen thus, is a characteristic of the modern world system from its inception. There is, consequently, a permanent tension between national political actors and international economic actors. Equally, domestic political struggles and structures have often hinged on the nature of the international economic system and exchange. Both Wallerstein and Tilly contend that the emergence of grain trade provoked massive changes in agricultural organization in Eastern Europe.[3] The expansion of American grain production in the second half of the nineteenth century similarly had powerful political and economic effects in Europe. In the twentieth century, the world depression of the 1930s and its political consequences are attributed by some to shifts in the international economy, both the decline of trade and the absence of an international leader.[4] Thus, domestic vulnerability to changes in the international economy is a basic part of modern history. The terms or nature of international interconnection are, of course, in constant evolution. What, then, have the past few years brought? What is, in fact, unique about the postwar world in which the French found themselves?

One can argue that the interconnections now are broader, affecting more sectors of society, and that they are more profound, affecting the very well-being of the entire economy as well as those engaged in foreign trade. It has also been suggested that organizational forms such as the multinational corporation increase the vulnerability of the nation-state. The question is, what new conditions does that create? An expansion in foreign exchange, of goods, services, and capital, may make one economy sensitive to another. Short-run fluctuations abroad can affect the level of domestic production, and developments in foreign industry may affect national firms. Yet a nation is vulnerable, not merely sensitive, by the definition of

---

[2] Immanuel Wallerstein, *The Modern World System* (New York: Academic Press, 1974).

[3] Charles Tilly, "Food Supply and Public Order in Modern Europe," in Tilly, ed. *The Formation of National States in Western Europe* (Princeton, N.J.: Princeton University Press, 1975).

[4] See in particular Charles Kindleberger, *The World in Depression* (Berkeley: University of California Press, 1974).

Keohane and Nye[5], only if domestic costs of external shifts cannot be avoided by policy changes at home. Not all sensitivities result in vulnerabilities. Less developed domestic or international markets might be more vulnerable to the impact of small shifts. Each point of contact with the international economy might be a vulnerability, even if the range of sectors sensitive to external shifts is quite limited. Growth in trade may generate capacities to absorb trade fluctuations and shifts. Thus more elaborate and larger markets may absorb fluctuations more effectively. Sensitivity might increase as vulnerability declines. For example, the recent evolution of international capital markets allowed the recycling of OPEC earnings, though creating problems. The capacities of the nation-state to adjust, to protect, to insulate have developed along with the interconnections. Nation-states may therefore be no more vulnerable to international changes than they were before. Vulnerability is a function of domestic structure as well as the international environment.

Equally, not all sensitivities or vulnerabilities have the same domestic economic or political consequences. When the impact of events abroad threatens the power of the nation, the stability of the state, the organization of the regime or the coalitions on which it rests—then the country might be judged *critically exposed*. Thus, just as a distinction is made between sensitivity and vulnerability, a second distinction must be made between ordinary and critical interconnections. One must separate, then, those interconnections that directly affect political stability from those that constrain the options of national actors. The constraints of ordinary interconnection establish the playing field the nation encounters or the minefield it must maneuver through. Critical exposure, though, can compel vital domestic changes and alter the political game, not simply limit the tactics. Domestic adjustment may occur in society or in politics. In the nineteenth century the Danes responded to grain price changes with farming innovation while in Germany the response was a policy of protection that rested on the infamous iron-rye coalition. A nation may be able to choose to insulate itself against an international shift, to reach some international agreement to control the change, or to accommodate itself by domestic shifts. The choice will rest on the costs and consequences of each decision; and, as De Gaulle so vividly demonstrated, the decisions can be changed.

Historically, basic national political arrangements have been overturned by pressures generated abroad. The critical exposure of national politics to international economic events or the activities of private actors beyond their borders has always been important. There have been, of course, periods of critical exposure. One might hypothesize, moreover, that such intense vulnerability occurs with the rise or decline of a major player or a shake-up of the relative standing of the national players. The emergence of new players affects the price of raw materials as has been demonstrated by the decline in grain prices when US wheat hit the

[5] Robert O. Keohane, and Joseph S. Nye, *Power and Interdependence: World Politics in Transition* (Boston: Little, Brown and Company, 1977), p. 13.

nineteenth century markets and by the increase in oil prices when supply and price began to be controlled by OPEC. The conditions of industrial competition are likewise affected by new players. The national adjustment to these changes will affect a country's position in world politics and its relative take from the international economic order. Also affected will be the ability to achieve a variety of national goals and the ability to affect the basic economic rules of play. The problem of the decay and regeneration of industrial societies in response to changes in the international economy is as interesting a problem as changes in their decision-making autonomy or their growing entanglement with other nations.

Emerging from the war broken and divided, French leadership faced the problem of renewal. It sought to regenerate the economy and the society and to reestablish France as a power among nations. Industrialization—as much as reconstruction—was required. Monnet, in his memoirs, refers to the period as one of modernization, not simply reconstruction. Before the war France was still heavily rural with an industrial sector that was protected, cartelized, and restrictive. The economy, as many have noted, was a delicate sort of plant preserved in a carefully tended hothouse. The hothouse walls were maintained by the highest prewar tariffs in Europe and the internal temperature was adjusted by restrictive business practices. The choice in essence was whether to reinforce the hothouse, which in a period of world growth and expansion would insure a decline in France's national position and augured ill for the well-being of the people. The alternative was to set France on a new path, which meant opening the hothouse without destroying the plant, neither permitting it to wither from competition nor to be uprooted by political turmoil. At the same time it was necessary to ensure French security, first against a revival of Germany and later against the Soviets. Military position served as well to reassert French autonomy and pride, but those military expenditures were drawn from resources that might otherwise have been devoted to economic growth.

This industrial revitalization was an instrument of French glory to some, an end in itself to others; but, for all, domestic and international purposes were linked. The economic transformation was led by the state, and foreign economic policy served as one of its instruments. Consequently, when attempting to establish and rejuvenate industries that formed parts of the international markets, the state found itself a player in the game. At times it attempted to restructure the international rules to suit itself. Often it sought to use political support for French firms to override the international marketplace. Other times, it sought simply to find a French niche in the international market. Equally, it sought access to raw materials and markets by negotiating directly with other governments. When De Gaulle and later Jobert sought to reorder international rules and markets to suit their purposes, France appeared disruptive. De Gaulle's choices of disruptive tactics to support a strategy intended to reorder the rules emerged in part from his vision of France, an image of politics that runs deep even among his domestic opponents. The recent choice of a more collaborative language is as much a recognition of the limits of French power as a principled renunciation of the strategy of reordering economic affairs on French terms. French government tactics and strategy were permitted and encouraged by the internal organization of the state and its relation to the bureaucracy.

## II Institutional structure and economic policy

Since the argument centers on the effect of the particular organization of the French state on its economic strategy at home and abroad, the structure and operation of the state will be dealt with next. Specifically, consideration will be given to the question of how the arrangements in the state bureaucracy and its ties with the other institutions in the economy and society affect its choice of strategy, its definition of goals, and its tactics for the implementation of that strategy. As I have argued elsewhere, the capacity of any state to implement particular policies and to have an impact on domestic economic outcomes is systematically affected by the patterned set of institutional relationships in the economy, the structured institutional setting in which it attempts to act.[6] The specific capacities—distinctive competencies, difficulties, and weakness—of each network are thus the focus. Again, some policies may be easier to define and implement in a specific network than others. Whether, in fact, a state is "strong" or "weak" depends not only on its internal organization but also on its links to other institutions. Society, in this analysis then, decomposes into the institutions that directly affect production and distribution. Two elements in this institutional network will be the focus of this discussion. The first is the organization of the state, both the formal arrangement of power within the bureaucracy and the relation of the bureaucracy to the legislature and executive, and its accessibility to the political community. The second element is composed of the relationships among the financial systems, the business community, and the state bureaucracy. Two examples indicate the influence of these factors on policy choices and execution.

In Britain, as in France, the government supported a merger drive in the 1960s that resulted in increased industrial concentration. In France, the state often acted in alliance with the *banques d'affaires,* institutions experienced at the initiation and sponsorship of industrial reorganization, the nationalized deposit banks that provide the bulk of available investment capital, and such vital para-public institutions as Crédit National, Crédit Hotelier, and Crédit Agricole. The *banques d'affaires,* though, are a distinctive product of continental industrial development with no real counterpart in England, and the Ministry of Finance has both a direct and indirect power of disposition over investment capital unequaled by the English Treasury. The financial community in England, by contrast, grew by servicing

[6] Part of this section, particularly the notion of the institutional structure in the economy and the description of the state bureaucracy, and part of section III, particularly the discussion of three cases of industrial intervention, draw heavily from John Zysman, *Political Strategies for Industrial Order: Market State and Industry in France* (Berkeley: University of California Press, 1977).

English trade and commerce, not government or industry, and, during the years that sterling served as an international reserve currency, even acted as the institutional support for world commerce. The country's financial institutions, concentrated in London's "City" district, reflect that heritage and are more embroiled, it often seems, in international commerce than domestic industry. Consequently, when an effort was made to reorganize British industry, a government agency had to be created to provide an instrument that could affect the financial organization of industrial capital. The Industrial Reorganization Corporation and, subsequently, the National Enterprise Board, established as part of the Labour government's drive to modernize British industry, were composed of bankers and businessmen who could draw on state resources to support favored merger efforts even against the opposition of other segments of the banking and business community. The continuing evolution of the "City" in response to government actions and the debate on how to reorganize financial institutions emerges from the same logic. In a sense, this government agency was created as a substitute for the banking-state business complex born naturally of industrialization in France. In a reversal of the Gerschenkron logic, the industrial firstborn is found imitating the institutional arrangements of the latecomers to cope with the difficulties of managing the organization and reorganization of large-scale capital. Problems of this nature simply did not exist when England first industrialized but were issues from the beginning on the continent.[7]

In a different vein, the character of the Italian state bureaucracy paralyzes government efforts to implement macroeconomic policy. As La Palombara argues, the bureaucracy is not organized to make or implement general policy but only to give or deny concessions, authorizations, or tax exceptions.[8] This bureaucracy, as is often noted, is the product of the electoral base of the grab-all Christian Democratic Party that has ruled Italy since the war. That party harvests votes through patron-client relationships in which political support is exchanged for special favors, a particular tradition in the South where political elites mediate between peasants and the political system. The consequences, as many economists note, is that fiscal policy, resting as it does on the even-handed and rational administration of tax and expenditure policies, is ineffective in Italy. Efforts to achieve macroeconomic stability thus rest almost exclusively on monetary manipulation, a mighty weight to be borne by any single policy instrument.

It shall be argued here that the structure of relations between economic and political institutions in France produces essential continuities in the domestic and international economic policies of the French state, whatever government is in power and often without seeming regard for the problem at hand. The institutional structure of the economy can thus be taken as a mediating variable or a system parameter that

[7] Alexander Gerschenkron, *Economic Backwardness in Historical Perspective* (Cambridge, Mass.: Harvard University Press, 1962).

[8] Joseph La Palombara, *Italy: The Politics of Planning* (New York: Syracuse University Press, 1966).

patterns government responses to both domestic and international economic pressures. Moreover, since that structure is a product of the particular national route from feudalism to the modern world, international economic policy must be seen as a function of the structure of the domestic economy. Certainly, the pattern of international economic life produces pressures and episodes a nation must cope with, but the responses are conditioned by domestic institutional arrangements. Whether in the domestic or international arena, when the capacities of the French state match the requirements of the problem at hand, policy has been successful.

Together, the firms, organized producer associations, the banks, and organized labor constitute the economy's institutional structure. The strategies, choices, and behavior of any of these actors are formed in an enduring pattern of constraints and opportunities created by these structured relations. Structure, in this sense of the term, means more than the economic issue of the number and size of firms or the conditions of competition that prevail in any industry. It points to the pattern of control and influence that exists among the various institutions. It is this pattern that determines such matters as entrepreneurial initiation of new business activity, the reorganization of sectors in difficulty, and the organization of day-to-day business activities, on the one hand, and remuneration, conditions of work, and the political power of labor on the other. It points as well to the instruments of formal organizational relationships, the legal possibility of restraint, and the actual control of critical resources that serve these institutions in maintaining or seeking to change any particular pattern of power and control. (The question is one of who controls *which* decisions and directs particular actions. This is ultimately an empirical, not a theoretical, question.) Just as the structure of a single organization, with its particular distribution of tasks and responsibilities and its set of rules and procedures, sets the strategies which any group or individuals within the organization can adopt to achieve any aim, so the institutional structure of the economy implies an enduring division of labor and a set of rules of play. The structures themselves are initially established during the process of industrialization and modernization, with the particular route to the present establishing a nationally specific pattern of relationships. The confrontation between the demands of industrialization at a specific historical moment and the existing organization of politics and the state bureaucracy is most important in defining the strategies open to the several actors within the economy.

A crucial issue is whether any one institution can exert industrial leadership, that is, consciously influence and guide the pattern of investment, competition, and exchange between sectors or the industrial organization of particular industries. If such industrial leadership requires a concentration of financial and economic power, the existence or creation of a point at which industrial investment, production, or organization could be negotiated or decided. Such a mechanism might be created politically by an association among producers, a cartel, or, under the influence of the state, by planning. It might also be created economically by the concentration of industrial investment in universal banking institutions that gather savings, loan funds, and invest in business undertakings, as is the case in Germany. In France, where a modern state with a centrally controlled bureaucracy existed before industrialization, the state developed a powerful, but not predominant, role in economic life. What is meant by a strong state may, in fact, be one which can exert industrial leadership.

Can one, though, even speak of the state as a coordinated and directed institution apart from the social groups that attempt to use it, the agencies that are its instrumentalities, or the political executive who seeks to direct the bureaucracy? In France, in fact, one does speak of the state (*l'état*) as a powerful, independent force in political life, and the almost metaphysical notion of *l'état* as the unified authority of the society has a powerful symbolic value in French politics. The state bureaucracy was created by the kings in their efforts to control the provincial nobles and administer the society without aristocratic mediation through agents directly loyal to the throne. Thus, from the beginning, the state was an instrument of centralizing power created apart from the society, almost in opposition to it. As such, it was at least partially autonomous. Mass political movements and the industrial bourgeoisie in France both had to adapt to existing government structures while, in the United States, the structures were created in an epoch of democratic and, later, mass politics. Thus the French state often seems to reach out to capture private allies for its own purposes, and certainly in many economic affairs the initiative lies with the state.

An elite wishing to direct or even influence the course of industrialization must be able to coordinate its activities and directly affect the behavior of the industrialists. Equally important, it must insulate itself from or repress the political reaction to dislocations inevitably provoked by industrialization. Therefore, the centralization of the state bureaucracy, its at least partial insulation from outside interference by pressure groups or parliament, and its instruments for channeling industrial investment are the features of the French system critical to this discussion. Centralization provides the possibility of unified and concerted government action while partial autonomy allows it to initiate and direct events. At the same time, its policy instruments permit it to intervene directly in the affairs of particular industrial sectors and companies on very specific industrial decisions. The state does not direct or administer the society or the economy, and nothing here should be taken to suggest that. The views of bureaucrats are not formed in isolation. The industrial services of the Ministry of Industry often act as an internal lobbyist for certain sectors against the harder views of the Trésor and sometimes the Industry Minister's personal staff. Yet views are formed which do not simply reflect industry's wishes, and once views are formed, the state bureaucrats can impose their position. The state is an autonomous and powerful player in the game, often able to force its will against the immediate wants and wishes of particular industries or businessmen. This does not imply that the government acts against business interests, simply that it can achieve collective outcomes not otherwise possible. This power is not, it must also be emphasized, used in all industries or in all firms.

Organizational behavior, though, cannot simply be inferred from organizational structure. One might properly interpose that formal centralization, to consider the first of these features, does not mean capacity for action, let alone unified action. In fact, one popular image of the French state and French bureaucracy in general is of a gargantuan paralyzed by hierarchical and functional barriers between tasks, formally centralized but informally incapacitated. This paralysis is often claimed to contribute to a general inability of the French government to respond to social problems without crisis. While continuing reforms that might avoid crisis are difficult to implement, commentators on French bureaucracy suggest that crisis, when it comes, is met by a powerful, unified, and centralized response tolerated in the face of chaos and collapse. Less dramatically, mechanisms do exist to coordinate the decisions of the highest echelons of the state bureaucracy, and if those decisions can be implemented, then the unified weight of a centralized state can be massed for particular purposes. While ongoing reform at lower level initiative may be difficult, coordination of strategy on critical issues is not precluded. As during a period of crisis, though, such coordination may require the arbitration and intervention of the high executive authority. In fact, once a choice is made, strategic coordination led by the chief executive may be simplified in a centralized state because the number of individuals who are involved in the choice and whose active cooperation is required is substantially reduced. Furthermore, as a practical matter, the sharp formal differentiation of responsibility within the bureaucracy is blurred at the top by the system of *Grands Ecoles* and *Grands Corps*.[9] School ties and attachments to the *Grands Corps* cut across the bureaucracy. This opens channels of communication and influence at the top of the state bureaucracy just as it provides informal ties between state and business. In this manner the capacity to coordinate high-level decision making is increased. Admittedly, of course, the struggles among *Grand Corps* divide the bureaucracy. Yet, unlike the American system of autonomous agencies and shifting elites, the mechanisms for coordination exist even if they are not always easy to use. One official remarked rather casually about the world of political power in France, "It is a small village; I know everyone that matters." ("La France, c'est un tout petit village; je connais tout le monde.")

The *Grands Corps* system serves as well to insulate the state bureaucracy from society because the mechanism of recruitment severely restricts access to high positions within the bureaucracy. Only the Minister and Junior Minister for less prestigious assignments (*secrétaires d'état*) are direct political appointments. The Minister, in turn, names a "cabinet" of personal staff assistances. Though powerful, the "cabinet" does not form part of the line bureaucracy. By contrast, in the American system, political appointments extend to the position of Assistant Secretary, some three or four echelons deeper in the government structure. Since particular *Corps* have virtual monopolies on particular responsibilities and jobs within the state system, they can autonomously organize the careers of their members. A decade in advance, one can identify the handful of potential candidates

[9] Ezra Suleiman, *Politics, Power and Bureaucracy* (Princeton, N.J.: Princeton University Press, 1974).

for crucial posts.[10] Access to the *Corps* depends on admission and position at two schools, the Ecole nationale d'administration (l'ENA) and Polytechnique. Consequently, entrance to the core group of the state is determined very early. Success elsewhere or later in life does not provide easy access to this bureaucracy. From positions in the state, many of the graduates of the *Grands Ecoles* and members of the *Grands Corps* leave for high positions in the private business community, dominating many crucial firms and even sectors of industry. Since top civil service positions are available only to graduates of the *Grands Ecoles,* the flow is almost exclusively from the state toward the business community. The top members of the state bureaucracy, holding positions of enormous political importance, represent a socially and even politically coherent and enduring body within French life whose personal careers within the state and in the business community, if they choose to leave public service, rest ultimately on maintaining and extending state power.

The autonomous state bureaucracy was created to serve the kings and reinforced to serve Napoleon; but while such a system creates the potential for state initiative, it in no way implies such initiative will be taken or what ends will be pursued. In the Third Republic, as Hoffmann argues, the state served to arbitrate conflict within the society and to maintain social balance and political calm. After the Second World War, when the political decision was made to alter the structure of the French economy, this bureaucracy was once again used as an instrument of executive power. The structure of the Fifth Republic, which insulates the political executive from interest group influence, and the Gaullist party system, which provides ambitious civil servants with routes to political position, have reinforced the autonomy of the state bureaucracy. The bureaucracy, somewhat insulated from political pressure and staffed by an enduring and coherent group of bureaucrats, can develop an interpretation of the public interest that is more than the sum of particular pressures. Government policy never accords precisely with the wishes and intentions of the groups that compose its constituency, but the discretion open to the French bureaucracy and to the government in the Fifth Republic has been, on some issues, most remarkable. The French state has the structural potential for autonomous action, but structure does not determine how or whether that potential is used. A political explanation will always be required to explain the direction of state activity.

Perhaps the easiest thing to coordinate in such a centralized system is the allocation of capital, either for private investment or for public infrastructure development. This is so because such decisions do not require the reorganization or agreement of the lower level bureaucracies. At the heart of this centralized system is the Direction du Trésor in the Ministry of Finance, what more than one ranking official has called the sanctuary in the temple, the holy of holies. Here, banking and capital market regulation, stock market management, public enterprise financial policy, and lending to private industry of public funds are all to be found. The

[10] Ibid

instruments to assemble any specific financial package for industrial intervention are all there. Therefore, when the government chooses to affect the organizational structure of a particular industrial sector, the character of the financial system, the second factor in this analysis, provides it, in most instances, with a powerful policy instrument. Through the nationalized banks, the Banque de France, and state institutions such as Crédit National, the government can exercise selective control over the allocation of credit to industry by the financial community. Alternatively, it can make special investment credit at subsidized interest rates available from public funds to particular industrial projects. This instrument is now used more in particular cases than in a systematic way to influence the course of an entire sector. In fact, some sources estimate that one-half of all private investment is made by government loan or subsidy.[11] The enduring tradition of private bank involvement in the initiation and management of business enterprise is as important as the capacity of the Ministry of Finance to influence directly conditions in particular sectors. The banks are now vital intermediary institutions between the state and industry whether they followed or led the creation of industrial enterprise in the second half of the nineteenth century. In particular, the *banques d'affaires,* which made their profits from the establishment, growth, and reorganization of industries rather than by enlisting widespread private deposits to be loaned to service the financial needs of companies, are experienced at the task of the financial reorganization of industry often required to rationalize production. The role of the Banque de Paris et des Pays-bas, for example, in the affairs of oil and electronics is important to note. Significantly, many of the deposit banks also play the role of industrial intermediary. This occurs despite the fact that after the Second World War their right to hold industrial shares was severely restricted. In 1966 they regained this right.

In the more modern and capital intensive industries of the greatest concern to the state, the banks' influence is extensive, while bank voices are less often heard in traditional industries such as textiles. Family-owned firms, seemingly quite resistant to bank and government influence, are not simply small or middle-sized companies. Indeed, of the 200 largest firms in France, nearly 40 are still in family hands (majority control) and in another 60 the owning family still seems dominant. An additional 40 are foreign multinationals, and thus also outside this state-bank network. Equally important, the banks do not pursue identical strategies. For example, the Suez Bank group has been said to be more independent of government maneuverings. The influence of the banks in French industry, thus, is uneven, varying from industry to industry, and from firm to firm.[12]

Similarly, though the state's power is potentially enormous, its weight is not uniformly felt throughout the private sector. In some sectors such as textiles, the

[11] Raymond Vernon, *Big Business and the State* (Cambridge, Mass.: Harvard University Press, 1974).
[12] François Morin, *La Structure Financière de l'Industrie Française* (Paris: Calmann Levy, 1974).

trade association stands as an intermediary between the government and the firm, trying to force the government to treat the industry as a unit and to preserve the position of each firm. In this arrangement, the government might be seen as an arbitrator settling conflicts within industries and between industries. Such arrangements, as the experience in electronics suggests, are difficult to maintain in the face of international competition. Even so, McArthur and Scott found that in the mid-1960s industry-wide cartel-like arrangements were still prevalent.[13] In industries where firms are managed by technocrats, many of them former civil servants, the state plays a more directive role, though even here the pattern is not uniform. The state's role as initiator is clearly seen in an industry like electronics where for many years it virtually made product choices inside many firms. In other industries, however, such as glass, it has left matters pretty much alone. When the state is a primary client, its influence is great. One must not forget, either, that major sectors, including utilities and certain oil firms, are nationalized and that the state's influence in the private sector is supplemented by its control in the public arena.

Clearly, the French state, even in its most *dirigiste* guise, is certainly not omnipotent in the economy nor does it even attempt interventionist strategies in all sectors. Yet, equally important, the French do not see a sharp and clear-cut choice between state control or direction and a free market, a dichotomy that often creeps into British debate. For the French, there are three decisions, not two. The state can do (*faire*), incite others to do (*faire faire*), or simply leave be (*laissez faire*). Leaving things to private forces, moreover, does not necessarily mean allowing free competition. It may imply, on the contrary, allowing *private* actors to negotiate market arrangements. The anti-market tradition runs deep in France, despite liberal protestations. Unfortunately, the state is often defined narrowly in economic affairs to mean the Ministries of Industry and Finance. Consequently, recent shifts in the allocation of public funds away from the Trésor in the Ministry of Finance to industry via para-public institutions (as well as the increase in public borrowing to provide such funds) to some portends a liberal change. It is a change, but certainly not a liberalism that Adam Smith would recognize. Thus, French economic debates are often misleading to outsiders. Liberalism does not always mean that the state is about to get out of matters. Rather, it often means that the state is choosing to incite rather than direct, to set basic lines and leave the day-to-day matters to others, or simply to focus its power on selected arenas.

## III Policy approaches and policy problems

The French have coordinated foreign economic policy with their domestic strategies, using the state's role as mediator between the national and international markets to further specific domestic economic goals. They were not able to fashion

---

[13] John H. McArthur, and Bruce R. Scott, *Industrial Planning in France* (Boston: Harvard University Division of Research, Graduate School of Business Administration, 1969).

the international order after their own design but were able to disrupt and complicate the purposes of others. Not a maker of the system, though an occasional breaker, the French situated themselves to take and maintain the benefits of an order others had established.

Postwar French politics divides itself quite conveniently into the years before De Gaulle, De Gaulle's reign, and his succession. In each period, domestic requirements and international constraints forced different problems to the fore. In each, a different issue was salient and critical. Each period will, then, be used to frame a different problem, though, of course, most of these issues threaded their way throughout the entire postwar epoch. In the Fourth Republic, the crucial problem was to establish a framework for reconstruction and growth without disrupting agricultural sectors. When De Gaulle took power, the time had arrived to bolster critical French industries, whatever his vision of his world role. Throughout Europe, the presence of American corporations, enormous and with a seemingly invulnerable technological advantage, became the issue of the day. De Gaulle's successors learned from the years of mergers and outright resistance to American corporations. They found that their own companies had begun to move abroad, and they evolved new tactics to cope with the multinational. The sudden jump in oil prices and the resulting need to increase exports accentuated an emerging policy of supporting industry through export financing and state promotion of country-to-country trade deals. Our focus throughout is on the way the state fastened pieces of policy together to attack particular problems, not on the category of policies themselves. Monetary policy, which emerges in each epoch, is something of an exception, reflecting both changes in the international order and shifts in the French stance toward it.

## The Fourth Republic

During the Fourth Republic, the government made a commitment to growth and expansion and created national and European institutions that would support such a policy.[14] The Planning Commission and the Common Market, which were conceived and nurtured in the Fourth Republic but not born until the Fifth, had common origins and, in a sense, a common fate of important achievements that seem modest next to the claims of proponents.[15] The Planning Commission was

---

[14] For a discussion of French growth that focuses on the new mentality created by new men and institutions, see Charles Kindleberger's article, "The Post-War Resurgence of the French Economy," in Stanley Hoffman et al., *In Search of France: The Economy, Society, and Political System in the Twentieth Century* (Cambridge, Mass.: Harvard University Press, 1963). See also Stephen Cohen, *Modern Capitalist Planning: The French Experience* (Berkeley: University of California Press, 1976). Recent memoirs of Jean Monnet, *Memoires* (Paris: Fayard, 1976), and Francois Bloch Laine, *Profession Fonctionaire* (Pairs: Editions du Seuil, 1976) add substantially to our understanding.

[15] The American literature on integration certainly maintained a vision of the European Community as a bold new venture, a view that is no longer shared by the Europeans or the authors themselves.

established to direct the postwar reconstruction. It gained power from its control over the allocation of Marshall Fund credits and import licenses. Reconstruction took place with firm government control of monetary movements. In the credit- and material-short economy, this gave the Plan and Trésor almost a veto over many corporate affairs in the early years. At the same time, an independent source of funds gave it autonomy from parliament. When credit eased and the Marshall funds ended, the Planning Commission's direct power ended and, over the years, its influence eroded as well. The Plan initiated the state's postwar role as economic leader committed to industrial expansion. Before, it had been an economic guardian seeking simply to preserve privilege and position in a static order. In later years, other agencies and different instruments would serve this changed purpose. The crucial element in the state's industrial strategy has been freedom from broad political scrutiny. This has left the state free to justify itself and negotiate with a narrow constituency on particular issues and tactics. Furthermore, during the Fourth Republic the bureaucracy was reformed and became increasingly insulated from electoral politics. The institutional instrument of a state-led economic strategy, an effective and independent bureaucracy with tools to affect the business decisions of industrial enterprise, was constructed. The purposes and organization of the state were in evolution, and these changes in domestic policy were tied to foreign economic policy.

The Common Market and its predecessor, the Coal and Steel Community, were supported and in part designed by French bureaucrats and politicians who had established the Planning Commission. In turn, the Common Market reinforced the position of the planners and their growth strategy by providing crucial support for French farmers from German money and driving French companies to seek support from the government to meet the competition they feared. As institutions, more- over, both the Plan and the Common Market were committed to continuous expansion and growth.[16]

Support for European integration arose initially as much from defense as from economic concerns. The European Defense Community had been an attempt to tie allied-controlled Germany to the Western Community. When the effort was defeated in France by a coalition of Gaullists and Communists, seeking different reasons to avoid European military integration, the Europeanists tried to substitute economic seduction for political commitment. They hoped that integrating the economic systems would encourage political integration by creating problems best solved at a regional level. Their logic proved false and their hopes were deceived. Nation and state building has historically been more a matter of force and conquest than of allurement and voluntary association to resolve economic problems. In France and Russia one ethnic group conquered the others, and the ruler, king, or tsar created a bureaucracy to impose its will on the aristocracy and local com-

---

[16]One can find evidence for these views both in the logic of the choices and in contemporary and current interpretations of the period.

munities. In Germany the Prussians manipulated an outside threat to coerce the other German states into an alliance that was to become a nation. Their economic alliance, the Zollverein, was unlikely to become a nation on its own. The American states, of course, joined themselves together, but they were hardly established sovereign units to begin with. One can argue that it is the Defense Community alliance in the face of a military threat, rather than the Economic Community, which paralleled the historic German experience.

The lesson, of course, is that there are many political solutions to increasing economic ties. There is no inevitability to the continuous expansion of economic, let alone political, integration. Expanded international trade may make national economies more sensitive to events in other countries and perhaps stir the sleepy to find more effective corporate and production organization. Yet those solutions will most often be found within the existing network of institutions that affect business, particularly banks and the state. Trade may force innovation but it does not necessarily alter the basic organization of business life. The relations between banks and business, for example, are profoundly different in England, France, and Germany. Establishing a common set of financial institutions would require far more than mutual sacrifices—it would demand that some and perhaps all fundamentally alter the way they do business. Evolution would not be smooth, proceeding in small indistinguishable steps toward common institutions and ways of doing business. Rather, it would require an explicit domestic political choice to alter the institutions of economic life. Integration could not be invisible and piecemeal, creating an economic and political fact. In fact, competitive advantages created by institutional differences have been compensated by domestic policies of the national states, often reinforcing their authority, rather than by eliminating the differences. Clearly the compensations, though often controversial, are not extensive enough to disrupt the entire game. Rather than supranationalism, the French chose domestic compensation.

The European effort, then, has stopped at a common market of free trade and partial factor mobility inside a common tariff wall. While joint external positions have been developed as a response to common trade threats, these efforts have not as yet spilled over into internal community arrangements. Europe has not advanced far toward an economic community of shared institutions. Instances of supranationality represent discrete choices that have not produced accumulating pressure for further grants of national power to supranational organizations. The Coal and Steel Community is such an instance. To this observer, it represented a reconstruction of the interwar cartel with national states and an official arbitrator joining the game. Government involvement meant that corporate stability would not endanger national economic expansion, since companies would not restrict production to avoid destructive competition.[17] A series of specific consignments

---

[17] This argument is developed in Zysman, Chapter 3.

of power to community institutions can occur without building momentum toward integration.

The Common Market itself rests on three specific intergovernmental deals, three political principles that preceded the technical details. Each had important implications for French economic strategy. The first two principles were a trade between the French and Germans. The Germans subsidized French agriculture in exchange for the respectability Community membership could provide and the market for German industrial goods it would offer. The third principle, insisted on by the Americans, was that direct foreign investment would not be restricted. American concern with the Cold War rivalry with Russia meant that the US was willing to subsidize European development by permitting the Europeans to discriminate against American trade. The Europeans could discriminate in trade if they would treat American companies as national companies and not restrict their investment. This created a critical difference between Western Europe and Japan. The Europeans could not as effectively play the Japanese game of separating the multinational package of technology, management, and capital. They confronted the multinationals on their own territory as national companies. The Common Market deals affected industrial organization, the multinationals, and agriculture. The first two will be considered in later sections. The agricultural deal reflected French political needs to maintain the traditional while the modern was emerging and the continuous danger that the traditional would block the modern.

The agricultural deal was the most important at the beginning. French agriculture supported the EEC because the Common Market was seen as a solution to its problems. The EEC promised expanded markets and security of price. The Common Agricultural Policy (CAP) helped the French government escape a difficult trap in its drive for industrial growth. Growth, as Kindleberger and others have since argued, hinged on a transfer of manpower from the countryside to industry. Although the basic structure of ownership and production was left in place, underemployed labor was drained away and more labor freed by mechanization. Though the number of peasants was reduced, the structure of peasant life was not disrupted nor its well-being threatened. Had the French been forced to support their own agriculture, funds would have had to be drawn away from industry or from the pockets of other groups who might also resist expanded industrialization. The CAP may have meant that the French could maintain industrialization without rapid, forced reorganization of the agricultural sector.

The Fourth Republic stumbled in the colonial wars, toppling finally over Algerian policy. Perhaps a settlement required De Gaulle, a man of the army and the right, but De Gaulle indeed needed the executive authority with which the institutions he designed for the Fifth Republic provided him. Whether a parliamentary regime could have sustained rapid industrialization is, of course, undemonstrable, but it does seem doubtful. At any rate, the continued autonomy of the executive and the state bureaucracy were basic features of economic life in the Fifth Republic.

## De Gaulle

De Gaulle had two purposes. The first was to reorganize France at home; the second, to reorganize the world of nations to reestablish the French place. He sought to create a domestic executive that could provide leadership to the state bureaucracy and a state bureaucracy that could mobilize the nation. This required that the chief executive, the president, be invested by direct popular election with the political authority of the nation and that the real power of parliament to control money and make policy be curbed lest it interfere with the executive and the bureaucracy. Democratic procedures served more to legitimate the makers of policy and to influence the direction of policy by the threat of withholding authority than to formulate policy and legislation. The bureaucracy became a route to political power, linking the ruling party and the administrative elites.[18] The strengthened executive was an instrument to build a modern France with an independent place in the global order.

De Gaulle sought a multipolar order which provided lesser powers enough maneuvering room to avoid domination by the "greats." His policy, as Stanley Hoffmann has argued, was to change the milieu of policy and the order, rather than simply to increase France's holdings. A multipolar world would have multiple lines of alignment. Necessarily, there would be shifting alliances, as the division of nations would depend on the issue and principle. There could not be a single alliance family on all issues determined by a position on a single issue and headed by a great power. Consequently, De Gaulle tried to avoid binding ties which restricted future action and realignments and sought to intervene in issues that had previously been the concern of the great powers alone. As Hoffmann argues, "De Gaulle was never foolish enough to confuse national independence with self-sufficiency or with a total absence of commitments or ties to other nations. His argument was, rather, never to accept bonds that cannot be removed and that might submit your nation's fate to the decisions of others long after the ties are no longer in your interest . . . the same dislike of alienating one's fate explains De Gaulle's hostility to supranational integration, in Western Europe or within the Atlantic Alliance."[19] De Gaulle never sought to avoid joint action or alliance, only ventures which subordinated the interests of France to those of others. Similarly, as Hoffmann puts it, De Gaulle denied that interdependence meant harmony and sought to use the economic and technological interconnections among nations to his ends. Thus, De Gaulle did not see the European Community as a value in itself or as an economic necessity. He would participate when the Community could

---

[18] This is not to say that the administrative elite of the Fourth Republic suddenly was transformed into a political bureaucracy in the Fifth. Not at all. Simply the form of political involvement changed as the focus of political authority shifted from parliament to the executive.

[19] See Stanley Hoffmann, "De Gaulle's Foreign Policy: The State and the Play, The Power and the Glory," in *Decline or Renewal: France Since the 1930's* (New York: Viking Press, 1974). As so often Hoffmann's idiom supports and augments his analytic argument. This discussion draws heavily on that article.

serve as an instrument of the policies he pursued and equal deals could be arranged with his partners.

De Gaulle understood that a capacity to block the plans of others meant that they might be forced to acknowledge and incorporate his own purposes. He saw clearly, as well, that political symbols can produce real results. For example, the independent nuclear force was the ante at the table of nuclear card players. Similarly, he sought to displace the dollar from its position as an unchallenged reserve currency. He did so because, in his view, it permitted the Americans to displace the costs of policies he opposed, such as the Vietnam War, onto others, and gave them economic advantage by facilitating the purchase of undervalued foreign assets and allowing them to define the economic rules of play.

Although the dollar subsequently crumbled, this effort to overturn its pivotal position in the Bretton Woods monetary order was markedly unsuccessful. The French continuously tried to tie world reserves directly to gold, thus preventing liquidity needs from being met by foreigners holding dollars. Foreign dollar holdings, they correctly argued, simply increased the American command over foreign resources. Foreigners took dollars as payment for their goods and services and then held them, or exchanged them among themselves. America never faced exchange discipline because the dollars were never returned for collection. Indeed, the debate on liquidity dominated monetary negotiations in the 1960s and the French-led defense of gold against the dollar was a fight over who would control and who would benefit from increases in liquidity.

The French positions were largely ignored, and when Debré replaced Giscard at Finance the French slowly adopted the position of embattled isolation. They insisted on an entirely gold-based system which would put great pressure on the US. By the Spring of 1967, however, they had moved away from their extreme positions and were willing to strike a deal. The issues, in general, were whether there would be some limit on the seemingly endless American deficit and whether European and, more particularly, French, influence would be acknowledged in the running of the monetary system. The technical particulars circled around these political basics. The French pushed hard to achieve a deal favorable to themselves, but their resistance was finally broken by the student-led strikes of May 1968 which tumbled the franc and drained reserves. The system of Special Drawing Rights was then pushed through by the Americans. As Susan Strange argues so well, it was not the perversity of De Gaulle that permitted the French to obstruct the implementation of a new system. Rather, "On certain key points France was supported by other Europeans . . . [about the end of 1966] . . . the General rightly discerned that there was quite a lot of common ground among the Europeans and concluded that it could be used to elicit support for French opposition to American wishes on certain questions, provided compromises were sought on others."[20] Had

[20] Susan Strange, "International Monetary Relations," in Vol. 2 of *International Economic Relations of the Western World 1959–71*, Andrew Shonfeld, ed. (London: Oxford University Press, 1976).

this not been so, the French would not have found it worthwhile to desert their splendid isolation. The French were not able to make the system to their liking, but, when possible, they used a strong reserve position and consummate negotiating skill to influence the settlement that finally was reached. Throughout these other arguments, the French sought to maintain a franc parity that would encourage exports but often had to choose between domestic and international purposes. When De Gaulle came to power, he immediately devalued the franc by 17.5 percent, which both encouraged exports and relieved him from any immediate pressure from the outside. Yet later, when the German-French trade balance pushed for a currency readjustment, De Gaulle stubbornly refused to adjust. He resisted any appearance of concession to outside pressure even though it required expenditure cuts and bank and exchange regulations. Quite clearly, in this instance, domestic growth was sacrificed to his foreign purposes. Ironically, it was then Pompidou who resolved the second mark-franc confrontation brought on by De Gaulle's resignation with a unilateral devaluation.

Jean Yves Haberer, as of January 1977 director of the Finance Minister's cabinet, has argued that with different and diverse tactics the French have consistently pursued three objectives since 1961. They have sought to insulate French exchange rates and reserves from external disturbance. They have contested the dollar's hegemony by supporting orthodox positions which have as their principal merit the echo they create in certain international financial milieux. Finally, they have attempted to make the struggle against the dollar and the organization of monetary security an element of the mobilization of Europe,[21] a mobilization presumably led by the French. Fred Hirsch sees a longer and deeper continuity. He argues that the French have replayed, toward the Americans, the policy and strategy found in their relations to the English in the 1920s. That is, they sought to amass financial power and then use it to assert France's position. In both periods, interestingly, an undervalued exchange rate promoted exports and drew gold. "Gaullist glosses apart," Hirsch writes, "traditional French financial policy has not been more nationalistic, self seeking or obtuse than British and American policies. Rather France has conceived its financial interests in a narrower frame. . . ."[22]

Whatever his monetary wheelings and dealings, De Gaulle's foreign policy required a strong domestic economic base and the industrial capacity to resist dependence on other nations. The symbols and realities of power require industrial resources. Michel Debré, a Gaullist committed to the General's vision of France and the world, replaced Giscard in 1966 to launch a policy of restructuring French industry,[23] partly to provide particular strategic goods and partly to increase its

---

[21] Yves Haberer, *Les Fonctions du Trésor et la Politique Financiere* (Paris: Institut d'Etudes Politiques de Paris 1975–1976).

[22] Fred Hirsch, *Money International* (Harmondsworth: Penguin Press, 1967).

[23] Giscard's own policies as President have down-played the open role of the state in reorganizing French industry, but there is no reason to argue he would have opposed the 1960s policy of expansion and reorganization. It is unclear whether he was replaced because of his economic philosophy, his previous deflationary policy, or some other political issue.

economic competitiveness. The political effort was a drain on the economy, taking not only resources, but often supporting non-commercial technological development and reinforcing the production bias of French industry. Certainly some value was recovered in exports, particularly arms exports. Many industrial choices made for strictly political and strategic reasons, such as computer and aircraft policy, were costly to the government and damaging to the industry. Despite De Gaulle's posturing, too much can be made of the military effort, and indeed Germany's military expenditures in 1976 were $15,220 million while the French spent $12,857, virtually equivalent percentages of their respective GNPs.[24]

The effort to reorganize critical French industries took place as a response to, and in an environment of, increasing regional and international trade competition. The French ability to reorganize and redirect its industry thus becomes a test of sorts on the nation-state's ability to control the domestic evolution of industries engaged in international markets. These efforts were politicized and publicized in the Gaullist years as a central piece of industrial strategy. The policies, as in the oil industry, had begun earlier and were to continue after the Fifth Plan and De Gaulle. Many would argue that the vital element was the transformation of the attitudes of French businessmen and consequently of the strategies of their firms. French industry was pushed out of an era of protection into one of international competition. To judge the efforts in particular sectors one must recognize that many of the failures of French policy resulted from a poor understanding of the necessary tactics, not from the impossibility of the endeavor. De Gaulle has often been accused of substituting form for substance, but as noted earlier, he indeed understood that form could become substance if the form affected the choices made by one's rivals and partners. In the industrial area, though, it can be argued that De Gaulle and his advisors did not have an understanding of how to translate form into substance. Furthermore, in many cases they seem to have misunderstood the basis of industrial power. In essence, they only partially understood the logic of profits, markets, and competition, and the ways in which a government could intervene to achieve different outcomes as well as the limits on state power.[25] A more sophisticated understanding produced more satisfactory outcomes, a proposition which will be examined in greater detail in the next section. Yet the pattern of success and failure in state intervention suggests the relative competencies of the French state apparatus and the requirements of successful intervention in an economically interconnected world.

Oil, steel, and electronics provide three cases that the state defined as critical to the national well-being because each provided inputs vital to industrial production and national defense. Because each industry was defined as vital, the state sought to insure a structure of ownership and production that would allow French

---

[24] *Military Balance 1976–1977* (London: International Institute for Strategic Studies, 1976).
[25] This general argument is based on a reading of policy documents analyzing industrial organization and industrial strategy. It is elaborated in Chapter 5 of *Political Strategies*.

national control over the industrial operations. The strategy in each instance was similar. A state alliance with financial holding companies was promoted to initiate new firms or to amalgamate old ones for particular policy ends. This arrangement was often backed by one or several of the *banques d'affaires* or by the direct control of access to financial markets. The striking difference among the three industries is that policy for oil and steel was successful while that for electronics was not. Success is defined here as the establishment and maintenance of an industry structure satisfactory to the state. In other words, success is the ability of the state to make the industry conform to some acceptable version of the state's original goal without being stymied by political opposition or economic difficulty. The different policy *outcomes* resulted from differences in both the *requirements* of success in the three industries and the possibilities of state leverage, suggesting the strengths and difficulties of state industrial intervention in France.

Organizational structures, which facilitated state intervention in oil and steel, were distinctive handicaps in electronics. In all three cases, the state pursued the same strategy, creating operating companies, channeling capital flows, and establishing guaranteed markets by wielding state power and manipulating the web of school and social ties between the top echelon of businessmen and government officials. This strategy was successful in technically stable, heavy investment, production-oriented industries and generated problems in a technically unstable, market-oriented industry.[26]

The three cases suggest that when an industry's problems can be remedied by massive, directed investment and when the appropriate strategy can be selected by a centralized organization, the case in the oil and steel industries, the initiatives of the French state can be expected to be effective. Both oil and steel are capital-intensive basic industries producing relatively homogeneous goods. The product of one firm is little different from the product of another. This both makes price the only basis of competition and eases the problems of managing the market, a task falling to the state in oil and the trade association in steel. If adequate natural resources are available, then the critical problem is to assure sufficient and appropriate production facilities. In these industries, production technologies are relatively stable, both because fundamental technical changes are not an everyday occurrence and because the heavy capital investment inevitably locks the firms into long-term choices. The massive investment required to implement basic technical change requires high-level choices within an organization; and because the technical evolutions are slow, the central management can reasonably acquaint itself with the choices. Essentially, centralized decision making is appropriate in industries such as these.

The task in steel was first to force a structure of ownership that could accommodate the most modern technologies and then to insure the public and private investment to create them. Massive new seaside facilities made the myriad small firms extremely inappropriate. Financial difficulties in the industry, the result of declining demand and strict price controls, allowed the state—in this instance

---

[26] Ibid., Chapters 3 and 7.

acting through the trade association—to restructure the industry. The new production facilities are being built by the coordination of public capital improvements investment and long-term low interest loans provided by the state. The problem in oil was to create French oil companies where none existed. Once again, the state initiated and guaranteed the existence of wholly French firms, one a semi-public company created in alliance with a *banque d'affaires* and the other an entirely nationalized firm. In both instances, the capacity to direct capital investment was critical.

The vital tasks in electronics are quite different. Success in this industry depends on rapid technological innovation continuously adapted to shifting market possibilities. This is not a capital-intensive industry. Many of the dominant international firms have been built by rapid expansion rather than mergers. In fact, mergers that disrupt the organization and interfere with ongoing product development can ultimately be self-defeating. Thus, a capacity to direct massive capital investment and initiate and promote mergers that concert public and private efforts is of limited value. The rapid pace of technological and market evolution, furthermore, makes it extremely difficult for a central executive within a firm, let alone in the state, to make appropriate product and process decisions. Similarly, cartelization in such an industry is quite hard. American government aid was important in promoting technological evolution because different agencies were effective in picking up and supporting privately initiated efforts. This was possible, in part, because the fragmentation of responsibility, particularly the division in the military between itself and NASA, created a variety of independent funding sources. Equally, the ready availability of venture capital in the 1960s was important in allowing a multitude of private efforts to push ahead. The diffusion of American efforts was critical to the success of this industry. The centralization of the French state and the pressure felt by a relatively small state to coordinate limited resources pushed exactly the opposite way, toward state-initiated mergers, involvement in technological strategies, and concentration of public and private efforts.

Extraordinary international competitive pressure as much as any mistaken tactics of state intervention produced the difficulties of the French electronics industry, and the focus of discussion must now move from the domestic to the international arena. The French, unable to control the international development of this industry or to insulate their firms from it, were unwilling to adjust to the constraints of the market. In fact, one might argue that the critical difference between the electronics case and that of oil and steel was not the specifics of sectoral policy, but rather the ability of the French state to mediate the access of foreigners to the national marketplace.

In the case of oil, the French were able to wrench back control of their domestic market from foreign companies, but they were unable to maintain an acceptable degree of control in electronics. *In both cases, the critical problem was not simply defending against a post-World War II wave of foreign penetration, but rather, when oil and electronics suddenly appeared to be crucial industries requiring national control, reversing a pattern of control and production that had been established for the most part between the wars.* Multinational oil companies had long supplied the bulk of the French market, at one time, before the Compagnie Française des Pétroles (CFP) was set up in the 1920s, virtually all of it. The decision made in 1959 to use oil as a transitional energy source in the shift from coal to nuclear power seemed to require even greater direct French influence. Similarly, in electronics, IBM had long held an important share of the business equipment market in France; although, in this instance, the collapse of Machines Bull during the transition of office machines from electromechanical to electronic equipment and the intense competition of other United States firms expanded the American market share. The actual and mythical importance of the computer industry, however, as much as the expansion of American market shares, focused attention on the industry. The concern over the penetration of national economies is raised as much by increased demands for national control, the result of increased pressures for political control of domestic economic events, as by fundamental changes in the pattern of international economic activity.

The three cases can be reexamined, then, with the focus on the state's capacity to mediate between domestic industry and the international economy. In the petroleum industry, the French state was able to assure an adequate supply of crude oil and control the distribution of refined products to provide guaranteed markets for companies of its choice. Crude oil supplies are, as has been discovered recently, ultimately in the hands of the governments controlling the territory where they are produced. Thus, successive French governments were able to negotiate for oil supplies on a state-to-state basis, tying oil purchases to a package of relationships between governments. Whether private companies could strike a better bargain during those years or not is really of little importance; the French could and did operate on a bilateral political basis. Since the import of massive quantities of oil requires special facilities, the government can easily monitor the import of refined products and the origin of crude supplies, requiring companies to build facilities in France if they wish access to the French market. Those refineries, in turn, provide a second monitoring point, and, in fact, control over the number and ownership of these facilities amounts to control of the final products market. The characteristics of final products, moreover, are relatively stable and can be affected only by altering the technology of refining, a slow process at best. Finally, within a very wide range, product costs are not critical, assuming balance-of-payment problems are not generated in paying for the crude supplies. The costs can be passed on to consumers without serious distortion of the economy. By contrast, in electronics, the state could not itself assure a supply of the critical electronics products, components, or final goods. It had to depend on private companies to develop and manufacture a constantly evolving range of goods at a pace set in the international marketplace. The capacity of the firms to respond, finally, depended on their ability to compete in the international market because the state was unable to insulate them from its pressure or restructure the international industry. Over the years, adequate *supplies* could only be assured by healthy firms, but the products of greatest immediate interest to the state were those where product competition was the greatest. The technological goals of the state weakened the competitive position of the firms while erosion of the firms' market positions diminished the capacity of the state to pursue its technological goals. Nor could the state assure *markets* to the firms for the bulk of their production. Most of the product purchase decisions were in private hands as well. The state could have only a limited impact on their choices, in part because the decision makers were diffused and partly because price and quality of products could not be equated at a single point such as a refinery. French firms and their foreign competitors were not selling identical products, and price and quality differences in these goods mattered to the purchasers. Unable to assure supply or control markets, the state was essentially helpless.

Steel is somewhat more confusing. The state could assure an adequate domestically produced supply and control its price. International and, particularly, inter-European trade in steel did increase after the war. It is of vital importance, however, that such trade was never so extensive that it threatened the existence or well-being of the French industry. The international steel market appears to be a competitive, often high-cost, supplement to domestic production during periods of upswing, not a threat to national producers' control of their domestic market. Several explanations are possible. The simplest would be that location advantages, assuming reasonably parallel production costs, are of such advantage that traditional sales patterns will be disrupted only by massive shifts in supply or costs. This would imply that the state need only assure reasonably efficient production, and the market will act to preserve national patterns of production. Extensive international trade in steel, and particularly the Japanese success, does suggest, however, that location does not firmly fix market patterns. The question remains whether the French did act directly to assure and protect national markets despite the elimination of inter-European tariffs. State influence is enormous in major steel-consuming industries such as aircraft, naval construction, automobiles, and the like. Market patterns may be sustained, therefore, by pressure on purchasers. Alternatively, pressure might be brought on foreign producers or governments to prevent an invasion of the French market. There is no direct evidence of such efforts, nor were they probably required. Any temptation a more efficient foreign producer may have had to invade the French market, assuming transport costs did not eat too deeply into the product advantage, would be dampened by the clear willingness of the French to protect the well-being of their firms. A real invasion of the French market, replacement of French producers in their own market, would necessitate the expansion of production facilities, a costly and potentially dangerous undertaking. The French could respond by subsidizing domestic production, whatever the restrictions of the Rome Treaty, or subsidizing exports to the invading country. Such a potential would discourage the massive risk involved in the expansion of plant capacity. The European steel industry is a stable oligopoly supported by national policy. Unless one element withers, leaving a vacuum, no one would seem to have much advantage in destabilizing the present arrangements. Furthermore, the dependence of the other European steel companies on their national governments would mean that a rival state would have to approve, if not finance, an invasion of the French market. Such an action would be a serious provocation. Thus, in some ways, the oligopolistic structure of European steel companies dependent on national governments creates a situation in which power never need be directly extended to keep out foreign production.

The essence of this discussion, then, is that the state can stand as intermediary between a national industry and the international market. It can virtually cut off the national economy from the world economy when, by its own actions, it can assure a stable supply of the product and control the market in which it is sold. Such an intermediary role depends, it would seem, on an autonomous capacity for leadership in domestic industry and the ability to coordinate and direct diverse state powers in support of politically defined economic outcomes. This is easiest for stable products sold to a handful of consumers open to influence from the state and most difficult for rapidly evolving products sold to a diverse and diffuse consuming public. This analysis, as noted earlier, should not imply that only goods such as oil and steel that are inputs to other products meet these standards. Civilian radar, electrical generating equipment, railroad equipment, and even television systems all evolve at steady, but not blinding, paces and can be sold only to governmental or semi-governmental bodies. Even in an interdependent world, then, a nation-state may be able to influence the terms of trade in a wide variety of essential industries.

Whether the French strategy of state intermediation, if not direct trading, to affect the terms of international exchange is successful or not, it certainly ran against the grain of the structure of the international economic system in the 1960s. In that liberal system, the states established and guaranteed the rules of the game but left the actual play to private firms. Did this handicap them in the international competition? The French thought they would be able, and often were able, to match state formulated political strategy against a privately formulated economic strategy. They hoped to create selective power mismatches favorable to themselves. Such a strategy, one might guess, is more likely to be successful when the French are the only, or the predominant, political actor. When an economic issue is politicized for everyone, bringing other states into the game, then the French lose much of their advantage, being simply one medium-sized power among others. Again, it must be emphasized that these cases suggest the French willingness and ability to operate a state directed strategy. It does not mean the policy was attempted throughout the economy, nor that the strategies were always wise ones.

## After De Gaulle

De Gaulle's successors, it would seem, have increasingly accepted the structure of the international system or at least accepted the seeming limits on their ability to change it. Certainly, at moments of crisis and breakdown like the Arab oil embargo, the French sought to transform a system wobbling around an American pivot into a multipivoted one in which the French would exert leadership. Similarly, the French have not felt bound by rules others set for them, following an independent policy in areas such as the Middle East and nuclear plant sales. They have also pursued their own line on monetary matters. Indeed, until the recent ascension of German and Japanese industrial might, France was the only industrial country able and willing to assert itself against the United States. Nonetheless, the essential thrust of French policy now seems to be to use France's ever-asserted autonomy to obtain the best possible deal within the existing order rather than to overturn that order. Of course, there is less of a regime to attack. Yet, while emphasizing the change, one young ranking finance official, by no means a traditional Gaullist, remarked quite insistently, "One must not forget, we live in the shadow of De Gaulle."

The persistence of earlier themes is clear in monetary policy. As suggested before, there is a continuity in policy since 1960. It is aimed at protecting the French exchange position and preventing American domination in the monetary system. In the 1960s, the primary concern was the excessive purchasing power of the dollar. Now, following a monetarist analysis, the French worry that world inflation was generated by the uncontrolled liquidity that the export of dollars in the 1960s produced. The great fear is that the expansion of international lending and liquidity would make the domestic French economy more vulnerable to international money movements. In fact, all international borrowing requires government approval, and though automatically granted, funds flowing in can be tracked. Some effort is reported to even out such borrowing in order to provide a stable impact on domestic money supply.[27]

Since the dollar crisis of 1971, a system of floating exchange rates has replaced the old fixed rate system. The French have resisted, adhering, in principle at least, to a fixed exchange rate system but conceding, of necessity, in practice. They have at least won the paper argument that the fixed system should be resurrected sometime. Monetary discipline continues to preoccupy the French. The overwhelming strength of the German mark does not leave the French much room for financial leadership within Europe. They have advocated a fixed system within Europe, the so-called snake, but they have played the game only when it was convenient. They maintained a fixed rate against the mark when it did not require substantial domestic adjustment. In November 1976, they sought to seize the monetary initiative by supporting Britain's request to be aided in easing sterling out of its position as a reserve currency. At the same time, this permitted the French to reassert their claim that no national currency should play a reserve role. Most important, a weakened Britain seems to provide a perfect ally to counterbalance Germany within the European Community. The purposes of such a link to Britain are not so different from those of De Gaulle's German connection. The Germans, unfortunately for the French, became too powerful too quickly. If an arrangement could be made, the English should prove reliable for some time.

[27] See, for example, Thierry de Montbrial, *Le Désordre Economique Mondiale* (Paris: Seuil, 1974).

The institutions De Gaulle built and many of the tactics he used have been turned to somewhat new ends. Foreign economic policy once more sustains and emerges from domestic needs. The tactics of state intervention have also shifted, moreover. The Planning Commission's influence is diminished. A high level planning group that includes the President, the Ministers of Finance and Industry, and the Planning Commission now meets monthly to consider specific problems of industrial and economic policy. While the Plan's influence seems further eroded, the present system does not appear to break with the high-level interministerial committee system used by Pompidou. Beginning with Pompidou, moreover, state financial support has been increasingly passed through para-public banking institutions. Partly, this serves to take these expenditures out of the budget and, partly, it seems to reduce administrative pressure on the Trésor itself. One must acknowledge that the Trésor is an administration organized to make political choices, while the Crédit National, for example, is a banking institution prepared to distribute funds on more strict profit criteria. One commentator summarized the situation as follows: "The financial supports distributed by the public authorities have been widely diversified in recent years. The changes concern both the means of intervention and equally the beneficiaries of this aid . . . an elimination of direct loans, a growth of support in the form of grants and subsidies, much of which is financed outside of the budget or treasury, and a growth of assistance in the form of guarantees and interest subsidies."[28] He argues this has meant a more rapid increase in support than would have occurred if one simply had continued direct loans. Support may have increased while direct administrative involvement in corporate affairs declined.

The emphasis, at any rate, seems to be more on coordination of state power toward specific and selected ends rather than on a continuing effort to maintain coherence in the economy. One might, of course, contend that nothing has changed except the pretensions of the language of planning. The industrial commissions of directive planning aside, the weight of state intervention has always been on selected sectors and problems. The Plan, many have argued, never had much influence outside the few sectors chosen for emphasis. Equally important, the emphasis in the 1960s was on mergers and reorganization, which often deeply involved the state in company affairs. Now, the emphasis is on exports and export financing, allowing the state and industry to remain more at arm's length. Partly, the corporations are themselves stronger, having increased their potential for self-financing since the war. Nonetheless, with heavy borrowing a basic part of the strategy of many, and profit margins dipping during the recent recession, many firms find themselves financially vulnerable again. In the steel industry, hard hit by recession, a crisis has developed. The firms are heavily in debt and the state will intervene. The economic reins may have been loosened, but the state has in no way relinquished the means or right to intervene when it chooses.

---

[28] François Eck, *Le Role Monetaire et Financier du Trésor 1960–74* (Thèse pour le Doctorat, Université de Paris, 1975).

At any rate, the Bretton Woods order has partly unraveled, though it is not entirely clear whether American power has indeed eroded all that much. The late 1940s and early 1950s and the Fourth Republic were dominated by American power as the Europeans and Japanese rebuilt. The late 1950s and the 1960s saw the full fruition of an international economic system led by America. French policy is made now, however, in an era in which multinationals are said to be more vulnerable and nation-states are emerging again as agents of trade. We therefore need to ask, how is France dealing with multinationals and what role is developing for the French state as trader?

The French appear to have adopted a more sophisticated policy toward multinational companies in recent years. There is still a preference that companies with power in the French economy be French-owned and controlled; for example, the decision to invest billions of francs in a renovation and expansion of the telephone system has forced ITT to sell part of its French-owned companies. Otherwise, it would not have been allowed to share in the electronics bonanza. Yet purely French companies and entirely French technology seem costly luxuries in many industries. War against the multinationals simply because they are foreign entities no longer seems necessary or possible. Furthermore, French companies such as Michelin have begun to invest abroad, opening them to retaliation for national policies at home. The limits on the power of a state to intervene in an international industry are more clearly understood. Yet the possibilities of state action are also more acutely perceived. Seemingly, the French feel able to minimize the problems and take advantage of the opportunities the multinationals represent. The policy began to evolve under Pompidou and seems to have crystalized with Giscard. It is reported to be as much a response to events as an explicit shift in direction.

Simply, the government seems prepared to make the best use it can of these companies. It will try to influence them with the same array of policy instruments it uses to influence French companies: assured markets, subsidies, and investment funds. Since multinationals are often stronger and more flexible than French companies, that will mean the state's resources must be used judiciously and at vulnerable points. When the French state can offer solutions to problems the foreign companies face, it may gain influence on their policies. As part of this shift, the French seem willing to accept a junior role in industrial partnerships as long as their interests and purposes are satisfied. This means, significantly, that the French no longer demand joint European efforts which they control but can seek out attractive arrangements with American partners. A series of cases provides the evidence for these propositions, and some French officials openly articulate these principles.

In the Summer of 1975, the French government arranged the sale of Compagnie Internationale pour l'Informatique (CII), the state-sponsored computer company, to Honeywell. This was an ironic turn in the French computer adventure. A little more than a decade earlier, the French had blocked the sale of Machines Bull to General Electric (GE). A year after that, the steadily declining fortunes of the French company forced the sale anyhow, this time on much poorer terms that gave GE complete control. When GE went out of the computer business, its worldwide activities in the industry were sold to Honeywell. In the meantime, the French responded to this invasion by launching a state inspired company, CII. CII soon became an albatross. It required increasing subsidies and guaranteed markets to remain alive but offered ever-diminishing prospects of a profitable future. The company belonged to two electrical and electronics equipment holding companies, so the sale involved negotiations among the French as delicate as and, ultimately, more difficult than those with the new American partner. Along with CII came not only a continued state subsidy, to ease a transition that would phase out CII products and integrate its personnel into Honeywell-Bull, but also a substantial expansion of state markets.

The French, many thought, were paying Honeywell to take CII from them and were giving up any position in the world computer market. In fact, the French, who ended up with a majority position in the Honeywell subsidiary, seem to be playing a very subtle game to put themselves in a position to influence directly the policies of this major multinational, the second computer company in the world. The CII purchase, combined with the existing Bull holdings, increase Honeywell's financial stake in the French holding to 53 percent. The government argues that Honeywell-Bull is now a French company, and indeed it is. Moreover, the research and development (R & D) capacity and the guaranteed state-controlled markets, which could assist Honeywell's introduction of new product lines, give the French substantial bargaining power on product and manufacturing policy. Honeywell-Bull is, in fact, a much sounder long-term proposition than CII and has extensive commercial as well as government markets. Indeed, Honeywell was concerned enough to arrange assurances that the parent company would still have the right to establish a single coherent product strategy that it could still dominate. Indeed, the formula to determine control of the interlinked board is still not fully settled. By any interpretation of the contracted formula, Honeywell would retain control now; but some arrangements, which Honeywell would almost certainly resist, could result in French control in the future. The French have not captured a multinational, but they hardly stand helpless before this one.

The French arrangements with Westinghouse, and the negotiations in the aircraft industry to find a joint American-French undertaking, strongly suggest that the Honeywell deal was not an isolated case. First the government chose Frama-tome, a joint French-American venture, over a Compagnie Générale d'Électricité (CGE)-Germany undertaking, as the instrument of French nuclear energy policy. Then, when Westinghouse had taken substantial losses in the European elevator market and found the cash attractive, they purchased an important share of the Westinghouse holdings. This left the French in full control. The two moves represent something of a reversal of earlier French insistence that technology had to be entirely French conceived and developed. One electronics executive, speaking of the earlier policy, had said: "For De Gaulle everything had to be French." Aircraft provides a third case. After the defeat in the "fighter deal of the century" both Dassault and Sud-Aviation are seeking American industrial partners.

There does, though, seem to be a sharp change in policy. The French are no longer trying simply to block American companies or to replace them with French ones. In essence, they are seeking to break up the multinational packages of technology, management, capital, and marketing, to obtain influence—not control. The presence of foreign investment remains a critical concern. Whatever arrangements are made with particular companies, foreign firms abound. Overall, companies where foreign holdings are 20 percent or more represent 26 percent of sales, 24 percent of investments, and 18 percent of the jobs. Well over half (60 percent) are from other members of the EEC. Only one-fifth (20 percent) are from the US, and a good portion of the rest is Swiss. In some vital sectors such as oil, electrical and electronic construction, and chemicals, the total of foreign ownership is over 30 percent. A system of investment control is in place, but it is used more for information than dissuasion. French investment abroad, interestingly, is still less than that of foreigners in France. Of that overseas investment, about one-third goes to oil exploration and nearly half to investments in the EEC.[29]

French government policies to promote and directly arrange exports, often on a state-to-state basis, have blossomed with the expansion of the Middle Eastern market. The French state has attempted to play trader in the international markets, either by creating public or para-public companies or by negotiating the terms of trade for private companies. State trading as an instrument of policy has often seemed linked to bilateral trade arrangements in the French case, although it is not at all clear whether the existence of a state-owned company encouraged or simply facilitated such dealings. The political administration is separate from a productive unit, whether ownership is private or public, and must find ways of influencing company behavior. Within a single country and even within the same sector, the relations between the central administration and public companies differ. The outline of French state trading policy is clear nonetheless. For example, French oil policy has been conducted through a public company (Elf-Acquitaine, formerly, Elf-ERAP) which serves as an instrument of the administration and through CFP, which is partly state-owned but quite independent. Before 1973, oil relationships with Algeria, for example, were negotiated on a state-to-state basis with Elf-ERAP serving more as the conduit for the trade flows and less as an independent actor. Indeed, during the 1973 oil crisis and its aftermath, French policy urged bilateral, state-to-state arrangements. Certainly, part of the ploy was an effort to push American oil companies from their central role in the organization of the international oil industry. This was suggested by the French effort to organize a European bloc as an alternative to an American-led Western bloc and then to organize producer-consumer conferences. The French, a cynic might remark, were willing to organize anyone, as long as the Americans couldn't. Nonetheless, bilateral dealings by the state or by para-public companies have been a basic part of French

---

[29] Diana Green, "Economic Decision-Making in France " (Ph.D. Dissertation, London School of Economics, 1976).

domestic oil policy, and it is not surprising that they advocated these approaches during a crisis.

There has been an important controversy over whether the French government actually controlled these companies during the boycott. Some have suggested that the oil companies, in defiance of French policy, simply ignored the demands to favor France.[30] This may have been the case with CFP, said to have participated in the multinationals' supposedly even-handed distribution of oil throughout the world. It was almost certainly not true of Elf-Erap (now Elf Acquitaine), and talk has begun that the government will exert closer control over CFP policies. Crippling shortages never developed, so it is difficult to judge how deeply French interests were compromised or whether they were at all. For domestic purposes, the French government had to assert its Middle Eastern policy. It achieved substantive results, and did not, therefore, place restrictions on domestic consumption of fuel. Consequently, it was impossible openly to approve any oil-sharing arrangements. If France's partner countries were to have been sharply inconvenienced, let alone damaged, because of French refusal to make oil available, the international effort might have been compromised. Whether oil company actions to distribute oil evenly slipped a fast one past the government or whether the government tacitly approved those actions is not clear. Internationally, however, the French were trying to assemble a consuming bloc under their leadership. It is quite possible that they simply had the best of both worlds; symbolic gluttony at home and actual sharing in their dealings with other governments.

In industrial sectors in which public companies predominate, bilateral state dealings are also evident. In one instance, it appears a French administration is promoting the creation of a public firm for domestic uses by seeking service and product contacts with other governments. Reorganization in the nuclear field, a separate case, seems designed to facilitate state trading. Nonetheless, French announcements of multi-billion dollar trade deals with the oil-producing countries require a certain scepticism about the precise character of the agreements and the exact role of the government in the arrangements. Such deals would promise some mix of goods for oil, thus settling the problem of markets, terms of trade, and trade deficits at once. Unlike the Japanese trading companies discussed by T.J. Pempel, the French cannot really promise to deliver such complex arrangements. In fact, there are reports that contracts have been lost in the machine tool industry because the companies involved would not agree to Renault acting as overall negotiator, in essence, as general contractor.[31] The grandiose figures are reached by adding together contracts already signed with or without state help, those in negotiation, and those in which discussions are just beginning. Whatever the government says or does, though, final agreements must be negotiated directly with the individual

---

[30] *L'Expansion* (November, 1976): 203.
[31] Yves Laulan, *Le Physiologie de la France* (Paris: Cujas, 1976), p. 97.

companies. Thus, although the French bureaucracy takes an active and public role in negotiating trade deals, the precise relationship between the government and the private companies in these arrangements is obscure. The companies often insist quite convincingly that they would have found the markets and made the deals on their own. The government, for its part, emphasizes its role in searching out deals, maintaining the relations required to settle them, and providing the financing. The historical weakness of the export sector, a result of the years of insulation and protection, makes governments worry that, left to their own, the companies will not adequately expand exports.

French bureaucrats have regularly engaged in all the activities required to assemble a trade package. They have prospected markets, often claiming a role in settling the deals themselves. Financing that subsidizes exports has been arranged, thus providing a selective devaluation. Finally, by a selective use of export credits, the government has the power to decide which companies will bid for which contracts. These various tasks are divided among several ministries. Market prospecting has been done by the Ministry of Industry, and, since the oil crisis, a special office has been established to promote the export of large-scale French projects. This section of industrial redeployment is run by the former Ministry of Defense official concerned with arms exports. The same diplomatic skills of state-to-state trade negotiation are, presumably, important. There is a Minister of Foreign Commerce but this department does not rival the Ministry of Industry nor in any way correspond to the Japanese Ministry of International Trade and Industry (MITI). One official remarked that market prospecting often is assisted by the exchanges during ministerial visits, and, consequently, there were constant requests to visit trade fairs or to simply visit. The Minister of Foreign Commerce provides just such a person, a traveling minister for a traveling trade show.

Promotional efforts aside, the arrangements for export finance are often the key to an economic package. The terms of finance which settle the actual cost of a good are an important part of international price competition and are inevitably part of aggressive trade practices. French truck manufacturers complain that they are unable to compete with the lending terms that American and Swedish companies are able to offer. Financing arrangements involve more than price, however, and can protect companies against default and exchange rate risks. The individual elements of finance are stitched together in the division for foreign economic relations of the Ministry of Finance (DREE). This financing net is linked to the Industry Department's export drive both through personal contacts of the operating officials, and in a formal inter-ministerial committee that, on a regular weekly basis, provides a forum for resolving policy differences. The policy instruments are designed to be selective, not intentionally evenhanded, and thus give the bureaucrats discretion and, consequently, power. How often and when this discretionary power is exercised is not clear. Japan projects the image of a coordinated national trading policy arranged between MITI and the private trading companies. France does not even approach such an operation, though it can operate a selective and directed policy in specific sectors.

At any rate, the Banque Française pour le Commerce Extérieur (BFCE), the Caisse Centrale de Cooperation Economique, and, above all, the Compagnie Française d'Assurance pour le Commerce Extérieur are the instruments. Even before the oil crisis, one source suggests, the funds for guarantees of finance to French firms grew from 39 million francs in 1960 (the first year the Crédit National and the BFCE were involved) to 848 million in 1973. One sharp increase came in 1964, with a jump from 29 to 209 million francs; a second, in 1969, with a jump to 479 millions, and a third in 1971.[32] Figures since 1973 are not available, but there is every reason to assume they jumped again. There is a second instrument. Direct loans to other governments, primarily Tunisia, Morocco, and India, but also Turkey, Indonesia, and Pakistan, have financed their imports from France. Haberer, now one of the senior finance officials, gives a figure of 2.5 billion francs, about $500 million at today's exchange, but closer to $600 to $700 million at the time, as the annual financial assistance provided to exports. He contends, moreover, that this has resulted in exports leading French growth. From 1969 to 1973, exports grew from two to three times faster than investments or consumption.[33] Funds for such financing are not unlimited. Guidelines for their use come from Finance's Direction of External Economic Affairs and any difficult decisions will certainly be settled there. The proportion of funds provided automatically according to a predetermined set of criteria is not clear. In other words, the range of discretion the Ministry of Finance exerts on a continuing basis is not evident. Certainly, there is an endless effort to reduce its commitments in any particular instance. In some cases, competing French companies do have their respective claims vetted before they enter international competition, and, clearly, such an arrangement allows the Ministry of Finance extensive influence within domestic industry. How extensive such specific and directed tactics are is, again, unclear. In some industries, including electronics, electrical equipment, and nuclear reactors, there is overwhelming evidence that the state's market prospecting and financing produces trade. In other industries, company officials make a prima facie case that their high-level links with government are limited and do not affect product, production, or market strategy. Such state trading arrangements are most evident in the armaments industry where the French are third, though a distant third, only to the Soviet Union and the United States. Over 7 percent of all French exports are arms, a figure exceeded, according to French figures, only by the United States.

In recent years, then, the French have tried to build their growth strategy on exports. Using both direct and indirect policy tools, this, of course, makes a nation dependent on the health of foreign markets. The French are less dependent on external demand than their European or Japanese peers, but, turned around, this means their firms have not been as successful exporters. Current comparisons must not hide the switch in the French economy from domestic protection to international competition.

[32] Eck, pp. 133–200.
[33] Haberer, pp. 193–99.

There is a general issue amid the details of bureaucratic arrangements. State trading, exchange in which one of the partners is a government agency or firm, has increased substantially in recent years. The commodity-exporting countries, of which the OPEC nations are the most visible and powerful, and the Socialist nations have confronted the private traders in the West. To exaggerate, one might say that the private traders in the core of the industrial countries have been surrounded by state traders. In many cases, such as the French oil dealings and the American grain arrangements with the Soviets, Western governments have been pulled into the game. French state trading seems less anomalous therefore. One issue is whether state trading will deeply alter the terms of exchange among nations, either between developed and developing countries or in trade shares of the advanced nations. This seems doubtful. Direct trade relations among governments may, though, affect the domestic arrangements between business and the state. Ultimately, then, the *method* of exchange may be of as much importance as the *terms* of exchange. When the state is the intermediary between two trade partners, it could substantially increase its power in its relations with business. The question is whether private companies in the industrial countries must depend on their national state to deal with foreign state traders. If so, the parent government becomes a veil between private companies and state markets, mediating the relation between domestic and international economies. If the industrial state controls international access in certain sectors, it presumably gains a bargaining counter with which to influence domestic business activity. The domestic consequences, though, will depend on the existing structure of business-state dealings. In the American splintered polyarchical bureaucracy where government bureaus are often the fiefdoms of particular private interests, a government bureau of state trading may be less likely to serve as an instrument of government policy in the economy than as a support for particular private interests. In France, where the power of the veil has, in the past, allowed the government to shape industry organization, an extension of that veil will likely improve the position of the state in any bargaining. Whether the improved position would be used and, if so, what for, would depend on the government in power.

## IV Conclusion

A state bureaucracy partially able to shelter itself from parliament and to influence the industrial sector directly has been able to maneuver to protect national interests in an economically interdependent world. It struck a regional bargain that committed agriculture to the European Community and, in effect, provided a German subsidy to French farmers. It mediated between the national and international market to promote industrial modernization and to force a restructuring of critical industrial sectors. It has grown increasingly sophisticated in its dealings with multinational companies, attempting to exploit their needs and dynamics to affect their corporate policies. Early efforts to insist on purely French operations have been abandoned. This has permitted the state to negotiate more effectively with the multinationals and to obtain substantive, not symbolic, goods. These foreign economic policies have served to cushion agriculture's transition into an industrial world and to help the state pressure a previously protected industry to modernize. Finally, the state has played trader, trying to market French goods directly and assure payment for imports in package trade deals. Of course, the French have not been able to impose their own rules of play on monetary and energy matters. Yet their efforts suggest that a nation-state can use administrative or domestic economic resources to reduce its vulnerability to international developments, though it cannot escape from the game.

Foreign economic policy has been so entangled with domestic strategies that its contribution to the immediate well-being of the French people, as distinct from the vulnerability of the nation to the international arena, cannot be separated from a general discussion of postwar French growth. Per capita income spurted ahead, and between 1963 and 1970 personal incomes in France grew at a pace second only to Japan. Indeed, some calculations suggest that domestic production (GDP) grew faster in France during the 1960s (1961–72) than in any other West European country.[34] French policy must be judged to have succeeded in its basic task of promoting rapid growth and the modernization of industry and commerce. However, one can argue now that the conditions that permitted growth in these years have passed. The movement of labor out of agriculture into industry, which provided one important impetus, is being completed. The absorption of state of the art technologies is another transient growth source that was important in these years. Equally, the reorganization of many industrial sectors, which often involved adopting more competitive strategies rather than more efficient structures, has left awkwardly organized firms which may ultimately prove neither competitive nor efficient.[35]

Most critically, perhaps, French policies were effective in an international economy of rapid growth and relatively stable prices and in a domestic political environment where growth could be pursued without careful attention to distribution. The French economy may have inherent inflationary pressures which are all the more difficult to curb when the burden of government and the benefits of growth are central political issues. Economic privilege, resulting finally in higher costs, has not been wrung out of the French system, and a substantial and inefficient secondary sector has been tolerated. In a different vein, the heavy corporate debt linked to the French strategy for rapid growth has meant high fixed costs during the economic downturn, as have policies to maintain jobs. Economic instruments and policies which seemed to hinge on the exclusion of labor from arrangements between business and the state to promote growth may prove less effective in controlling inflation.

[34] These statistics are from Green, and Robert Bacon and Walter Eltis, *Britain's Economic Problem* (London: Macmillan Press, 1976), p. 2.
[35] Mr. H. Aujac, former director of the BIPE, has advanced precisely this argument, which parallels my conclusion based on an analysis of the electronics industry.

With a challenge from an allied Left, the distribution of growth has become a central issue. This makes it more difficult to contain demands from labor for increased labor shares. Although the economic and political contexts have shifted, the problem, it must be noted, is not new. The enormous squeeze on workers' incomes required to have both reasonable price stability and adequate investment undoubtedly contributed to the explosion in May 1968. Indeed, there is little to suggest that the benefits of growth were spread at all evenly. In fact, a recent and controversial OECD study contends that France has more unequal income distribution than any Western country, including Spain, both before and after income transfers.[36] The burden of government, moreover, falls unevenly as well. France is virtually the sole industrial country with only the most nominal of capital gains taxes. Equally, a toleration of tax evasion by peasants and small shopkeepers lightens their burden, though indirect taxes inevitably make up some of the gap in direct taxation. How much income would in fact be raised by tax changes is less important, politically, than the tax inequality itself. In sum, whether rapid expansion reduced or exacerbated income and wealth inequalities, the advance of the Left has given the issue increasing salience.

The roots of the inequalities are in domestic policy, not foreign economic policy. Certainly, political symbols such as Corcorde and CII drained resources that could have been used for other social or economic ends. So, almost certainly, did efforts to overthrow existing monetary rules. The European Community's Common Agricultural Policy set food costs above world market levels, but it did shift part of the costs of the peasantry from the French to the Germans. Accommodating multinationals and playing the role of trade seeker, with whatever success, can be argued to benefit the French community as a whole at the expense of someone else, and do not have automatic distributional consequences within France.

France faces serious economic problems whether the current majority retains power or the Left attempts to implement its policies. The precise mix of problems and objectives will, of course, depend on which particular coalition is in power. Giscard is now struggling through a political valley with the revitalized Gaullists, headed by Chirac, organizing a challenge from the Right built on traditional themes. The precise balance between Communists and Socialists on the Left is unclear, let alone the international response to their possible victory. In this political setting and with uncertain economic conditions, any projection is simply speculation. Nonetheless, some strategy to manipulate consciously the power of the state bureaucracy to contract the best possible deal for France will almost certainly continue whoever governs France. The structure of state power pushes toward certain tactics, even if it does not determine the objectives.

---

[36] OECD, *Income Distribution in OECD Countries* (Paris: OECD, July 1976). The controversial section is by Malcolm Sawyer.

# 9
# Conclusion: Domestic Structures and Strategies of Foreign Economic Policy

*Peter J. Katzenstein*

An inventory of the objectives and instruments which characterize the differing political strategies of six advanced industrial states in the international economy yields three groups of states: the two Anglo-Saxon countries, mercantilist Japan, and the states of the European continent. Corresponding differences exist in the distinctive elements of domestic structure: the coalition between business and the state and the policy networks linking public and private sectors. An historical explanation of these differences is most appropriate. In the future, stresses in the relations between business and the state and contradictions between ruling coalitions and organized labor may lead to changes in political strategies.

At no time since the late 1950s did the advanced industrial states jointly confront a threat as serious as the one in October 1973. The oil embargo and the ensuing price increases aimed at the core of their industrial economies and endangered the stability of their societies. However, even this common crisis led them to pursue divergent strategies of foreign economic policy. Blessed with a relative abundance

Earlier drafts of this paper have benefitted from the comments, criticisms, and suggestions which I have received from the authors in this volume; from the participants in the workshop and in the conference on Domestic Structures and the Foreign Economic Policy of Advanced Industrial States; from my Cornell colleagues Douglas E. Ashford, Theodord J. Lowi, T. J. Pempel, George H. Quester, Richard Rosecrance, Martin Shefter and Sidney Tarrow; and from Robert Gilpin, Peter Gourevitch, Miles Kahler, Peter Kenen, Robert O. Keohane, James R. Kurth, David D. Laitin, Leon N. Lindberg, Edward L. Morse, Wolf-Dieter Narr and Hans-Jürgen Puhle. I have also learned much from discussions of early drafts of this paper by the seminar on "State and Capitalism Since 1800" at Harvard's Center for European Studies; from a seminar of the International Finance Section at Princeton University; and from a panel held at the XVIII Annual Convention of the International Studies Association.

of indigenous sources of energy and constrained by the strategic position of its Israeli ally, the United States adopted a hard line towards OPEC producer states. Britain increased its efforts to become self-sufficient in energy before the end of the decade by intensifying the development of its North Sea oil reserves. West Germany and France countered with a commercial offensive. Italy relied on direct foreign assistance. And Japan accelerated its investment program in countries exporting raw materials.[1] The oil crisis thus points out an important question of contemporary international political economy. Why, in the face of a common threat, did the strategies of advanced industrial states differ so much?

This divergence in political strategies is not confined to questions of energy. On issues of international monetary reform, for example, conflicting national strategies date back to the early and mid-1960s. In the area of non-agricultural trade especially, divergent national strategies have appeared since the late 1960s. Questions such as the proposed commodity stabilization fund or the sale of certain types of nuclear reactors are only now revealing the fundamentally different strategies which advanced industrial states are pursuing.

This divergence in foreign economic policies is surprising. The growing entanglement of advanced industrial states in the international political economy resulted from the liberal political framework which the United States established after 1945. It was reinforced by advances in the technology of communications and transportation which drastically lowered the economic costs of international exchange. But this process of economic entanglement did not, in and of itself, lead to unquestioning acceptance of the dictates of the international market place. All major advanced industrial states developed different strategies to manage the terms of interdependence.

In the early postwar years the political and economic predominance of the US was so great that its presence or preference deeply affected these strategies. Charles Maier's paper shows that these constraints were most evident in the policies of the defeated Axis powers. Extending the American vision of the "politics of productivity" to West Germany and Japan required direct intervention in many spheres of domestic political life.[2] American intervention in Italy and France aimed primarily at containing Communist labor movements but did not attempt seriously to affect the organization of political parties, the state bureaucracy, and the business community. Although American policy makers may have disdained the Labour Party's efforts to build a social welfare state in Britain after 1945, they were primarily concerned with replacing the Commonwealth system of Imperial Preferences with a truly international economic order. The anti-Fascist, anti-Communist, and anti-Imperial imperatives of American policy in the immediate postwar era thus affected, in different forms and to different degrees, the strategies which the advanced industrial states could use to manage the terms of interdependence.

Although still dominant today, America no longer holds the position of overwhelming power which it enjoyed in the immediate postwar era. To a greater

---

[1] See the special issue "The Oil Crisis in Perspective," *Daedalus* Vol. 104, No. 4 (Fall 1975).
[2] See the essay of Charles Maier in this volume.

extent than in the 1950s and 1960s the strategies of foreign economic policy of advanced industrial states now reflect their domestic structures. This essay, like those that precede it, argues that the divergence in foreign economic policies in the 1970s is due principally to differences in domestic structures.

This chapter is not a summary of the previous ones but a comparative analysis of political strategies in the international political economy. Part I makes an inventory of different strategies of foreign economic policy which shows three distinct patterns. The United States and Britain follow a liberal strategy in permitting market forces to operate and in giving policy makers few instruments to apply directly to particular sectors or firms. Japan, on the other hand, pursues a neo-mercantilist strategy which favors active intervention in the market and gives policy makers a large number of instruments with which they can impinge directly on specific sectors and firms. Finally, the European states occupy an intermediary position between Anglo-Saxons and the Japanese, with West Germany and Italy adopting a more liberal and France a more neo-mercantilist strategy.

Part II of the paper explains these three types of political strategies in terms of different domestic structures. In the two Anglo-Saxon countries these give private actors a powerful role; while in Japan the state bureaucracy and the Liberal Democratic Party (LDP) join the business community in determining the policy-making process.

Part III offers an historical explanation of contemporary differences in the domestic structures of advanced industrial states. A comparative analysis of the elimination of feudalism, the Industrial Revolution, and the process of state-building in these six advanced industrial states yields the same three groups of states as in Parts I and II. It distinguishes between the United States and Britain, with their democratic tradition and early industrialization, and Japan, with its authoritarian past and late industrialization. Once again, the three continental states occupy an intermediary position between the Anglo-Saxon countries and Japan.

Finally, Part IV addresses the sources of conflict and the potential for changing strategies of foreign economic policy. Conflict in domestic politics within the business community, and between business and labor is increasing. Directly or indirectly, governments and state bureaucracies get involved in these conflicts and thus may exacerbate developments in the international political economy.

## *I Strategies of foreign economic policy: objectives and instruments*

For purpose of analysis it is helpful to distinguish between two aspects of strategy—policy objectives and policy instruments. The definition of objectives reflects a choice among values which differ from state to state. Throughout the postwar years, for example, the United States has vigorously pursued policies to support a liberal international economic order. Japan, on the other hand, has self-consciously sought to maximize its rate of economic growth. The instruments which policy makers command largely determine whether stated objectives can be achieved in the process of policy implementation. Throughout the 1960s the lack of tools for sectoral economic policy impeded the British government's efforts to improve export performance. Without these tools, France's policy of sectoral transformation would have been unthinkable. The distinction between policy objectives and policy instruments is no more than a convenient analytical device; in reality the ends and the means of a policy always fuse. The case of West Germany illustrates that some objectives, such as price stability, can become instruments to attain other objectives, such as export-led growth. And the defense of particular policy instruments, like sectoral policy, can itself become an objective of policy, by which states like Japan and France hope to maintain control over their own economies.

The essays in this volume provide a good starting point from which to construct a descriptive inventory of the objectives and instruments of foreign economic policy. To be sure, a great deal more careful, descriptive work needs to be done, some of which will undoubtedly lead to the revision, extension, and refinement of the brief inventories presented here. But future characterizations of different strategies in the international political economy will benefit, I believe, from the development of categories which are grounded in reality rather than abstraction.[3] An inventory of policy objectives and instruments yields three distinct patterns. Policy makers in America and Britain, subscribing to the principles of a liberal international economic order, have at their disposal policy instruments which only indirectly affect particular sectors and firms. Japanese policy makers aim for a high rate of economic growth; they can command selective policy instruments which have a direct impact on particular sectors and firms. The three states of the European continent, finally, mix elements of Anglo-Saxon liberalism and Japanese neo-mercantilism in a third, hybrid pattern.

*Policy Objectives:* The analysis of policy objectives in these papers differs in three ways from the old concept of the national interest.[4] (1) The description of a particular set of objectives is used solely as an analytical device. The normative connotations which identify the national interest with the public good in the traditional international relations literature are thus avoided. (2) Unlike the earlier literature, these essays do not postulate policy objectives deductively under broad categories such as "national security" or "national welfare." Instead they trace them inductively, by closely observing several areas of foreign economic policy. (3) Finally, the authors in this volume explore policy objectives by looking not only at policy makers' rhetoric but also at their actions.

The two Anglo-Saxon states and Japan differ greatly in their policy objectives. The United States' and Britain's deep and abiding commitment to the principles of a liberal international economic order has shaped their commercial policies. It also led them to defend the parity of their currencies even when, until the late 1960s and early 1970s, they were overvalued. Finally, it facilitated capital exports and imports. Japan has intervened actively in the play of market forces, and

---

[3] See the introduction to this volume.
[4] Stephen D. Krasner, *Raw Materials Investments and American Foreign Policy* (Princeton: Princeton University Press, forthcoming), Chapter 2.

defended the parity of its currency tenaciously, even when it was undervalued. It has actively encouraged capital exports only in very recent years and has tried to restrict capital imports.

Grouping the United States and Britain in one category does some injustice to the distinct way each of them has defined its objectives in the international political economy. American policy makers have viewed the liberal international economy abstractly in terms of the unhindered flow of trade and capital organized by private corporations. For British policy makers the meaning of a liberal international economy was more concrete, tied directly to the defense of sterling. Until the mid-1960s America's power was so overwhelming that it could tolerate some deviations (both by itself and others) from the principles of an open, international economic order. Britain's power base, by comparison, was relatively small and rapidly shrinking. The defense of the reserve position of sterling was essential for claiming the position of a world power. The differing meanings which American and British policy makers attached to the concept of a liberal international economy are important for an analysis of foreign economic policy. In commercial policy, for example, America showed a somewhat greater commitment to export promotion than did Britain; and American import restrictions have traditionally been somewhat more stringent than British restrictions.[5] In monetary matters, economic criteria may not have justified American support of the dollar's parity from the mid-1960s on. But compared to the political and economic costs the British incurred in defending sterling, American efforts to shore up the value of the dollar look paltry. Indeed in comparison to Britain it is striking how quickly American policy makers initiated and adjusted to a new set of monetary rules in 1971. Finally, the current American debate on foreign investments indicates a greater readiness to explore policy alternatives than is true of Britain, with its long-standing commitment to further capital exports.[6]

Compared to Japan, though, these differences between America and Britain are minor. Economic growth was more important to the Japanese than defending a liberal international economy or aspiring to great power status. After 1945 growth required a thorough modernization of the Japanese economy through a continuous transformation of its industrial structure. In its commercial policy Japan thus adopted an energetic program of export promotion and followed an export drive to increase Japan's share in world markets for manufactured goods and to restrict imports to vitally needed raw materials and high technology goods.[7] Furthermore,

---

[5] On the neglect of British industry in particular, see the essay by Stephen Blank in this volume.

[6] For example, see Robert Gilpin, *US Power and the Multinational Corporation: The Political Economy of Foreign Direct Investment* (New York: Basic Books, 1975). Despite that commitment, the British government was of course compelled to impose some restrictions on the outflow of sterling from 1966 on. See Fred Hirsch, *Money International* (London: Allen Lane, the Penguin Press, 1967).

[7] Lawrence B. Krause and Sueo Sekiguchi, "Japan and the World Economy," in *Asia's New Giant: How the Japanese Economy Works,* Hugh Patrick and Henry Rosovsky, eds. (Washington, D.C.: The Brookings Institution, 1976), pp. 398–402 discuss the reasons why the Japanese

since 1949 Japanese policy makers have tenaciously defended the yen even when it was undervalued. Unlike Britain, that defense was not tied directly to largeı political aims, but served the prosaic purpose of strengthening the position of Japanese products in world markets. And until the late 1960s Japan did not favor capital exports. Large increases in domestic wage levels and the appearance of a surplus in the balance of payments have contributed to a change in policy only in recent years. Despite some recent relaxation in Japan's traditional restrictions on capital imports, policy makers' desire to maintain control over all important sectors of the Japanese economy has not flagged. Foreign investment policy illuminates what is striking about Japan's foreign economic policy more generally: the continuity in the state's defense of the economy in the face of numerous external challenges.

The basic objectives of West German, Italian, and French foreign economic policy fall somewhere between the two Anglo-Saxon countries on the one hand and Japan on the other. West Germany and Italy approximate the Anglo-Saxon model; France follows the Japanese pattern. West German and Italian policy makers have encouraged export-led-growth, through which, until recently, they have achieved full employment and social stability. Although the strategy of these two states is viable only in a liberal international economy, West Germany's economic success in the existing international economic order makes it, more than Italy, opposed to any basic changes in the rules of the game. West Germany's success rests on an unfailing belief in the virtues of price stability, which strengthens the position of West German products in world markets by simultaneously dampening domestic demand and increasing the competitiveness of exports. Italy's foreign economic policy, on the other hand, must tolerate higher levels of domestic inflation, which undermines its position in world markets by reducing the volume and competitiveness of exports.

In their commercial policy both West Germany and Italy share an export orientation and extend selective protection to import-competing industries.[8] Despite two moderate revaluations of the Deutsche Mark in the 1960s, the Federal Republic, like Japan, has preferred an undervalued currency in order to strengthen its export performance. The Italian lira, on the other hand, did not experience pressure to revalue upward in international money markets, and Italy has favored selective devaluations of its currency whenever these have seemed opportune. On questions of foreign investment the objectives of West Germany and Italy were close to the liberal stance of the United States and Britain. Throughout the 1960s West German policy makers hoped to ease the upward pressure on the Deutsche Mark by encouraging capital exports. But in trying to maintain its competitiveness in the international political economy the Federal Republic has preferred to import

strategy is not one of export-led growth.
[8] With regard to import restrictions these three member states of the European Communities (EC) show relatively few differences.

foreign labor rather than to export capital. Large wage increases in the early 1970s, the revaluation of the Deutsche Mark under floating rates, and the growing scarcity of raw materials have accelerated the move of West German capital abroad. Iran's acquisition of one quarter of Krupp stocks in 1976 again underlined West Germany's traditionally permissive stance on questions of capital imports. In its openness to foreign investors West Germany was, however, surpassed by Italy which has taken perhaps the most liberal attitude of all advanced industrial states.[9] Although Italy's large corporations, both public and private, have exported more and more capital in recent years, throughout most of the postwar era Italy has tended to export labor rather than capital.

The objectives of French foreign economic policy show a close affinity to the Japanese emphasis on economic growth based on the transformation of key industrial sectors. But unlike Japan, and like Britain, Gaullist France subordinated this growth objective to broader political aims in the 1960s. This is the main reason why France has shown less continuity of purpose in its foreign economic policy than Japan. French commercial policy is distinguished by a program of export promotion through which the government has attempted to modernize key sectors of French industry. Like Italian monetary policy, French policy before and after de Gaulle was flexible in seeking maximum trade advantages from selective devaluations. But in the mid- and late 1960s the question of the franc's parity became a cornerstone of de Gaulle's attack on the international monetary system. In the face of increasing economic pressures, de Gaulle followed British precedents in preferring domestic deflation and foreign exchange regulations to devaluation of the franc. A similar stiffening of France's posture was notable in the mid-1960s in reference to foreign investment. For a brief period French policy tried to discourage the inflow of foreign capital for political reasons. But the economic and political costs of that policy were too great, so French policy returned quickly to extracting maximum benefits from the multinational corporations. Unlike West Germany and Italy, it did not grant uncontrolled access to domestic markets but, especially in recent years, unravelled the package of technology, managerial know-how, and foreign capital. The export of capital has not been one of France's main objectives. In recent years these exports have increased, but as in Italy the most sensitive political aspect of this change has been the growing "flight" of portfolio investment abroad, induced by fears of a left-wing government seizing power in the near future. The differing policy objectives of these six advanced industrial states are summarized in Table 1.[10]

[9] Joseph LaPalombara and Stephen Blank, *Multinational Corporations and National Elites: A Study in Tensions,* A Research Report from The Conference Board's Division of Public Affairs Research (New York: The Conference Board, 1976), pp. 13–17.

[10] A search for patterns of policy should focus on the rows rather than the columns of Table 1. But such a search promises results only if the policy objectives were characterized more abstractly than is appropriate for this concluding essay.

Table I The objectives of foreign economic policy

| | I | | II | | III | |
|---|---|---|---|---|---|---|
| | UNITED STATES | BRITAIN | WEST GERMANY | ITALY | FRANCE | JAPAN |
| Trade | export orientation | export orientation | export-led growth | export-led growth | export promotion to increase competitiveness of French industry | export drive to meet import needs |
| | selective protection | liberalization of imports | selective protection | selective protection | selective protection | general regulation of imports |
| Balance of payments | defend parity even when overvalued (mid 1960s–1971); flexible (since 1971) | strongly defend parity even when overvalued (until 1967 and to a lesser extent between 1967 and 1976) | defend parity even when undervalued and revalue by no more than a minimum margin | flexible | flexible; defend parity even when overvalued (in the mid and late 1960s) | strongly defend parity even when undervalued |
| Foreign investment | encourage capital export (except for temporary restraints in the mid 1960s) | encourage capital exports | encourage capital exports | tolerate capital exports | tolerate capital exports | restrict capital exports; encourage it only since the early 1970s |
| | welcome foreign investment | welcome foreign investment | welcome foreign investment | welcome foreign investment | tolerate foreign investment (and impose temporary restrictions in the mid 1960s) | restrict foreign investment |

*Policy Instruments:* The instruments which policy makers can command in the pursuit of their objectives also condition strategies of foreign economic policy. Collectively, these essays point to an impressive array of instruments from which policy makers can choose. These include traditional instruments such as licenses, tariffs, quotas, exchange controls, and export insurances. But they also cover the whole range of monetary and fiscal policies, including interest equalization taxes, tax credits and direct subsidies for exports, and incomes policy affecting the domestic economy via budgetary decisions or interest rates. Finally, there are some novel instruments: constitutional innovations such as the National Economic Development Councils (Neddies) in England, sectoral policy in Japan and France, or bilateral, "voluntary" export agreements between other countries and the United States. Faced with such a bewildering variety of policy instruments, it is necessary to group them into fewer descriptive categories.

Many of the policy instruments at the disposal of American and British policy makers are also employed elsewhere. At one point or another since 1945 the two Anglo-Saxon states have used quotas, peril points, escape clauses, invisible tariff barriers, direct subsidies to import-competing industries, tax concessions for exporters, and different forms of foreign exchange controls. But more than elsewhere, policy makers in these two states have relied on three distinctive types of instruments. The first is an appeal to ideology. America's liberal ideology grew out of Wilsonianism and, after 1947, anti-Communism. Stephen Krasner argues in his essay that this ideology was important in rallying the American public in support of the establishment and maintenance of a liberal, international economic order. According to Stephen Blank, Britain's fundamental consensus on the beneficial effect of its role as a world power was, until the early 1960s, similarly important in the defense of sterling.

A second instrument distinctive of the two Anglo-Saxon states is the creation of new institutions or a major shift of power between institutions. The forty-year period of liberalism in American commercial policy between 1934 and 1974 was made possible by a change in the institutional arena of policy making.[11] The shift of power from the legislative to the executive branch of government partly insulated policy makers from protectionist groups and thus facilitated the steering of a liberal course in the international political economy. Britain, on the other hand, experimented in the 1960s with a large number of new institutions such as the Neddies and the Industrial Reorganization Corporation (IRC). Institutional innovation was originally undertaken to benefit exports through a general increase in the productivity and competitiveness of British industry. Institutional changes in Britain were potentially far-reaching, for their aim was to develop a price and incomes policy and a restructuring of the economy.

---

[11] Theodore J. Lowi, "American Business, Public Policy, Case-Studies, and Political Theory," *World Politics* Vol. 16, No. 4 (July 1964): 677–715. Elmer E. Schattschneider, *Politics, Pressures and the Tariff* (New York: Prentice-Hall, 1935).

Both Anglo-Saxon states have relied on a third, distinctive policy instrument. In the commercial and monetary area, American policy makers have often preferred bilateral, "voluntary" agreements with major trade partners over domestic adjustments. In an attempt to protect import-competing industries, America has, since the late 1960s, negotiated an increasing number of bilateral export control programs with other states. In the latter half of the 1960s the defense of the dollar would have been more difficult without West German cooperation; the purchase of so-called Roosa bonds, off-set agreements on troop stationing, and the assurance that West German dollar holdings would not be converted into gold all added strength to the dollar. On questions of foreign investment American policy makers have adopted a similarly "voluntarist" attitude toward America's own business community when, for balance of payments reasons, they sought to slow the outflow of capital from the early 1960s on.[12] In contrast, British policy makers have used macro-economic policy in their defense of the pound. The external strength of sterling was taken as almost the sole guiding principle in determining macro-economic policy at home. Throughout the last two decades domestic demand, and particularly domestic investment, was curbed repeatedly in a breathless alternation of stop and go for balance of payments reasons. Changes in the government budget or the discount rate of the Bank of England affected the entire British economy.

The situation was strikingly different in Japan. Policy makers there use a wide range of instruments which directly affect industrial sectors or firms. In Japan's integrated tool kit two instruments hold a key position. First, Japanese policy makers have effectively used instruments of sectoral policy directly to restructure a number of key sectors of the national economy. Relying on numerous policy instruments such as concentration policy, indicative planning, export promotion, and most importantly the channeling of public investment funds, that restructuring was central to Japan's export drive after World War II. In addition, Japanese policy makers have had at their disposal a wide range of highly effective administrative tools.[13] These have been of critical importance for restricting Japanese imports largely to raw materials, controlling the inflow of technology, excluding private direct investment, and linking recent capital exports with the search for new sources of raw materials.

The instruments available to policy makers in West Germany, Italy, and France fall somewhere between the extremes of the two Anglo-Saxon countries and Japan. That intermediate position reflects a particular blend of policy tools at the disposal of each of the three continental states. Speaking generally, West Germany approximates the Anglo-Saxon pattern of indirect control; France resembles more the Japanese pattern of direct intervention; and Italy holds a position somewhere in

[12] Gilpin, *US Power and the Multinational Corporation.*
[13] On the system of administrative guidance in Japan see Philip H. Trezise with the collaboration of Yukio Suzuki, "Politics, Government, and Economic Growth in Japan," in Patrick and Rosovsky, p. 784.

between. In the West German arsenal of instruments neither the Anglo-Saxon emphasis on institutional changes nor the Japanese emphasis on state-supervised industrial reconstruction figures prominently. Yet there is an undeniable affinity between the West German and the Anglo-Saxon approaches. West Germany's export mystique was an ideological formula to which virtually all segments of West German society, including organized labor, have subscribed throughout the postwar era. And despite West Germany's objective of export-led-growth there existed, in contrast to Japan and France, relatively little direct export promotion. The Export Promotion Act was rescinded as early as 1955; other instruments of export aid, such as credit guarantees, tax rebates, and interest rate subsidization by the state bureaucracy were used less in West Germany than in most advanced industrial states. Instead West German policy makers put a great emphasis on macro-economic policy. In comparison to Britain that policy had a more monetarist cast. West Germany's preoccupation with price stability was reflected in the strict limitations which the constitution set to the deficit of the government budget. Fiscal conservatism was reinforced by a deflationary monetary policy and measures such as the acceleration of import liberalization in the 1950s and the import of foreign labor in the 1960s. All of these measures tended to keep domestic price increases down.

Two small revaluations of the Deutsche Mark notwithstanding, the defense of an undervalued currency was, until the early 1970s, a central instrument of West German foreign economic policy. The absence of other usable policy tools made the undervaluation of the Deutsche Mark the lynchpin of the Federal Republic's strategy in the international economy. The dearth of policy instruments is illustrated by the fact that in the 1950s and 1960s foreign trade policy became a substitute for sectoral policy. Conditions on the world market, rather than in the West German state, shaped the structure of the West German economy. In fact the very concept of sectoral policy (Strukturpolitik) is mired in ambiguity. It refers to improvements in the social infrastructure of the welfare state (for example, schools, universities, hospitals, and roads), as well as deliberate efforts to develop high technology sectors of West Germany's economy.

In contrast, French policy instruments resemble those used in Japan. Sectoral policy in France applies to critical parts of the economy which the government has singled out as deserving industrial reorganization. For that task of reorganization, policy makers in France can command a wide array of instruments, including control over a substantial portion of investment funds directly affecting particular sectors and firms. The distinction which John Zysman makes between an incentive ("faire-faire") and a control ("faire") approach to policy points to a possibly important difference between France and Japan.[14] Although both approaches are used in France as well as in Japan, French policy makers have relied more on an incentive approach, especially in recent years. In addition, the French state's organizational structure and its characteristic use of administrative regulation have

[14] See the essay by John Zysman in this volume.

proved, at times, to be incompatible with the technical requirements of production. We can see an example in the case of the unsuccessful reorganization of the French electronics industry. No comparable instance of "failure" has yet been recorded in Japan. Finally, France, more than Japan, has relied on resources from international institutions such as the EEC. Although the number and range of French policy instruments look impressive compared to those available in other continental states as well as Britain and the United States, they still lack Japanese scope and effectiveness.

Italian policy makers mix measures of direct intervention with elements of indirect control. Public corporations such as Ente Nazionale Idrocarburi (ENI) or Istituto per la Ricostruzione Industriale (IRI) give the Italian state a potentially very strong means with which to intervene in the economy. But despite the large size of these corporations it is surprising how little use policy makers have made of them in Italy's foreign economic policy. In fact, these public corporations act relatively independently of the Italian state, whose planning efforts are still embryonic. Indirect measures of control, particularly monetary policy, are at least equally important.[15] In addition, policy makers have often relied on the improvisation of a few key individuals in government. More important than in any other advanced industrial state is the strategic location of industrial and financial *condottieri*—the Carlis, Agnellis, and Matteis—who implement Italy's objectives in the international political economy to the best of their individual abilities. Table 2 summarizes the main policy instruments available in the six advanced industrial states.

Despite their summary presentation in Tables 1 and 2, policy objectives and instruments are not ineluctable or unchangeable. Strategies of foreign economic policy result from policy makers' choices among alternative objectives and instruments. These strategies are not predetermined nor do they occur within a vacuum. Tables 1 and 2 reveal systematic differences in the objectives and instruments of foreign economic policy in three groups of states. We shall explain these differences through an analysis of the different domestic structures in which policy makers operate.


## II  Domestic structures and strategies of foreign economic policy: coalitions and policy networks

The ruling coalition and policy networks in domestic politics condition strategies of foreign economic policy. The definition of policy objectives is shaped largely by the ideological outlook and material interests of the *ruling coalition*. Such coalitions combine elements of the dominant social classes with political power-brokers finding their institutional expression in the party system and in a

[15] Banca Commerciale Italiana, "The Italian Economy: Monetary Trends," produced by the Research Department with the collaboration of Mario Monti (Università Bocconi and Università di Torino) 1 (September 1975): 11.

**Table II  The instruments of foreign economic policy**

| | *I* | | | *II* | | *III* |
|---|---|---|---|---|---|---|
| | UNITED STATES | BRITAIN | WEST GERMANY | ITALY | FRANCE | JAPAN |
| | appeal to anti-Communist ideology | consensus ideology | export ideology | nationalized industries | sectoral policy | sectoral policy |
| | shift institutional arena | institutional innovation | deflationary macro-economic policy (primarily monetary) | macro-economic policy (primarily monetary) | administrative regulation | administrative regulation |
| | "voluntary" bilateral agreements | macro-economic policy (both fiscal and monetary) | defend undervalued currency | improvisation by key individuals | extract resources from international institutions | |

variety of institutions a step removed from electoral competition—government ministries, banks, industrial associations, and large public or private corporations.

Policy instruments are a second aspect of strategies of foreign economic policy. It is the character of the *policy network* spanning both the public and the private sector which conditions them. The number and range of policy instruments emerge from the differentiation of state from society and the centralization within each. Varying degrees of differentiation and centralization create a distinctive combination of instruments in each of the six advanced industrial states.

In the next three sections we examine ruling coalitions and policy networks and advance an explanation of the objectives and instruments of foreign economic policy summarized in Tables 1 and 2. In that explanation we face two tasks. We should account for the main differences between the three groups of states identified in Tables 1 and 2: the two Anglo-Saxon countries, Japan, and the states of the European continent. At the same time, though, our explanation should also make intelligible the differences in strategy which distinguish the United States from Britain, and West Germany, Italy, and France from one another.

*United States and Britain:* Public officials have played a major role in tailoring American and British foreign economic policy to the defense of a liberal international economy. Government officials do not define these objectives single-handedly but in conjunction with business and financial leaders. However, the political rationale underlying their calculations is very much in evidence. This is especially clear for the American case.[16] The anti-Communist strategy which gave American foreign policy its overall focus in the postwar era required a liberal, market-oriented international economy uniting the Western Alliance. Similarly, British officials derived from the three circles they sought to unite—Europe, America, and the Commonwealth—a mandate for internationalism. Britain's waning influence in international politics also reinforced her ideological commitment to the principles of the Atlantic Alliance.

In both states, politically motivated support of a liberal international economy ran parallel to and was reinforced by the economic interests of the business community. But the latter term is imprecise: by all measures the American business community is large and heterogeneous. On questions of international economy it has contained both isolationists and internationalists.[17] The isolationist elements of the American business community tend not to locate on the East Coast, are outside of both the old Establishment and the financial community, and represent medium-sized corporations and small firms focusing on domestic investments. The internationalists, on the other hand, tend to be on the East Coast, are often part of the financial community, and represent large corporations heavily involved in international operations. During the last decade these distinctions have become less sharp. The

---

[16] Samuel P. Huntington, "The Democratic Distemper," *The Public Interest* 41 (Fall 1975): 23–28.

[17] Franz Schurmann, *The Logic of World Power: An Inquiry into the Origins, Currents, and Contradictions of World Politics* (New York: Random House, 1974), Part I.

gradual shift of industrial and financial power away from the declining East toward America's "new South" and the growing internationalism of the farm belt in the Midwest have led to a blurring of distinctions in the economic realm. In the area of foreign policy, the socio-economic "Establishment" has been supplemented and to some extent supplanted by the professional foreign policy "Community."[18] But despite these changes, it still remains true that America's international corporations have more tolerantly accepted the occasional violation of the market-orientation to which both segments of American business subscribe. Their toleration has in turn facilitated the joint definition of objectives by a coalition which has united business "interest" with state "ideology."[19]

Although it is smaller and less heterogeneous than its American counterpart, the British business community is also internally differentiated. Put concisely, the British definition of policy objectives reflects a "banker's" rather than a "business" view of the world.[20] The former view has found its most ardent proponents in London's City, whose economic survival, it was thought until the mid 1960s, depended on defending the position of sterling as a reserve currency. But the banker's view extended far beyond the City; subscribed to by the "Overseas Lobby" in the Treasury, it totally dominated the thinking of a succession of occupants of 10 Downing Street whose decisions ultimately counted most. The single most important source of the banker's view has been the Bank of England, which links government with the financial district and British industry beyond. Despite the devaluation of the pound a decade ago and its accelerating decline in recent years, the banker's view has retained a remarkable strength in the definition of policy objectives. It is perhaps the major asset which Britain commands today as it confronts an increasingly restive international financial community.

The dominance of the multinational corporations in the American business community and the City in the British business community explains why policy objectives are subtly different under the common veneer of market liberalism. The economic interests which entered into the definition of policy objectives were "real" in America and "monetarist" in Britain. This explains why the promotion of exports and selective protection have ranked somewhat higher in American commercial policy than in Britain. It also makes intelligible the British policy makers' rigidity in defending the pound.[21]

International forces also help to explain why both Anglo-Saxon states favored a liberal orientation in defining their objectives and why American goals tended to

---

[18] J. Kirkpatrick Sale, *Power Shift: The Rise of the Southern Rim and its Challenge to the Eastern Establishment* (New York: Random House, 1975). Leslie H. Gelb, "The New American Establishment is Called the Community," *The New York Times,* December 19, 1976. Section 4, p. 1. See also Fred Block, "Beyond Corporate Liberalism," to be published in *Social Problems,*1977.

[19] Schurmann, pp. 8–13.

[20] William Wallace, *The Foreign Policy Process in Britain* (London: The Royal Institute of International Affairs, 1975), pp. 156–88. Jeremiah M. Riemer, "Challenging the Banker's View in Britain and West Germany " (Ithaca: Cornell University, 1976).

[21] The overhang of sterling assets held abroad was of course an additional factor constraining British policy.

be cast in "real" and British objectives in "monetarist" terms. The access-to-market form of interventionism which has characterized Imperialism in its British and American incarnations and the management of an international reserve currency which accompanies hegemonic leadership in the international political economy both reinforce a liberal definition of policy objectives. The monetarist cast of British foreign economic policy has been conditioned by the very duration of Britain's imperial past and the prolonged decline in international power which it has experienced. Although the institutional effects of American hegemony since 1945 have also been profound, the American Empire is, in comparison, much younger, and the definition of American objectives is consequently less rigidly focused on intangible international obligations which cut across tangible claims at home.

The centralization of state and society and the differentiation between them affect the character of the policy networks and policy instruments. The British state has only one apex. The shift of authority from Parliamentary, to Cabinet, to Prime Ministerial government which has occurred during the past century has made 10 Downing Street the central decision point which controls, at least formally, the entire apparatus of the British state. The elected representative of Britain's system of responsible government can command the loyalty of a unified civil service. By comparison, the organizational fragmentation of Britain's private sector is striking. Business organizations have comparatively little impact on foreign economic policy.[22] In undermining the centralization of organized labor, the shop steward movement has greatly impaired the capacity of any government, be it Conservative or Labour, to wage an effective policy. The absence of a handful of leading private banks reinforces the decentralization of the British banking sector, with its sharp division between clearing banks (which provide liquidity to the money market for short-term credit) and merchant or investment banks (which offer long-term credit to British industry).[23] The clear differentiation between state and society is the third feature characteristic of Britain's policy network. In the early 1970s, for example, the threatened involvement of the state in collective bargaining almost precipitated a general strike. Another example of this differentiation is the fact that officials of private banks are barred from serving on the Board of Directors of the Bank of England. Throughout Britain's system of interest group representation, a "single-minded attention is paid to the maintenance of jurisdictional boundaries" between state and society. The sharing of information, consultation, and bargaining

[22] Stephen Blank, *Industry and Government in Britain: The Federation of British Industries in Politics, 1945–65* (Westmead, England and Lexington, Mass.: Saxon House and Lexington Books, 1973).
[23] Ulrich Immenga, *Participation by Banks in Other Branches of the Economy*, Competition–Approximation of Legislation Series No. 25 (Brussels: Commission of the European Communities, 1975), pp. 20–25. Due to the high rate of self-financing of British corporations the industrial and financial sectors of the British economy are less intimately linked than in other countries. See Derek F. Channon, *The Strategy and Structure of British Enterprise* (Boston: Division of Research, Graduate School of Business Administration, Harvard University, 1973), p. 38.

distinctive of Britain's "collectivist politics" takes place at a table which separates public from private sectors.[24]

Federalism, the separation of powers, judicial review, the committee and seniority system in Congress, and the absence of a disciplined two-party system illuminate the contrast between the centralized British and the fragmented American state. Organizational decentralization also marks America's private sector. The National Association of Manufacturers (NAM) and the Chamber of Commerce are weak national organizations representing the interests of the corporate sector. Trade associations are of greater importance but suffer from political atrophy in industries dominated by large firms. Even where they are strongest, these associations are a far cry from the peak associations and cartel arrangements so common on the continent and in Japan.[25] The decentralization of the American labor movement is also striking, for the uneasy alliance between crafts unions and industrial unions excludes major parts of organized labor such as the Teamsters but cultivates close ties with Canadian labor. Although it looks remarkably centralized when studied by itself, America's banking community is nothing like the kind of finance capitalism which Hilferding analyzed in the European context at the beginning of the twentieth century. Whether measured in terms of direct ownership of industry or financial market share, in comparative perspective America's banking sector looks relatively decentralized.[26] Finally, in contrast to Britain, the differentiation between state and society is not fully developed in America. Business groups and large corporations enjoy easy access to members of Congress, who act without the protection of strong national party organizations. The character of the American bureaucracy and regulatory commissions encourages in practice a symbiosis between public and private actors which is widely condemned in theory.

The successful conduct of foreign economic policy in the American and British state is difficult. Policy makers in both countries have few instruments of limited range to pursue their objectives. Although they take pride in their pragmatism, in both America and Britain, ideology has been an important instrument in the pursuit of liberal objectives. In addition, both countries' limited range of policy instruments typically leads to problems of institutional design which often transcend the particular issue at hand. In America's decentralized state a perceptible line has

[24] Andrew T. Cowart, "The Economic Policies of European Governments: Part I, Monetary Policy," prepared for delivery at the 1976 Annual Meeting of the American Political Science Association, The Palmer House, Chicago, Illinois, September 2–5, 1976, p. 7. Michael J. Brenner, "Functional Representation and Interest Group Theory: Some Notes on British Practice," *Comparative Policies* Vol. 2, No. 1 (October 1969): 125. Samuel H. Beer, *British Politics in the Collectivist Age* (New York: Random House Vintage Books, 1969).

[25] Grant McConnell, *Private Power and American Democracy* (New York: Random House Vintage Books, 1966), pp. 246–97.

[26] Eli Shapiro, Ezra Solomon, and William L. White, *Money and Banking*, 5th ed. (New York: Holt, Rinehart, and Winston, 1968). Paul M. Horvitz, *Monetary Policy and the Financial System* (Englewood Cliffs, N.J.: Prentice-Hall, 1969). Lester M. Salamon et al., *The Money Committees: A Study of the House Banking and Currency Committee and the Senate Banking, Housing, and Urban Affairs Committee* The Ralph Nader Congress Project (New York: Grossman Publishers, 1975).

separated a relatively protectionist Congress from a free-trade oriented Executive during the last forty years. The victory abroad of the executive-centered American "ideology" of liberal internationalism was possible only because of the defeat of American "interest" centered in Congress at home. This dualism mirrors that in the American business community. The culmination of America's postwar commercial policy in the 1962 Trade Expansion Act showed that political and economic dualism in and of itself did not stalemate foreign economic policy. The jurisdictional authority of Congressional committees and the effect of single-member constituencies (which Krasner argues permitted interest-group liberalism to feed on Congress as the carcass of the body politic) had shrunk while that of the Imperial Presidency had enlarged. The secondary effects of this institutional shift, which excluded Congress and import-competing industries from policy, has often been overlooked in recent years. In American foreign economic policy the role of the "internationalists" remains strong. The new Trade Reform Act of 1974 is remarkable, not for how much but for how little power it has shifted back to Congress.[27]

In Britain the conduct of foreign economic policy is not impaired by a decentralized state selectively infiltrated by private interests, but by a decentralized private sector differentiated sharply from the state. Because the rigidity of the British policy process does not allow for the kind of institutional shifts characteristic of American commercial policy, questions of institutional innovation have been crucial to the implementation of Britain's foreign economic policy. Once policy makers understood that the problem of sterling could only be solved through British exports, requiring increases in investment and productivity, they had to create institutions such as the Neddies to bring about these increases. Because it raised broader constitutional issues about the role of the British state in the economy, the experiment of the Neddies was a failure at least in terms of Britain's foreign economic policy. The consensus and stability orientation of Britain's collectivist politics, rooted in the political strategies of successive cabinets as much as in the system of private "veto-groups," made it highly improbable that policy could go beyond the stop-go cycle of Keynesianism. Thus the British Treasury was not "steering" the economy but bailing it out.[28] In summary, the immobility characteristic of American policy and the rigidity distinctive of British policy simply reflect the fact that in these two Anglo-Saxon countries questions of foreign economic policy lead more quickly to issues of institutional design and constitutional practice than in either Japan or the states of the European continent.

Faced with these obstacles, American and British policy makers have often chosen the path of least resistance. But the international context in which they have operated has led American policy makers to choose a path abroad, while

[27] Robert A. Pastor, "Legislative-Executive Relations and US Foreign Trade Policy: The Case of the Trade Act of 1974," paper prepared for delivery at the 1976 Annual Meeting of the American Political Science Association, The Palmer House, Chicago, Illinois, September 2–5, 1976.

[28] Samuel Brittain, *Steering the Economy: The Role of the Treasury*, revised edition (Harmondsworth: Penguin Books, 1971).

British policy makers have had to arrive at workable strategies at home. The sale of US government bonds to foreign central banks and the increases in Special Drawing Rights (SDR) with the International Monetary Fund (IMF) are examples of how American officials defended the parity of the dollar during growing balance-of-payments deficits in the 1960s without having to restrict their policy options. Since the late 1960s, the United States has negotiated a large number of "voluntary" export restriction agreements with other states in order to protect uncompetitive domestic industries and endangered jobs. In the pursuit of their objectives British policy makers lacked such international crutches. They have, instead, relied heavily on the lever of Keynesian macro-economic policy. The Treasury and the Bank of England could easily use this method; it required no direct cooperation from Britain's decentralized private sector; and it was supposedly apolitical, since it affected the whole economy at once rather than selected sectors.[29]

*Japan:* Among all advanced industrial states, the neo-mercantilism of Japan's objective of national growth provides the greatest contrast to the two Anglo-Saxon countries. The strength of the Japanese state derives from the intimate relations between the governing Liberal Democratic Party (LDP) and the state bureaucracy. As the most powerful spokesman of the conservative business community in Japanese politics, the LDP has held power ever since its formation in 1955. In a spirit of partnership the LDP has joined a prestigious and cohesive state bureaucracy, staffed largely by graduates of Tokyo University who were not taught the doctrines of laissez-faire liberalism. Japan's dependence on imports for virtually all of its raw materials and policy makers' perception of its relative isolation in the international community have reinforced the predilection of Japan's top party officials and senior civil servants to equate *raison d'état* with *raison d'être*.[30]

The growth orientation of Japan's foreign economic policy was actively supported by the business community and, in particular, its largest corporations whose economic interests it served most directly. Well into the 1960s commercial expansion abroad was important for achieving large increases in corporate earnings. In contrast to the British and American cases, a sizable sector of Japan's small businesses was politically frozen out of the process of defining policy objectives. Therefore, fewer important disagreements, such as the 1970 textile dispute, can be detected in the coalition between business and the state. It is thus impossible to ascertain the degree to which political aims have prevailed over economic ones, or vice versa. To construe the Japanese case in such language is in fact to mistake its

---

[29] Andrew Shonfield, *Modern Capitalism: The Changing Balance of Public and Private Power* (London: Oxford University Press, 1970), pp. 88–120. Trevor Smith, "Britain," in Jack Hayward and Michael Watson, eds., *Planning, Politics and Public Policy: The British, French and Italian Experience* (London: Cambridge University Press, 1975), pp. 52–69.

[30] Nathaniel B. Thayer, *How the Conservatives Rule Japan* (Princeton: Princeton University Press, 1969). Haruhiro Fukui, *Party in Power: The Japanese Liberal Democrats and Policy-Making* (Canberra: Australian National University Press, 1970).

very essence: the absence of serious conflict over policy objectives among the business community, party leaders, and senior civil servants.[31]

The international context in which Japan found itself after 1945 supported the neo-mercantilist course which it charted. Ironically, Japan's dependence on liberal America acted like a dam to protect it from the rising tide of antagonism and muted opposition among the member states of the Organization for Economic Co-operation and Development (OECD). Until the early 1970s American officials put broader political and security considerations over the narrower concerns of American multinational corporations wishing to enter the Japanese market and domestic industries increasingly threatened by Japanese exports.[32] A mercantilist state, furthermore, was likely to adhere to its chosen objectives in a liberal international economic order as long as it refrained from challenging the rules of the entire system. Unlike Gaullist France, Japan's objective in the international political economy never smacked of status diplomacy but revealed a single-minded export "atavism" instead. This was reinforced by import restrictions, an undervaluation of the yen, and a tight regulation of foreign investment.

The conduct of Japanese foreign economic policy has been greatly facilitated by the high degree of centralization of both state and society, as well as the lack of differentiation between them. In contrast to both the United States and Britain, the coalition between business and the state commands a large assortment of wide-ranging policy instruments. In comparison to America, Britain, and the continental states, Japan knows relatively few ethnic, religious, or regional cleavages. In its unitary system of government the central bureaucracy clearly controls lower levels of the state bureaucracy, headed by elected officials whose party has succeeded in monopolizing public office for the last two decades. This unified structure does not encourage infiltration from the bottom but rather invites accommodation at the top.[33] This feature bears more resemblance to the bargain struck between Ameri-

---

[31] A number of readers of earlier drafts of this paper have pointed out to me that this interpretation of Japan's domestic structure is in partial disagreement with recent writings which stress the pluralist character of Japanese politics. This disagreement, I believe, is due to the difference in perspective. Japan specialists rightly point to the numerous and intense political conflicts which accompany policy making as evidence speaking against the interpretation of "Japan Incorporated." What is striking, though, in comparative analysis is the fundamental underlying consensus which unites business, the government bureaucracy, and the LDP leadership, and which contains these conflicts. For a discussion of Japanese pluralism, sectionalism, and factionalism see Hugh Patrick and Henry Rosovsky, "Japan's Economic Performance: An Overview," in Patrick and Rosovsky, pp. 48–51; Trezise and Suzuki, pp. 761, 786. Ezra F. Vogel, "Introduction: Toward More Accurate Concepts," in *Modern Japanese Organization and Decision-Making*, Ezra F. Vogel, ed. (Berkeley: University of California Press, 1975), pp. xv–xviii. See also Gerald L. Curtis, "Big Business and Political Influence," ibid., pp. 33–70.

[32] For contrasting interpretations see, for example, *The Japan-US Assembly: Proceedings of a Conference on Japan-US Economic Policy*, 2 vols. (Washington, D.C.: American Enterprise Institute, 1975–76) and Jon Halliday and Gavan McCormack, *Japanese Imperialism Today: Co-prosperity in Greater East Asia* (Harmondsworth: Penguin, 1973). See also Donald C. Hellmann, *Japanese Foreign Policy and Domestic Politics* (Berkeley: University of California Press, 1969).

[33] Chitoshi Yanaga, *Big Business in Japanese Politics* (New Haven: Yale University Press, 1971). Kozo Yamamura, *Economic Policy in Postwar Japan: Growth versus Economic*

ca's large corporations and the executive branch of government than the organizational isolation of the British Prime Minister and the party elites in his Cabinet. The centralized character of the Japanese state helps explain why it has been able to act as a doorman, controlling the economic traffic entering and leaving Japan.

In contrast to Britain, a comparable degree of centralization also marks Japan's business community. The bifurcation of this community bears some resemblance to the American pattern. But in contrast to the United States, the gulf separating the giant corporations from small and medium-sized firms is bridged in two ways. A very large proportion of these smaller firms consists of subcontractors of the large corporations and has permanent affiliations with them. Organizational unity, furthermore, is assured by an elaborate network of overlapping peak associations dominated by the large corporations; this arrangement casts most parts of Japanese business into one centralized mold. The small number of Japan's commercial banks and the *keiretsu* system, by which industry and finance are linked, are similarly centralized, for they are all directly tied to the Bank of Japan and its monopoly power in regulating the supply of credit. The one exception to the centralized character of Japan's private sector is the dual organization of the unions, which leaves enterprise unions and national organizations largely independent of one another. But this has had little direct effect on Japan's foreign economic policy. In contrast to Britain, Japan's organized labor has been systematically excluded from positions of authority and has played at best only a limited role in policy.

The lack of differentiation between state and society is the third feature of the Japanese situation which facilitates policy implementation. In contrast to Britain and, to a lesser degree, America, relations between business and the state are so symbiotic that it is virtually impossible to determine where one stops and the other begins. Multiple connections exist. Common school ties in Japan's elite universities, especially Tokyo University, are reinforced in subsequent stages of life by an extensive system of advising committees, linking business, the LDP, and the state bureaucracy.[34] Upon retirement prominent senior civil servants frequently "descend from heaven"; that is, they leave the service of the state in order to join business corporations or to become LDP members in the Diet. Business representatives, in turn, help draft legislation in the influential policy committees of the LDP. In the tight interlock between business and finance the state is always present, for the government owns a majority of the shares of the Bank of Japan which provides the capital for Japan's industrial machine. In contrast to the nationalized-yet-autonomous Bank of England, the de facto nationalization of the Bank of Japan

---

*Democracy* (Berkeley: University of California Press, 1967). Eugene J. Kaplan, *Japan: The Government-Business Relationship* (Washington, D.C.: US Department of Commerce, 1972).

[34] Chalmers Johnson, 'The Reemployment of Retired Government Bureaucrats in Japanese Big Business," *Asian Survey* 14 (November 1974): 1–28. T.J. Pempel, "The Bureaucratization of Policymaking in Postwar Japan," *American Journal of Political Science* Vol. 18, No. 4 (November 1974): 647–64.

gives institutional expression to a policy network which in comparison to the United States and Britain is highly integrated.

The systematic reconstruction of specific sectors of Japan's industry in a planned sequence has been most important. Thus sectoral policy has been executed most often through administrative regulations issued by the powerful state bureaucracy. Japan's successful sectoral policy is in sharp contrast to the failure of the British Neddies; it is the functional equivalent to the mixture of economic robustness, market size, relative economic isolation, and international hegemony which has been the major substitute for the limited range of American policy instruments.

*West Germany, Italy, and France:* In their policy objectives and instruments the domestic structures of the two Anglo-Saxon states and of neo-mercantilist Japan represent the end points of a scale whose center is occupied by the three states of the European continent. Although the differences among the latter are less sharp, the coalitions which define objectives and the policy networks which condition the instruments of policy give West Germany's domestic structures an Anglo-Saxon cast; French structures resemble those in Japan; Italy, finally, occupies a middle ground.

From its beginning in 1949, the West German state has subscribed to an ideology of economic liberalism (*Soziale Marktwirtschaft*) which has been more strictly adhered to in defining international objectives than in domestic economic policy. Although this ideology justifies temporary state interventions in the market, West German governments have consistently advocated a liberal international economy.[35] Concrete political gains have gone along with West Germany's strategy of export-led-growth. The new West German state was compelled to compensate for the loss of its former export markets in East Germany, Poland, and Eastern Europe through an aggressive commercial offensive in the West. In addition, measures such as the early reestablishment of free convertibility and unilateral tariff reductions were useful for creating international goodwill and improving the international standing of the Federal Republic. The preference of the West German state for commercial expansion in a liberal international economy won out over political desires for European unification. On this important foreign policy question the views of the Economics Ministry have atypically prevailed in West Germany's "Chancellor Democracy."

The West German business community has fully agreed with the state's objective of export-led-growth and has been the main driving force since the initial political choice was made. As in America and Britain, however, West Germany's business community has been internally divided. The voice of the export industry has carried great weight on questions of commercial policy, favoring swift expansion in world markets. Smaller and more traditional firms have barely succeeded in their push for selective import controls. But the real contest concerned the issue of

[35] Carl-Joachim Friedrich, "The Political Thought of Neo-Liberalism," *American Political Science Review* Vol. 49, No. 2 (June 1955): 509–25.

the chronic undervaluation of the Deutsche Mark.[36] The advocates of monetary stability in the banking community argued that a strong export performance depended on domestic price stability, which an undervalued currency and the influx of speculative funds systematically eroded. In a situation of stalemate, international pressures tipped the scale and the export industries had to accept a very modest revaluation of the Deutsche Mark in 1961 and 1969. The managed float, to which the international monetary system has agreed since 1973, has reduced this long-standing irritant dividing West Germany's business community. In times of high inflation throughout the world, West Germany's domestic deflation policies offset and in some instances possibly exceeded the margin of revaluation of the Deutsche Mark in international money markets. In this manner the growth objective of export industries and the stability orientation of parts of the banking sector were well served. Economists may tell us that drastic deflation in 1974–1975 was "technically" wrong, but it was "politically" right.[37]

The social coalition which has defined policy objectives in postwar France to some extent resembles Japan's and offers a sharp contrast to the Federal Republic. Throughout the Fourth and Fifth Republics the French bureaucracy has been the key actor in defining the growth objectives of French foreign economic policy. For a brief period in the 1960s, though, these objectives became subordinate to the larger diplomatic aims of General de Gaulle. Cabinet instability in the Fourth Republic and the organizational weakness of the Gaullist movement in the Fifth Republic have given the French bureaucracy the dominant voice in policy delibera- tions.[38] The *dirigiste* outlook of the state bureaucracy is reinforced by an elabo- rate, institutionalized system of indicative planning which clearly spells out the state's policy objectives (although less so in the area of international economic questions) and tries to avoid internal contradictions between different objectives. Nothing comparable exists in either the Bonn Republic or in Italy.

French business has participated in the process of specifying growth objec- tives in a privileged but subordinate role.[39] The consultative mechanism through which the Planning Commission prepares its major statements gives business, and

---

[36] Franz-Ulrich Willeke et al., "Die Aufwertungsdebatte in der BRD in den Jahren 1968 und 1969," *Hamburger Jahrbuch für Wirtschafts-und Gesellschaftspolitik* 16 (1971): 287–316.

[37] Wilhelm Hankel, "West Germany Before and After the Oil Shock: Crisis Management or Adjustment of a Free Market Economy?" (Washington, Georgetown University, 1976). Wilhelm Hankel, "Germany's Postwar Economic Policy: The Case for a Neo-Mercantilist Approach," prepared for delivery at the XVII Annual Convention of the International Studies Association, February 1976, Toronto, Canada. Charles P. Kindleberger, "Germany's Persistent Balance-of- Payments Disequilibrium Revisited," *German Studies Notes* (Bloomington, Institute of German Studies, Indiana University, 1976). For a more general and somewhat dated but still useful discussion see Malcolm MacLennan, Murray Forsyth, and Geoffrey Denton, *Economic Planning and Policies in Britain, France and Germany* (New York: Praeger, 1968).

[38] Ezra N. Suleiman, *Politics, Power and Bureaucracy in France: The Administrative Elite* (Princeton: Princeton University Press, 1974), pp. 352–71.

[39] Shonfield, pp. 71–87, 121–75. Hayward and Watson. John Zysman, *Political Strategies for Industrial Order: Market, State and Industry in France* (Berkeley: University of California Press, 1977). Stephen Cohen, *Modern Capitalist Planning: The French Experience*, 2nd ed. (Berkeley: University of California Press, 1976).

particularly big business, very considerable weight. The French *tutelle* system, which links particular ministries vertically to a number of important industrial sectors or large corporations, makes the contribution of French business to the definition of policy objectives more explicit than is true in the case of the Japanese business community. But like Japan, and unlike West Germany, the powerful actors in French industry, commerce, and finance have been in basic agreement with the objectives of French foreign economic policy. This is not surprising in commercial policy, for the French "concentration policy" and an energetic program of export promotion helped the modern industrial sectors and large corporations most. When confronted with General de Gaulle's status diplomacy, the quiescence of French business illustrated the dominance of the state. The attempted restrictions on capital imports in the mid-1960s and the defense of an overvalued franc in the late 1960s were largely detrimental to the more narrowly conceived economic interests of French business.

Like West Germany, Italy has adhered to the objective of export-led-growth. That the Italian state would put so much store in the principles of a liberal market economy is in a way surprising, since the 1865 legislation on Italy's administrative unification was modelled after Napoleonic law. Although the electoral base of Italy's Christian Democratic Party (DC) was narrower than Japan's LDP, Italy has been uninterruptedly governed by a broadly-based conservative party. The passivity of the Italian state is due to a deeply ingrained personalism and fragmentation. That fragmentation in turn is congruent with and reinforced by the DC's "interclass coalition for patronage" which has sustained it in power for the last twenty-five years.[40] With the DC's 'Opening to the Left' in the early 1960s, the Italian government began to debate the merits of state planning more seriously. It rapidly became clear that the state bureaucracy and the right wing of the DC were adamant in their opposition to any new policy departures which might smack of Socialism. Italian planning was thus not "indicative" but wavered between being suggestive and projective.[41] In many instances such elementary obstacles as inaccurate data collection impaired the attempts of state bureaucrats and elected officials to set forth specific targets of action.

As in West Germany, in practice the task of defining and pursuing foreign economic policy objectives was thus assumed by other, parastatal institutions such as ENI, the Bank of Italy, or large private corporations such as Fiat or Pirelli. After the experience of Fascism and World War II, pent-up entrepreneurial instincts have led these organizations largely to disregard whatever objectives the state bureaucracy set forth. The large corporations have supported the market principle in the international political economy, and to a lesser degree, in the domestic economy as

---

[40] Sidney Tarrow, "The Italian Party System Between Crisis and Transition," *American Journal of Political Science* (1977).
[41] Gianfranco Pasquino and Umberto Pecchini, "Italy," in Hayward and Watson, pp. 70–92. Romano Prodi, "Italy," in *Big Business and the State: Changing Relations in Western Europe*, Raymond Vernon, ed. (Cambridge: Harvard University Press, 1974), pp. 45–63.

well. Neither ENI nor IRI, for example, has opposed the extremely liberal provisions governing foreign investment contained in the Vanoni Law of 1956. Italy's
private business community, and in particular the large industrial enterprises represented by their peak association, the *Confindustria*, have strongly supported an
export-led-growth strategy, especially when tempered by selective state subsidies,
tax credits for exports, selective import protection, and a flexible exchange rate
policy designed to strengthen Italian exports. Corporations such as Fiat or Olivetti
charted a course of corporate expansion in the international political economy.
They wished nothing more than to be left free of arbitrary state intervention.

The international context in which the ruling coalitions have defined the
objectives of West German, Italian, and French foreign economic policy has, in
most instances, reinforced the predilections of policy makers in these three states.
The defense of private property and the market principle which acceptance of the
politics of productivity promised was of critical importance to the West German
coalition, especially in the early postwar years when it found itself in the front
trenches of the Cold War in a divided nation. The pursuit of French objectives in
the 1960s was possible only after the establishment of the EEC generated West
German transfer payments which were important in modernizing France's industrial
structure. Similarly, Italy's political stability and "economic miracle" were helped
by the EEC's liberalization of international labor movements, which siphoned off
surplus labor in the South and improved the Italian balance of payments. At times,
though, the international context contradicted the preferences of the ruling coalitions. The liberal attitude which all three states have taken toward the influx of
foreign, and especially American, capital can be traced to United States government's insistence that American companies in EEC member states would be treated
no differently than West German, French, or Italian "national" companies.[42]
French policy makers have bridled under this restriction, especially in the mid-
1960s, and since then have sought to protect critical French industries with various
means falling short of government restrictions. In private, West German policy
makers may well have applauded French efforts, for the "imported inflation" of
the 1960s was largely the result of the rapidly growing Eurodollar market in which
American multinational corporations and banks operated freely.

Policy networks in West Germany, Italy, and France differ in the number and
range of instruments they offer to policy makers. As was found in the analysis of
policy objectives, West German and Italian instruments bear some resemblance to
those in the United States and Britain, while French policy instruments are not
unlike Japan's. By all accounts the West German state is decentralized.[43] Its lack of
a field system of administration is only partially offset by the smooth administrative coordination which links the federal bureaucracy with the provinces. Institu-

---

[42] Gilpin, p. 108.
[43] Renate Mayntz and Fritz Scharpf, *Policy-Making in the German Federal Bureaucracy*
(Amsterdam: Elsevier, 1975). Nevil Johnson, *Government in the Federal Republic of Germany:
The Executive at Work* (Oxford: Pergamon Press, 1973).

tions such as the Federal Employment Office (*Bundesanstalt für Arbeit*) or the Cartel Office (*Kartellamt*) are endowed with a constitutional mandate but in effect operate outside the regular bureaucratic chain of command. Bolstering the important role they play in policy implementation is a specialized court system which deals with a large number of social and economic problems. "Departmentalization" within the federal bureaucracy in Bonn, furthermore, was the major focus of an unsuccessful administrative reform movement in the early 1970s. West Germany's private sector, on the other hand, is highly centralized. Business is organized in a number of powerful peak associations, uniformly dominated by its largest members, which offer an institutional mechanism for articulating the views of business and, very occasionally, affording the government an additional instrument in the pursuit of its policies.[44] Even though the exclusive club of West Germany's "Big Three" private banks has grown somewhat during the last decade, West Germany's financial community is even more centralized than West German industry, and far more centralized than either the British or the American financial communities.[45] The same can also be said of West German labor, which is organized by industrial sectors and united by a strong national organization. Finally, the differentiation between state and society in West Germany is a mixture of British theory and American practice. West Germany's Bundesbank, for example, operates within a constitutionally-designed power vacuum in which technocracy appears to control the mixture of public pulls and private pushes. Selected in the past from the directors of one of the three big private banks, the chairman of the Bundesbank is expected to protect the nation's holy grail—a low inflation rate. It was in the nature of things that until the early 1970s the *Bundesbank* tended to look for allies to the stability-oriented banking community, rather than to the big-spending federal bureaucracy.

The centralization of the French state, the decentralization of its private sector, and the symbiotic relations between the two, offer a contrast to West Germany. The distinctive characteristic of the French state is its centralization. It commands a field system of administration which reaches into the most remote corners of society. In contrast to West Germany, the central bureaucracy staffs and fully controls all institutions concerned with policy implementation. Centralization and the immobile, byzantine bureaucratic conflicts and rigidity it engenders have been the most important concern of France's administrative reform efforts since 1945. Unlike West Germany, France's private sector is decentralized. The collective organization of business in the past has not been notably successful.[46] Even today

[44] Gerard Braunthal, *The Federation of German Industry in Politics* (Ithaca: Cornell University Press, 1965). Walter Simon, *Macht und Herrschaft der Unternehmerverbände BDI, BDA und DIHT* (Cologne: Pahl-Rugenstein, 1976).

[45] William P. Wadbrook, *West German Balance-of-Payments Policy: The Prelude to European Monetary Integration* (New York: Praeger, 1972). See also the special issue of the *WSI Mitteilungen* Vol. 28, No. 7 (July 1975).

[46] Henry W. Ehrmann, *Organized Business in France* (Princeton: Princeton University Press,

the Conseil National du Patronat Française (CNPF) has not been altogether success-ful in mediating the conflict between large corporations and medium-sized and small firms. Large corporations with privileged political access have thus established direct contact with the state bureaucracy. In this they have been encouraged by the favorable treatment which the French state has extended to its "national cham-pions" since the mid-1960s. French banking knows no equivalent to West Ger-many's three big private banks, since private commercial banking has always been an unrewarding business.[47] And unlike the West German unions, French labor is split into competing groups which still are not cut off from their roots in a syndicalist past. The differentiation between state and society, finally, is less complex than in West Germany, for the symbiotic relationship between the two takes place within the state bureaucracy rather than outside it. French banks are a good illustration; institutions such as the Caisse des Dépôts et des Consignations are intimately tied to the Finance Ministry and important for capital formation and the shaping of corporate investment decisions. And the Caisse is, of course, only the most prominent example of a host of public or parastatal banks which link the French state to the industrial sector.

Organizational characteristics such as degree of centralization do not ade-quately describe the distinctive character of the Italian state. In its original imita-tion of the Napoleonic state, in its size, and in involvement in the private sector, the Italian state resembles France. But in the systematic neutralization of its own power it can be likened to West Germany. French bureaucracy has been compared to a closed "honeycomb" structure which facilitates the criss-crossing of horizontal, vertical, and diagonal contacts in policy making.[48] The Italian state bureaucracy could be likened instead to a "sieve" which is particularly susceptible to the formation of clientelistic arrangements with the private sector and political par-ties.[49] As a result the Italian state bureaucracy prefers short-term, ad hoc arrange-ments to the long-term activist involvement characteristic of the French state or private (or semi-public) institutions in West Germany. These restrictions on policy instruments are reinforced by the incomplete centralization of Italy's private sector. The country's ideological fragmentation into Catholic, Socialist, and Communist political camps, for example, is reflected in the deep split of the Italian labor

---

1957). John H. McArthur and Bruce R. Scott, *Industrial Planning in France* (Boston: Division of Research, Graduate School of Business Administration, Harvard University, 1969).

[47] Charles-Albert Michalet, "France," in Vernon, *Big Business and the State*, pp. 105–25. Gareth P. Dyas and Heinz T. Thanheiser, *The Emerging European Enterprise: Strategy and Structure in French and German Industry* (Boulder: Westview Press, 1977).

[48] Jean-Claude Thoenig, "La Rélation entre le Centre et la Périphérie en France: Une Analyse Systematique," *Bulletin de l'Institut International d'Administration Publique* 35 (December 1975): 77–123.

[49] Joseph LaPalombara, *Interest Groups in Italian Politics* (Princeton: Princeton University Press, 1964). Luigi Graziano, *A Conceptual Framework for the Study of Clientelism*, Occasional Paper 2, Ithaca, Cornell University, Western Societies Program, 1975. Luigi Graziano, "Patron-Client Relationships in Southern Italy," *European Journal of Political Research* 1 (1973): 3–34.

movement. Italy's commercial banking system is weakly developed and it "plays a smaller part in Italy than in any other Western country."[50] The organization of Italian industry, though, is of considerably greater importance for an analysis of foreign economic policy, as it deviates from this pattern of fragmentation. The institution which represents small enterprises, *Confapi*, is virtually frozen out of policy making. On the other hand, *Confindustria*, the spokesman of larger firms, represents more than 100,000 enterprises and is led by powerful individuals such as Agnelli of Fiat or, now, Carli, formerly of the Bank of Italy. The Italian business community includes also Italy's enormous nationalized industries run by corporations such as ENI or IRI. This nationalized sector is just one illustration of the low degree of differentiation which more generally characterizes state and society in Italy. The Italian model of differentiation combines the French model of incorporation of the private sector into the state with the West German model of delegation of public power to parastatal organizations acting mostly autonomously. The result is a distinct form of "clientelism" which includes both the colonization of society and the privatization of the state.[51] The very size of ENI's and IRI's payrolls has made them increasingly susceptible to the DC's politics of patronage. Public enterprise and political entrepreneurship have thus become more and more intertwined; the result has been "patronage without political purpose."[52] The same cannot be said of Italy's financial institutions, which are closely integrated with industry and only formally dominated by the state. The apolitical image cultivated by the Bank of Italy strongly resembles that of the West German Bundesbank and has succeeded in removing the Bank from narrowly defined partisan politics. By the same token, though, Italy's banking sector is an instrument which is not easily manipulated by the government or the state bureaucracy. The great power which the Bank of Italy wields, together with institutions such as the *Cassa dei Depositi e Prestiti*, is thus directed largely to objectives of its own choosing.

West Germany's reliance on an export-mystique, an undervalued currency, and a deflationary monetary policy result from the delegation of authority to powerful, "non-political," parastatal organizations such as the Bundesbank, which link a decentralized state with a centralized society dominated by peak associations of industry and the banks. The centralization of the state and the osmotic relations between state and society have favored in France, as in Japan, a strategy based on sectoral policy and administrative regulation. Although the decentralized character of French society has rendered French efforts less successful than Japan's, the bureaucracy has countered this liability by extracting resources from international

[50] Shonfield, p. 180.

[51] Luigi Graziano, "Center-Periphery Relations and the Italian Crisis: The Problem of Clientelism," in *Territorial Politics in Industrial Nations*, Sidney Tarrow, Peter J. Katzenstein, and Luigi Graziano, eds. (New York: Praeger, forthcoming, 1978).

[52] Prodi, in Vernon, p. 61. See also Joseph LaPalombara, *Italy: The Politics of Planning* (Syracuse: Syracuse University Press, 1966). Stuart Holland, ed., *The State as Entrepreneur: New Dimensions for Public Enterprise: The IRI State Shareholding Formula* (London: Weidenfeld and Nicolson, 1972).

institutions such as the EEC. The internal fragmentation of the Italian state voids the use of the nationalized industries as an instrument of policy. That fragmentation, however, rewards and requires the improvisation of key individuals. As in West Germany, the reliance on monetary policy results from the prominent position of the Bank of Italy, which seems to stand above the political entrepreneurship pervading Italy and vitiating other instruments, such as fiscal or sectoral policy.

The character of the governing coalition conditions the objectives of foreign economic policy. Since the objectives of state policy and the interests of the business community are rarely in sharp conflict, it is impossible to talk of one prevailing, in general, over the other. But perceptible differences exist in the terms of accommodation between state and business, permitting some tentative rankings. In the definition of policy objectives these terms seem favorable to the Japanese and the French and unfavorable to the Italian state, with the West German and the two Anglo-Saxon states (whose powers were "unnaturally" enhanced by the side effects of international hegemony) falling somewhere in between.

In addition, though, strategies of foreign economic policy are conditioned by networks which provide the instruments of policy. Each of the six countries reveals a particular combination of centralization in state and society as well as differentiation between them. Table 3 summarizes the degree of centralization in the public and private sectors in these states. These six countries also differ in the degree of differentiation which separates state from society. Differentiation is low in Japan, Italy, and France; relatively high in Britain and West Germany; and at an intermediate level in the United States. This schematic summary suggests that, with regard to the instruments it can command, the role of the state in policy networks is strongest in Japan (with its centralization of state and society and lack of differentiation between them). The role of the state is also strong in France (which, however, lacks a degree of centralization in the private sector comparable to Japan). Suffering from different liabilities, the American, British, West German, and Italian states have fewer instruments at their disposal. And these instruments have only an indirect effect on particular sectors of the economy or on particular firms.

## III  The historical evolution of domestic structures

A comparison of the two Anglo-Saxon countries and Japan yields clear differences in the character of the governing coalitions defining the objectives of foreign economic policy and the policy networks which provide policy instruments. The three continental states occupy an intermediary position between the United States and Britain on the one hand and Japan on the other. But in a narrower range of variation, West Germany, Italy, and France also reveal some of the same differences in strategy and structure which distinguish the United States and Britain from Japan. Since the clash of political strategies in the international economy is attributable to different domestic structures, it is worthwhile to examine the foundations of these structures in greater detail. These foundations are historical. The contemporary structures of advanced industrial states are rooted in some of the major historical transformations of the past: the elimination of feudalism, the unfolding of the Industrial Revolution, and the building of a modern state. Except

Table III The degree of centralization of state and society in
six advanced industrial states

STATE CENTRALIZATION

|  |  | High | Low |
|---|---|---|---|
|  | High | Japan | West Germany, Italy |
| CENTRALIZATION OF SOCIETY | | | |
|  | Low | France | United States |
|  |  | Britain |  |

in the most extreme circumstances, negotiations on current issues in the international political economy will probably reflect, rather than reshape, these histori-
cally-evolved domestic structures.

How can one uncover the historical roots of the governing coalitions and
policy networks of advanced industrial states? The logic underlying Samuel Huntington's political comparison of the United States and Britain, Alexander Gerschenkron's economic comparison of Britain and continental Europe, and Barrington
Moore's historical comparison of America, Europe, and Asia suggests a mode of
analysis which relates political and economic changes to one another.[53] An analysis
of the historical evolution of state and society in these six countries points to three
alternative routes, corresponding to the three types of domestic structures which
distinguish the Anglo-Saxon countries, the continental countries, and Japan. This
array has a geographic dimension, stretching from West to East. But it has also a
chronological dimension. It distinguishes between countries with a democratic past
which experienced the Industrial Revolution early and a country with an authoritarian past which experienced it late, with the continental states occupying an
intermediary position. The Anglo-Saxon states featured parliamentary forms of
government and "atomistic" forms of capitalism favoring liberal strategies in the
international political economy, while Japan experienced executive-based forms of
government and varieties of "state capitalism" conducive to mercantilist strategies.
These differences in historical evolution can be traced to the smaller differences

---

[53] Samuel P. Huntington, *Political Order and Changing Societies* (New Haven: Yale University
Press, 1968), pp. 93–139. Alexander Gerschenkron, *Economic Backwardness in Historical
Perspective: A Book of Essays* (Cambridge: The Belknap Press of Harvard University Press,
1962), pp. 5–30. Barrington Moore, *Social Origins of Dictatorship and Democracy: Lord and
Peasant in the Making of the Modern World* (Boston: Beacon Press, 1966). This historical
analysis of domestic structures has also been influenced by Reinhard Bendix, *Nation-Building
and Citizenship: Studies of Our Changing Social Order* (New York: John Wiley, 1964). Leonard
Binder, et al., *Crises and Sequences in Political Development* (Princeton: Princeton University
Press, 1971). Gabriel Almond, Scott C. Flanagan and Robert J. Mundt, *Crisis, Choice and
Change: Historical Studies of Political Development* (Boston: Little, Brown and Company,
1973). Charles Tilly, ed., *The Formation of National States in Western Europe* (Princeton:
Princeton University Press, 1975).

which distinguish today's "competitive" and "organized" forms of capitalism in advanced industrial states.[54]

Why does the coalition between business and the state in the United States and Britain give industrial and financial leaders such a prominent role? Why do the policy networks in these two countries fail to generate effective policy instruments? Louis Hartz has offered an answer for the United States. Because the "first new nation" did not have to rid itself of a feudal past, the American business community prevailed easily.[55] Although American business faced some scattered opposition, between the end of the civil war and the 1930s it reigned supreme. For two generations it had only a weak state and a weakly organized Left to contend with. In the process of industrialization the firm was the central actor; the principles of private property and the market went unchallenged. The total victory of American business left a deep mark on both victor and vanquished. The absence of any important organized opposition for so prolonged a period reinforced the decentralized structure of the business community and deepened hostility toward all forms of business or state organization. The seeming contradiction between the widespread antipathy of American business to the state and the intimate relation between top business leaders and the state is rooted in the very magnitude of the business community's victory in the nineteenth century. Without a feudal past, America was unconstrained in fully developing its capitalism, becoming the center of "the enterprise system" first and, later, of "the free world."

The organizational decentralization of American business is related to the organizational decentralization of the American state, which for so many decades it had dwarfed. The process of bureaucratic penetration of America at the federal level occurred late. It began in earnest with the cumulative impact of the Great Depression, World War II, America's international hegemony, and the social welfare programs of the 1960s. This belated beginning occurred in a business civilization which reluctantly came to tolerate the federal bureaucracy as long as the pursuit of the state's objectives in the international arena did not conflict with business interests. That reluctance severely circumscribed the instruments of state power.

Unlike the United States, the British bourgeoisie had to rid itself of the shackles of feudalism inhibiting its entrepreneurial drive. But in contrast to the continental countries and Japan, British feudalism was defeated relatively early. Even though it lost the political struggles over the capitalist organization of the

---

[54] Philippe C. Schmitter, "Still the Century of Corporatism?" *The Review of Politics* Vol. 36, No. 1 (January 1974): 85–131. Henrich A. Winkler, ed., *Organisierter Kapitalismus: Voraussetzungen und Anfänge* (Göttingen: Vandenhoeck and Ruprecht, 1974).

[55] Louis Hartz, *The Liberal Tradition in America* (New York: Harcourt, Brace and World, 1955). Seymour Martin Lipset, *The First New Nation: The United States in Historical and Comparative Perspective* (New York: Basic Books, 1963). David Vogel, "Why Businessmen Mistrust Their State: The Political Consciousness of American Corporate Executives," Paper prepared for delivery at the 1976 Annual Meeting of the American Political Science Association, The Palmer House, Chicago, Illinois, September 2–5, 1976.

economy and the constitutional supremacy of Parliament, the economic and political base of the British aristocracy diminished only very gradually in the nineteenth and twentieth century.[56]

In matters of economic policy, however, the views of the British bourgeoisie, in the form of Benthamite and Manchester Liberalism, reigned supreme. The free interplay of demand and supply determined production and distribution in all markets and the central economic actor was the firm. The passivity of the state in economic affairs gave the British bourgeoisie the same luxury of organizational decentralization characteristic of America. Its most formidable opponent arose, in fact, not in Whitehall but in the City. Over time, political power shifted from industry to finance with its international orientation. Unlike German banks, the growth of a powerful financial community was geared not to financing investments at home but to facilitating capital exports. As was true of America after 1945, both business (that is, finance) interests and state ideology converged, preferring liberal imperialism. But in contrast to America's "Tudor polity,"[57] modern Britain became a party state, with political parties controlling the institution which embodied the sovereignty of the nation and party leaders, rather than industrial or financial magnates, becoming the *classe politique*.

Parliamentary sovereignty and the early extension of suffrage signalled the democratic character of the British state and circumscribed the growth of its central bureaucracy. In contrast to the United States, where political participation preceded bureaucratic penetration (as well as the continental countries and Japan, where that order was reversed), the creation of a modern British civil service coincided with the political mobilization of a mass electorate in the latter part of the nineteenth century. Situated in the capital and designed to support the government in carrying out its policies, the centralized character of Britain's modern bureaucracy inhibited the osmosis with private groups characteristic of American bureaucracy. On the other hand, its previous history of administrative decentralization and its prescribed role as neutral arbiter, rather than creative shaper, of society inhibited the cultivation of policy instruments which, to different degrees, are at the disposal of the continental countries and Japan.[58]

Japan has traversed a very different route. The difference in historical evolution helps to explain why the state bureaucracy and party leaders have become such powerful allies of the business community, and why the policy network which spans public and private sectors gives policy makers a wide range of effective instruments.

The strength of Japanese feudalism and its belated rejection in the last third of the nineteenth century are in striking contrast to America and Britain. Feudal-

---

[56] Moore, pp. 3–39. J.E. Christopher Hill, *Puritanism and Revolution: Studies in the Interpretation of the English Revolution of the 17th Century* (London: Secker and Warburg, 1958). John U. Nef, *Industry and Government in France and England 1540–1640* (Philadelphia: The American Philosophical Society, 1940).

[57] Huntington, pp. 93–139.

[58] John A. Armstrong, *The European Administrative Elite* (Princeton: Princeton University Press, 1973).

ism's strength was due to the centralized and bureaucratic institutions which led to the ossification of Japanese society in the Tokugawa era. But the legacy of this bureaucratic feudalism was the pacification of the nobility and the consolidation of Japan's administrative structure. The centralized bureaucratic regime which has marked modern Japan ever since the Meiji Restoration thus has very deep historical roots. The Meiji Restoration is a classical example of what Barrington Moore calls a revolution from above.[59] To allow for capitalist development the shackles impeding the mobility of factors of production, including labor, under feudalism were loosened. The state invested heavily in rapidly expanding an economic infrastructure of transportation and communication which was a necessary precondition for industrialization. Although the state played a direct entrepreneurial role in some industries which it regarded as critical, such as steel, on the whole it preferred to mastermind an indirect industrial development strategy. It could then quickly transfer directly-operated pilot ventures or risk-sharing arrangements to private entrepreneurs. Critical to the success of this form of "indirect management" was a state-controlled credit market. In contrast to America, in Japan the state, not business, enjoyed hegemony in the delayed Industrial Revolution. Unlike Britain, the instincts of the banking sector were directed toward industrial investment projects in the home market rather than capital export. For Okubo, Japan's Colbert, as for most of his generation, industrial wealth and state power were mutually reinforcing. The slogan of the time was "a rich country and a strong army," symbolizing an industrial samurai spirit which, in demilitarized form, is also characteristic of modern Japan since 1945.

The centralized structure of Japan's business community and its intimate links to the public sector reflect the organizational presence and active involvement of the Japanese state in charting the country's path into an industrial era. A system of centralized holding companies (*zaibatsu*), dominated by a small number of prominent families in the late nineteenth century, joined the state bureaucracy and the military in charting Japan's future. Under American occupation the military was eliminated as an important political actor and the *zaibatsu* was dissolved after 1945. The business community in contemporary Japan is thus left without a rival in the private sector.[60] In contrast to both America and Britain, the penetration of Japanese society by the state bureaucracy preceded organized political participation. The growing influence of political parties in the 1920s provided a brief interlude, as the "military-bureaucratic" complex proved its decisive power with the first stirrings of crisis. Only since 1945 have party leaders of the conservative camp, united since 1955 in the LDP, become permanent members of Japan's governing coalition. In Japan's expanding oligarchy, they are relative newcomers.

---

[59] Moore, pp. 228–313. William W. Lockwood, *The Economic Development of Japan: Growth and Structural Change 1868–1938* (Princeton: Princeton University Press, 1954). William W. Lockwood, ed., *The State and Economic Enterprise in Japan: Essays in the Political Economy of Growth* (Princeton: Princeton University Press, 1965).

[60] Yanaga, pp. 32, 87–88.

The contrast between the historical evolution of the early industrializing, democratic Anglo-Saxon countries and a late industrializing, authoritarian Japan can also be found among the three continental states. While West Germany's affinity to the Anglo-Saxon mold largely results from occupation and partition in 1945, the resemblance between France and Japan is rooted in the long, if intermittent, tradition of activism of the French state bureaucracy. Italy's delayed national unification and industrial development mix elements which, in a different context, can also be found in the German and French patterns.

Why does the coalition between business and the state in West Germany elevate the business community to such a prominent position? Why does the network linking state and society deny West German policy makers, like those in Britain or America, powerful policy instruments?

The main answer to these questions lies in the very recent past. In its historical evolution, as Barrington Moore has noted, in many respects Germany resembles Japan.[61] As was true of Japan, Germany's feudal past weighed heavily on its industrial revolution. The Prussian aristocracy, for example, participated in "the second founding" of the German Empire in 1879—the (in)famous coalition between iron and rye—which united conservatives in the industrial and agricultural sectors and propelled Germany toward economic protectionism, the naval arms race, foreign expansion, and World War I. But partition after 1945 was brutally effective in removing the *Junkers* from West Germany's political scene. The consequences of defeat and occupation were thus more visible and lasting in Germany than in Japan. The prominence of the West German business community today is not due to an early bourgeois revolution but to a belated military occupation.

This prominence results, at least in part, from the organizational centralization which business imposed on itself in the late nineteenth century. The Great Crash of 1873 spurred German business to form its first peak association in 1876, some ninety years before the creation of the Confederation of British Industries (CBI) in 1965. Industrial strategies were mapped by large firms, often organized in cartel-like organizations, masterminded by investment banks which, unlike Britain's, formed an economically integrated whole with the industrial sector. These organizations, unlike Japan's, were less open to direct or indirect state intervention.[62] Two world wars, Nazism, occupation, half-hearted efforts of deconcentration and decartelization, and a generation of economic prosperity have done very little to diminish the integrated industrial-financial structure as West Germany's central economic actor.

---

[61] Moore, pp. 433–52. F.L. Carsten, *The Origins of Prussia* (London: The Clarendon Press, 1954). Alexander Gerschenkron, *Bread and Democracy in Germany* (Berkeley: University of California Press, 1943). Theodore S. Hamerow, *Restoration, Revolution, Reaction: Economics and Politics in Germany, 1815–1871* (Princeton: Princeton University Press, 1958).

[62] Heinz Josef Varain, ed., *Interessenverbände in Deutschland* (Cologne: Kiepenheuer and Witsch, 1973).

The impact of the occupation has also weakened the erstwhile powerful bureaucratic core of Germany. The federal government's creation in 1949 occurred after a number of important jurisdictional claims in economic, cultural, and social policy had been made by other public actors, such as the Bundesbank and the state governments.[63]

World War II was then a decisive watershed in German history which has contributed greatly to the remaking of German industriousness in America's image. As a "people of plenty," West Germans have come to subscribe to America's "politics of productivity."[64] But it took the elimination of the Prussian Junkers, a great weakening of the central bureaucracy, and the rise of stable party government to achieve that end. Even today, though, there are traces in the West German policy network which resemble the Japanese model more than the Anglo-Saxon one. The tight interlock between business and finance and their occasionally intimate relations with the state bureaucracy remind us that after only one generation West Germany's historical convergence with the West remains superficial.

Although smaller than the gulf separating the two Anglo-Saxon countries and Japan, the difference in the political strategies and domestic structures shaping West German and French conduct in the international political economy is also striking. Why does the coalition between French business and the state accord the state bureaucracy such a prominent place? Why does the policy network spanning state and society provide a much greater array of policy instruments than can be found in the hands of West German policy makers across the border?

The history of the French administrative state is the most prominent feature of French political development and provides part of the answer. The French king subordinated his aristocratic opponents earlier than did the Prussian king. Like Japan and unlike Britain, the landed aristocracy was induced to choose social status over political power by leaving the estates in the countryside, attending the king at court, and thus squandering its economic resources.[65] The French Revolution tried to relegate the aristocracy to a stance of political opposition from which it failed to escape either into the world of politics, as in Britain, or of industry and finance, as in Japan.

The Napoleonic reforms at the beginning of the nineteenth century endowed France with a modern, centralized state machinery which has operated since then in a milieu in which state activism has, alternately, been expected and dreaded. At least since Colbert's mercantilism Frenchmen have subscribed to the view that the engine of industrial progress is the state, not the market. In some historical periods,

---

[63] John D. Montgomery, *Forced to be Free: The Artificial Revolution in Germany and Japan* (Chicago: University of Chicago Press, 1957). Edward H. Lichtfield et al., *Governing Postwar Germany*, 2 vols (Ithaca: Cornell University Press, 1953).

[64] David Potter, *People of Plenty: Economic Abundance and the American Character* (Chicago: University of Chicago Press, 1954).

[65] Moore, pp. 40–110. Franklin L. Ford, *Robe and Sword: The Regrouping of the French Aristocracy after Louis XIV* (Cambridge: Harvard University Press, 1953). Theodore Zeldin, *France, 1848–1945* (Oxford: The Clarendon Press, 1973).

including the present, France has developed what Weber called a "politically oriented capitalism" in which the state was centrally involved in economic affairs.[66] But in other periods state activism was less evident. In entrepreneurial zeal, the "absolutist coalition" still controlling the state bureaucracy in the Third Republic never equalled the Japanese samurai-administrators.[67] Unlike the German business community, French business operated in a conservative national climate of peasants and shopkeepers and failed to overcome its position of relative economic backwardness (compared to Britain and Belgium) in the industrial revolution. With some notable exceptions, French business continued to operate on a small scale, remained relatively decentralized, and adhered to a very traditionalist outlook. The French equivalent to Prussia's coalition between iron and rye, the Méline tariff of 1892, typified the way in which different social sectors were balanced, international competition was neutralized, and civil tranquility and peace were insured. Only since 1945, and with increasing rapidity since 1958, has France experienced its Meiji Restoration.[68] The conservative orientation toward the market is being supplemented by a still small but rapidly growing group of modern industrialists who view the state bureaucracy as an indispensable ally in charting French foreign economic policy.

In a comparative analysis of political strategies and domestic structures, Italy appears to hold an intermediary position between West Germany and France. Why, despite its size, is the state so passive in its coalition with the business community? Why does the network linking public and private sectors leave Italian policy makers without instruments despite considerable state involvement in the economy?

Unlike France and Germany, Italy's uneasy accommodation between feudalism and industrialism includes a territorial conflict between the industrially developed North and a backward South. Southern landowners did not enjoy the combination of political power and social prestige characteristic of the Northern aristocracy and, to a much greater degree, of the Prussian Junkers. But neither did they suffer the momentous defeat which the French aristocracy experienced in 1789. Although the influence of the Southern aristocracy in the development of Italy's industrial development remained small in the nineteenth century, the South has left an indelible mark on the development of the Italian state bureaucracy and party system.

---

[66] Max Weber, *The Theory of Social and Economic Organization* (New York: The Free Press, 1964), p. 315.
[67] Martin Shefter, "Patronage and its Opponents: A Theory and Some European Cases," paper prepared for delivery at the Conference on the Scope and Practice of Social Science History, sponsored by the Western European Area Studies Program, University of Wisconsin, Madison, and the Social Science History Association, April 23–24, 1976, Madison, Wisconsin.
[68] I would like to thank Miles Kahler for pointing out to me this connection between the Gaullist reform period and the Meiji Restoration. His comment was prompted by Ellen Kay Trimberger, "A Theory of Elite Revolutions," *Studies in Comparative International Development* Vol. 7, No. 3 (1973): 191–207.

This was not altogether surprising; the meekness of the Italian bourgeoisie was due not simply to its small size but to the late arrival of the Industrial Revolution south of the Alps. As in Germany, Italy's belated national unification was not tied to the middle class and the *Risorgimento* but to the diplomatic maneuvers of Cavour. But Piedmont lacked Prussia's power. Faced with the determined opposition of the Vatican and Southern indifference, the Northern reformers (both aristocrats and bourgeois) needed support. The *blocco storico*, the Italian equivalent to the coalition between "iron and rye," united a gradually industrializing North with a semi-feudal South.[69] Compared to Britain, France, and Germany, Italy's industrialization occurred late and lacked vigor. Despite the liberal orientation of some segments of the Northern bourgeoisie, the market principle lost out to cartel arrangements among industrial producers, heavy involvement by investment banks, and government assistance and subsidies.[70] Southern landowners became, then, an indispensible ally in the coalition which was formed after 1871. They were rewarded by noninterference in local affairs, police protection, funds for patronage, and, later, favorable access of the Southern middle class to jobs in the central bureaucracy.

The consequences of the bargain between North and South are still pervasive today in the character of the Italian state and party system. In the absence of indirect mechanisms of social control, such as the market or the state, the system of directly exchanged favors between patron and client was not seriously challenged in Italy's South. The extension of Southern political practice to Rome also, with the passage of time, appeared in the large, decentralized, patronage-ridden state bureaucracy, which, linked intimately to private groups, lacked the administrative tradition and *ésprit de corps* of the French state. World War I, Fascism, and World War II have brought enormous changes. But they have failed to overshadow the political consequences of Italy's incomplete conquest by the South.

Each of these six advanced industrial states has traversed a distinct path to the present. A comparison of the United States and Britain on the one hand and Japan on the other suggests a number of differences. Within a smaller range of variation, the historical experience of the three European countries also yields some of the same differences. But the exceptions (which are more numerous for the second set of countries than for the first) remind us that reality only approaches to varying degrees the ideal types described here; it never coincides with them.[71]

---

[69] Antonio Gramsci, *Selections from the Prison Notebooks* (New York: International Publishers, 1971), pp. 44–121. Graziano, "Center-Periphery Relations."

[70] Gerschenkron, pp. 72–118. Alexander Gerschenkron, *Continuity in History and Other Essays* (Cambridge: The Belknap Press of Harvard University Press, 1968), pp. 98–127. James R. Kurth, "Industrial Structure and Comparative Politics " (Cambridge, Center for European Studies, 1975), pp. 6–12.

[71] Besides the sources in footnote 57, this section is also heavily indebted to Gerschenkron, *Continuity in History*, pp. 77–97.

Early industrializers like Britain and the United States, which created parliamentary institutions, have weak or nonexistent feudal structures; they experienced an early commercialization of agriculture and early elimination of a dominant aristocracy. Late industrializers, with executive forms of government, like Japan, feature strong feudal structures, late commercialization of agriculture, and late elimination of a dominant aristocracy. Early industrializers are distinguished by gradual economic growth, relatively small-scale enterprises, low industrial concentration, few restrictions on competition, and an emphasis on consumer good industries, at least in the initial stages of industrialization. Late industrializers like Japan show spurts of explosive growth, relatively large-scale enterprises, high industrial concentration, numerous restrictions on competition, and an emphasis on heavy industry. Because the technological and financial requirements of production are small, the firm is the central economic actor among early industrializers. Among late industrializers the capital requirements of large firms were so great that the banking sector came to occupy the commanding heights of the economy. Since foreign competition often threatened the development of infant industries of these countries, the state was thrust into the midst of industrial development. Thus the central economic organizations among late industrializers are the firm, investment banks, and the state bureaucracy.

The character of state activity influences the organization of business and unions in both early and late industrializers. The passivity of the state in directing industrial growth makes for an organizationally decentralized business community. On the other hand, state activism in managing the economy, characteristic of late industrializers, facilitates a centralized organization of business. Labor movements among early industrializers tend to be decentralized, reformist, detached from political parties, and politically incorporated into a state apparatus which, consequently, needs to be less repressive. Among late industrializers, labor movements tend to be centralized, radical, attached to political parties, and excluded from a state machinery which must therefore be more repressive.

At the root of these differences lies the different character of the state in early and late industrializers. Among early industrializers political parties were instruments of political mobilization from the bottom; a progressive coalition focused on political participation rather than bureaucratic penetration. Among late industrializers political parties were instruments of political implantation from the top; an absolutist coalition concentrated its efforts on bureaucratic penetration rather than political participation. Parliamentary-based state authority favored strategies of non-intervention and "laissez-faire" in the economy among early industrializers. Executive-based state authority preferred strategies of intervention and "faire-faire" among late industrializers. These institutional differences have behavioral consequences. Early industrializers tend to focus their resources on consumption and wages: late industrializers emphasize investment and profits. Government programs among early industrializers emphasize short-term goals, distribution, and large social welfare expenditures, while late industrializers emphasize long-term goals, accumulation, and small welfare expenditures.

## IV  Conflict and change in foreign economic policy

Change in foreign economic policy partly results from conflict in domestic politics. Strategies of foreign economic policy are reflections of the "stress and contradiction" in domestic structures;[72] but they are also attempts to cope with stress and contradictions. The very concept of domestic "structure" is in fact ambiguous. It describes the stress in the relations between business and the state as well as the contradiction between organized capital and organized labor. Taken as a whole, the papers in this volume show that the main pillars of power in the advanced industrial states—the state, business, and organized labor—have largely reinforced one another throughout the postwar era with organized labor playing a marginal role. For a few decades pluralist bargaining seemed supreme. Recent developments are usefully reminding us of the stresses and contradictions which are inherent, although at times invisible, in the domestic structures of advanced industrial states.

One source of stress in the relations between business and the state derives from the conflict between export-oriented, technologically advanced industries and import-competing, technologically backward ones. In all advanced industrial states industries such as textiles clamour for protection. The basic logic of the international division of labor in the postwar international economy has tended to weaken technologically backward industries in advanced industrial states. This conflict has not been restricted to the business community. In their defense of jobs unions in declining sectors typically enter into alliance with producers. Furthermore, when confronted with a united front of business and labor, the state is normally forced to take action. But the objectives and instruments of policy are crucial in determining the character of the state's response. The use of tariffs and quotas characteristic of the Anglo-Saxon states and some continental countries responds to domestic political pressures by buying time without addressing technological change as the root of the problem. The pursuit of a sectoral policy in selected parts of the economy, which is characteristic of Japan and France, emphasizes long-term over short-term considerations, even at the cost of temporarily intensifying domestic political conflict. Irrespective of the state response, technologically advanced, competitive, export-oriented industries in all major advanced industrial states have prevailed. The very success which leading firms in these industries have enjoyed in the 1950s and 1960s explains why the forces of protectionism have scored only a few, peripheral victories since the early 1970s. In a future promising lower rates of economic growth, the conflict between export-oriented and import-competing industrial sectors and firms—and with it the conflicting demands made on the state—will probably intensify.

---

[72] Leon N. Lindberg et al., eds., *Stress and Contradiction in Modern Capitalism* (Lexington, Mass.: D.C. Heath, 1975).

A second source of stress in the relations between business and the state derives from the muted conflict between industry and finance. The creation of the Euro-Dollar market has to some extent freed large firms from the constraints imposed by national banking institutions. Free access to a large capital market was particularly important for firms with an unfavorable debt-equity ratio, as, for example, in the Federal Republic. At the same time, though, the growth of the Euro-Dollar market has led to a subsequent increase in the international operation of banks.[73] The British experience in particular suggests that the effect of these international operations on total profits is less important than the increase in the political power of central banks, who now, among other things, manage the flow of Petro-Dollars.[74] In an era where currency values are determined by a system of "managed floating," the strategic importance of central banks has increased in all advanced industrial states. Recent changes in these complex relations between industry and finance often affect the state, as in West Germany, where they seem to have decreased state power. In Japan, on the other hand, the effect of these changes is less easily gauged: they may have affected only the relative standing of different sections in the Finance Ministry.

Another potential source of conflict and change in foreign economic policy is inherent in the relation between organized labor and business. The exercise of American power after 1945 reinforced domestic political impulses in Europe and Japan to assign organized labor no more than a marginal role in the postwar international political economy. The American formula of the politics of productivity was organized around the key concept of aggregate welfare which, to different degrees, gave organized labor some of the dividends of economic growth. As a result, the absolute level of per capita income increased while relative income differentials remained largely unchanged.[75] As long as this institutional arrangement delivered the goods, the uneasy accommodation between Anglo-Saxon mass consumption and the European and Japanese inclination toward investment was successful. But when, for a variety of reasons, these dividends of growth diminished from the early 1970s on, the internal contradictions of the entire

[73] Gerd Junne, *Der Eurogeldmarkt: Seine Bedeutung für Inflation und Inflationsbekämpfung* (Frankfurt: Campus Verlag, 1976).

[74] Janet Kelley, *Bankers and Borders: The Case of the American Banks in Britain* (Cambridge, Mass.: Ballinger, in press), Table 8.1.

[75] Malcolm Sawyer, "Income Distribution in OECD Countries," *OECD Economic Outlook: Occasional Studies* (Paris: OECD, 1976). See also United Nations, Secretariat of the Economic Commission for Europe, *Incomes in Postwar Europe: A Study of Politics, Growth, and Distribution*, Economic Survey of Europe in 1965: Part 2 (Geneva: United Nations Publications, 1967). Frederic L. Pyror, *Property and Industrial Organization in Communist and Capitalist Nations* (Bloomington: Indiana University Press, 1973). Martin Schnitzer, *Income Distribution: A Comparative Study of the United States, Sweden, West Germany, East Germany, the United Kingdom, and Japan* (New York: Praeger, 1974). David R. Cameron, "Inequality and the State: A Political-Economic Comparison," paper prepared for delivery at the 1976 Annual Meeting of the American Political Science Association, The Palmer House, Chicago, Illinois, September 2–5, 1976.

institutional arrangement centered around the concept of aggregate welfare became increasingly obvious.

In none of the six advanced industrial states analyzed here has organized labor been an important part of the governing coalitions which have defined policy objectives. Consequently it has played little more than a marginal role in the process of policy implementation. With the possible exception of Britain, until the early 1970s organized labor delicately mixed tacit assent with active cooperation in backing the foreign economic policy strategies of the dominant national coalitions.[76] In America and West Germany in particular, unions have accepted economic gains without worrying unduly about questions of long-term political strategy. As long as the overall performance of the economy was relatively satisfactory, they have, as producers, participated in a silent "great coalition" favoring a liberal export policy. Even when the political influence of organized labor was rising in West Germany after 1966 and 1969, changes in policy were not observable. In Italy, France, and Japan, on the other hand, the contradiction between organized labor and business was much sharper. Strong, indigenous Communist parties and labor movements explain labor's exclusion from participation in any aspect of foreign economic policy making. Worker militancy was, to varying degrees in the different countries, diluted by the dividends of growth. The growing strength of the Italian and French Left in recent years and the continued radicalism of the Japanese Left illustrate the contradictions in the domestic structures of "late industrializers" that have remained closer to the center of politics than is true of "early industrializers."

Changes in the structure of domestic labor markets have severely limited the success of the liberal international political economy and the acquiescence of organized labor on which it was partly based. The slowdown in rural-urban migration, the achievement of full employment, and an accelerating rise in wage levels in the 1960s made all advanced industrial states confront the problem of orchestrating manpower shifts from low-productivity to high-productivity sectors in industry. Japan and France have responded with a policy of sectoral transformation which has relied primarily on the allocation of state-controlled investment funds. In the other countries state bureaucrats have generally been more cautious and union hostility could not be as easily discounted. Nowhere in these six states does one encounter an active manpower policy with which smaller states, such as Sweden, have attempted to confront technological change head on. Instead, in search of greater profits, American and British multinational corporations (later followed by German and Japanese firms) have followed a strategy of capital exports while European governments, in particular, have acceded to the import of cheap labor. Both these measures have weakened the role of organized labor in domestic politics.

---

[76] The role of labor movements more generally is discussed in Solomon Barkin, ed., *Worker Militancy and its Consequences 1965–1975* (New York: Praeger, 1975) and in two issues edited by John P. Windmuller dealing with European Labor and Politics. See *Industrial and Labor Relations Review* Vol. 28, No. 1 (October 1974) and Vol. 28, No. 2 (January 1975).

These stresses and contradictions in domestic politics complement increasingly important sources of conflict and change in the international political economy. Many of the conflicts result from an incremental accumulation of political and economic changes over the last twenty-five years. Uneven developments in the division of labor among Northern countries have encouraged a projection of domestic impulses into the international political economy. American and French exports of conventional weapons and West Germany's aggressive search for international outlets for its nuclear reactor industry are motivated largely by considerations of export performance, employment, and profits rather than international security. Japan's foreign investment strategy reflects its insecure access to raw materials as well as the rising domestic opposition to the environmental hazards of an unrestrained policy of economic growth. Political stalemate in Britain and Italy seems to point to continued reliance on international credit arrangements in the years ahead.

The oil crisis and less developed countries' pressures for a New International Economic Order (NIEO) have accentuated these uneven developments among the major OECD states, creating further sources of conflict. The British "letter of intent" submitted to the International Monetary Fund (IMF) in 1969 and the conditions attached to the 3.9 billion dollar IMF loan in 1976 have generated widespread resentment of external interference in British politics especially among the left wing of the Labour Party. In lending money to Italy, West Germany's thinly veiled insistence that the Italians follow a policy of deflation and continue to exclude the Communist Party from government has had a similar effect. France and Japan, which depend heavily on their export markets, are under pressure from their trading partners to divert an increasing amount of resources to preserve a liberal international economy in order to achieve their more narrowly-defined national growth objectives.

Multiple sources of conflicts are bound to change foreign economic policies of advanced industrial states in the years ahead. The tranquility in which the politics of productivity experienced its greatest triumphs in the 1950s and 1960s is rapidly disappearing. The domestic structures which we have identified as characterizing the Anglo-Saxon states, the continental states, and Japan will have major importance in determining political strategies in the international economy. In comparison to the Anglo-Saxon countries and West Germany, the concentration of political and economic power typical of industrial late-comers has left them better equipped to cope with external challenges. At the same time, though, that concentration of power makes the domestic structures of these late-comers more brittle and their political strategies more susceptible to fundamental change. Political strategies reveal the character of the domestic structures which they are designed to strengthen. West German stability and the British crisis illuminate what holds true for the advanced industrial states in general: foreign economic policy raises basic questions about the legitimation of power and the accumulation of plenty and thus shapes the future governance of advanced industrial states.

# Index

Acheson, Dean, 75, 76
Adenauer, Konrad, 199, 205
Advanced industrial states, 3, 4, 5-7
AFL (American Federation of Labor), 28, 42
Agricultural policy: in Germany, 203; in Italy, 244-245; in France, 273
American Federation of Labor. *See* AFL
Anti-Communism: as U.S. foreign policy motive, 25; and U.S. foreign aid, 40-44; and the Marshall Plan, 75; in German-Italian relations, 253

Balance of payments: United States deficit, 54, 76; attempts of U.S. to redress, 80; and oil crisis, 81-82; British policy toward, 108-9; and Britain in the 1950s, 111-12; and Britain and North Sea oil, 134; and Japan, 186; and Italy, 251. *See also* Monetary policy
Balance of trade: U.S., 67, 68-69, 70; British, 94-95
Banking: in Japan, 152-53 (*see also* Bank of Japan); in Germany, 210-12 (*see also* Bundesbank); in France, 268 (*see also* banques d'affaires). *See also* Finance
—, U.S.: 70; expansion of, 71; on World Bank and IMF, 74; decentralization of, 311
Bank of England: and parity of the pound, 105-6; influence of, in eco-

nomic policy making, 106; and Harold Wilson, 118
Bank of Italy: role of, in coordinating economic policy, 234-35; policy instruments of, 235; influenced by political considerations, 236
Bank of Japan: role of, in economy, 152-53; as policy instrument, 165-66, 315
*Banques d'affaires*, 262, 268, 278, 279
BDI (Bundesverband der Deutschen Industrie [Federation of German Industries]): and protectionism, 198, 203; elements within, 201; and East-West trade, 204-5; and revaluation of the DM, 214-15; and *Strukturpolitik*, 222
Belgium, 37, 38
Bretton Woods system, 10-11, 13; and U.S. foreign aid, 39; ending of, 54, 81; and Germany, 196
Britain, 89-137; economic performance of, 90; foreign economic policy making of, 91, 103; economy of, compared to France, 93, 113; economy of, from late 1930s to late 1940s, 93-95; economic performance of, affected by World War II, 94, 132-33; postwar military policy of, 96, 108; economic performance of, as a result of deflationary policies, 112-14; from 1968 to 1975, 123-24; and the EEC, 133; economic future of, 134-37. *See also* Conservative governments, of